THE POWER OF DIALOGUE BETWEEN ISRAELIS AND PALESTINIANS

THE POWER OF DIALOGUE BETWEEN ISRAELIS AND PALESTINIANS

Stories of Change from the School for Peace

NAVA SONNENSCHEIN

EDITED AND TRANSLATED BY DEB REICH

R

RUTGERS UNIVERSITY PRESS

New Brunswick, Camden, and Newark, New Jersey, and London

A British Cataloging-in-Publication record for this book is available from the
British Library.

Library of Congress Cataloging-in-Publication Data

Names: Sonnenschein, Nava, 1953– author. | Reich, Deb, translator.
Title: The power of dialogue between Israelis and Palestinians : stories of change
    from the School for Peace / by Nava Sonnenschein ; translated by Deb Reich.
Description: New Brunswick : Rutgers University Press, 2019. | Includes
    bibliographical references.
Identifiers: LCCN 2017059909| ISBN 9780813599229 (cloth : alk. paper) |
    ISBN 9780813599212 (pbk. : alk. paper)
Subjects: LCSH: Multicultural education—Israel. | Neve shalom (School) |
    Arab–Israeli conflict—1993—Peace. | Jews—Israel—Interviews. | Palestinian
    Arabs—Israel—Interviews. | Conflict management—Israel. | Israel—Ethnic relations.
Classification: LCC LC1099.5.I75 S6513 2019 | DDC 370.117095694—dc23
LC record available at https://lccn.loc.gov/2017059909

♾ The paper used in this publication meets the requirements of the American
National Standard for Information Sciences—Permanence of Paper for Printed
Library Materials, ANSI Z39.48-1992.

www.rutgersuniversitypress.org

Manufactured in the United States of America

CONTENTS

PREFACE

Working on this book was a very empowering and moving experience for me. It began with an interview I conducted with Michael Sfard in 2007, and ended more than two dozen interviews later, in April 2016. During these years, we have witnessed a troubling reality, with Israeli society moving in some deeply worrying directions: humanitarian and democratic values are further eroding, human rights are less and less honored, and the path toward peace between Israelis and Palestinians is increasingly neglected. In this context, the interviews in this book with graduates of School for Peace courses provide a glimmer of hope that change is indeed possible.

The process of conducting the interviews became a fascinating journey during a difficult period in relations between Jews and Palestinians in this land. The period between 2007 and 2016 is framed by the fortieth anniversary of Israel's conquest of the Palestinian territories occupied in 1967, the end of the second Intifada, Israel's second war in Lebanon, the subsequent wars waged by Israel against Palestinians in Gaza, and the deteriorating situation in Gaza under Hamas rule. At this writing (spring 2016), all negotiations between Israel and the Palestinians are frozen and the violence continues to intensify, alongside increasing manifestations of racism in Israeli society. The people interviewed for this book were born into the post-1967 era of occupation, and many of them, experiencing it daily, have dedicated their lives to promoting peace, ending the occupation, and achieving equality between Jews and Palestinians in Israel. You can read about this in detail in the interviews.

In my daily work, facilitating long-term programs of dialogue and action that bring together Jewish Israelis and Palestinians from both sides of the Green Line, I sometimes ask myself what kind of change these encounters can generate, what purpose they can have, when reality indicates that things are going in an entirely different direction. The answer emerges from the dialogues I facilitate. I renew my strength to keep working by seeing the transformation undergone by the participants. There is an amazing, dramatic moment when something perceptibly shifts for a participant or for an entire group, and I have witnessed such moments innumerable times while teaching courses and facilitating groups. This is what has prompted me to look more deeply into the nature of the changes I have witnessed. The shift that people experience always involves pain, because it demands that they relinquish old attitudes and ideas to make room for new ones. Throughout this book, people talk candidly about the formative moments in this change process and their translation into action in the quest for peace, human rights, and equality. These first-person accounts have sustained me in my own work.

I am often asked about the impact on participants. After all (people tell me), the political map is continually shifting to the right—so what impact can you be having on reality? This series of interviews offers a fascinating window into these inner transformations among participants.

Every School for Peace graduate I approached for this project agreed wholeheartedly to be interviewed. The book was to include all the interviews; two of the participants, however, both of them women in counseling professions, subsequently withdrew, citing the need for anonymity in their work. The participants as a group do not comprise a scientifically representative sample of School for Peace graduates; on the other hand, I can state with confidence that there are numerous other graduates whose stories are no less compelling and who could have been included alongside, or instead of, the actual participants. In arranging the interviews, I sought people with interesting stories, asked for an interview and described the planned book, and then conducted an interview of approximately ninety minutes with each participant. The interviews were recorded and transcribed.

During the interviews, participants describe how the School for Peace courses they took have influenced their lives. Their stories allow us to see what motivates this kind of change in people and how the dialogue in which they were immersed has spurred them to act. They describe the formative moments in the encounter, explaining how the changes in their awareness came about; how they have been able to hold on to their changed awareness during a period of such unending conflict; and how they have succeeded in translating their inner transformation into action "out there." They all spoke in some way of feeling a kind of internal spark that, once ignited, drove them to action aimed at changing the reality shared by Jews and Palestinians. This is the power of dialogue: a real dialogue, one that places issues lying at the very heart of the conflict right there on the table; a dialogue of deep listening, a dialogue that investigates and challenges the asymmetries of power;

a dialogue that examines the processes occurring between the two national groups and investigates them fearlessly; a dialogue that makes possible discussion on an equal basis, shorn of privilege; a dialogue that enhances critical thinking about our reality; a dialogue that can allow participants to expand their identities to include "the other."

In the remainder of this preface, I will briefly describe the work of the School for Peace, an institution I founded together with colleagues at Wahat al Salam–Neve Shalom, in 1979. I will note some key aspects of the working method we developed for facilitating groups in conflict, which is the method used in all three types of courses attended by the participants in the interviews for this book. I hope that the book will provide a model for others of an alternative path that is most certainly accessible to those willing to do the work of walking it.

The School for Peace (SFP) at Wahat al-Salam–Neve Shalom was one of the first educational institutions in Israel to address the vast chasm between Palestinians and Jews in Israel, working intensively with both groups to bridge the divide and develop a healthy democratic state based on equality and equity for all citizens. Established in 1979, the SFP is continually developing its unique approach to building a shared future, an approach based on dialogue courses, research, theory, evaluation, and the development of best practices in the field of conflict resolution.

The School for Peace is located in an unusual setting at Wahat al-Salam–Neve Shalom (WASNS), which is the only intentional shared community in Israel where Jews and Palestinians live together by choice, in peace and equality. The community strives to function as a shared home whose residents draw encouragement from the village's model of equality, pluralism, and partnership. Since the founding of the School for Peace, some 65,000 Jews and Palestinians have participated in its various programs. For more current details, see the school's website (www.sfpeace.org).

The working method used at the School for Peace has evolved over the years and has created a unique approach to working with groups in conflict. This approach focuses on how two groups relate to each other, stressing intergroup rather than interpersonal processes. The SFP sees the group as a microcosm of the larger society; through the group experience, participants attain deep learning about the dynamics of the relationship between the two groups in the wider society.

The SFP acknowledges the asymmetry in the power dynamics between groups. This asymmetry shapes self and group image and behavior. The model intentionally puts the conflict squarely on the table, making it clear that participants have come together to discuss the conflict and providing an opportunity to address real issues and negotiate difficult topics.

Participants explore their national and ethnic group identity in a way that enables them to understand how the group identity forms their perceptions and behaviors. They undergo a process of change as they discover how their group identity influences the way they think and act. They are empowered to address conflicts and differences and to take responsibility for their perceptions and actions. In later phases, the groups work together at identifying issues of common concern and implementing projects addressing those concerns. The aim is to catalyze societal change so as to move toward a more equal and just society. For more details about the method, consult *Israeli and Palestinian Identities in Dialogue* (R. Halabi, ed., 2004).

Everyone interviewed for this book was a participant in one or more long-term School for Peace courses, which lasted from 120 hours to 18 months in duration: the Course for Facilitators of Groups in Conflict; the University courses offered by the School for Peace in conjunction with various universities and colleges; and the Change Agents courses. The basis of all those programs is the unique intergroup method for dialogue between Jews and Palestinians developed at the School for Peace.

The following are brief descriptions of each of the three types of courses.

FACILITATORS TRAINING COURSES

The training for facilitators of groups in conflict is the flagship program of the School for Peace. Since it began offering this course in 1990, the SFP has trained more than 1,000 facilitators for groups in conflict who are now in leadership positions in many peace and human rights NGOs (nongovernmental organizations) in Israel and in Palestine. In this four-month intensive training course, participants attend lectures, read academic materials, and undergo intensive experiential group processes addressing aspects of the Jewish-Palestinian conflict and the role of their own identity in that conflict. They also learn to analyze intergroup processes and acquire the skills needed for facilitating groups in conflict by practicing peer facilitation.

UNIVERSITY-LEVEL ACADEMIC COURSES

Pioneering the field of peace studies in Israel's universities from 1990 onward, the School for Peace has been teaching undergraduate and graduate students the theoretical and practical aspects of building peace in the Middle East. These courses take place at Tel Aviv University, the University of Haifa, Ben-Gurion University, the Hebrew University and others. Combining experiential and theoretical study, these courses impart a deep understanding of intergroup conflict generally and the Jewish-Arab conflict in particular. The students who participate, all of whom are working toward undergraduate or graduate degrees in the social sciences, bring this unique preparation with them to their participation in decision-making and policy formulation in all kinds of organizations later on. Course graduates with advanced degrees are now among the faculty teaching similar courses at Ben-Gurion University, the Interdisciplinary Center Herzliya, and the College of Tel Aviv–Jaffa.

CHANGE AGENTS COURSES

The change agents program has trained hundreds of individuals to promote social change in their own communities and in the governmental and non-governmental agencies where they work. This innovative model engages citizens of Israel (Jews and Palestinians) and Palestinians from Palestine in shared groups geared to their specific professional fields, building on their professional expertise. In the advanced phase of these courses, the participants develop joint projects addressing shared concerns of Israeli and Palestinian society. Programs have been tailored especially for lawyers, mental health professionals, journalists, environmentalist, architects and planners, physicians, young politicians, teachers, and other professional groups. Each course lasts from 12 to 18 months, meeting once a month, with additional intensive workshops of 2 to 5 days' duration. Each course, comprising twenty-five to forty participants, has four components: ongoing participation in a group dialogue process using the SFP method; the acquisition of theoretical and practical knowledge relevant to the connection between a group's specific profession and the conflict; guided field trips; and practice in the skills needed to design and engage in effective action for change.

Following this preface is a theoretical introduction to the interview material written by Professor Tamar Saguy; my own close analysis of the interview contents appears as an afterword. Between those two are the twenty-five interviews, loosely arranged in groups by participants' field of endeavor, and introduced by brief bios written by the participants themselves.

Our hope is that this book will lend strength to human rights and peace organizations so that they may persevere in the struggle for a more just and equal society in which the two peoples who share this small bit of land can live side by side in harmony.

—Nava Sonnenschein, Ph.D.

THE POWER OF DIALOGUE BETWEEN ISRAELIS AND PALESTINIANS

INTRODUCTION

When Groups Meet—Understanding How Power Dynamics Shape Intergroup Encounters

TAMAR SAGUY, INTERDISCIPLINARY
CENTER (IDC) HERZLIYA

This book tells a unique story. It is a story of the personal transformations that individuals have undergone through their participation in a dialogue project bringing together members of their own group and members of an outgroup with whom their group is in conflict. I have undergone such a transformation myself, and I found echoes of my own experience in many of the personal testimonies you will read in this book. As part of my M.A. studies at Tel Aviv University in 2000, I took part in a dialogue group of Palestinians and Israelis. The group met weekly over the course of a year, and was facilitated by a Jewish facilitator and an Arab facilitator—precisely the type of encounter this book addresses. The uniqueness of the model employed, which was developed by the School for Peace at Wahat al-Salam–Neve Shalom (Halabi, 2004), is especially evident when considering the literature on intergroup encounters. Perhaps the most unusual element in this model of encounter is its explicit focus on the power dynamics between the groups.

In this introduction, I locate the personal transformations that this book is revealing in the larger context of intergroup encounters, which has been a focus of research for decades within the social sciences. Indeed, hundreds of studies have been dedicated to understanding how best to construct intergroup encounters so that their impact on intergroup relations will be positive. Understanding this background is essential for analyzing the transformations this book documents. As will become clear through reading this chapter, the experiences outlined in this book are unique also in the scholarly sense, because they are linked to a type of intergroup encounter that is focused on power dynamics. Such encounters have been tested empirically only rarely, and might intuitively seem counterproductive. However, as the personal stories in this book suggest, careful examination of the literature indicates that even though such encounters are not considered mainstream and might be challenging, they can have considerable impact in promoting social change. The goal of this introduction is to analyze this potential with a scholarly lens.

I will begin by outlining the key tenets of research on intergroup encounters, while considering how this research has (or has not) dealt with the issue of power asymmetries. I will then move on to describe a synthesis I have developed with my colleagues over the years, which analyzes psychological processes that occur in intergroup encounters from a perspective that considers the power dynamics between the interacting groups. This synthesis relies heavily on my personal experience in the Israeli-Palestinian dialogue program that I mentioned in the opening paragraph, which was based on the model developed by the School for Peace at Wahat al-Salam–Neve Shalom. The research approach that connects power dynamics with intergroup encounters is strongly linked to the stories told in this book, by pointing, albeit sometimes indirectly, to the potentially powerful impact of encounters in which power dynamics are exposed.

EXISTING RESEARCH ON INTERGROUP ENCOUNTERS

One of the most pressing questions faced by policy makers and researchers alike is how to attenuate intergroup animosity and advance more peaceful and just relations between groups in society. Solutions to problems associated with intergroup tension occur at various levels, ranging from the political level—which includes policy formation and resolutions to conflict negotiated among leaders—to the grassroots level, where it is aimed at promoting better relations between individuals from the communities of the opposing sides (e.g., via dialogue groups, educational programs, and joint initiatives in professional and cultural domains). Many such approaches to conflict resolution involve some form of encounter, or interaction, across group lines.

Among the most influential theories in shaping the thinking about, and the planning of, interactions between individuals from opposing sides is contact theory (Allport, 1954). According to this theory, positive interactions between members of opposing or conflicting groups can reduce prejudice and improve intergroup relations, particularly when they occur under optimal conditions. Encounters that have traditionally been considered optimal involve a focus on a common goal or cooperation between groups (Allport, 1954), through which individuals have an opportunity to get to know one another as equals. Power differences, which often characterize the relations outside the encounter, were considered an obstacle to a productive encounter and hence as something that should be removed during the interactions (Allport, 1954; Amir, 1969). As a result, optimal encounters often involve direct attempts to eliminate power differences or any mention of asymmetries between the groups.

The notion of cooperation between equals dates back to classic work by Allport (1954) and Sherif (Sherif, Harvey, White, Hood, & Sherif, 1961), and was systematically investigated under the framework of processes associated with categorization (Dovidio & Gaertner, 2010). In their classic studies of the basis of intergroup conflict, Sherif and colleagues (1961) demonstrated that animosity between groups can be reverted by having members of both groups work together toward a common goal. This notion was later developed by Gaertner, Dovidio, and colleagues in their work on the common ingroup identity model (Gaertner & Dovidio, 2000). The principle behind the model is that inducing people to think of themselves as sharing a common, superordinate identity with members of another group can overcome fundamental intergroup bias. A superordinate identity may be, for example, a common school, organization, or national identity, and can be also induced by providing people with goals, tasks, or even simply cues that emphasize elements common to both groups (Dovidio, Gaertner, & Saguy, 2015).

Indeed, field applications of contact theory have typically resulted in encounters that are centered on superordinate goals and afford opportunities for the formation of acquaintance and friendships between group members (Dixon, Durrheim, & Tredoux, 2005). Notable examples are the jigsaw classroom (Aronson & Patnoe, 1997) and the countless encounters between groups in conflict (e.g., Palestinians and Israelis) that center discussions on common themes and similarities between the groups (see Nadler & Saguy, 2004). The primary goal of such encounters has been to lead to improved intergroup attitudes that enable more harmonious relations to develop.

The contact hypothesis has stimulated a vast amount of research and received a great deal of empirical support: indeed, a comprehensive meta-analysis, considering data from over 500 studies on contact, has demonstrated that contact reliably predicts reduced prejudice (Pettigrew & Tropp, 2006), an effect that can be largely explained by reductions in intergroup anxiety and increased empathy, as well as by increases in participants' knowledge about outgroup members (Pettigrew & Tropp, 2008). Moreover, the benefits of positive contact have been shown to extend beyond the boundaries of the specific interactions. It has been shown that improved outgroup attitudes can transfer from the outgroup with which one has experienced positive contact to other groups with which one has not (Tausch et al., 2010). Furthermore, in recent years, researchers have begun testing the benefits of intergroup contact beyond the scope of physical face-to-face interaction. Even imagining contact with outgroup individuals has been shown to result in improved attitudes toward the other side (Crisp & Turner, 2012).

Nevertheless, despite this impressive evidence, until recently at least two fundamental questions regarding contact remained unanswered. First, who benefits from such encounters, and from an emphasis on commonalities? This question was rarely raised, reflecting the assumption that advantaged and disadvantaged group members alike are benefiting from these optimal encounters. The second, closely related question is about how power dynamics, which shape the relations outside the encounter, might still impact the optimal encounters, even when attempts are made to achieve equal status. In the remainder of this chapter I describe research that attempts to answer these questions, and thus provide critical insights as to the effectiveness of intergroup encounters.

INTERGROUP ENCOUNTERS FROM A POWER PERSPECTIVE

With rare exceptions, societies are hierarchically organized such that at least one group controls a greater share of valued resources (e.g., political power, economic wealth, educational opportunities) than do other groups (Sidanius & Pratto, 1999). Reflecting this hierarchical structure, high group power is traditionally defined as having relatively greater control of resources, with decreased dependence on the other side (Emerson, 1962; see Saguy & Kteily, 2014). Group-based hierarchy is reflected in almost every aspect of social life, with members of advantaged groups enjoying better outcomes than disadvantaged group members in a range of domains, from poverty rates and school attrition rates to prison sentences and mortality rates (Feagin, 2006; Smooha, 2005; Ulmer & Johnson, 2004). Members of disadvantaged groups, compared to members of advantaged groups, also encounter discrimination and social injustice across a wide spectrum of social contexts, such as when interviewing for jobs or being quoted a price for a house or a car (Ayres, 1991; Bertrand & Mullainathan, 2004).

Greater control over resources as well as preferential social treatment produces divergent daily realities for members of advantaged relative to disadvantaged groups. Whereas members of disadvantaged groups find many doors to economic opportunities closed, have a difficult time climbing the social ladder, and experience legal authorities as a source of intimidation, advantaged group members experience far more economic security, opportunities to advance, and social acceptance. Moreover, members of advantaged groups also benefit psychologically from being part of a socially valued group. According to social identity theory (Tajfel & Turner, 1979), individuals derive their social identity, which is an important part of their self-concept, from their membership in social groups. Because people strive for positive self-worth, they are motivated to achieve a positively valued and distinct social identity: a need that can be satisfied by favorable social comparisons to other relevant groups. Given their dominant position in society and their control over resources and positions conferring high status, social comparisons to other relevant groups typically yield favorable outcomes for members of advantaged groups, promoting a positive social identity. By contrast, members of disadvantaged groups are more likely to experience a devalued or threatened social identity when making social comparisons to other groups.

Thus, relative to members of disadvantaged groups, members of advantaged groups benefit both practically and psychologically from hierarchical social arrangements. These different group-based experiences often translate to contrasting views, preferences, motivations, and strategies regarding the status quo. Members of advantaged groups—who benefit from the situation as it stands—are likely to have little opposition to current status arrangements, and indeed may be threatened by the possibility of changes to a system that advantages them. Members of subordinate groups, however, experience relative disadvantage under the existing state of affairs; as such, they are generally more likely to perceive the status quo as problematic, and to desire social change. These group-based orientations toward the status quo are described in prominent theories of intergroup relations such as the group position model (Blumer, 1958; Bobo, 1999), social dominance theory (Sidanius & Pratto, 1999), realistic group conflict theory (LeVine & Campbell, 1972), and social identity theory (Tajfel & Turner, 1979), and have received substantial empirical support.

For example, a long tradition of research in social dominance theory (Pratto, Sidanius, Stallworth, & Malle, 1994) demonstrates that individuals who hold more dominant positions in society tend to view the social hierarchy as natural and necessary, whereas members of disadvantaged groups are more likely to see the hierarchy as in need of change. This effect has been replicated in a variety of intergroup contexts, including ethnic groups in Israel (Saguy, Davidio, & Pratto, 2008, Study 2), India (Saguy, Tausch, Dovidio, Pratto, & Singh, 2010), and the United States (Pratto et al., 1994), and also among artificial groups for whom group position was experimentally manipulated (Saguy et al., 2008, Study 1).

These group-based, or power-based, motivations are critical for understanding processes that occur within contact situations. As described earlier, even though attempts are made to "cancel out" power differences during encounters, such group-based motivations, which are highly linked to individuals' social identities, are unlikely to disappear during intergroup encounters. Yet the classic literature on intergroup contact provides little insight as to how such motivations might play a role in the encounter itself. Together with my colleagues I have attempted to develop such an understanding, which I will describe next.

POWER-BASED MOTIVATIONS AND PREFERENCES FOR THE CONTENT OF CONTACT

Consistent with their group-based motivations toward the status quo, advantaged group members are likely to behave in ways that would help them maintain their relative dominance and undermine change, such as by promoting ideologies that make hierarchy seem legitimate and reasonable (Knowles, Lowery, Chow, & Unzuetta, 2014; Reicher, 2007; Sidanius & Pratto, 1999). By contrast, members of disadvantaged groups are more likely to engage in behaviors that would challenge current social arrangements, such as by supporting or participating in collective action efforts aimed at promoting equality (van Zomeren, Postmes, & Spears, 2008). These different tendencies are dependent on a variety of factors and can be attenuated or intensified as a function of different contextual elements (e.g., the extent to which the hierarchy seems stable; Saguy & Dovidio, 2013), however, all else being equal, differences between advantaged and disadvantaged groups in their attempts to sustain or change social arrangements can be expected.

Such tendencies were found to manifest in what individuals regard as the preferred form of intergroup relations (Dovidio, Gaertner, & Saguy, 2009). Advantaged group members show relatively strong support for relations in which differences between groups are minimized and the emphasis instead is on common ties among the groups within one, superordinate, category (e.g., "we are all Americans, rather than Blacks and Whites"; Wolsko, Park, Judd, & Wittenbrink, 2000). Conversely, even though they might also appreciate cross-group commonalities, members of disadvantaged groups show a consistent preference for relations through which group differences are also acknowledged and valued (Richeson & Nussbaum, 2004; Wolsko et al., 2000). For example, native-born Dutch (the advantaged majority) have been shown to prefer assimilation of immigrants to the host culture, whereas immigrants prefer to become part of the dominant (host) culture while retaining their original cultural identity (van Oudenhoven, Prins, & Buunk, 1998). Similarly, Blacks in the United States have been shown to endorse an emphasis on racial identities more than color blindness, whereas Whites tend to endorse color blindness more than Blacks (Ryan, Hunt, Weible, Peterson, & Casas, 2007).

In my research, I examined whether such orientations are also reflected in how individuals approach intergroup encounters. This work demonstrated that group power systematically predicts what group members wish to talk about when interacting with members from the other group (see Saguy & Kteily, 2014, for a review). For example, members of advantaged groups were found to prefer to focus the encounter on topics of cross-group commonalities, and to de-emphasize topics that bring to light differences between the groups, including differences in power. This effect was initially found among Ashkenazi Jews (Jews whose ethnic origins are in North America or Europe), who constitute a high-status group in Israeli society in relation to Mizrahi Jews (Jews whose ethnic origins are in Asia or Africa; Saguy et al., 2008). When asked to simply choose topics for an encounter with Mizrahim, Ashkenazim showed a clear presence to address topics that dealt with commonalities across group lines (e.g., "Discussing cultural similarities between the two groups") over those that dealt with power differences between the groups ("Discussing affirmative action aimed at promoting Mizrahim"). Similar effects were obtained among Muslims in Turkey (in relation to both Kurds and Armenians; Bikmen & Sunar, 2013), and among Whites in the United States (in relation to both Blacks and Asians; Bikmen & Durkin, 2014). Given the strong emphasis on commonalities in optimal encounters, these findings suggest that optimal encounters might align well with advantaged group members' motivation to focus on commonalities and avoid discussions of power.

In contrast, members of disadvantaged groups were found to have an equivalently high interest in focusing both on commonalities and on power differences. For example, the Mizrahi Jews in the work by Saguy and colleagues (2008) wanted to discuss issues related to cross-group commonalities with Ashkenazi Jews to a similar extent that they wanted to address issues related to power differences between the groups—with the latter preference being significantly higher than that of Ashkenazi Jews (Saguy et al., 2008). These tendencies are further reflected in the analysis of conflict resolution workshops involving Israelis and Palestinians. Rouhana and Korper (1997) found that Israeli participants expressed a desire to participate in the workshop if the interactions were based on interpersonal processes that could lead to attitude change, whereas Palestinians wanted to address structural and political issues during the encounters (see Maoz, 2011; Nadler & Saguy, 2004; for additional qualitative evidence). Related findings were observed in a study of interactions between Jewish and Arab educators in Israel (Maoz, 2000). When discussing issues related to the educational system, a topic clearly common to both groups, Jewish participants were more active and dominant in the interactions, whereas Arabs were passive and uninvolved. However, when the discussion shifted to issues concerning the political conflict in the region, Arabs were more involved in the interaction and also expressed more positive attitudes toward it (Maoz, 2000).

There is also an abundance of anecdotal support for such differences. For example, in November 2005, an Israeli peace center brought together Palestinian and Israeli architecture students to design hypothetical joint-housing projects. In the course of the encounters, the students learned about housing prototypes in Palestinian and Israeli societies, and then worked in mixed Palestinian-Israeli groups to design a building that could house both Palestinian and Israeli families. Interviews with the participants a few months later revealed that while the project seemed to have had a positive impact on the perceptions and feelings of Israelis, who reported enjoyment and satisfaction with the encounters, it did little to change those of the Palestinians, whose main reactions were frustration and disappointment (Zandberg, 2006; see also Nadler & Saguy, 2004). These dynamics are consistent with meta-analytic findings that show that even though contact relates to improved intergroup attitudes among both advantaged and disadvantaged group members, it has been shown to be significantly less effective for improving the outgroup attitudes of disadvantaged group members (Tropp & Pettigrew, 2005).

Together, these findings raise the question, "Why is that the case?" What is it about a focus on commonalities (coupled with a de-emphasis on power) that makes advantaged group members feel favorable toward it? I offer an answer to this question in the next section, in which I consider the content of contact as strategic in the sense of serving, or not serving, group members' motivation for social change (versus stability).

THE CONTENT OF INTERGROUP ENCOUNTERS AND CONSEQUENCES FOR THE STATUS QUO

As stated earlier, the question of "who benefits" from encounters that are focused on commonalities was rarely raised. In recent years, however, scholars have begun to explore the possibility that optimal forms of contact might not necessarily promote social change toward equality. Specifically, these scholars have pointed to a potential disjuncture between optimal forms of contact and the development of attitudes pertaining to changes in the group-based hierarchy (Dixon, Levine, Reicher, & Durrheim, 2012; Saguy, Tausch, Dovidio, & Pratto, 2009; Wright & Lubensky, 2009). The central argument in this line of thinking is that the focus on pleasant and cooperative relations works to diminish the tendency to view the groups in "us" versus "them" terms. Instead, optimal forms of contact promote either an individuating view of outgroup members (Brewer & Miller, 1984) or a view of the outgroup as part of a common superordinate category (Gaertner & Dovidio, 2012).

These orientations, even though they may drive positive outgroup attitudes and emotions, are at odds with the psychological processes needed for collective action to occur. Indeed, efforts to promote social change emerge from an awareness of group-based injustice and the recognition of differential intergroup access to important resources (van Zomeren et al., 2008). Moreover, collective action among the disadvantaged is motivated by anger toward advantaged groups over group-based injustice (Simon & Klandermans, 2001) and by strong identification with one's subgroup (Wright & Lubensky, 2009). These orientations (awareness of group-based inequality, injustice, and outgroup-directed anger) are much less likely to develop when intergroup encounters draw attention away from intergroup comparisons and differences (Dixon et al., 2012; Saguy et al., 2009).

These ideas point to a troubling gap between the ultimate aim of contact intervention, which is to transform social injustice at a broad social level, and the changes it was shown to produce, which are mainly reductions in individuals' prejudices. Improvement in individuals' attitudes may not necessarily promote the political reforms that are essential for the reduction of injustice. Furthermore, positive contact may impact minority group members' political consciousness in ways that can lead them to become less concerned with current discriminatory practices. Thus, by focusing individuals' attention on commonalities between the groups, what is considered optimal contact may, inadvertently, have the ironic consequence of reinforcing existing status relations.

Several lines of work, which have primarily focused on members of disadvantaged groups, offer support for this idea. For example, for South African Blacks, intergroup contact was associated with less support for policies that can promote the rights of their ingroup (Dixon, Durrheim, & Tredoux, 2007). These effects were replicated in another study conducted in South Africa (Cakal, Hewstone, Schwär, & Heath, 2011), while further indicating that for Blacks, the negative association between contact and collective action was mediated by decreased perceptions of one's group as unjustly deprived. Consistent findings were also obtained among Arabs in Israel (Saguy et al., 2009). We found that having more Jewish friends (a form of optimal contact) predicted better attitudes toward Jews and less attention to the inequality between the groups. Moreover, these outcomes were associated with greater perceptions of Jews as fair, which in turn were associated with less support for egalitarian policies. The negative association between positive intergroup contact and collective action intentions was further supported by longitudinal data from a study of college students in the United States, which showed that for Latino-Americans, more friendships with Whites were negatively associated with collective action intentions, with a similar (albeit marginally significant) association emerging among African-Americans (Tropp, Hawi, Van Laar, & Levin, 2012).

To shed more light on the mechanism accounting for these effects, Saguy and Chernyak-Hai (2012) examined the association between friendly intergroup contact and the tendency to attribute social disadvantage of minority groups to discrimination—a perception that is a key factor in mobilizing subordinate groups to act for social change (Walker & Smith, 2002). Participants were Ethiopian Jews in Israel who, compared to non-Ethiopian Jews, suffer notable, enduring social disadvantage (Central Bureau of Statistics, 2013) and encounter discrimination in various life domains. They were asked to judge a hypothetical scenario which described an Ethiopian Jew whose application for a desirable job was turned down for no obvious reason. Participants then indicated whether they attributed the rejection to discrimination, or to the applicant's lack of qualifications. Results revealed that experiences of optimal contact with non-Ethiopian Jews were associated with lower tendencies to make such attributions to discrimination, and with greater perceptions of the social system in Israel as legitimate. Consistent findings were obtained among members of the Maori, a disadvantaged group in New Zealand, for whom having more friends from the dominant group (New Zealand Europeans) was associated with the legitimization of inequality, which in turn predicted less support for reparative social policies (Sengupta & Sibley, 2013).

As for members of advantaged groups, research suggests that a sole focus on commonalities, even though this is sometimes associated with support for policies that can promote equality (Hayes & Dowds, 2006; Pettigrew, Wagner, & Christ, 2007), can also have the paradoxical outcome of reducing sensitivity to injustice across group lines. This latter notion comes from experimental studies which attempted to detect the causal influence a commonality focus may have on members of advantaged groups. For example,

Banfield and Dovidio (2013) demonstrated that White Americans for whom common-group (American) identity of Blacks and Whites was emphasized were less sensitive to racial bias relative to participants for whom separate identities were emphasized (or relative to those who were exposed to neutral information). In a different laboratory experiment we found that whereas advantaged group members indeed had more favorable attitudes toward disadvantaged groups following a commonality-focused encounter, such favorable attitudes did not translate into egalitarian resource allocation toward the disadvantaged group (Saguy et al., 2009).

Taken together, this research suggests that an emphasis on commonalities in intergroup encounters—and the blurring of power differences— occurring in many of the applications of contact theory might, indirectly, contribute to the maintenance of the status quo. This can occur by reducing the desire for social change among low-power groups and by reducing sensitivity to injustice among high-power groups. As such, the choice to focus intergroup encounters on commonalities versus differences is not to be considered simply a question of taste or abstract preference, but can be an important strategic tool that benefits one's group, the advantaged group, over the counterpart.

Thus, by emphasizing commonalities and de-emphasizing power differences, high-power groups may reduce tension and avoid contentious issues, while further reinforcing the status quo favoring their own group. By contrast, addressing issues that are at the heart of the power relations may pose a threat to current hierarchical relations because bringing them to light can promote awareness of the inequality. Stated differently, relative to issues that are rooted in commonalities, addressing topics that are at the heart of power differences between groups may be more contentious and difficult to discuss, but at the same time, may promote the possibility of changes to the status quo.

IMPLICATIONS

The research reviewed in this chapter raises a pressing question for both academic work and practical efforts: how should intergroup encounters be constructed so that they would not involve demobilizing effects on disadvantaged or advantaged groups? The model developed by the School for Peace at Wahat al-Salam–Neve Shalom (Halabi, 2004) is highly relevant to this question because it places power dynamics at the heart of the encounter. Emerging studies support this emphasis. Vezzali, Andrighetto, and Saguy (2016) have shown that direct contact does not undermine motivation for social change, and might even increase it, when the content of the contact is focused more on differences than commonalities between groups. In their work they found that among native Italians (advantaged group members), cross-group friendships with immigrants were associated with increased social change motivation, but only when contact was focused more on differences than commonalities. Results were replicated with another sample of both advantaged (Italian) and disadvantaged (immigrant) group members.

These results are consistent with the "critical intergroup dialogue approach," which advocates an explicit focus on power relations during a structured contact situation. These power relations constitute the basis of the model developed at the School for Peace at Wahat al-Salam–Neve Shalom (Halabi, 2004; Zuniga, Nagda, & Sevig, 2002). Similarly, Becker, Wright, Lubenski, and Zhou (2013) demonstrated that when the content of contact involved (versus did not involve) a focus on power differences as illegitimate, contact did not have a demobilizing effect among members of disadvantaged groups.

Future research can productively develop a systematic model of contact that involves a focus on differences, and/or differences in power; such a model will be evidence-based, and will enable critical theoretical and practical advancement in this field of intergroup contact, and harmony more generally. When thinking of such a model of contact, a great challenge that arises is how to get members of advantaged and disadvantaged groups to be willing to openly address their differences, and particularly their differences in power. As evident throughout this book, such a discussion is challenging on many levels. This is not surprising given the well-known tendency of advantaged groups to avoid such discussions in order to protect their moral image (Knowles et al., 2014; Saguy & Kteily, 2014). The development of such a model should therefore be based on a fruitful integration of social psychological insights about the psychology of high-power and low-power groups, together with field applications of creative encounter models such as the one developed at the School for Peace at Wahat al-Salam–Neve Shalom.

CLOSING REMARKS

One of the most critical aims of social psychological science is to inform practical solutions to pressing social problems, many of which are associated with tensions between groups in society (Demoulin, Leyens, & Dovidio, 2009). Among the most studied interventions for ameliorating tension between groups is intergroup contact (Allport, 1954; Paluck & Green, 2009). The central notion in contact theory is that intergroup bias can be substantially reduced via positive encounters between members of different groups. Decades of research within the framework of intergroup contact have focused on the processes that are responsible for the effects of contact on attitudes, and on the underlying principles of what constitutes a "positive," or optimal, encounter (Pettigrew & Tropp, 2006). A central element that emerges from this work is that in order for contact to be effective, it needs to give rise to a sense of common identity, shared by members of both groups.

Harmony-inducing strategies can have positive consequences for intergroup attitudes that are both obvious and relatively immediate. Nevertheless, as the research reviewed in this chapter suggests, even though the consequences for the advantaged group are sometimes positive, members of disadvantaged groups are likely to become more supportive of the very system that disadvantaged them as a result of optimal contact. This dynamic is important to recognize because, first, without such recognition, many prejudice-reduction interventions might reinforce the status quo even though they aim to achieve the opposite outcome. Second, it is critical to attempt to find and provide solutions to such contradiction. The as-yet meager work that has begun to provide solutions clearly points to the importance of having members of advantaged groups be willing to address differences during contact, and more importantly, be critical of their own power position. This can maintain pressures for social change by disadvantaged group members while providing an avenue for communication and exchange with advantaged group members. In addition, to the extent that recognizing both commonality and group-based differences and inequality helps people extend principles or morality across group lines, advantaged group members may become more motivated to advance change themselves. Future research can focus on how to enhance the ability of members of both advantaged and disadvantaged groups to address such topics in a way that would promote sensitivity to inequality, while not undermining potential harmony between the groups.

PART 1　HUMAN RIGHTS AND POLITICAL ACTIVISM

1 · MICHAEL SFARD

Human Rights Advocate

Born in 1972, Michael Sfard is an attorney specializing in international human rights law and the laws of war. Sfard grew up in Jerusalem and served in the Israeli Defense Forces (IDF) as a military paramedic. Sfard was a conscientious objector and spent three weeks in military prison because of his refusal to serve in Hebron in the occupied West Bank. He obtained his law degree from the Hebrew University in Jerusalem, after which he apprenticed with Attorney Avigdor Feldman and worked in Feldman's office for five years. Meanwhile, during a year in London, he completed a master's degree in International Human Rights Law at UCL. In early 2004, Sfard opened his own legal practice in Tel Aviv. Today Sfard is the legal adviser to several Israeli human rights organizations and peace groups (including Yesh Din, Peace Now, and Breaking the Silence) and represents Palestinian communities (like the Village of Bil'in) and Israeli and Palestinian activists. Sfard led, and continues to lead, legal campaigns for the evacuation of illegal settlements and outposts built in the occupied West Bank (most notably, his successful litigation for removal of the Migron outpost), and he has handled numerous petitions concerning the Separation Barrier. He has represented many conscientious objectors, led the case against the Israeli policy of "targeted assassinations," and represents Palestinian detainees before parole boards. Michael Sfard attended the School for Peace Course for Facilitators of Groups in Conflict in 1994 at Wahat al-Salam–Neve Shalom. He was interviewed for this project in spring 2007.

At Neve Shalom, I finally understood my connection to all the conquests and expulsions: not a legal connection, but one of silence, of acquiescence, of resigning myself to let it happen. It's about responsibility.

Michael, tell me about how you were affected by the course you took at Neve Shalom.

The bottom line, completely without exaggeration, is that it unequivocally changed my life. It is the point of reference for all my development as a human being and certainly as an Israeli. I was just out of the army; I was twenty-two. I was actually still on unpaid termination leave from the Nahal Brigade and, since I was a group leader, I was sent to take the School for Peace Course for Facilitators of Groups in Conflict, and they even paid my fee. This came at just the right time for me because the army years are exceedingly problematical from a personal development standpoint; at the end, I was starved for both emotional and intellectual challenges. The course provides both, in one concentrated and generous serving.

The work you do as you struggle with the things you encounter in the course stays with you for a long time afterward. It's like that toothpaste commercial about how it keeps on working. . . . It keeps on working because what I felt I got from that course was not only about Jews and Arabs. I got a complete set of equipment, tools, lenses, I don't know what to call it, which allowed me to examine the behavior of groups of people in all sorts of cross-sections. I think that my understanding concerning men and women changed: it improved amazingly, even though the Neve Shalom course did not deal directly with gender issues. Even now when I look at social situations, sociological situations of one sort or another, the tools I use to analyze them, my most basic tools, are from Neve Shalom.

Meanwhile, the course is not just a pleasant memory: I shed a lot of my innocence during that period, thanks to the course, because of the course. Two kinds of innocence: One was my Zionist innocence. I'm saying this as clearly as possible; it's not simple at all. And the other kind was the sort of innocence that permits us to say, hey, we are all human beings, this too shall pass and then everything will be fine. So in a certain sense, confronting this actually reinforced my identity as someone who was coming from the perspective of wanting to ignore differences, to say let's all dance together in one circle and we are all human beings and the differences between us are not important, and there is absolute equality. It was this kind of simplistic liberalism, this very superficial leftist stance.

I came to understand that the fact that we are all human beings is only part of the story, that my being a Jew is significant; it's not a question of good or bad, but it is significant. The fact that someone else is an Arab is signifi- cant and it has significance for how we relate to each other, whether I want that to be the case or not. This understanding, this insight is very powerful and has stayed with me, maybe even having an inverse effect . . . on my sense of belonging to this place. It's very strange.

MULTIPLE PERSPECTIVES

This brings me to the next important point, which is the ability to accept that there can be several aspects to a single story. This is something you don't understand until you notice it, until a day comes when you see the light. . . . One fine day you understand that different people can see the same reality differently and that we don't necessarily have to decide that one person is wrong and another is right. People can live together in that reality and see it differently, and what's important is that they see it differently. It's less impor- tant to try to find out what really happened because the very fact that they see reality differently has implications for their living together. And this thing is simply part of me in everything, everything I do, in work relationships, every- thing. In other words, it doesn't just involve conflicts between peoples, between the sexes or between races; it addresses the relations between people in general. In the specific Neve Shalom course that I took, there was a practice of trying to understand that while I am looking at something and seeing it as square, the person sitting next to me in the room is looking at the same thing and seeing it as round, and my job is not to blame him for having terrible eyesight, but to try to understand that he sees it differently. It took me a very long time in the course to accept this; but after you accept it, it really does change the way you look at all relationships between people, and I take this with me wherever I go.

Talk a little more about the impact of this in your
personal and professional life.

Consider the example of the relationship between two people who are a couple. . . . Today I am more interested in the fact that someone feels some- thing, feels, let's say . . . hurt by me. Today it's more important to me to under- stand what he feels than to try to persuade him that he's wrong because he wasn't supposed to feel that way. It's less important who is right, because there really is no such thing. When I am having an argument with someone and they see something differently than I see it, the fact is that we have a disagreement about how things look. That's what interests me: that this is our situation. I'm less interested in the fact that I can or cannot persuade that other person to see things the way I do. Our human story is the fact that we see things differently and we have to let this manifest itself and not negate the other person.

I am a lawyer now. My profession deals all the time with different narratives. I am always representing one side and the other side is representing the other party. We deal all the time, nonstop, with stories. I think this greatly helps me to understand the situation, because sometimes the sense that you are right can blind you. You feel so strongly that you are right that you cannot really step into the shoes of your opponent, which is a loss, because you are unable to fully understand. In my profession, in the end, if you cannot fully understand the other side, you won't be able to see things the way the other side sees them, and you also won't be able to properly appreciate the strength of the other side's case.

Another thing is that today, a large part of what I do is representing the Palestinian narrative, and I feel like someone who can speak two languages. . . . That is, I am certainly an Israeli Jew and as such I know very well that I'm coming from the Israeli Zionist discourse. I know exactly what pushes people's buttons in that narrative, I know the weaknesses of that narrative, I know its strengths, I know all of that. I know that in a lot of cases now I represent "Palestinian interests," in quotation marks, but I don't really think that these are Palestinian interests: I think that they are Israeli interests to the same degree. . . . But I represent interests that are perceived as Palestinian interests, and I am able today to see things from that angle. I feel like someone who previously spoke only French and now has also learned English, so he transitions into the possibility of communicating with more people, and his capacity for creative thought has grown. A language is not just a tool for communication, it's actually also a tool for your own communication with yourself. So the more languages you know, the more you can express yourself, the more creative your thinking becomes, and that's how I feel in this context. But I feel uncomfortable in that I seem to be giving myself compliments now.

IDEOLOGICAL METAMORPHOSIS

Both in practice and ideologically, the course influenced me enormously. When I got to Neve Shalom, I already knew that I was going to study law, but thanks to the course, the realms in which I wanted to change the world also shifted. Originally I aspired to petition the Supreme Court on cases of freedom of expression that would change the world. Later I realized that the things that are most important to me involve the Israeli-Palestinian conflict. I already saw myself as a leftist in every respect—one of what I call in hindsight the "soldiers with blankets": when right-wingers are beating a Palestinian prisoner, these guys bring him a blanket against the cold. But the fiction that you can be an enlightened occupier really blew up in my face at Neve Shalom. That revelation marked a very significant new stage for me: it led me to choose to refuse a military call-up, long before the second Intifada began in the fall of 2000 and before the influential Courage to Refuse group was established in 2001.

For someone who goes through the course at Neve Shalom wholeheartedly, there is a stage when you know that you are continuing to play a role and you know that you're lying; you continue to say the same things but, deep inside, you know that there is a gap between what you are presenting outwardly and what is happening inside of you. For me, this feeling was very, very difficult, because I don't like to lie. I remember one specific session when I got angry at some image about a donkey and its rider, with the donkey being the Palestinian people and the rider being the Zionist entity. I have forgotten the details but I remember having been very angry at this image. Afterward, at home, I was even angrier when I realized that I had not said anything about it; I went back determined to crack that open, at least that one phrase, so that they wouldn't say it anymore. And even as I was speaking, I already knew that I didn't believe what I was saying.

JAIL TIME

In 1998 when I was called up for reserve duty in Hebron, I refused to report for duty and went to jail instead. From that point to defending conscientious objectors was not much of a leap, and it already seemed very natural.

The formative moment is not when you represent someone else who is a conscientious objector, but rather your own refusal. That's the formative moment. That moment was undoubtedly a product of the process I had gone through, and the main catalyst for it was the course at Neve Shalom. I found that things suddenly fall into place. Everything; suddenly. You realize things that maybe already were there, but suddenly you understand them differently. Suddenly I was trying to really think about how it feels to be an Arab citizen in Israel. This isn't something you really ask yourself about, because you are captive to these concepts of we have a state, everything is democratic, there is equality here and there's no law preventing an Arab from becoming the prime minister or defense minister or chief of staff. Not only are you inside of this thing; you're also in total segregation in Israel. I was born and grew up in Jerusalem, a mixed city where I did not see a single Arab in my entire life. What does this "I did not see" mean? They passed in front of my retina but I did not really see and I did not connect, of course. Well, here and there, the [left-wing political party] Ratz youth movement, left-wing activism of one sort or another, so there were encounters but they were fleeting and superficial, not serious.

Then suddenly you are thrust into this consciousness at Neve Shalom with all the tension that goes along with it, and you really have to be authentic at some point because by now you are sick of the perpetual pretense. Little by little you start to understand what it is actually like, to be a citizen who belongs to a minority that is in conflict with the majority. The moment I understood, there was a natural progression to where I could no longer be a part of this. I am talking on purpose about the Arab citizens of Israel. Of course when we are dealing with the territories, then the story is much simpler from that standpoint. So it was a tremendous catalyst, there's no doubt of that. Until I got to Neve Shalom, I was a combat soldier. I don't want to say that I regret it: I was a combat soldier who was in the territories and did not refuse and did not think about refusing, on the contrary, I argued against what were relatively marginal phenomena of refusal and I never imagined for a moment that someday I would refuse.

You said: "I was always asking myself, if I did not refuse, then how could I look at myself in the mirror afterward?" That was the real question.

Yes . . . I was telling myself things that related to other things . . . things like: I am talking really well and I've never had a problem with expressing myself, so I am talking really well, but now is the time when I have to stand behind the words I speak, and standing behind the words means not to be part of the machine.

I had this moment in front of the officer . . . the moment when the officer said, "Look, I can't promise you that I won't put you up for a disciplinary hearing but I want to ask you, just so I know. . . . If we give you a role that has no contact with the population there in Hebron, without touching the population at all, then would you retract your refusal?" Never mind that an affirmative answer to that proposition is immoral in my view, and also kind of cowardly. Like, it's OK for others to do the "dirty work"! That made me say no, immediately. But later I tried to think about it and to really try to imagine doing things there that would not involve direct contact with the population . . . and then came this matter of being a cog in the machine . . . and in the context of Neve Shalom, it's fairly clear. It's awfully clear. I am the good leftist who comes from a good home and wants peace and wants brotherhood. I come to Neve Shalom and suddenly I am fielding all these accusations as if. . . . What? Excuse me, but am I the one who started the Six-Day War? Did I do the conquering there? Did I expel people from Jaffa? What does all that (pardon the expression) shit have to do with me? And at Neve Shalom, I understood what my connection is: It does not have to be a legal one, involving criminal thinking that can be proven in a court of law beyond a reasonable doubt; it can be a connection of silence, of acquiescence, of coming to terms with letting it happen. All of these things definitely arose at Neve Shalom. It's the feeling of responsibility.

Incidentally, there's something else that's connected, an intuitive connection, via the "school of identities" that I encountered at Neve Shalom. There were things that I was learning on my own back then about the banality of evil and the dangers of modernity and things relating to bureaucracy and being a cog in the system that does evil and whether this cog is responsible or not responsible. All these things brought me, in the end, to some kind of understanding about a human being who wants not to feel that he is a cog in the machine. Given a kind of determinism dictating that he will be part of some kind of big machine, he has to know, he has to constantly look around and say: Do I agree or do I not agree to do what I'm being commanded to do? It's not especially problematical to say no when they are telling you to shoot an unarmed child waiving a white flag. The trick is to say no when you are ordered into a guard tower, and the guard tower is part of a huge system that ends with the child being killed. The connection between these two things is problematical. Yet the moment arrived when all these things came together for me. It could have happened to me on an earlier round of reserve duty when I was in Gaza; it could have happened to me on the next round of reserve duty. It happened at a point when things had reached some kind of . . . when the circle had closed.

CRITICAL VISION

The ideological change is very connected with the issue of thinking critically. You develop the ability to be critical about the obvious, about the self-evident things broadcast by the society around you. There's a lot of danger in that [critical stance] and I'm afraid that a lot of the Neve Shalom graduates could be prey to that danger. You receive a powerful tool that you are capable of using to look critically at social phenomena that you formerly saw as self-evident, as things that were just part of your culture. With your new critical stance, you can easily become a refugee and totally stop belonging. The hardest thing is to go on being critical while still belonging, even when you suddenly see how awful everything is. When you suddenly discover that everything you saw as rosy is actually blacker than coal, the simplest thing is to lose any desire to be connected with the culture and with the people and with the nation and with the gender that you are supposed to belong to . . . to say that everything is so awful, to suddenly discover that they sold me a bunch of fairy tales in history class, they sold me a bunch of myths, they brainwashed me about a million and one things . . . to say I want no part of this place . . . that the Israel Defense Forces is also my enemy.

This almost happened to me, but in the end it did not, and I am very glad. I did reach a situation where I felt that I didn't belong to the collective; I had an identity, a cultural identity, but I did not feel that there was a group, a collective, that I could say I am a part of.

But now you are very involved in the collective?
Yes, that's my solution; that's my cure. It's not for everyone, certainly. It's like when they say that freedom of expression could be dangerous, like the freedom of expression to tell lies: The solution is even more freedom of expression. Flood everything with free speech and then the truth will emerge; that's

the liberal theory. So by the same token, if there is a sort of belongingness problem, then become even more involved. That's how it is for me; and for me it is also very, very important to belong.

Around the time I was at Neve Shalom, I worked as a researcher for the current affairs TV programs Erev Hadash and Musaf Hamosafim on Friday evenings. I began studying law and moved back to Jerusalem (where I was born) from Tel Aviv, to continue my law studies at the Hebrew University. I was also the legal affairs reporter for the Kol Ha'ir newspaper in Jerusalem. Toward the end of law school, I began working less at Kol Ha'ir and writing long articles, analyses, and features. After law school I moved back to Tel Aviv for an apprenticeship with Avigdor Feldman in 1998–99 and then stayed on as an attorney until 2000, when I went to London with my partner Nirith Ben Horin. There I did a master's degree in international human rights law and international humanitarian law, which deals with the laws of war. I finished the degree in three semesters. We returned to Israel with great ambivalence.

I went back to work for Avigdor Feldman. Broadly speaking, the firm handles two main areas: criminal law and High Court of Justice cases with an emphasis on constitutional human rights law. I was dealing with both areas but generally was more involved with the High Court cases. We represented a lot of human rights organizations in Israel, both Israeli and Palestinian. The main projects I was involved in included the High Court petition against the Israeli government's policy of targeted assassinations, and High Court and other court cases involving conscientious objectors.

What does your law practice encompass today?

I represent Courage to Refuse, an organization of reservists who refuse reserve duty in the Occupied Territories. I am the legal consultant to the movement, and I also represent the refusers themselves individually when they come to trial and go to jail. I represent them even for small things. So I remain involved, which is very, very important to me. It's a kind of therapy. Because I also remember that feeling: The loneliness is the greatest price you pay for refusing. There is tremendous power in the existence of a movement that also provides legal services, and you can consult with them, and that helps a lot. On the targeted assassinations issue, we submitted a case to the Supreme Court (sitting as the High Court of Justice), a petition on the July 2002 targeted killing of [Salah Mustafa Mohammad] Shehadeh in which fourteen innocent people were killed, mainly children. The cases vary widely. And of course there is Yoni Ben-Artzi [Sara Netanyahu's nephew], whom I represent as a pacifist and whom the IDF would like to hang from the tallest tree.

I have an office now in Tel Aviv with three attorneys and apprentices. The firm represents several Israeli human rights and peace organizations and Palestinian communities, plus individuals who have been injured by the Israeli regime in the West Bank or Gaza. I am also a legal consultant to Yesh Din, to the settlement monitoring team at Peace Now, and to Breaking the Silence, among others, and I represent the Palestinian Village Council of Bil'in in various legal struggles. My law office is handling petitions against the construction of the Separation Barrier and petitions seeking to repel incursions by settlers into Palestinians' land; it represents Palestinians injured by settler violence or by the security services; and it handles cases for peace activists. The office also deals with copyright law and represents directors, screenwriters, authors and other artists.

I could not have been one of those attorneys who make a lot of money from real estate because I am incapable of doing things that don't interest me. Articles about real estate just put me to sleep, so it's not really a question of choice, but a question of capability. I simply can't do those kinds of things. I am happy being someone who can make a living doing what interests him and what he feels is also, beyond a livelihood, something of value. One cannot ask for more.

2 · SUHAD HAMMOUD DAHLEH

Human Rights Advocate

Born and raised in Acre, Suhad Hammoud Dahleh hosted her own radio talk show and was co-anchor for a TV magazine about the Middle East while she was still an undergraduate law student at Tel Aviv University. After qualifying to practice, Hammoud Dahleh began a New Israel Fund leadership training program in human and civil rights law and social justice, subsequently completing a master's degree in international human rights and humanitarian law at American University in Washington, DC. During her training there, she worked at the American Civil Liberties Union and other human rights organizations in Washington, D.C. Returning from the United States, she joined the legal division of Adalah, the Legal Center for Arab Minority Rights in Israel, during a very tumultuous period—October 2000. Together with her Adalah colleagues, she monitored the deliberations of the Or Commission, the state committee of inquiry established to investigate the events of October 2000 and more broadly the relations between the Arab minority in Israel and the State. Subsequently she partnered in setting up a private law firm in Jerusalem specializing in the defense of the human rights of Palestinians in the occupied territories, including East Jerusalem. Suhad Hammoud Dahleh took the joint SFP-university course, "The Jewish-Arab Conflict and Theories of Inter-Group Conflict," at Tel Aviv University in 1994–1995. She was interviewed on September 15, 2001.

We are of course an integral part of this land, yet in this country we live on the margins, politically, economically and otherwise. . . . You can't just complain all the time about the reality without trying to do something about it; we have to go out there and try to change the reality, our reality.

I don't really come from a uni-national, monolingual background. I am from Acre, an ethnically mixed city. I can't say that Acre is a beacon of coexistence; on the contrary. But the daily contact is there. I was even educated in Jewish preschools. I may have been the only Arab girl there. This made a lasting impact on me, both for better and for worse.

So when I reached university, contact with Jewish students wasn't new for me: that was just how things were. But the SFP course at the university was special. First of all, the people were there because they wanted to be. It wasn't a required course. Certainly the Jewish students you meet there—with the friction, the argument and the dialogue—are highly motivated for the encounter with Arab students and looking to address all kinds of things connected with the Arab-Jewish conflict.

So the profile of that specific group was unlike what I experienced ordinarily in Acre. There, the experience was fairly negative, due to the realities of life in Acre, and definitely as the only Arab girl in a Jewish kindergarten class. It was really a tough experience. Maybe it strengthened me for the future, I don't know, but in the near term it was very unpleasant for me as an Arab girl in a [mostly] Jewish city where Jews have a certain orientation. But to return to the SFP course: The period we were living through at the time, 1994–95, was not an easy time. It was not long before Rabin was assassinated, and we should consider everything that preceded that, all the incitement. That was the context while we were taking the course. Plus, as a female Arab student coming to live in Tel Aviv and looking for an apartment—that wasn't easy either. We were insulted repeatedly because apartment owners refused to lease to us; it took a lot of time and effort until we finally found ourselves an apartment near the university. Even then, the landlord stipulated all kinds of things relating to my national origin. His ideas were so biased. And this was north Tel Aviv, supposedly full of open-minded leftists, but we had problems there anyway. The hassles we go through in finding a place to live are not like what Jewish students go through. They've finished with the army by that time whereas we are younger and relatively inexperienced, arriving straight from home to encounter all these problems and a lot of insults. Not easy.

So we started university and I guess I was drawn to your course because it spoke to me. I don't think there's even one Arab in Israel who wouldn't feel that this course spoke to him. Maybe Jews in Israel wouldn't be as attracted because they have the privilege of skipping such courses, but every Arab in Israel I think has to pay his dues, so to speak, by experiencing an encounter like this. I also think that it's in his interest to do it. Jewish students who are attracted to the course come, I think, because they want to see [Arabs], to talk, to meet. They come to argue and they come to listen.

This desire is of interest to us. As Palestinian citizens of Israel, and as a national minority in this country, we have a dream: to live in dignity. To me, that means to achieve full equality and attain our collective rights as a minority, and at the same time to assist our people, to secure a national home for the Palestinian people through the establishment of an independent free Palestinian state alongside Israel. I believe that we should aspire to achieve those goals through peaceful struggle, through dialogue with people, and through a legal and public process. Naturally we are interested in these encounter groups as a forum for sitting down with people and looking for ways to change the dreary reality here.

So let's say it was a journey, maybe. I remember some really tough arguments; they couldn't be glossed over. I remember things we talked about, fifteen years ago. The Arab group, as I recall, was not homogeneous. People held a range of views. I remember Rabah Halabi talking about how we were feeling, about the connection between the feeling of belonging and the pride that an Arab citizen feels. That is, the more I feel that I am connected with my group, the more I become accustomed to it and feel pride, as if I am conserving something that belongs to me, and I go on with it. That's my clearest memory. I recall that there were very difficult conflicts. I remember that there was some very sensitive and highly charged material that you raised for us there. You and Rabah were, of course, completely objective and tried, as I recall, to move the discussion forward without personal involvement from either of you. The goal is wonderful, of course. Encounters like these between university students, forums where they can meet, argue, talk things over, these are very important. I remember that the period we were going through at the time was quite difficult.

What did this encounter do for you, at twenty, this opportunity to talk with people in a somewhat more equal way?

It was a different time, and each period is different, and people change for political, social and economic reasons, or whatever. It was a natural progression for me. It wasn't that I didn't know that such groups existed; actually, I always believed that they were there. If you don't have faith, you really despair and just curse the dark. That's not me. I wanted to light a candle. Even given the tough reality we lived in, even after all kinds of unpleasant (to put it mildly) encounters that I experienced as a Palestinian woman in Israel, I still wanted to make a difference, to change public opinion and to influence the reality we live in. This fighting spirit has been with me all my life. Today the reality has deteriorated further. People in Israel are becoming more racist and less tolerant towards other racial and ethnic groups, and when it comes to the Palestinians inside Israel or in the Occupied Territories, the situation is even worse.

IT ALL BEGAN IN PRESCHOOL

The truth is that it all started in preschool. When I showed up with my name they would say, "Oh, Suhad, that's an Arab name." And you know that children are like sponges; whatever they absorb at home, they will say openly to you, without filtering. They were rude, racist and violent. Those racist incidents also happened when I was studying in an Arab school but living in a Jewish neighborhood. Our whole reality was rather strange. You're a Palestinian Arab girl living in a mixed city; your family is choosing to live in a Jewish area because it has better amenities and infrastructure. By coincidence you find yourself, a Palestinian, living on a road named "Golani Brigade Street." And since the neighborhood community center is the closest one to our house, your parents register you for summer camp there. This was during the Lebanon War. Summer camp that is supposed to be fun, with a swimming pool and games, but suddenly you encounter the reality that you are in. I remember the Lebanon War in the background and I'm in a classroom where they are teaching about loving the homeland. The instructor, who is a soldier, has come home from some battle in the Lebanon War and suddenly vents all of her rage because she assumes that everyone is Jewish and has a certain orientation. Then the children discover that I am an Arab and wham! They are like, "We've beaten you Arabs," and all of that. You have all this baggage. The truth is that it was a really tough period, really tough. You just want to ignore them, not to come near them, because you haven't grown up yet or learned how to deal with this. Until you have the maturity and are able to cope, you simply swim as best you can. But it was very hard. In the long term, I think it made me stronger. I knew that this existed. I remember when [Meir] Kahane came to Acre. He went to a shopping center, talking to the crowds, giving his usual racist speech, "Hello Jews and goodbye to the dogs." I remember that, too. This was the background, and despite all of that I was drawn to these encounters [with Jews].

I simply believed there is a better reality than this one, and so why wait, why not work to bring that reality into being and try to find other people to work with. As a law student I despaired when I discovered how many racist laws are on the books. Even in my work as a lawyer I came face to face with institutionalized racism, and it made things even harder. We're not talking about a kindergarten now or about that awful summer camp I went to. We're talking about something much bigger, about the state where we live; this is the establishment here. So what can you say and what can you do and where can you turn? How can you educate your children, what can you tell them? Every word has to be carefully weighed. We don't just chatter; everything has to be thought through, about where we can turn and whether there is hope and believe me, it seems that there is none. This internal dialogue, of course, still goes on inside me, even today.

*Do you feel that the one-year course reinforced your
connection to your identity?*

I wanted to say earlier that, yes, it reinforced my identity. As I think about it, though, I'm not sure about some aspects of this. Did I come with this baggage just to try to promote my cause? To try to raise the consciousness of the Jewish public about the reality we live in? To try to make that whole process happen? Apparently, and of course even with all the arguments, all the feelings, yes, it reinforced that. You believe in it and you're also proud of belonging where you belong and you suffer from the reality you are living in. So there's no doubt that the answer is yes.

Suhad, do you think that you were influential in the group there?
I remember your doing a large share of the work in the
Arab group in the course.

Yes, well, I don't know. The truth is, I have believed and still believe in myself, I believe in the cause that I'm representing, but more than that I believe in the power of women. I feel that women, when they speak out, have a considerable impact on everything. I am totally convinced of that. So what I work on follows naturally somehow, in terms of human rights, the encounter with the establishment, protection of human rights, the rights of Jerusalem residents, and before that the Or Commission, Adalah, after the October [2000] uprising. I couldn't see myself in any other place; it would be impossible; this is who I am. Maybe it has to do with my home environment, or maybe my father, who was also this way, like me. I'm like him. Furthermore, I can see myself for example in all kinds of professional capacities in the area of law because I want to be a liberated human being, a person who works openly and freely for the advancement of this cause I believe in. We are of course an integral part of this land, yet we have not been integrated into the establishment. We live on the margins, politically, economically and otherwise. Our lives have a glass ceiling. I think there is a lot of work to be done internally, inside the establishment in order for us to be integrated. We have to work to change some basic things in people's understanding, their worldview, their political outlook, their understanding of the value of human beings and human rights. As long as the state does not consider itself a state for all its citizens, we will not be fully integrated.

SPEAKING TO AMERICAN JEWISH AUDIENCES

I did my apprenticeship in a private law firm in Haifa, but I was already leaning toward moving ahead on this issue of human rights. I applied for a human rights scholarship that the New Israel Fund offers, which includes studying for a Masters in Law in Human Rights in the U.S.; they accept both Palestinians and Jews as applicants. I was the first woman. So naturally I felt that I've been carrying this burden ever since my childhood, up to and including when I finished university. I went to the United States and lectured extensively to Jewish audiences. Mostly it was to people considered the new generation there, something like the American Jewish Left, but not the mainstream.

I felt that you can criticize anything there except Israel. It's easier for me to be critical of Israel here than in the U.S., and it was very interesting. Sometimes people were enraged, there were provocations from various generations, both younger people and older people, all Jewish.

I wanted to influence public opinion there, in various locations. I went to Washington, to Boston, New York, San Francisco. It was a fairly long trip. It brought my whole experience there into sharper focus. I understood that the NIF was very interested in trying to give the Jews in the U.S. a better understanding about the legal status of Arabs in Israel. After all we went there as jurists through the NIF. Believe me, it wasn't simple. But I always had this urge to go and talk and explain and give speeches to diverse audiences. It was actually a challenge that the audience was not always sympathetic, although even when it was energizing, it was also exhausting. But it was part of that dream of trying to have an impact. You can't just complain all the time about the reality without trying to do something about it; we have to go out there and try to change the reality, our reality.

It was very energizing. I don't know, something about the stress of the encounter ignites a flame, and this flame illuminates a lot of things. That's how it felt to me. When we went out to speak and we would stay afterward and argue, it was interesting, even fascinating, especially when it wasn't just the general population but was an interesting audience of students who came especially to that forum.

RAISING CHILDREN IN THIS REALITY

After that, I went back to the personal realm and was married, and today I have a family. Now I'm responsible for their education; it's not just me anymore. How shall I give them an understanding of life, of this hard reality here? It's very difficult. I told you—every word has to be carefully considered; I can't just throw words around without foundation, because they're listening. They hear the news broadcasts. They are aware of their impossible reality, living in a country that oppressed their people, occupied their land and discriminates against them as citizens.

I want my children to carry on the culture of their people, to be its emissaries in the struggle for equality inside Israel and freedom and self-determination for our people in the Occupied Territories. That's what I would like them to be. So I make some very difficult choices, because I worry that I'm forcing on them a reality they have not chosen. Starting with the choice of school, and including what happens when we watch the news together. When they watch a news broadcast, they ask me about it. We've been through this quite a lot, where they ask a lot of very tough questions about the Lebanon war or the war in Gaza, and you have to cope with them somehow. Meantime you know that this is where you are living: you are living in this country. As a Palestinian in Israel, how can you make a normal life for a child here?

My son already has the beginnings of a critical outlook on reality. I see him as a political creature already. He even has solutions for the conflict and he talks about them. I am happy to hear them. He seems to be utterly welded to the conflict; it's amazing to me how he gets into this so strongly and thoroughly.

Meantime I was working at Adalah—the Legal Center for Arab Minority Rights in Israel. I worked there for a year. Working with a human rights organization was part of my commitment to the scholarship. When the October 2000 protests happened, I was at Adalah. It was about a week or so, and everything just exploded. We had a conference, I remember, in Rhodes—Adalah met there with two Palestinian organizations of human rights lawyers from Jerusalem. Then we got into that whole legal mess that just descended on us one fine day, when the Or Commission [state-appointed committee of inquiry] convened afterward to look into the disturbances and the authorities' response.

WORKING WITH THE OR COMMISSION AND THE FAMILIES OF THE BEREAVED

Let's say that for the Or Commission, I oversaw the matter of values. We couldn't do much as lawyers representing clients, since this was a commission that investigated the public, the police of course, and some of the Arab public including heads of local councils and members of Knesset who are symbols of the Arab public and had a role in those events. We monitored the proceedings. We accompanied the bereaved families [who came to testify], otherwise they would not have come. We explained the legal significance of the proceedings. It was very important to us, too. We coordinated the work.

I handled the media aspects. You have to deal with the media if you want an immediate impact on the evidentiary process, the testimonies in progress. The families were there at a very emotionally charged and difficult time. It all ended with the Commission's report, which they [the authorities] refrained from utilizing in any way. That was terribly, terribly unfortunate. In truth, I can't really blame the Or Commission, I can only blame the establishment, the branches of government, who simply wanted to ditch this commission. As if to say, OK, this is what you decided, we're just going to throw out all this paper with all the ink used to write the commission's conclusions, just throw it in the trash. It was really very aggravating.

When I finished my one-year commitment, I began practicing law with my husband, with whom I had opened a law office by that time, as co-founders. Although the firm has a very diverse legal practice, it deals largely with cases of human rights violations against Palestinians in Jerusalem, the West Bank and Gaza, including petitions to the Supreme Court against the separation wall (the leading case being the Beit Sourik case in 2004, in which the Supreme Court declared 30 kilometers of the wall around Jerusalem to be illegal), land confiscation, residency rights of Palestinians in Jerusalem, prisoners' rights, civil lawsuits against the Israeli army for bodily harm to innocent civilians, and house demolition cases. I also had a dream to set up a human rights organization in Jerusalem. I believe in that kind of organization. I wanted to be able to give legal services for free to Jerusalem residents who suffer terribly from never-ending experiences of racism and discrimination on the day-to-day level.

PLACEMENTS FOR ARAB PROFESSIONALS

While all this was happening, I also ran a project aimed at placing more Arab professional people in private and public companies in Israel. We worked very hard on this project, with funding assistance from a very committed American donor. We attempted to work with leading human resources agencies, offering no-fee training seminars for Arab academics to coach them on writing a CV and handling interviews. Meantime I was meeting with CEOs of companies; we pulled out all the stops, particularly in the private sector. Private companies showed little interest apart from one man, the CEO at

Clal Insurance Company, who was very positive. Apart from pleasant conversations, however, that didn't produce results either.

We found that people's hearts weren't too open and the doors weren't open much at all. You constantly need to get people to help you get in, to go in deeper and get past these problems, to enable people to understand the significance of hiring Arabs into these companies. I think this is an Israeli goal of the highest priority but they did not understand that either. This showed me even more clearly that hate, racism, revulsion, and alienation seem to be the lot of the Israeli [Jewish] public.

I still have a burning passion for these issues. Only a small person can live without protest in a reality [like this]; I can't. I'm proud of who I am and the groups I belong to. A proud person cannot agree to submit to such a reality. You want to change it, no matter the cost. So I have this impulse to assert blame, yes; I have this powerful will to change the reality, by raising my children and bequeathing them my heritage, and also simply through the struggle for our collective rights as a national minority and also by going and struggling against all the racism, not accepting it but rather fighting against it.

A lot of people give way to despair or lose hope. Your vitality and determination not to give in, these are unique.

They used to tell me it was because I was young that I still had the strength for this. They said that it was natural for young people to want to fight back and that's why they always build revolutions on students. But that can't be the whole story, because I still have it.

Earlier you mentioned the power of women. Do you see something special in your power as a woman, your ability to have an impact and change things?

As a Palestinian woman in Israel, I face discrimination on different levels. I wear a minority hat as a woman and as a Palestinian inside Israel, and I face discrimination as all women do from the general public. I face discrimination from my own conservative society as a female and on top of that, I suffer discrimination as a Palestinian from the state and its agencies. I have to be stronger and empowered in order to cope, to survive, to strive. I'm continually needing to fight for my place.

*Now, about 15 years after your course at the SFP, you are completely
wrapped up in this kind of work and you haven't given up. Do you think
that being part of the group in that course had an influence on your
deciding later on to be engaged with these issues?*

Well, this is one of several layers: one level, one route. I've been on this tra-
jectory in some way ever since, at the age of three, I first heard the phrase
"dirty Arab." It began there, and now we are sitting here and talking about it.
The whole thing is one entire process that emerges from those moments
when any Palestinian citizen of Israel has contact with the Israeli Jewish public. What's left is the individual's own personality. Maybe some people are
more passive and are prepared to live in this kind of society, but I don't give
up and I'm not passive. I'm a fighter who wants to change the way things
are. That workshop, that group, encouraged me, let's say. Maybe because of
the type of people I met there. And the way you [facilitators from SFP] presented things to us was comfortable for me.

Sometimes it was hard because there was stress, there were tensions, and
there was some unpleasantness within the group, but something changes
when you grow up, when you're not a stubborn student anymore with that
need to always hang on to your position and advocate for it. In hindsight my
feeling is completely positive, and I hope you keep on going with the work.

Sometimes a person feels things, but when they talk about them, they are
venting their feelings; it's more than just having feelings and also talking; they
are speaking from what they have inside. They aren't lecturing about an academic subject that they researched. When you are living this, the simple act
of talking, getting it out, expressing it, including things that are hard to put
out there in the room in front of people who have completely different perspectives than yours—this by itself is a constructive thing. Maybe it did something to us that we weren't aware of; maybe in the depths of my soul it did
something we didn't notice and weren't aware of. But I'd guess that we really
were aware of it, because any process like that, any encounter like that, all
the things that are said, all the groups, all of that does something to your
worldview and your awareness and your insights and everything.

Do you see your children carrying on with this direction in some way?
Without any doubt whatsoever. I couldn't possibly see it any other way. We
are people who come with the intention of contributing to humanity and to

the society in which we live—otherwise life has no meaning. We are bringing children into this world and giving them the best we can, in order to change racist and depressing realities. We are waiting for the new Martin Luther King.

We are facing a very hard reality; the future is not bright at all. Racism is running rampant in Israeli society, and people aren't ashamed to be racist. Speaking Arabic in public has become challenging. Some Jews refuse to sell or rent property to Arabs. Not a single Arab town was built [in Israel] since 1948. Discrimination against Arabs is growing daily. The Arab education system is far behind the [Jewish] Israeli one. And racist laws are increasingly being legislated. The Arab minority is becoming more marginalized. On the other hand, we are proud of belonging to our people, and proud of our language, our heritage, and our knowledge of this homeland. So what else can we do, except share this land, live together, and make it a better place for the children of both peoples?

3 · MOHAMMAD ABU SNINEH

Human Rights Advocate and Group Facilitator

Mohammad Abu Snineh has had a private law practice in Jerusalem since 2000, focusing on cases involving the military, compensation, security and police restrictions, family unification, and home demolitions. He is licensed to practice law in Israel, Jerusalem, and the West Bank. Among the organizations he works with are the Jerusalem Legal Aid Center, the Civic Coalition for Defending Palestinian Rights in Jerusalem, and Rabbis for Human Rights and, in Ramallah, Al Haq and the Ramallah Prisoners Club. He holds a high diploma in law from the Institute of Arab Research and Studies in Cairo (2004), a B.Sc. in law from Alquds University, Jerusalem (1997), and a Tawjihi matriculation diploma from Al Ebrahmiah College, Jerusalem (1993). Fluent in Arabic and Hebrew with functional competence in English, he is also a trained group facilitator and has pursued broad additional training in diverse areas including human rights, children's rights, conflict management and resolution, documenting the abuse of civilians, and statistical and economic field research. Mohammad Abu Snineh took the SFP Course for Facilitators of Groups in Conflict in 1997–1998. He was interviewed on September 19, 2009.

The idea of human rights law beckoned. It spoke to me as a human being. But I enjoy facilitating groups even more; it makes you feel that you can take someone to a different place. You help one person, or two, or three, and

*incrementally you are building a good society, a group of people. You build
people. That's how I feel, that I build people. It's amazing, that feeling.
I really love this work.*

I did the facilitators course in 1997–1998 while I was at university. During
that era, the course met on weekends for around six months. The experience affected my personality and the way I relate to people in general, not just
in terms of Israelis and Palestinians, but also to people in my own society and
my own group. The course touched on foundational questions about how I
behave with others, no matter who; how I listen to others and understand
where they are coming from. All of that has influenced me deeply.

For me, it was about how to behave with people. I was young and didn't
understand people very well. Mostly I saw things only from my own perspective, as people tend to do. If someone makes a mistake, if he is wrong, we
often behave as if it doesn't matter why. I never wondered why someone did
something. If he made a mistake, that was it.

But if someone affects you, for better or worse, you need to look at that
more deeply. Then you reach a new, more humane level that encompasses
more than just your own personal interest. This whole idea changed me
greatly. I sat with people I never thought to sit down with, with the enemy.
You hear him and he hears you, he sees that you are listening to him and he
listens to you; this has an impact. Suddenly, behind the picture you see, you
discover a human being whom you didn't really see earlier. And beyond
how I related to Israelis in the SFP course, it affected how I relate to my own
friends.

After the course, while I was at university, I did not begin working as a
group facilitator right away, but I remained enthusiastic, and subsequently,
via Muhammad Joudeh, I reconnected with Neve Shalom and the School for
Peace. I came for a job interview and observed one or two workshops and
then began doing facilitation. That step would finally take me to somewhere
else entirely. Facilitation work takes you as a human being to a higher level
in your own humanity so that you're not just fitting in with life the way it is,
anymore.

Meantime, after I began working as a facilitator with binational groups
and groups in conflict, I finished my legal training and did an apprenticeship as an attorney. My father's law office deals with civil law and damages,
and I worked there for a while: nothing to do with human rights yet. But

having begun facilitating with groups, incorporating this very different idea about how you work with someone irrespective of where he is from or what his prejudices are, I found myself leaning toward working in human rights law. After three years doing ordinary civil cases, that was no longer enough for me.

HUMAN RIGHTS LAW BECKONED

While facilitating, I had begun to hear stories about Palestinians living in the territories. I'm a Palestinian too, but this was something else. I felt impelled to help people, as an attorney, as someone who could really do something. The idea of human rights law beckoned. It spoke to me as a human being. It's true you earn a lot less, but that's not crucial. I began working with Al Haq on freedom of movement issues, helping get permits for people who have problems entering Israel. We helped many people but of course not everyone, because of all the obstacles created by the Civil Administration and the DCOs (District Coordination Offices).

I continued working with freedom of movement. That included helping people who sought to leave the country but had been refused exit permits on various security-related grounds. I made contact with a Belgium-based international organization, Lawyers Without Borders [LWOB], and began taking courses with them through Al Haq. LWOB offers joint courses in human rights law for Palestinian and Israeli lawyers. Their approach is different from the School for Peace mode. They don't touch on the conflict at all. The two sides sit together and hear lectures about a given topic, which is not all that great but OK, it still had an impact on me.

I then began working with Rabbis for Human Rights, an Israeli human rights organization, which is where I met Neta Amar, who had also done the facilitators course at Neve Shalom. I actually asked her, Neta, Why are you working on behalf of Palestinians' rights and she said, Well, I took a facilitators course at Neve Shalom, I became acquainted with the issues, and I just plunged in. So I worked with her at RHR-Israel, where she is now a legal adviser. Much of their focus currently is on human rights in the South Hebron Hills area and all the problems there: freedom of movement, home demolitions—all kinds of demolitions. There are Bedouins living there in tents and when some international aid organization built them toilets, they got demolition orders on the toilets.

I don't think it's only due to the sorts of problems we Palestinians face every day that I decided to get involved in human rights law. Many Palestinian lawyers are themselves living this situation, yet it doesn't occur to them to work in human rights. I really think that it was the influence of the facilitators course and other Neve Shalom courses I took that put me on that path.

How did that influence you? In what ways?

When you take a course like that, you really do end up afterward with a different mode of thinking. As someone living under occupation, and having lived a while in Jerusalem, I am aware of the problems facing Palestinian children and youth in Jerusalem, given the policy of Judaizing the city. What we face is not identical to what goes on in the territories. When I was at university, I was never politically involved, nor affiliated with any political organization like the PLO or Hamas, nothing. My thinking was in a different direction. During the SFP course, my entire way of thinking changed. I began thinking differently about people and confronting problems I hadn't considered before. Maybe it's only natural for young men and women to do that, but in my case it was the course that catalyzed it.

In terms of your own identity, did more nationalist components emerge?

Yes, but not just politically: also in terms of understanding my place, exactly who I am, that I'm a Palestinian, not just an Arab. I really woke up to an understanding of where I am, I'm a Jerusalemite with a blue Israeli ID card, not a green Palestinian ID card. Or, I'm a person without Israeli citizenship, holding a Jordanian passport. Or, I'm stateless. All those complexities. I never thought much about all that before, as a university student. It's true that when I began studying law, it did influence my thinking somewhat, so I wasn't like someone who doesn't think at all. But it was the IFP course that gave me a strong sense of where I am. I saw how people look down on others, and realized that we have felt this. As if there is a ranking in status, as if the Jews are at the top looking down on the Palestinians in Israel, and the Palestinians living in Israel are looking down on the Palestinians living in the territories, as if they're inferior. I thought so too, more or less. I met Palestinians from the territories at the SFP course and that also had a major impact on me, because my Jerusalem peers don't generally develop friendships with Palestinians from the occupied territories, even at university.

Of course there were Palestinians from the territories who studied with me, but we didn't hang out much or talk in depth. We didn't seriously discuss all these kinds of things with one another and try to understand them in detail, together. This sort of discussion is not easy. Let's say you have met someone from the territories, you can't just tell him these things. On his part, he can't just say to you, I feel that you are looking down on me and not seeing me as an equal. To get to the point of being able to say such things would take a long time. This interested me, to consider all of these people in that context. I met people who were Palestinians and also Israelis and that was important—I always say this—because you really do come to identify with people, including the other. I went through this in the course, and afterward I understood it better, after I had worked in group facilitation and after I had also read books about it. Before, it had never occurred to me that there were books about all this.

You identify with the oppressed?

Yes, and also with myself, self-identity. And with the nationalist parts of myself. Once upon a time, I realized that if I were to go in the nationalist direction, I would end up in prison. During the first Intifada, it was clear that throwing stones was our nationalism. If you wanted to act, to acknowledge and feel your own national affiliation, you threw stones; there seemed to be no other way back then. I didn't want to go that route, and I simply didn't understand that there is another way. Stone-throwing is not the approach of the entire Palestinian people; some do, but others are moved to pursue a different direction. They move toward a greater national feeling, while understanding where it may be found, having a positive influence on our society, in the process of creating Palestine as a whole. And in the SFP course, I understood this; I connected with a different way of understanding and acting on one's nationalism. This definitely enhanced my understanding of myself, my identification with myself and also with the enemy, and with a different side of being Palestinian that I didn't know about, and with the Palestinians living inside Israel. There is a certain complexity there, and you can discuss the three realms, three components of being Palestinian— with the Jerusalem Palestinians in the middle between the other two. I know Palestinians from Jerusalem who still look at Palestinians from the occupied territories as inferior to them, and some inside Israel who look at other Palestinians as repulsive. They don't say they are better than us, they don't consider that maybe we've gone in different directions. They look at West Bank Palestinians that way because they look at us Jerusalem Palestinians that way, from above.

All of this new understanding evolved for me during the group process and during my own process in the course itself, and afterward in my work. So I identified with myself, got to know myself, got to know my society, understood that there is something that we can do to help people, something that I can do. Unfortunately, we don't have a lot of Palestinian lawyers who deal with human rights; to my regret, there are probably more Israelis than Palestinians doing that work. There simply aren't enough. In my case, the humanitarian aspect worked on me, and I went with it.

So you got to some very deep insights, and you also acted on them.

Yes, I really felt that. In general as Muslims, we have to understand the other side. There are a lot of verses in the Qur'an and also hadiths of the Prophet Muhammad saying that you have to understand the other side. Many Muslims do not fully realize this. If you want to say that someone has made a mistake, or not made a mistake, you first must put yourself in his place and think that way, as if you were him, and then you can talk about him or judge him or say if he was right or not. From the facilitators course, I got something very much like that, because you think about the other, you think why he acts as he does, so you put yourself in his place, and it's not about material things, it's about spiritual things.

This is also a legal approach they taught us at university: If a man comes to you complaining of certain things, you cannot form an opinion until you have heard the other side. You must do that. And you must not let your preconceptions interfere. What was correct the last time around may not be so in this case. You simply cannot reach an opinion after hearing only the one side; your judgment will be faulty. You must listen first to the other side.

There are security-related cases when I go to court and defend people, some of them in administrative detention. About administrative detention I don't even want to talk; it's a game and there's nothing to be done, but sometimes in court you can see the file. For example, a file has been closed in the case of a complaint against settlers. In 90 percent of such cases, the police simply abandon the investigation; the case is closed.

Once they closed a case that we were sure had merit. If you don't think about hearing the other side and getting the complete picture, the file would simply be closed and that would be that. You tell the plaintiff who was beaten, or whatever was done to him by the settlers, that you can't help him. In this one case, we photocopied the file, we looked at everything, all of the testimonies, and we found one statement by the accused in which he confesses that he did the deed. But he claims that he did it because the Palestinian stole something from him and therefore he took the law into his own hands. That is, of course, illegal. They closed the file anyway. Still, for a lawyer it's very important, in his work, to observe from all angles, to try to find a point of entry so that he can do something. That's our work as lawyers.

How do you keep on doing this? Why haven't you lost hope?
Maybe we don't have much hope, but there is something important here. As Palestinians, we have a lot of problems internally, both because of the occupation and maybe also because of the complexities, and the most important thing is that you feel free, feel that you are a human being, even under occupation. I don't know how to explain this. Under occupation you don't feel your humanity as clearly, but you can feel it; I believe that you can. Maybe it takes a long time, but you can free yourself of military occupation. Maybe historically there are not that many examples of success, but . . . you can free yourself spiritually.

Let's say my son goes to school to take an exam and he fails the exam, and we could say he failed the exam because of the occupation, but that's not true. There are a lot of things that the occupation does, but there are things that we do, too, and we have to consider that not everything is about the occupation. You have to feel that you are free. If you want to be free, so that later you can have a state, you have to free yourself inwardly. You can't be free without being free inwardly. Inside yourself, you can be free, even under occupation.

You can't just go in one direction and think: That's no good, and there it ends. You must also pursue other directions and think in other ways, and look around. Generally, I think that the Palestinians are not free inwardly, because of the occupation, yes, but also—you know, I don't really want to go into these theories from the literature, I want to rely on my experience that you can free yourself inwardly, and one way is through these courses.

How does that happen through the course?
Well, first of all, many Palestinians have not had an opportunity to sit with the other side, except as an employee with his boss, or as a defendant with a

policeman, which is not enough. Secondly, we have a lot of fear, and it impacts not only ourselves but the society around us, our children, our spouses. So it may take generations to reach the place I'm thinking of, but this fear of the occupation, of the enemy, the fear of being afraid, the fear that you won't be able to find your own voice—all those fears have an impact on you spiritually. There are a lot of people who need a psychologist or psychiatrist to address all of this. Now, if someone sits with the other side as happens in these courses, and can sit in front of him coming from strength, and can open up and talk about what's inside him—that is very healthy.

I see this from my own experience. I see that it's healthy, when someone is in pain, to do this. I've done it with groups and also for myself. If you can't get the pain out, it eats away at you from the inside. The complexity and difficulty don't get clarified. Not all pain is physical; pain is also emotional and spiritual. Letting it out, coming from strength, opening up—this changes the way someone thinks, and it's a process—as we say, it's part of the process he undergoes.

In the course, we can look at a particular person in the group in terms of how he started out, and then later how he speaks, telling his story. He may have started out being afraid, but the uni-national sessions bring more clarity. He moves beyond his fear, expresses it, tells his story, speaks differently. Often without being aware of it, the person is able to say things later in the process that he was unable to say at first. I did this kind of work a lot: eight years.

As a lawyer I do help people, but I am more enthused by facilitating with groups than by my work as a lawyer. Human rights lawyers do help people, it's true. People call you and say: We don't know where our son is. And you have to try to help, and it's hard. Personally for me it's very hard.

Once some parents called me, saying: We think our son is being held at the Russian Compound in Jerusalem, he was arrested at Ma'ale Adumim, at the Dead Sea, can you find out for us? So I went there. I told the parents that I wanted a fee but I still haven't taken any money from them. They might not give me anything, they are from Qalqiliya, not from here. I don't know them, but it doesn't matter. I really do love to help people, and I make my living from the organizations that I work for as a lawyer. But in group facilitation, you are working with your feelings all the time, it's not like preparing a motion for the court, or a letter to the police, or going to visit someone in jail. Yes, that also has certain feelings around it. But working with groups, doing facilitation, all your emotion is invested in it. There are a lot of things that are not ordinarily expressed, things you don't think about in your usual day-to-day work. In the group, you are wholly involved, your brain, your heart, your feelings; you have to be attentive to everything that happens in the room. I really love this work, maybe more—no, not maybe—I love it more than legal work, even more than the human rights law that I'm doing now.

YOU BUILD PEOPLE

Working with groups is great because you feel that you are able to take someone to a different place. Maybe later he will be frustrated, after the course ends, when he goes back to the difficult reality he knew from before, and he finds it hard, but he is healthier inside, even so. In these complicated times, you can't do more than that at first. Little by little, you can do more. You help one person, or two, or three, and incrementally you are building a good society, a group of people. You build people. That's how I feel, that I build people. It's amazing to experience that feeling. I really love this work.

Sometimes you look at what you have been doing and you can see what's been built, and sometimes you don't see it, because it also depends on the participants, not just on you as a facilitator. Overall, I think that this work is wonderful, even if it doesn't have an immediate impact on the terrible reality around us and on our daily lives.

I'm also living with this suffering myself part of the time. When I go into the territories and return through a checkpoint, for example, and a soldier comes and sometimes does such inhuman things. You get aggravated. Sometimes I look at him and think, poor guy!—him, not me. Yes, I really do, sometimes. It's not a simple thing, to be thinking that way, but if you do, you can feel really comfortable there. OK, so he'll check me, he'll do what he wants, it's his loss because he's afraid of me, he does it out of fear or because his commander told him to. He gets orders; he doesn't deal with me as a human being, and that's not good from his point of view either. Sometimes I even say to the soldier, You poor guy, sitting here all day in the sun, while I'm in my car; maybe I do it on purpose because I want to feel more comfortable, because I get aggravated by him. So instead of being nasty to him, I say a good word to him. Those guys are really unfortunate sometimes; if they only understood better what they are doing.

I just remembered something else about the importance of our work. It's true that the Palestinians identify with and are building and are liberating the other side as well, the Israeli side. The process improves the Israelis' capacity as Israelis to understand the Palestinian side. A lot of Israelis are against what Israel does; that's very important. It's amazing sometimes, because you see people who don't go to the army because of what their government is doing, or because of what soldiers do at the checkpoints. And they feel the suffering that is caused to the Palestinians, they know about it because of these courses. There's no other way to know about it, unless someone is thinking at a higher level and going in that direction, thinking about it and looking at alternative media, not just at Israeli television. But in this kind of course, you influence a lot of people: maybe not 100 percent of them, but let's say 60 percent, or 50, or 40. If even 40 percent of the people in the course come to understand the thinking of the other side, the Palestinian side, and don't go to the army and try to have an impact, that's major. This is how you are liberating the Israeli side. That's why I say "poor guy" about the soldier at the checkpoint, because he doesn't understand, he just gets orders and carries them out, and doesn't think. But an Israeli who has once participated in a course, and understood the other side, and the other side's pain, maybe he won't enlist. Or he enlists but treats people better; he doesn't refuse to serve in the territories but treats the people there better. Naturally, this is not exactly my goal nor that of the Palestinian people. But in everyday life, it's still better to have a policeman who treats people well. In these courses, how much exactly do you influence the other side to persuade his society to go in a different direction? We don't know. It will take time. But from where I sit, the work is important, and it's good.

Do you want to talk a little about the situation in East Jerusalem and how you would like it to be for your children, during your lifetime?
Right now in East Jerusalem, we are living a very difficult reality, not in terms of physical suffering but in terms of emotional suffering and the impact on the next generation of Palestinians, the children and young people who have to build the future. It saddens me that if I walk in the street today and meet someone eighteen or nineteen years old from East Jerusalem, and if he is one of the many who haven't gone to university, then he works for Israelis. Driving in his own car, he listens to Israeli music that he doesn't even understand.

These young people are losing their identity, and I look at this and find it frightening and painful.

It's really wonderful that there are so many people who, when we sit down together, will say: Look at our young people—where are they headed? This is crucial. Israel, or the Israeli government, or someone, has succeeded in taking over Jerusalem and Judaizing it, or Israelifying it, as if the whole city is [only] part of Israel, like what happened with all the mixed cities within Israel. This is painful, really heartbreaking. And we see it happening day by day.

As if that were not enough, they also started demolishing houses in Jerusalem, and there are no places for us to build, even for someone who has land. I actually have dealt with this. I was in a course for lawyers on planning and building in Jerusalem. Some people say that we have to plan but not build, because they will demolish it. But you run into a lot of difficulties. In the end, a person with land builds on it, and it's not good because it's illegal, but why is he doing it illegally? Because he can't do it any other way. They don't give building permits. And they make things terribly complicated for people. In one case I know of, a municipal clerk was sent to demand proof of ownership from a man seeking a building permit. So you prove ownership, OK, you see that the man is paying taxes, that's proof that he is using it, but not that he is the owner. When no one comes forward with an opposing claim, this is fine under the law. But the clerk said, that's not sufficient for me, I want more proof. So the man has no permit because they did not give him one. His application did not go anywhere, so he went to a lawyer and the lawyer went to the High Court, and three or four years along, he won there, so then his application had to start all over again. And this dumb clerk told him, I'm not satisfied. There are no places to build and the people just keep on going somehow, and now there are master plans done by the regional planning and building commission, and there are thousands of these cases, but meanwhile the authorities want fewer Arabs and more Israelis.

Another thing is the identity card. If you leave Jerusalem, you can't come back, even if you haven't actually moved away. Or the issue of family reunification: there are endless problems with this. In my work, I hear stories that you wouldn't believe, a great many such stories about the impact of this and the political situation. There are people working on it and they want to help fix it, but the laws are manipulated. So when the applicant is Palestinian, or Arab, the law is not applied as it would be applied for a Jewish applicant.

In the courts, if someone comes from Indonesia or Thailand, and wants to work here, and marries an Israeli, he gets legal status, but if someone comes from Ramallah, he doesn't get legal status, even if he was born in Jerusalem. They want the fewest possible Palestinians and the most Jews.

Moreover there are now very large areas that are still technically under the jurisdiction of Jerusalem but are physically separated from Jerusalem by the Wall and the checkpoints, like the Shuafat refugee camp, a very large camp, or Anata, or Dahat al-Islam. They are legally part of Jerusalem but if their residents want to come into the city, they have to get through a checkpoint, like say from Kafr Aqab. One thing I don't like to talk about is the Oslo Accords. Things with the Palestinian Authority aren't that good. It's very painful to contemplate what's left under Palestinian sovereignty. It's not my choice, and maybe it has shrunk our dream, but OK, we will make do with this, OK.

What about having a Palestinian capital?
Yes, all of East Jerusalem should be the Palestinian capital. There are people who still have keys to their homes in West Jerusalem. But OK, at least we've come to a situation where we want to live and we want the other side to live; but unless you get your rights, you can't live, period. And now in Jerusalem you hear that they are taking people out of their homes in Sheikh Jarrah. Yes, I know some of them. I was at demonstrations and people were arrested there, even Jews were arrested, [Rabbi] Arik Ascherman was arrested for twenty-four hours, and another young woman who volunteers with us was arrested for four hours.

RAISING CHILDREN IN THIS REALITY

In terms of the children, I try, consciously or not, I try to ignore the reality because it's just so bad.

We worry about the children's future, their studies, how they behave in general and how they behave toward others, whether they are respectful of one another. I have not thought extensively about how I ought to relate to them concerning the situation. I suppose I need to tell them not to be afraid, that things will be OK, that if something happens sometimes, if we get stuck at a checkpoint and can't get through, we will be together and we will deal with it. I sometimes say uncomplimentary things about the soldiers and tell them stories, trying to prepare them to deal with it, and sometimes they are afraid of what might happen. They ask me, for instance, why their aunt can't get here to visit them when she lives just a few dozen meters away. I answer, OK, yes, but something must have happened so they closed the road, or they are suspicious about something, and so we go around a different way and now they close that road, and we can't get through. And the child asks: "What are they? Who are they?" And I say they are the occupation and they shouldn't be here but they are here. But you don't go that route with a child too much. You try to protect him and keep it brief, for the child's benefit, and maybe it's good and maybe not, I don't know. It's important to me that the child not be afraid, that he be free, and me too. It's also important to bring weakness out into the open. When I was a little boy, I was afraid of the dark, afraid to go out at night; if something happens now at a checkpoint, if a policeman comes, I want my child not to be afraid of that person or that group. The man in the end is just doing his job, maybe it's correct, maybe not, OK, but don't be afraid of him. But he is afraid.

Once we were at the Al Aqsa Mosque with my father when he went there to pray on a Friday, and there was some kind of demonstration, and the soldiers went in, and my son was crying, he was little, just nine years old maybe, a year or two ago. I always make sure to sit with him and talk with him, to tell him don't be afraid, this is life, it's just life, don't be afraid and if something happens, be calm. And I am always thinking, there are going to be some hard times for them.

We try to minimize all this because it's unfortunate if they start living this reality now. They are little and they should be playing. He's a kid. He should live in his world.

Mohammad, do you see yourself going on with this human rights work?
Yes, I think I will go on with it. I will try to help people as much as I can, and also help the other side, by keeping on with my work in group facilitation. As I said, I love that work even more than my legal work, and I won't give it up.

4 · YONATAN SHAPIRA

Musician

Yonatan Shapira has been a captain and Black Hawk pilot in the Israeli Air Force. He served twelve years of regular and reserve duty, beginning in 1991. In 2003, he initiated what became known as The Pilots' Letter, whose signers declared their intent not to fly bombing missions over civilian areas of the Palestinian territories. Shapira was a founding member of Combatants for Peace in 2005. He earned an M.A. in Peace and Conflict Studies at the European Center for Peace Studies (EPU) in Stadtschlaining, Austria, in 2008. He has been a member of Boycott from Within (Israelis supporting the Palestinian civil society boycott project) since 2009. Yonatan was a participant in three attempts to breach the sea blockade of Gaza, in 2010, 2011, and 2012. He has been a facilitator at the School for Peace at Wahat al-Salam–Neve Shalom since 2011. He lives in Tel Aviv with Ine and baby Ella and is working on a music album. Yonatan Shapira participated in the School for Peace Cross-Border Project for Israeli and Palestinian university students in 2003, and in 2010 he took the SFP Facilitators Training Course. The following interview was conducted on February 9, 2009.

We always think that our conflict is the biggest and most terrible in the entire world, but it's not so. We are just one more place. I know by heart all the creeks and valleys in the Negev and in the north; my connection to this land will remain always, though it's not important to me that Israel, specifically, be around forever; it's important to me that humanity stop living off murder; it's important to me that people live. It's about belonging to the planet.

In 2003, when I was thirty-one, I signed up for a weekend workshop for Israeli and Palestinian university students. I was studying music at the Rimon School of Jazz and Contemporary Music. The other students at the workshop were from Jerusalem, Tel Aviv, and a group from Nablus. We divided into four groups of sixteen people in each, eight Jews and eight Palestinians, and our Israeli facilitator was Yael. There was a translator from Kaukab in the Galilee.

That was a very turbulent period for me. My inner turmoil about the whole situation was coming into focus; I was starting to ask questions about my part in this thing, including questions about conscientious objection. . . . This was more than six months after the assassination of [Salah] Shehade [by the Israeli Air Force], an event that figured in my evolving understanding of the reality and the brutality of the system in which I was serving.

Someone from school suggested that I come to the workshop, but I was really busy and didn't want to. I was doing reserve duty once a week as a Black Hawk rescue pilot, and also transporting troops. During the 2002 Defensive Shield campaign [in the West Bank; Israel's largest military operation there since the 1967 war], I was in the military. I thought I already knew what was going on out there, what was going on in Israel and with the Palestinian side. I was already against the occupation, the settlements, the targeted killings. I didn't feel a need for further explanations from anyone, including from the Palestinian side.

What happened at the Neve Shalom workshop on the weekend became another very important layer in my evolving understanding my own emotional turmoil, helping me articulate it and direct it more toward some kind of action. In hindsight, the process seems to change, or crystallize, one's identity. A great illustration was the first encounter, the getting-acquainted circle. We were each to introduce ourselves: name, home town, why I'm here, and some event that was very influential for me recently.

As people took turns one by one, I was rehearsing: "Shalom, my name is Yonatan, I serve in the reserves as a helicopter pilot in the Air Force even though I am very opposed to the occupation, to targeted killings and to the settlements. I want peace and so I am here to meet with Palestinians. The event that most influenced me was the targeted killing of Shehade when they also killed a lot of children and civilians, which I view as a crime. And I want you to know that there are people in the army who oppose these things and oppose the occupation."

Meantime, the introductions proceeded. The Palestinian guy next to me began to speak. He said he was a student from Nablus and was also very opposed to the occupation and wanted peace and thought it was important to talk with Israelis. The event that most influenced him recently was that his little sister had been crippled when an Apache missile struck their neighbor's house and since then she had been paralyzed from the waist down. Then it was my turn, and I couldn't say I was a pilot because suddenly it made no difference if I was the pilot of a helicopter that rescues soldiers or shoots missiles, or even an Air Force clerk. Suddenly, clearly, simply, I understood: All during my service it had been significant to me that I was doing the clean work, saving lives, at most transporting soldiers . . . I was doing the clean work, not the dirty work. Suddenly I saw that, from a different perspective, the distinction is marginal. So I said, "I'm here and I oppose targeted assassinations," but I did not utter the word pilot, or army or anything like that, and that's how it was for the whole weekend.

FROM SHAME TO COMMITMENT

I think I was ashamed. I was a very active participant. I always volunteered to sum up, talking confidently about what I thought and what my friends thought, and how much we needed to talk. We said we would go back to Israeli society and work against the occupation, and they would go back to their society and work against the suicide bombing—something very participatory, official, communal. I was always active in the movement and I did the extra year of volunteer service before the army. But meantime something so basic in my identity and in my life was hidden. One guy named Shimon told how he had been a paratrooper not long before that, during the Defensive Shield campaign. He stood on a hill outside Nablus as a sharpshooter, and shot at rooftop water tanks. When he decided to become a conscientious objector, he decided he would not go back there. The Palestinians in the workshop accepted him and appreciated his frankness. They nicknamed him Abu Jabel [Father of the Hill] because he stood on a hill. For me, though, he represented something I had yet to be capable of: to say exactly what I was and where I was coming from. I felt like I was undergoing a kind of commitment process, like taking a military oath.

Toward the end of the workshop, we discussed what role each of us would play, with his own people. We committed ourselves to do everything we could think of to end the occupation. I wasn't committing myself just to me and my friends; I was committing myself to the Palestinians, too. I may even have told Shimon (the paratrooper) that I planned to organize something within the Air Force. In hindsight, I think I needed to tell someone. I didn't disclose my Air Force connection in the uni-national group session, either. Only on the last day did I tell two Israelis, and one was a conscientious objector himself. At that point it wasn't yet completely clear to me what I was. I told myself I wasn't going to serve in the territories except to fly there to evacuate wounded or ferry in soldiers. It wasn't clear to me yet that if I served in the territories, I was part of the occupation. I didn't realize that my understanding was still embryonic; I thought I had a thorough understanding of the situation.

Then there was an evening session about halfway through the seminar. We sat on the lawn and played music and sang. I sang them a song from my student days at Rimon, from a competition where we sang well-known songs with a different interpretation. It was in 2001, at the beginning of the second Intifada. I wasn't thinking yet about conscientious objection or anything like. I don't think I knew the most basic concepts. I chose the song "Zion, My Innocent One"; you must know it. I always loved that song. I gave it to Peretz Dror Banai, an obscure but distinguished poet who also translates and writes in Arabic. He translated the song into literary Arabic for me and it came out very Palestinian, very strong. I sang it in Hebrew but switched in the middle into Arabic. It made the audience uneasy. I guess it was my way of expressing my inner turmoil about everything that was going on, only very preliminarily. So that evening at Neve Shalom, I sang that song. Everyone played and sang together; I was among the first. They didn't seem to be clear if I was singing about Israel as an Israeli or as a Palestinian. They were uncomfortable because I had translated a Zionist song. The Palestinian guys there asked me about it and I explained that it was precisely to show the love triangle, the tragic love story, of two peoples and the land. So then the group was very moved, and I was, too, and it was fun for me that I had something that shows my soft side, my civilian and humane side, that I was willing to expose. The weekend ended and I was very glad I had come, even though I was very busy and hadn't wanted to go.

DETAINED AT THE CHECKPOINT

That night after I got home, my girlfriend and I went to see a film in Tel Aviv and when I got back around midnight, I had a phone call from the workshop's translator, a young Palestinian woman from the Galilee. She said that Majd's whole Palestinian group had been detained at one of the checkpoints, after trying to go around it through the hills, and the Border Police beat them up. One guy I had become really good friends with, Tamer, who sat next to me that last evening while we were singing on the lawn, was still being held by the Shin Bet or whoever. That really pushed my buttons. I just lost it. It seemed almost foreordained. I had given this young woman a ride to the bus station and on the way we talked and got to know each other; it was really interesting. I didn't tell her, either, that I was in the military and a pilot; apparently I had some need to show her that I was on her side and against the occupation. I think my identity got another sort of push at that weekend. So it was comfortable and enjoyable to be talking with a young Palestinian woman. I think we even exchanged phone numbers. I also had a few phone numbers of the guys from Nablus and afterward I phoned. We didn't really know what to say but I wanted to know if Tamer had made it home OK or not. It wasn't entirely clear. Then I was imagining calling him at the refugee camp and talking with him in Hebrew after all his friends there had been beaten up, and he wouldn't understand what I wanted of him.

Anyway she phoned me and told me about this thing, and then I started telephoning to anyone I could, trying to get them to help get Tamer released and explaining that I'm an Air Force officer, that I had met these people at a peace encounter at Neve Shalom and that this guy hadn't done anything whatsoever and they should let him go immediately. I got to all kinds of Knesset members from Meretz, Mossi Raz and others. Everyone said they'd look into it. Through the squadron I was able to get the phone number for the Shin Bet facility where Tamer was. Wherever I phoned, I said that I was speaking from the squadron: I said, Hello, This is Captain Yonatan Shapira, I got this phone number from the clerk and we want to clarify what is happening with Tamer. It was hard for me. I even got to talk with an interrogations officer there, at that facility, and I told him all of this. They said Tamer had been arrested because his cousin was involved in some kind of activity, you know. So I called a few times, every so often, and they kept him for maybe six months, or maybe not. I don't know exactly. But he stayed in my head from that moment on.

I kept on going to the squadron, my usual Israeli life, but somehow I turned into—my identity expanded to include another image. I'm trying now to analyze it after the fact. I started looking at reality from a very specific and different point of view, not necessarily from the standpoint of the Palestinian people, or of a global citizen, or of an Israeli peacenik, but from the standpoint of a detainee at a Shin Bet interrogation facility, who's being tortured, or whatever is happening to him there, because his cousin is something or other—and this is after he had come to Neve Shalom to talk to me about ending the conflict, about peace.

So I was already not just a man, pilot, officer, music student, leftist, Zionist, good guy; I was also a Palestinian prisoner in a Shin Bet interrogation cell. A lot has happened since then, but that was kind of a one-two punch in the face: first with the part that, in the circle, I was unable to say who I was and what I was, and then the commitment to people that we are really going to do everything humanly possible. Until, finally, part of me is somehow there in an interrogation cell, detained there by another part of me. That's the magic of the dialogue. As if you incorporate something, somehow, even if you're unaware of it: You adopt something from the person you are talking with, especially if your exchange is not done in a macho, argumentative, militaristic way, but with real listening. Something gets into you, whether you meant it to or not, and you change, you are recalibrated. Your identity broadens and becomes something encompassing all kinds of other perspectives and identities.

COURAGE TO REFUSE

So that was the point when my path began to open out: the start of my "deterioration," so to speak. I went to a meeting of Courage to Refuse [their English-language website is www.seruv.org.il]. They met in Tel Aviv to tell stories. People told stories about their refusal and about going to jail for it. Suddenly I saw that there are a lot of people feeling the same thing I do who also come from the same background that I do: They love the country, too, they love the same things, and they are ready to do something. Their own solution for the distress or the anger they feel, for their disagreement with the consensus, is also a solution on the societal, national, ethical level. What I am feeling can be translated into something that could have an impact. For me this was like discovering a new law of nature.

I think I had always had an appreciation for people who said no, or who would not toe the line. Even before I was conscripted, I didn't see eye to eye with other people about a lot of things. And I was against the war, and against these military campaigns in Lebanon, and against remaining in southern Lebanon. But I didn't connect all of that with my part in it until later. When I finally understood, I described it this way: To connect the occupation and all of this needless death, this cycle of madness, and the obtuseness and stupidity of the government and the army—to connect all that with the exalted pleasure of working the helicopter's controls for lift-off from a field of chrysanthemums that are lying flat in circles around the helicopter from the downwash wind that it's producing; that tremendous power, to be in fearless control of such a mighty machine; knowing you can do whatever you want with it, and you're above everything; that rush, that high, like what a child gets from a toy he really loves to play with . . . but in this case it's a weapon, and you're part of the military. How could I connect this with what I hate so much, what I am so much against? One way was to sit in the circle there and understand that, for this young guy whose sister has been crippled by a missile from an Apache helicopter, it doesn't matter whether I'm against the occupation or not, I'm part of it, I have a part in that missile, whether directly or indirectly. And, well, it's much more direct than I thought, than I understood, until I saw myself through the eyes of someone else and saw reality through this other additional pair of eyes that I had now acquired.

RESPONSIBILITY AND COMMITMENT

The commitment created at the workshop was, I think, a commitment to them, to flesh-and-blood people. It seemed to be coming from looking into what I was feeling. There we were, with people sitting right there next to us, one guy who was shot in the leg or the rear end, and people with horrible stories. I started to feel a responsibility for what was happening to them, even if I wasn't directly involved. It came to me, somehow, that we were making a commitment. I remember saying so. I spoke freely in the name of everyone who was against the occupation; I said we were making a commitment to do whatever we could do. Whatever we could. I went back home with this whatever we could. This whatever we could was really getting to me now, and I had to figure out what we really could do, and how I could go on enjoying these flights with the squadron. They were a refined pleasure: I wasn't required to shoot anyone, to dirty my hands in any way or get blood on them. I only had to risk my life to bring back the wounded and to transport soldiers who had gone there to wound other people, while remaining aloof from all that myself. But meanwhile, I felt this commitment. And there were things that happened to my brothers in the army, in the infantry. I began to feel that I was living in some kind of detached world where I was enjoying playing with my toys of steel in these very comfortable conditions, and suddenly everything else also started to be a little irritating, like those comfortable rooms on the base. When you came to reserve duty to go out for night flights, you'd find that chocolate and the newspaper sitting on your pillow; this started to be a little troubling. You would sleep for three hours first and then there was a briefing. Everything was orderly, quiet, and clean. Right then my brother phones to tell me that he notified his commanders that he isn't going to do reserve duty in the territories. He was a soldier in the Special Forces unit of Sayeret Matkal during Campaign Protective Shield. He didn't want to do anything publicly at that point. He agreed to add his name to the list of Courage to Refuse but a while later he established the group of reservists from Sayeret Matkal who refused [to serve in the territories], and afterward the organization Combatants for Peace.

Later he told me about how troubled he was and how he came to his decision to resolve it. He told his staff colleagues and their officer that he wasn't coming. And then I left my air-conditioned room for the night flights, and I felt uneasy somehow, bordering on the betrayal of the principles of something or other, I don't know, uneasiness, a terrible uneasiness because I am having fun with this while my brothers, my little brother, have to roam around there amid all the horrible things that are the occupation and do all kinds of terrible things. It all came together into a kind of whirlpool. That eventually led me to organize the pilots' group.

THE PILOTS' GROUP

It was just a few weeks after the Neve Shalom weekend, and then came the event with Courage to Refuse, and I saw a lot of people who were like me there. So I phoned one of the guys and said that I would be happy to add my name, or something like that. And then suddenly they said, "Come to a meet-ing," and I met with two guys there from Yesh Gvul. Then the idea came up to find more people who feel the same way in the squadron. There were two more who felt the same, one guy from a different squadron who had been my instructor and someone else I knew from my neighborhood, so then we were around three people plus someone from Courage to Refuse. We drafted the letter [the "Pilots' Letter" of September 2003], more or less. After a while, not everyone who was involved opted to sign; people dropped out at vari-ous stages. One said, I can't because right now I'm in the career army; another said, Maybe I'll join later in the second round to increase the effect, but I never heard from him. So that was that, and I had the letter, and two guys from a different squadron who weren't at the meeting but said they would sign. Then there were two guys from the squadron, one of them had been a trainee of mine once and the other had also been my trainee at an earlier period, but there were other regular pilots from the squadron who also had already finished their compulsory career service and were now reservists. So we began looking. At first I was on my own, and toward the end they also helped. It was me and then later Alon, a guy from my squadron who really ran everything from this little penthouse apartment in Tel Aviv, like a little war room, with lists. Once he got into it, Alon got totally involved.

I started roaming around with all kinds of people I heard giving talks here and there. I met with Professor Joseph Agassi, a very interesting guy, after I heard him speaking at a Courage to Refuse event. I got there and he started telling me about [Martin] Buber and others. I did not have much perspec-tive because I wasn't very educated or well-read in the literature of political science. I started reading bits and pieces of all kinds of things. I started meeting all kinds of people, people with ideas and thoughts. I told them about the idea of recruiting a group of pilots from the Air Force who would refuse and they were very enthusiastic. They felt that, Ah, something's happening here. I realized that I had waited a long time for someone else to do something like this . . . not someone like me, because I don't fly combat aircraft at all, and I didn't bomb anyone, and I also don't know how to address an audience very well. I always get nervous. It requires a leadership type with a better façade and a richer combat history. But it didn't happen; no such person materialized.

And then—when you understand that, hey, you have to do this, and to develop these capabilities, even if you don't feel that you can or that you're qualified enough—you'll learn. It was like an intensive university course for a thousand professions at once. You get almost obsessed with coming to grips with what you're missing. You have to learn history and philosophy and learn about yourself and about identities and psychology; how to talk with people and how to make contact and how not to frighten people when you are proposing an idea like this. You also have to learn how to be tactical and strategic: at some point I realized that, if it were all discovered at an early stage, it would all go to hell. And I had to develop all kinds of methods; let's call them fishing methods. Because I told myself that this thing was too dangerous and the ramifications too immense for me to involve someone who wasn't persuaded, who was still ambivalent. I knew that I had to fish not only for people who were in this ocean, this potpourri, of the pilots with all their thoughts and feelings, but also that I had to find people who had already gone through a transition. Without knowing how it happened for them, but just that they had already gone through the process and now I would find them and they would sign on and it would be OK. When you first discover one or two more, even that is surprising. At first you feel alone, as though there are no other people who feel this way. And when you are alone, this insanity is stuck in your head; you start to feel maybe a little nuts because, if I am different from so many other people around me, then maybe I'm not OK. Yet you start to discover more and more, and especially older people, who suddenly gave me the perspective of all the previous wars and those other stories. I was in shock. Each thing like that gave me another shot of wild energy and I also exploited all my connections. I grew up in one of those pilots' neighborhoods with my father and mother. My father was a military pilot and it was easy for me to come to all the people from his generation and say, "I'm Shlomo's son and I thought maybe we could sit and talk," and that's how I was able to talk to Amos Lapidot [former commander of the Israeli Air Force].

How did your father respond?

I didn't tell my father until the night before the letter was to be published, so there was a period of several months when he had no idea. I was going fishing and I knew that he wasn't persuaded, so I didn't want to endanger the project nor put him into a dilemma of loyalties. My father I think is in transition, I think it's an ongoing process. But the moment I told him, even though he wasn't in the same place at all—I showed him the list with all those names of friends, and people he knew; I told him so-and-so knows, and this person and that person are supporting it—he supported me psychologically right away as a father, although he thought differently.

I heard from my mother about Yigal Schochat [a former IAF pilot and colonel in the reserves] who had published his opposition to the bombardment of Gaza in 2002. So I said OK, I'll go meet with him; I knew it would be interesting, and in fact I will always remember him there, this pilot, this doctor, this man. I got his phone number and called and told him, I am Shlomo's and Tzvia's son and all that. So he said, Oy, come!, and he was excited. When my father heard that I was going to meet him, I asked him, "Wait, do you know him?" And he said, "Sure, we flew together in the Six-Day War in one of the first sorties of that campaign. He's a really nice man and very smart, but in recent years he's gone off the rails, I think maybe because of his wife." That is so typical: as soon as people close to you decide something that's terribly different from how you yourself think, you have to blame something or someone, because one of our own Air Force good guys can't be saying things like this. Someone must have brainwashed him.

So when I opened the door at Yigal Schochat's house, I said that I had come to meet with Yigal Schochat who had gone off the rails. Yigal told me about his experience as a doctor volunteering in the territories with Physicians for Human Rights. He was very moved by my idea and said that of course he would sign on. At that point I wasn't sure if it should be only pilots currently serving, or also veterans who could give some kind of moral backing, fatherly backing, to the project. But he said that he was signing on and gave me contact information for another guy, [major in the reserves] Hagai Tamir [former fighter pilot, and an architect]. He mentioned a book written by a few people who had served in Lebanon and refused to do all kinds of things; Tamir had refused to bomb a school in Beirut. So, I went to see him too.

Each one sent out tentacles, so to speak, to all kinds of people, some still serving and some from an earlier generation. Hagai Tamir undertook to enlist his generation. We began making lists. I sat with Hagai with a little notebook—I titled it: "The Air Force Is in My lists," a reference to the slogan that "The Air Force Is in My Soul." Wherever I went, I took notes about the person, who he was, his rank, whether he is flying, and one sentence about the kind of case he represents for me, psychologically. I tried to actually map the people: the ambivalent; the good prospects; the ones who could give me someone's else's name; the risky ones to whom I couldn't reveal the whole project. I had to develop screening methods. I'd ask someone how he feels about the occupation or about targeted assassinations, progressing to how he feels about the guys from Yesh Gvul or Courage to Refuse. Until someone passed this screening, I didn't begin talking with him about a pilots' letter.

Hagai also told me all kinds of other difficult stories from the past about the Lebanon War [in 1982], about the Libyan plane that was shot down [in February 1973], a Libyan Air civilian plane flown by an Air France crew that they shot down in Sinai, killing 108 people. The [Israeli] soldiers in the nearby army bases looted their baggage afterward. All kinds of stories that don't fit the way the Air Force likes to portray itself. The pilot that shot down the Libyan passenger plane was a friend of Hagai who afterward committed suicide. They said it was an accident, but Hagai had always thought it was suicide. Suddenly I was seeing a new dimension of the Air Force, as being sort of my family. That's where I come from, a community of pilots on their bases, with my father and all that, and also my squadron.

Finally Hagai opened a cupboard and took out a photograph that I immediately identified, because it showed a large scene in my grandfather and grandmother's house. There's my father, standing with Hagai, who says to me now, "Do you see that? The guy with the long hair, that's me." Everything was suddenly turned inside out because, over the years whenever I had seen that picture, my father was that quiet, modest, gentle, down-to-earth man, a peace-seeker. For me, that photo portrayed peace and quiet and security. The guy next to him, Hagai, always represented for me the kind of boastful pilot I never wanted to be like. I wanted to be like my father. And suddenly Hagai is showing me this and now everything is upside down. This pilot isn't bragging at all about how he shot down others, but rather talking about how he was shot down over Sinai, and he's the one who is cooperating with me in something subversive. And I can't even tell my father what I'm doing.

Nevertheless it was the beginning of a fabulous period because I felt that I was connecting my feelings and my values to my actions. It's a powerful feeling. I rode this little yellow motorbike to all kinds of people's apartments in Tel Aviv to lobby them for refusal or check whether they would agree to it, and on the way—there's that song, the Air Force anthem, I think it must have been written by Naomi Shemer, who is very nationalist: "On Silver Wings." They always played that song on parade at the conclusion of pilot training, and as trainees we would march along, eyes toward the commanders, singing the words proudly. I knew the song by heart. There's a line there, something about "My brother flew toward the light" and a trail of fire and triumph, when the plane rends the air and writes a message of fire as we fly aloft in a flash. From my perspective the message of fire was refusal. I wanted to dispel that horror. I have a lot of stories; this could take a lot of time.

I began a long process of gradual exposure to reality, with sudden pushes, too: Shehade, Neve Shalom, Tamer. Gradually I approached a readiness to embrace refusal. Not just my own, but also enlisting others—because there comes a point when merely refusing isn't enough. You want to have an impact; you want to create something no one can be indifferent to. For me it came on Rosh Hashana in 2003, about six or seven months after the seminar.

You haven't talked at all about the price paid.

No, that wasn't really relevant. First of all I didn't pay any sort of major price. The process I underwent was exponential. Where I am now, in terms of how I approach the army and Zionism, is so distant from where I was when I first refused. The curve becomes almost parabolic as soon as you get involved and start meeting with people and talking with people, especially people from abroad. Somehow I was always receiving invitations to come and speak in various places. On the emotional plane, your frame of reference moves beyond the army, the family, the conscientious objectors, to encompass the people you meet from all over the world. I met someone who was at Sabra and Shatila. I met an Israeli who refused in 1967 after Sharon told them to throw grenades into a crowd of protestors in Gaza. You discover all kinds of things that are very far from the way they used to sound in the rhetoric about the occupation. I talked at the European Social Forum in London to about 4,000 people and someone asked me about the Palestinian refugees, and I hadn't thought at all about refugees. So then you have to learn things and decide what you think. Meanwhile, the people that I started hanging around with were more and more—what shall I call it?—more radical or more humane. From being unable even to think about a binational state or a return of the 1948 refugees, I got to a place where I am someone else completely than I was at the outset when I refused in the name of Zionism. The word Zionism appeared so many times in our letter—"we who were raised in the Zionist fold, to love our people, to love the homeland," and all kinds of flowery phrases—and although of course this was partly tactical rather than an authentic reflection of our feelings, still I'm in a completely different place now.

But you asked about the price: being fired from my job afterward, and people thinking I was the worst thing in existence. All that is insignificant compared to what I got: I was released. I was finally released from the army and released from militarism, from chauvinism.

You were released.

Yes. When I say "released" now, I immediately remember how I felt even before the Neve Shalom seminar, before all these things happened. I had already been released from being unconscious of reality. I have to remind myself that even now I am apparently still hampered in many ways by familiar aspects of reality, by things I don't really see comprehensively. So when you talk about paying a price, I would rather talk about what I've gained. The biggest thing is about our awareness: You learn to acknowledge the limitations of our way of perceiving things, which is so much a product of our identity. Some new component is added to your psychological space, to your consciousness, your way of thinking, when you realize that everything is subject to question. There's no framework that can't be questioned, queried, clarified—and that's freedom, a formative and empowering move toward freedom. So when you ask about the price, I could whine about all the painful, hurtful stuff—but really it was minor.

What job were you fired from?

I was working in a civilian Israeli helicopter company, a subsidiary of an Australian company. They claimed they no longer needed me. By then, the chief pilot was someone who was until recently the commander of the Israeli Air Force helicopter section and was responsible either directly or indirectly for a lot of targeted assassinations himself. He was in that position when Ahmad Yassin was assassinated, and later he came to work at the company where I was employed. Subsequently he was made chief pilot, after I had trained him and taught him the job; until then, I was the only pilot in the country authorized to perform this specific job so they couldn't fire me. I had done special training for it in Australia. It involves working with the Israeli Electric Company's high tension wires while you are hovering right next to them, and even attached to the electricity wire among other things. I trained him to do this work, tested and signed him off and a few months later he was made the company's chief pilot. He then announced that henceforth no one who signed any sort of refusal letter would be employed there. The parent company is Australian but the Israeli subsidiary has Israeli management and the pilots here are from the Israel Air Force. I went to court, and the case is coming up now; it's unpleasant, it's not fun, and I don't know if it's worth it or not, because it uses up so much energy that I could have invested in more positive things. I decided to do it anyway because it was a chance to establish a precedent. Michael Sfard, my lawyer, who's also a friend of mine, told me that no legal precedent has been established concerning what happens after someone is fired due to his political positions or activism here in Israel. There are stories of illegal firings, but no precedent. Women fired during pregnancy or following sexual harassment, yes; but not this. So we decided it was important to exploit the exposure I received and address this as a classic case of the intrusion of militarism into civilian life. It aligns with the objectives of New Profile, and they're helping me with the whole project. We sued the company and if it provides a precedent, that'll be important.

You said that today you're in a different place than you were. Can you say a bit more about that?

I think that it's mainly that I've read a lot now and seen films, and I've been in the [occupied] territories a lot, or at least a lot more than I had been before. I have Palestinian friends here and I have Palestinian friends abroad and Jewish and non-Jewish friends abroad who are activists, people who have given me a perspective on other opinions and positions and struggles, beyond the tiny mess that we have here. We always think that our conflict is the biggest, the most terrible, and the most important in the entire world, but it's not so. We are just one more place, and elements of our situation resemble so many others, elsewhere. Naturally the combination of factors here creates all kinds of unique phenomena. But still, someone from Burma or Sri Lanka will tell you about aspects of the conflict there that also incorporate religious issues, capitalism, militarism—all the isms you can think of. So today I see us as one more example. And the struggle that I feel myself to be part of is a much broader, more general struggle.

There's the struggle for equality, for justice, for dividing the pie into equal shares. Some of what's happening here doesn't come down to Israelis versus Palestinians; it's about some people having a larger slice of the pie. The pie can be money, water, food, land, military power, all kinds of things. And some people don't get any, or they get less: They could also be Israeli citizens, they could be foreign workers, and they could be Palestinians who live in Israel. And conversely, there can also be Palestinians who are taking a larger share of the pie, selling a lot of cement for construction of the Separation Wall when they are theoretically supposed to be representing the Palestinian people. So whereas I once looked at things in terms of us and them, or us and those who are with us versus them and those who are with them, now I see things dividing up differently. It's about how we share: Who is enjoying the pleasures of such resources as the reality here provides, and who is suffering, or is receiving less.

And this connects with the European colonialism of the last few centuries and also with examples today, of which Israel is an excellent case, or South Africa, and the attitude of various other regimes in South and North America. It's all part of a mix of struggles, and somehow maybe the pain has eased a little because the pain you feel at losing the vision or innocence or even the potential of a place, combines with a larger pain and all the things in the world that are not going that well. And it's about identity, too. Today I am not only an Israeli or a Palestinian; I identify with Indians and with Darfur. I've been freed a little from this thing about belonging to a flag or a national idea, although I still feel very connected.

I'm still connected to words, language, culture, and to the land too. I know by heart almost all the creeks and valleys in the Negev and in the north. You get very connected also to people and to family. This connection will remain always, even though it's not important to me that Israel, specifically, be around forever; it's important to me that humanity stop living off murder; it's important to me that people live. I don't care if everyone gets mixed up together and if they stop being careful about their religion; let people decide for themselves. My mother, for instance, finds it very painful that what my grandparents wanted to bring into being here is not exactly going to happen, but I don't feel that pain. I am stirred by the potential of what there could be here. When I ramble through all kinds of circles where all kinds of people are mixed up together, Jews, Muslims, Christians, atheists, there's a kind of excitement from something that's much greater. It's about belonging to the planet.

When I try to persuade people with this thesis, after the fishing stage, after the winnowing, when I try to find the compassionate parts of the soul of a good friend who commits murder, it's not about ideas and arguments or some kind of radical academic discourse. It's nothing like that; its light-years away from all that. If I could arrange for a friend of mine to meet someone like Tamer and see what Tamer is like, maybe experiencing that would touch his soul. But arguing is useless, it means nothing; I just get farther away in these arguments. I realized that I have to stop working on winning arguments against people, because that doesn't change anything.

PART 2 COMMUNITY ORGANIZING, EDUCATION, AND PLANNING

5 · AYELET ROTH

Director, Bilingual School Network

Married and a mother of three, Ayelet Roth lives in Adi in the Western Galilee. She is the director of the Hand in Hand network of bilingual schools in Israel. Her extensive experience in the fields of education and Jewish-Arab coexistence features an emphasis on planning and implementing educational programs for staff and students and developing courses and seminars focusing on multiculturalism and the promotion of peace. She has worked with municipal authorities, nonprofit associations, and the Israeli Ministry of Education. Roth has served as a director and consultant in both the formal and informal education systems in northern Israel, including key roles as co-manager at the Jewish-Arab Center for Peace, Givat Haviva; principal at Amirim junior high school in Kfar Vradim; director of the education department at IPCRI (Israel Palestine Center for Research and Information); and long-term research project manager at the Center for Research on Peace Education at Haifa University. In addition to holding an M.A. in Peace Education and a B.A. in Middle East Studies and History Education from Haifa University, Roth is also a certified professional mediator. She has led seminars for groups from EU regions affected by conflict (Balkans, Spain) and has founded and acted as the CEO of her own business for mediation and social educational projects. Ayelet Roth took the School for Peace Course for Facilitators of Groups in Conflict, at Wahat al-Salam–Neve Shalom in 2000. She was interviewed on November 26, 2007.

My family thought the SFP course was like a disaster, but for me it was a
kind of revelation, an epiphany. Wherever I am, whatever I'm doing in my
work with the children at school, this is there. I have been changed forever.
This is me, part of my identity, my agenda. It's part of what I try to promote
in the world I live in.

I began the facilitators course at the School for Peace in May of 2000,
when I was 36, and finished in November 2000.

When I came to the course, I was looking for something to help me make
some kind of change. I had been interested for several years in the field of
Jewish-Arab relations in Israel and in the Palestinian Authority, but I felt that
something was obstructing me, holding me back. It bothered me a lot, like a
screen showing only half the picture. I didn't seem able to fix it by myself; I
needed help. My ability to act was encumbered by this sense of not being able
to see some very important thing within the overall picture.

Today I know what it was, but back then, I didn't. I knew that something
not right was happening in my communication with people. I was working
with IPCRI [Israel Palestine Center for Research and Information; since
renamed Israel Palestine: Creative Regional Initiatives]. At the school where I
taught, I was running an encounter project but I felt that I wasn't getting
across the way I should. Something was missing in my dialogues with people.
The puzzle had a piece missing. The reality and what I thought about it didn't
match, as if I had the wrong eyeglasses, or something. Something needed
adjustment on the screen. I knew it wouldn't be easy. I knew it would have
costs, operationally and otherwise. At Neve Shalom there were all kinds of
options for facilitation courses, for going to encounters between Jews and
Arabs at university, and also at Oranim College at that time. I was looking
for something to open the way through. I expected the process to be difficult. Just going to Neve Shalom for two days would be hard, when I was
working full time and had three small children. The travel time alone was
two and a half hours each way and I had never driven anywhere father than
from home to work and back again, which was twenty minutes. So it looked
really difficult, or even impossible. The decision to go ahead was in itself
the start of a transformation, just getting into the car and driving to Neve
Shalom. For a lot of the sessions, it was as if I were driving in reverse the
whole way.

Meaning what?

It was so hard for me, so painful. I would get a terrible headache every Thursday morning and it didn't let up until I got to Neve Shalom. It was like a migraine, but I don't get migraines. It was something completely physical. If you ask me today, I'm not sure if it was about the process at Neve Shalom, or part of my driving to get there, because the distance frightened me; in both those respects it was very hard for me to embark on the journey and there were many obstacles to be overcome. Among other things, the course ran for six months and in the middle we had the events of October 2000. I noticed the changes in me immediately; I could still see what was happening through my old eyes, too.

So this process was very hard from the outset. The process at Neve Shalom was hard, and very cold, not empathic, it sliced right through things very harshly. That's how I experienced it. I don't remember all the names anymore, but the sessions were very difficult, even ruthless. Apparently I had to let go of something before I could enter into something new. It takes time to understand this. Something about identity, letting go of the story, letting go of the narrative you were raised on, that you have an interest in, wanting it to be correct. There was that article about the combat soldiers, and all the high school principals who say that their guys are the salt of the earth and that's why they're combat soldiers. The task was to let go of this story and be ready to do something new there, to get into something new, to look at things differently, to hear something different. At first I didn't grasp it that way; at first I just tried to compress the information I got at Neve Shalom to fit into the existing identity, into the existing ideas. I think anyone would rather see himself as a good person first of all. I thought of myself as a good person, who wants to do good, works in education, and so forth. And during this process at some point you have to look in the mirror and see something less good. However much you try to squash the [new] information, you begin to understand that it doesn't fit in with the existing information. And you have to decide, either to go with it or to let it go.

Midway through the course I also went on sabbatical and began looking for work in that field. It took me four months. While the course was still running, I began working in a binational women's organization called Nisan. I had an Arab woman boss. Nisan deals with women's empowerment and with what is usually called coexistence, a term which is already dead, in my opinion, but OK we'll use it because it's customary. I would prefer to say fair existence, in all senses, rather than coexistence. So the Neve Shalom process wasn't my only process; it presaged other things.

Neve Shalom offered a very direct encounter with a different reality, in a closed room. I had been in encounters, but the Neve Shalom group was relatively small. Though not my first Neve Shalom workshop, this one was different. I had decided to change direction and was seeking a major change, plus the rising tensions near my home in the Galilee made everything more powerful. I was ready to molt the skin I no longer needed, to change part of my identity. That's about more than just a story; it's also about the way you see and judge the world and the reality around you.

SEARING SELF-JUDGMENT

In hindsight, part of me was deeply racist. I thought I was a very good person, very open, very liberal, and it turned out that there were also other things there, deep inside, deeply entrenched. To look at them and acknowledge them was terribly hard. I saw a type of racism, at the ugliest and most basic level, in how I understood the other. I told myself out loud that all the participants were equal and would be equal no matter what might happen there. In that encounter, however, everything came out. It went even beyond stereotypes. We were already past the stereotypes, we knew they were there, but these things were deeper. I don't know how to explain it. You encounter the essence of who this other person is who is standing in front you, what he experiences, what he feels. Maybe he doesn't need you all that much; you're not there in order to give him something. He has his own existence with his own needs, and for you maybe it's the reverse. We went through a searing and difficult self-judgment.

The course ran in two chunks: May through the end of July, a break during August, and then we returned in mid-September. During the first part, from May to July, even with Holocaust Remembrance Day and Memorial Day and Independence Day, we could feel things, and people made all kinds of claims, but we didn't really know what was happening. Then, after the first two sessions in September, we got into October 2000 and entered a different reality. Each session was a volcanic eruption, an earthquake, the Syrian-African rift shifting, something like that, with such a powerful impact on reality.

Maybe there was even some of that during the first part of the course. As I got to October, it came over me gradually. There had been a session on Holocaust Remembrance Day that had been very meaningful for me, through the eyes of the other. That day is a sacred cow, a very fat cow indeed. How worthwhile it is to take a new look at that, to see what happens to me when I put myself in someone else's shoes for a moment as they look at this story, to see what that does to me, at home. Those two days, Holocaust Remembrance Day and Independence Day, were very hard for me at home. I refused to hang a flag in the parking area as people customarily do here, and we still don't put up a flag. At Neve Shalom, something happens over the course of two days, over eight or ten hours. At home, there's a process happening all week between one session and the next. There were huge difficulties. In my family at that stage, some people were having real problems with my opinions. I had had a completely proper Zionist education, by the book; it was very hard, with my family. There were even family meals I didn't want to go to. It was hard with my father. There were heartbreaking arguments. He thought of himself as a leftist, always a very humanistic kind of person, and indeed I was raised on a very deeply rooted humanism, and everything was OK—until it came to the point of Arabs and Jews. Meanwhile, my husband supported my going, supported my doing this, and yet he couldn't come to terms with the process I was going through; it was very difficult for him.

Today it's different. I think that the whole family changed. They sometimes talk about it like a disaster, but it wasn't a disaster. From my standpoint, it was a kind of revelation. Maybe it's a bit embarrassing to talk in those terms, but for me, it was an epiphany. The change radiated out from the initial encounter. My family started out and my children began growing up in one home, and ended up growing up in another. Not all the way. They attend a uni-national school. And I didn't end up running the binational school here in Misgav (not that I know if they'd accept me), although I made one attempt to initiate change there. It's located in an entirely Jewish community, but there has been some change. The person who was with me for this entire change process from beginning to end, in a very surprising and unexpected way, was my mother, who simply underwent a revolution along with me. If you ask her today, she'd tell you, Nonsense! I was always this way.

And then there was October 2000. That's when my identity was reborn, or shattered, or whatever you want to call it. I lost my faith—in the country, in the media; in our story, in our narrative, in the justice of our path, in everything.

It's like standing on the edge of the void. A decision is required, and I jumped. Then the initial period was very turbulent. Maybe it sounds overly dramatic, but I really felt that way. It was a drama for me. My life changed, from within. I had somewhere I could work through everything that was happening in reality, week by week. In November 2000 I began my master's in peace education, a degree I created—they didn't have it there, before that. I got to the university and looked for someone who would agree to build me an individualized degree in peace education. I didn't walk the usual path at university. I met with Professor Gaby Solomon and he agreed that we would build a program together, and we did. Now he has a whole [peace education] center.

What was it like, that jump into the void?
Where did the growth come from?
It was a slice of life. How can I lay it out so that it will be clear, and accurate, and illuminating . . . ? It's connected with the events of October 2000. We lived through something very hard, like a siege: for three days we could not go out. We wanted to take the children by way of the village of Kaabiya, but there was some kind of confrontation there, and we were closed off, we couldn't leave the community. The children couldn't go to school. One day we did go, and the bus was attacked. It was a group of people with sticks. We got into Shfaram, and they were burning the synagogue, they burned the bank, in the end they hurt Shfaram's own residents. But it started when they came up to the village, to here, with torches. About 300 people. It was a very frightening night. It was Yom Kippur. We spend Yom Kippur with friends, a few households from here, we play games all together on that night. At 11 P.M. they called—it's that Jewish story again, it irritates me so much now, even then it irritated me. They called all our men to come out. We have no fence, it's a community that was built without fences on land from Shfaram, which I think is extraordinary. Some of the community's land was confiscated, and some was purchased, from Bedouin and other Arabs living in Shfaram. There are actually Bedouin houses within the community itself. When they called all the men to come out, the Bedouin men came, too. It was complicated. They didn't give them weapons.

The Bedouin men were guarding the community during the day and some were working here. They weren't given weapons. We, the women and children, we stayed at home. It sounds hallucinatory, right? But there was a feeling that we were being attacked. There was a very big sense of threat. We are very close, within walking distance. Where we bought our house, the area is fenced. But the southern neighborhood that I showed you, there's part of it next to—at a place there called Umm a-Sahali, next to Adi, and the residents work here, they don't live together, but they've been living side by side for years. There were disturbances here that started with home demolitions and then people from Adi went up there and took the people home with them and hosted them. There's a web of relationships that developed over the years and it's different. So we had a very hard experience here and we got reports from the people living at the edge of our village that a group was coming up here from the [Arab] village.

Now at the same time, in Nazareth—there was someone in the facilitators course with me from Nazareth whose cousin was killed there. I can relate everything from a first-hand source, because I also had friends from my workplace at the school, people from the IPCRI project and also from the course, and I heard the stories from people, I heard the stories that were in the paper, and I was here and I saw what they wrote about what happened here with us. What happened here, also happened in Nazareth. Except that here, someone was a little smarter: a police representative or an officer. He didn't pick up a rifle. He went out to the people and spoke to them. So OK, they let off steam and then went and did something even worse in Shfaram itself, but no one died, not our people and not theirs. Still, there was property damage and that's not OK.

Then the following week when I was at Neve Shalom, each of us told their story. I told it very differently; not like what was in the newspapers. And the woman whose cousin had been killed told her story, of what happened in Arrabe, and someone else told more about what happened there, and at that time we had a very close working relationship. Something was amiss. I felt my divorce from the country. It's terribly hard; you're sitting there alone. People don't understand you. They don't get you; they think you're insane and they want you to wake up. From their perspective, you want everyone to be killed, because you don't understand what's required for security purposes. You're familiar with that.

To be cleansed, everything has to come out. It's like a big space in your identity, and when it's empty, it's very painful. Where do you belong? Who is yours? You're not an Arab. You're not a Palestinian. I understand myself as being Jewish, but even there, there were suddenly questions. What's that about, and why, and how? And you're Israeli, and to be Israeli is to be an occupier, someone bad. All these comparisons. And no one understands you. You feel that no one understands you. And here, at the workshop . . . I think I already said this, and I wrote it in the letters I sent to my facilitator (the Arab facilitator, a man): There was no comfort here. No strokes, no comfort, nowhere to curl up in. I anticipated finding that at Neve Shalom, and didn't.

The process went on mowing things down, digging into things. I think it even went over the line a little bit. I was left with this empty space until the end of the course. It wasn't Neve Shalom's problem. It was my problem, that I wasn't able to fill that space yet. It was a wound, that's all. A change in identity is a kind of wound because you have a decision to make; you are cutting something off and you have to replace it. To find a graft that will fit, and can be grafted on. I felt alone, felt that I had no one with whom to do that. Neve Shalom is very far from here, where I live, and in my course there was not one person from around here. It was really insanely isolated, a very great isolation, at a time when the right thing to say was that everyone should barricade himself in his own fortress, put up the barbed wire fences, balance the rifles atop the barbed wire and shoot anyone who comes near. And I should have been shot. I mean, how was I able to even see another side during a period like that when they were coming to kill us? Residents of Adi conducted a boycott. The community of Adi boycotted Shfaram. They stopped buying there, to the point where the hummus guy was going house to house here and knocking on doors to say it wasn't him doing those things. Like that, really. The pediatrician and the family doctor from Shfaram stopped coming. Even ordinary little things. Life changed. And amid all of that I kept going to Shfaram with my daughter. I wasn't the only one, but there weren't many. I was one of the only ones. And I was willing to say so among my own circle, and in my own circle it was a waste of time. I felt absolutely alien, on the social level I felt completely alien. Like I did not belong.

People from the community related to the things you said as if you had freaked out, or as if you just didn't really understand?
No one thought I didn't really understand. I am considered someone with a head on her shoulders, and they don't see me as stupid. I definitely freaked out, but I'm not crazy. They know that I'm an intelligent person, one of the good guys, but they don't know how to take me. I frustrated them, I annoyed them, I pushed their buttons, I said unacceptable things. From their point of view, I said things that endangered people's lives.

There's the way I understand the Palestinian side, for instance; the fact that I say "Palestinians" and not "Arabs." I, personally, Ayelet Roth, am endangering the existence of the State of Israel, because if there were a lot more like me, the state would no longer exist; I'm the enemy, a fifth column. It's so lousy. It's so hard. People talked to my family and were sure that if they just told me again, I'd realize that I was wrong, that I was confused. I have a very good friend who became Orthodox. She started the process of becoming religious when I started the process at Neve Shalom. It's a good comparison between the two processes, in terms of how the society responds to us. But my process had no outward signs, I didn't wrap my hair in anything or start going around in a long skirt. But from every other standpoint, a person who goes and starts walking a new path from that of the society where he lives, it's not something lauded. Think about what I did. I didn't go live in Shfaram. I went on living here; my children continued going to school in Nahalal, but still . . .

FILLING THE VOID

But you asked about the change, about the void, and the question is, how it gets filled up.

First of all, before this empty space in my identity, I needed a band aid and some salve for a wound. . . . I started studying for a master's degree in peace education. I had planned that even before. I worked on it a long time. I knew before I got to Neve Shalom that it was going to be the next phase of my life and that I would accomplish it at any price. I was still at a point I my life where I thought that what I decided was what would happen. So maybe that did something. In the Neve Shalom course they distributed one article that greatly influenced me, and I think helped to shape the stages of my identity. I completely connected with it; it gave me a place that I could grow from. We were given it toward the end of the course. I found out that wasn't alone. Other people, people who aren't living in this insanity, have the same experience. You [discover that you] are normal. And if I'm not mistaken, and I more or less learned the whole article by heart, there's some statement at the end about a description of someone else who did go through this transformation. And I could connect myself with someone who became a better person or who had uprooted from within himself some kind of racism.

So first of all I took another course in group facilitation, and I found empathy there, which is what I really needed: for someone to see me as a human being with the right to be better or worse, more racist or less racist, a human being who has taken some blows and needs a hug. I brought the entire [School for Peace] course there with me. It was also a mixed group. I am sure that they didn't intend for it to be a workshop of that type, but it was, and it was very interesting.

Do you generally bring this subject with you, wherever you participate in something or work on something?

I do. As soon as I made this transition, it was mine permanently. There is no child today in the school where I am principal, from seventh to twelfth grade, who doesn't know what the Nakba is. When I started there, doing things and saying things and explaining things, everyone went through a lesson on the expulsion from Tarshiha, with testimony, so that all the lesson plans on Jewish identity would mention the land issues. Wherever I am, whatever I'm doing in my work at school with the children, this is there. I have been changed forever; this is me, it really is. It's part of my identity now. It's part of my agenda. It's part of what I try to promote in the world I live in. It has become an article of faith with me. It changes, it evolves, the terminology changes, and as the years pass it includes more and more, but the foundation is there.

I worked for five years with an Israeli-Palestinian organization, and I have worked in the Israeli Jewish and Arab educational systems to instill views that see us all as human beings with equal rights, who can live accordingly, and that it's permissible for us to talk to each other, and that we should. First of all, I left teaching and went to work at Nisan, an appropriate place for me. I worked there for three months, but it was quite a small organization and dealt mostly with gender, which at the time did not really interest me. After that, I went to work at IPCRI, and for the next five years that's what I was doing. I was an emissary, I saw myself as a kind of emissary and my work as a mission, promoting dialogue and change and the attempts to change reality.

A lot of the people I guided and worked with in that department at IPCRI are now working in this field. The woman who is principal of the bilingual school at Misgav, who was in my group, I met recently after she began that job and she said to me, "You know, it's on account of you." . . . These people are still in touch with me. I touched their lives in some way, everyone I worked with, I touched their lives and they were changed, some in a small way, others in a major way.

I think what they got from me was the possibility of seeing through different eyes, to see the situation around them in the Jewish-Arab context, even in the Jewish-Palestinian context. And beyond that, most of those people, the hard-core for sure, but more than that—most of them found some kind of commitment to this issue, some need to go and do something. If you ask me what the goal was, I know that in various other organizations that work in this field (although less so at Neve Shalom), they talk a lot about awareness and leave it at that. The work we did after the Neve Shalom course did not stop there. If people couldn't go beyond that, they didn't stay in the group, but a lot of people did stay and are still active today. That's dramatic, I think. They see it as a mission. Some of them, in educational work, are not always doing it the way I wish they would and their messages aren't always the ones I would have chosen to convey, but for all of them the transformation grabbed them at a level that made essential changes. I know that the e-network we set up is still functioning on the internet.

A TYPE OF MATURITY

How is my transformation manifest in my work as a school principal? Let's start with my work during the course, and also afterward, switching from teaching to being a facilitator. The change around the Jewish-Arab issue is not the only change. There's also a change in the way you behave with people, in your way of conducting yourself, starting with how you listen, which ties in with both identity-related and facilitation processes. I remember that in the Neve Shalom facilitators course I was asked to sit in silently on several workshops. I was able to sit quietly for an hour and a half but after that, it seemed impossible, and that was extremely instructive for me.

So when I started working as a principal I had facilitation qualifications and I could listen a lot better than before. It's a type of maturity, and an ability to accept different stories. To know that there's always another version. There's always another viewpoint. Everything, every incident at school, let's say with a teacher who behaved improperly, or made a mistake, or did something irregular—I know that in his eyes, it will seem different, and I take it for granted that in his view he first of all did what he could, he did his best.

Before [the facilitators course], I would not have been able to understand that. I'm not an angel, but I listen a lot better to people. I'm a lot more sensitive to clichés and I can identify when something is an empty statement with nothing to substantiate it. I can sense when a story hasn't been examined all the way through. Even from the standpoint of the values we are trying to pass on, a lot of slogans are used in the educational sphere. Today they can't just bring me a work plan with a slogan without my demanding to open it up all the way and take a look. I want to know what's behind the slogan. We cannot work with slogans.

Another very dramatic change that the course brought about was in my coping with a class of special education students. We have mid-range developmentally disabled students in the school. Joint facilitation work changed the way I see those classes. It enabled me to see that these students see the world differently; they get something else from it, different messages, within an entirely different story. They are traveling through the same reality at the same school in the same building, and while each child individually is experiencing something different, these kids are also experiencing it differently. I understand better now that within the school framework, this group is doing the giving and we are those who are being given to, more than we are giving. It's not that they need us, but that we need them. We need them tremendously. Without them we are hard, and in some way sterile, in our relationships. That's another change for me.

I don't have a program about Jews and Arabs in the school today. I'm in my third year at this school, and I don't yet have a program like that, nor will there be one in the next couple of years. I don't think I'll get something like this in. I don't believe in the "let's have hummus together" thing anymore. I don't believe in programs that exist to satisfy the system. I was so afraid that in the first year they'd discover who I really am, what I really think. I entered a community which is surrounded, or which surrounds—depending how you look at it—that is within an Arab population, and it sits on [their] land, and there are stories there about Tarshiha, endless stories, and this place is different in the sense that it's a highly regarded community with a high-achiever image, and so on. I didn't know how they'd take it. They did choose me and they knew what I'd done before, but I wasn't certain about my relationship to officialdom, what was allowed me and what wasn't, and it took time for me to define the boundaries for myself. The other thing is that I learned to be cautious about big pronouncements and about getting into huge projects. I'm doubtful about their reliability and their readiness, and I decided to bring this in differently. In what way, differently? I set very modest goals for myself initially. Now, too. And I look carefully; I'm always checking. Hatem Darawshe comes once a year to the school and participates in a panel on Jewish identity. The assistant principal of the school in Tarshiha comes once a year to talk about the expulsion from Tarshiha and about the bombing of Tarshiha. I can say that all the children in my school get a lecture. It sounds like hardly anything, but it's a lot.

Once a year I go into each classroom and give a talk, and I introduce the concepts. It starts with this consciousness-raising, so that they'll know what we're talking about. But I don't do it confrontationally, the way I once might have. I don't say "you" in the plural and I don't claim to know more than they do, but it's part of the broader story. I sit with the history teachers and work with them on things. I insist that these things be part of the story, and I make sure that people who have something different to say also come to speak at the school. This is learning, in my view. Meantime, it's clear to me that I can't introduce these children to a [deeper] process. There's a lot of pressure on me to do joint projects: sculpting together; horseback riding. It's very lovely, and you know what I sometimes think? Those things are important, too. Because they do something, on another level. So reality sort of behaves the way we behave with it, and maybe we do need a little of those things. . . . But I have lost my faith in it. I don't do this stuff unless my staff makes a commitment that they're prepared to go into a process.

I don't come to talk about the Nakba. I come to talk about the 29th of November 1947 [when the UN declared an end to the British Mandate in Palestine and announced partition]. I present two approaches to the 29th of November; I explain how one people saw it, and how another people saw it. I tell about the Balfour Declaration [Britain's promise of a Jewish national home in Palestine], about McMahon-Hussein [correspondence regarding the political status of lands under the Ottoman Empire]. I explain. I don't know for certain that they remember. The children ask a lot of questions. It's a very interesting lesson and lasts for ninety minutes instead of forty-five. Afterward, if they want me to, I say I'll come again and talk about it, but I don't get a response. When I brought in the man from Tarshiha, though, I thought the sky would fall.

I respond to racist statements at school very sharply. The students know this and they don't dare. They know I will respond more strongly than to physical violence, even. First of all, it goes straight to the principal's office, and the parents are brought in immediately, and it's very difficult, with two parents. The discussions are very hard. This is a community-wide statement, the ability to contain this. And during the bar mitzvah year when the students do a trip to Safed, if they visit tombs, there's also some discussion of the identity of the Druze children, and some talk about the place as sacred and meaningful to them. It's about acknowledging the existence of more than one culture within the school.

Over five or six years, not just from that one SFP course, if I got something from the process it was a certain easing: an easing, and then a further easing; a kind of sponginess that I didn't have in me, before. Today I can hear any opinion offered, and maybe it will greatly annoy me, but whereas once I would have screamed, now I just listen, and sometimes I'll say OK, you can stick with your position and I'll stick with mine, and that's OK. I no longer have aspirations to convert everyone to my religion, although that is very characteristic of the early stages, but less so with me, that need for everyone to see things as you do. I'll compare it once again with the process of becoming Orthodox. You want them to see the light, as you do; maybe they will, if you only exert yourself just a bit more. It's a different set of eyes; things don't fit. But it does open some other space for seeing the world, for seeing everything that happens in the world, all relationships, even between intimate partners, everything.

6 · HARB AMARA

Educator, Therapy Centers Manager, and Facilitator Trainer

A married father of four, Harb Amara has a master's in social work, a diploma in business administration, a certificate in economic and social policy design, and training as a change agent for Jewish-Palestinian dialogue. An experienced therapist and social welfare manager and adviser, he initiates, operates, and evaluates a range of projects and programs in Nazareth. He oversees the city's master plan dealing with domestic violence and children at risk; he has developed and now manages several therapy centers serving the city's parents and children, and supervises a staff of community workers. At the School for Peace, meanwhile, he manages a project aiming to dramatically expand the reach of SFP programs. He runs SFP courses for facilitators of groups in conflict and for change agents in the workplace and the community. The meta-goal of this activity today is to give people hope that our situation here can be different and that we can make it so. Harb Amara took the Course for Mental Health Professionals as Change Agents in 2008–2009, at the School for Peace at Wahat al-Salam–Neve Shalom. He was interviewed in May 2015.

It's about emerging from the bunker and starting to think differently. You are acting not just for society but beginning to feel that you can contribute and can benefit from this on the personal level; you can taste something else. The fear hasn't disappeared, but it has diminished. I see myself as someone who has a partner. It's possible to take action together to influence what happens in this country.

I took the change agents course at Neve Shalom in 2008–2009 for professionals in mental health fields. I heard about it from a friend who had taken the first such course at Neve Shalom; he really encouraged me to go ahead and have the experience—an experience I now refer to as formative. Until 2008, while I was working, I kept fairly current with what was going on in the local community, in my neighborhood and my village, and with the people around me, but not beyond that.

During the course, I opened up more. It broadened my horizons and I realized that it wasn't enough just to think about and work for the empowerment of your own population, the Arab population, and your own village or the city where you work. We have to be thinking and doing more on the level of what's happening in our country and what's happening with the other side, Jews as well as Arabs. That's where I embarked on my journey: How could I contribute more to resolving conflicts, especially the Jewish-Palestinian conflict or Jewish-Arab conflict, broadly understood. I began taking more interest in what is happening on the Jewish side and with the Palestinians living outside Israel as well as the Arabs inside Israel. The SFP course gave me the direction and the tools to look at the big picture and strive to help change it.

The key was the approach to learning that the course used. As a social worker I'm coming from what are termed the therapeutic professions but, even so, the approach to learning used in this course was something different. The course provided directions. It highlighted points that I generally hear about but have not gone into very deeply, about my narrative and the other side's narrative; about the conflict from my standpoint and the conflict from the other's standpoint. In a personality context, too, something came into focus. I came to understand better where my place in this conflict is, what I lose by the continuation of the conflict, and what I could gain as someone who lives in this space if the conflict is resolved or if we are able to influence [for the better] what happens in this country. Aside from the learning style, the materials we were given were also good. The lecturers were good and the facilitation was good, addressing how we discuss the issues and how I can express what's happening with me and hear what's happening with the other side, and see the impact on each side. All of that began to change something for me; everything I'd been educated to believe, the values that had been to some extent clear to me, began not to be clear anymore.

For example, I always felt that I was the weaker side, the failed side in this equation; that there's not much I can change, that I have to wait, that sometime in the future someone will have the power to change this equation. Being on the victim's side of things, I felt that there wasn't anything I could do. Then I started taking a hard look at how these things were being shaken up for me [in the course]. I started thinking, wait a minute, in this equation I can break through the thinking around me that there's nothing I can do. I can do things to change the situation; I can at least not agree to this situation, at least present my side, hear the other side, try to change something there, see things from different angles, as they say. Where I had been deep in despair, now some signs of activism were sprouting, so to speak, and I could act, I felt that there are things I can do, I can have an influence on things.

This is a kind of empowerment, but what was causing you to come out of the despair and decide that you wanted to act? What moved you away from that place?

What moved me was first of all what you termed "empowerment." I saw it at the time as a sharper focusing of my identity. Until then I had perceived myself as a victim, a failure, without a future. I started to get signals that it wasn't me, I wasn't a failure, after all I'm living here, I'm living this situation, I have certain achievements of my own, so if I have these achievements despite the situation and despite the things I've gone through, then from the personal successes I've had, I can influence the space on a broader scale.

Another thing was the interaction with the other side, with the Jewish side. I began feeling from the discussions and the lectures, that it was possible to change the situation and to change people's ideas, that you can dialogue even with the opposition in Israeli politics, conduct a dialogue and reach a compromise, with everyone moving somewhat from his side. When I started to believe that it's possible to change people, to change an entire situation, then I began to believe in taking action, I called it a certain kind of activism, in which each act of mine had a part in making change.

That is a very powerful experience, when Arabs in the dialogue here discover that they have the ability to influence the other side in a profound way, not superficially or fleetingly.

Yes, and perhaps especially because we are coming from a situation of what I was defining as failure and despair. I meant that we are coming from a society that defines itself as a failed society. We went through wars. Our narrative is that we say we've been through a lot of wars. What came about while this state was being established was at the expense of the Arabs in the equation. The state was founded; the ones who lost, the ones who failed were the Arabs. My experience of living in a country that defines itself as a Jewish state is that, while I have certain civil rights, I don't have that feeling or that privilege that the state is there to protect me, that its institutions protect me.

That's the whole conflict between my being a Palestinian Arab living in Israel, and what I see when I look at a Jew: It doesn't matter where he comes from, he has all the state institutions coming to help him and empower him. In my experience, as an Arab here, everything I want to get ahead in, it's me who has to work hard, I have to invest resources and money and a lot of things so that I'll get somewhere on the personal level [without any of the various kinds of state aid available to Jews]. So given this equation, when I came here to Neve Shalom I started to feel that the other side was actually feeling my pain. First of all it was about that stigma, that all the Jews are looking to negate my rights or, if we put it in a less professional way: They're here to screw me. In the dialogue sessions here I began to see and feel that no, there are also some difficulties on the other side, from a different direction, on the Jewish side too, but from a different direction. I and the Jews, we are living in one space, and it's important to both of us that this space be good for both sides. So the price I'm paying for the existence of this conflict, the other side is also paying, but from a different direction. So these things started to become clearer to me and I started to think, and to feel the pain of the other side. And I started to feel that the other side was starting to understand my pain better, and my loss, in the existing situation here, and how together it might be possible to reach a different process that both sides could benefit from.

DISCOVERING JEWS AS PARTNERS FOR CHANGE

Before the SFP course, having chosen to live in an Arab village, my acquaintance with Jews was work-related, just business, ad hoc. I didn't come [to Jewish towns], I didn't know [them].

I chose to be more connected to the Arab side. I learned about Arab history, I learned about the pain and the narrative of the Arabs, I learned that if I want to live here I have to work harder and protect myself because this state, or anyhow the Jewish side, they don't want me [here] and don't think about my existence here. They think about what's good for them and how to get rid of me as an Arab in this country. That's what I understood, growing up.

When I came here [to the course], I felt that there was another direction; there are people who aren't like that. Just as I want to live and grow and prosper here, they do too, and they don't want me as an Arab to disappear. And I started to feel other things. Even though I had studied at universities in Israel, the Jews I had been in contact with were the teachers who taught me, and there were good teachers and [other] teachers like in any situation. My relationships with Jews were mainly, as I said, work-related. I kept my distance and learned not to get into politics with people, just to focus on the business at hand, but my political outlook was that I inclined more in the Arab direction, more what's called the Arab nationalist direction. I felt that I knew what was happening, and I never felt that I'd be part of the space that exists here in this country. I thought I needed to watch out for myself and my nationality and my identity and not get too much into the Jewish identity or do too much or think too much in common with the Jewish identity. But I didn't address these things much. I stayed focused; I would meet Jews in a professional capacity, something completely work-related, and I never even let myself think otherwise, even though there were attempts, I imagine, by the other side. But I was clear with myself that I wasn't interested; what interested me was my identity, my nationality, and how to protect myself from the other side.

The way I see it today is that, first of all, the fear hasn't disappeared, but it has diminished. I see myself as someone who has a partner. I have people I can think with, and share my thoughts with, and there are people on the Jewish side who think as I do, who want to change the situation as I do, to make it better for all of us. And it's possible to take action together to influence what happens in this country. These days I invest myself in this, really seeking this partner, to shift my positions a little, so that we can set something in motion or build action plans and make things good for us all.

I recently bumped into someone who said she had been with you in that course, and she said the thing that had most influenced her was when you talked about having gone with your daughter to buy ice cream in the city. You said that you couldn't even ask your child in her own language what flavor of ice cream she wanted because of what the Jewish guy selling the ice cream might think, or the other people in the grocery store, because the environment was so racist. For this young woman I met, that statement of yours had the biggest impact of anything in the entire course.

It's still true that in certain areas, I'm afraid to let my identity show. These days, though, if I go traveling with my family, my identity is obvious because my wife wears traditional clothing and has a clear Arab identity, and so do my daughters. Our Arab identity is clear even if I don't say anything. But the fear is there inside me, from experiences and situations that come up when there's a crisis or a war, and the media starts to feed the frenzy and ratchet up the racism. But today, honestly, I'm even more indifferent to it than before. I've begun dealing with the fact that I'm ready to pay the price if need be, or if I'm somewhere in a neighborhood that could be risky for me, I don't care. I need people to get used to my identity, my Arab identity. Nowadays I try insofar as possible to live with all this, without the fear.

Most Jews have no awareness of the fears Arabs have; they think that they themselves have a monopoly on this fear.

That's because they're afraid of any Arab, even if he isn't doing anything. The fear feeds more fear. Just his being an Arab in the same space, let's say at the mall or some entertainment venue or on an airplane, the Jews start to be afraid, thinking that this is someone who could hurt us.

Once I had an even worse situation. I was in a delegation with Jews and we were going to Berlin. A Jewish woman who was a friend of mine was also in the Israeli delegation. We prepared for the trip for almost a year, and spent time with each other getting ready for it. So this woman was sitting next to me on the bus and someone with a Persian or an Arab identity asked me in Arabic about which bus stop he should get off at. So I explained it to him. Suddenly this woman [from our group] sitting next to me said she wanted to get off at the next stop and go back to the hotel and not continue on to the meeting. She got off and I kept on, but later when I got back, I discovered from talking with her that she was scared to death that I was somehow in cahoots with that guy and she was in Berlin and something would happen to her. So you start to realize how deeply enmeshed people are in this, even someone you know personally from the other side. When your responses are driven by fear, you don't respond rationally to things.

The socialization is very powerful and it comes from the government, from the educational system, from the army. . . . We saw it in the most recent elections [March 17, 2015], when Netanyahu warned that the Arabs were "going in droves" to the polling stations.

That's the norm we are trying to change. Since 2009, when I finished the course, I've been active in all kinds of things at the School for Peace. I try to encourage a lot of people to go and have the SFP experience together. I'm active with my professional communities and I urge people to take SFP courses and come to SFP events, to begin to experience what this place is about. It's also influenced my work style on the job. What I've learned here, the years I've worked here, I've started to implement all that in my other work.

It's mainly about dialogue, and action: How it's possible to have a different dialogue, even different action, even in situations that aren't about the Jewish-Palestinian conflict. The tools I learned here included how to listen in a different way, to think in a different way; how to influence others in a different way. So I try to use these tools in my therapy groups, and with the trainees that I work with, and professional people I work with in all kinds of ways.

During the Lebanon war, for example, this led me to make a change in my staff at my workplace in Nazareth. The background is as follows: We had always had this very despairing discourse in the staff; everyone was in despair. My staff works with very difficult issues of domestic violence and parenting problems. I am in charge of a master plan for children at risk and domestic violence. Most of what I do is developing and initiating programs. I'm responsible for several treatment centers: a domestic violence center, family and couples center, parent and child center, and a supervised family visitation center. I oversee a staff of community workers whose goal is to work with the issue of raising awareness about domestic violence and also children at risk, to promote individual and family resilience, and to bolster resilience for potential crises like a major war. My staff prepares people in the community to deal with these kinds of situations.

The staff consists of twenty professionals, mostly social workers but also clinical psychologists and art and music therapists. Our work is mostly very stressful and requires staff to be able to make complicated decisions under pressure. We work mainly with the Arab population, in all its diversity: traditional people and religious people from various communities and a range of social groups and in that sense it is a population similar to the Jewish population.

So when the Second Lebanon War (2006) began, and the talk started, I felt that the discourse among my staff was a discourse of despair: What are we doing? What are we contributing? What good is it to try to treat this problem that some one particular woman is having, or the violence in one particular child's family, when meantime what's happening around us is much worse. The crimes and the violence are so much more massive than the domestic violence or child abuse we generally deal with. How shall we proceed in this situation? So I began initiating discussions about this among the staff. I said, "Let's think together how to proceed, as a professional community or as people whose declared motto is that we want to create social change. We want to change the situation and we feel that in our therapy sessions, despite the models we have learned, nothing much will change so long as the overall situation is one of comprehensive violence because that makes it hard to change people's behavior. So let's think together how we can first of all believe in ourselves, believe that we still have a purpose and can create change. Let's think what we have to do to influence this broader space and then start a dialogue from the point that we still want to have an influence, that I'm responsible for what happens with me and responsible for what happens around me, and we mustn't lose that awareness and lapse into despair."

So through these meetings and discussions, my goal was to use what I learned and the tools I got at the School for Peace to try to help my staff change their thinking. My life is not just about being someone who works as a therapist. My experience isn't limited only to what happens in the therapy room. How can I influence the client I am working with? I have to think more and be more proactive and say what else I can do beyond this therapy room. I have tools, so how can I use them to have an influence, to try to make change?

To connect with the macro, with reality.

Exactly, and turning people toward activist action, so they'll try to climb out of the despair and then look at how they can change what's going on around them, create change among their friends.

And it worked. People started first of all to look from different perspectives at what was happening. They started to see that really my own success is not enough, that it has to go beyond the personal and the family level, beyond what's going on at home, otherwise it's not enough. I have to be more active in what's happening around me and try to promote discussion and thinking among a wider circle that includes more people, deliberating about this situation and trying together with them to find a way to have an influence and change the situation, not to be thrown by the situation as if I can't change anything. What's happening is a lot bigger than me and there's no point in only looking at it and feeling bad about what I see. People started emerging from this bunker, where they were saying I'm only going to worry about myself and my children and that's it, and I'm closing my front door and what happens outside doesn't interest me. It even gave momentum to some of the women on the staff to seek to develop on the personal level, to start blossoming in a new way, to pursue further studies, to embark on broader action. Some of these staff members today are now instructors or have begun working in other circles beyond their workplace, doing things they had never been involved with before.

It's somewhat a parallel process to the one you yourself went through.

Yes. It's about emerging from the bunker and starting to think differently. This also means that you are acting not just for society but are also beginning to feel that you can contribute and can benefit from this on the personal level; you can taste something else. In terms of Maslow's scale, it's the embodiment of your self-actualization in a completely different way.

EMERGING FROM THE BUNKER

First of all, a lot of people from my staff in Nazareth came to the SFP to learn its approach. They participated in a lot of actions that were designed to stop the war. Some of them thought about how to do protest actions. And they were partners, together with the SFP, in mounting a conference for Jews and Arabs after the events of October 2000. It was a time when many of the Arab activists preferred to work more on Arab issues and the Israeli left began going its own way; there was a total disconnect, because the Arabs felt that they had been betrayed by the Israeli left when thirteen Arab youngsters were killed and there was a lot of resentment that no one showed up to protest and the state didn't do much about it, and so on. So we tried to set up a meeting between the leftist movements and leftist Jewish Israeli activists with activists from the Arab side, to try to see why there was no cooperation. This was in Nazareth in 2010. Some of them got into activism with Ossim Shalom (Social Workers for Peace); others worked on the professional level, trying to have an influence within their own professional niche. For example, some of the women social workers felt that more needed to be done about family violence besides what I was developing in Nazareth; they wanted to operate in a broader area around Nazareth and see how they personally could influence other social workers dealing with this subject. Each one focused on a different direction. But what I wanted to emphasize here is how, when someone breaks down the barriers and emerges from that bunker where he's barricaded himself, he can begin to operate in all kinds of directions. He can be a social activist, an activist who does battle against policies, and on the professional level he can begin to see things from a broader perspective.

This point you are making is a very important one, about being in the bunker. What percentage of the Arab population do you think is in that bunker?

Most of the Arab population is in that bunker. Why? Partly I think it's because they lived, and kept on living, in villages or anyhow in spaces where they were even more closed off, and it's also because of how the state relates to them and everything that's happened to them. All of that pushed them in that direction: what protects you is living in that bunker. I also think it's a policy from the top that aims to keep you where you are. It says: If you want to protect yourself or your work, you should stay in that bunker; you don't have to break out, or to think differently. I would guess that the majority of the Arab population [in Israel] is in that situation—aside from a few political activists or political parties, although there hasn't been very much of that activity. I don't see much action involving political parties within Arab communities. There used to be, in the 1970s and 1980s, but since the 1990s you don't see even a local branch office of a political party that's represented in the Knesset—maybe in Nazareth, but it's closed. This was how I once lived: there were political parties that weren't represented in the Knesset, and each one had its own direction, developing branches within the communities.

A lot of people were involved in the Sons of the Village movement and Al-Ard (The Land), for example. The Sons of the Village movement was never in the Knesset. There was the Progressive List for Peace (formed in 1984) with Mohammed Miari and others. A new movement would first start building itself and that was the big test, what kind of influence it achieved.

I don't know why today there are almost no political movements. What I see is that our society has regressed. These days if you ask young people, they'll tell you that what's important to them is their immediate circle, their family; and after that, their extended family. You can feel it, you can see that these young people, whatever their level of education, are prepared to sacrifice everything for their family or extended family.

So this is their bunker. This is where they draw their inspiration and their strength from. And they don't care about other circles. Political parties don't interest them; the state and what's happening in it are not of interest to them. What's important is what's happening in my family or my hamoula [extended kin].

This is a regression. That bunker is like regressing to the first stages of human development, even. I think these things are deliberately promoted, but before apportioning blame, I first want every society or every person to look in the mirror and see where his part in this situation is. I include blaming myself: Where is the part that I'm presenting to myself, the part that I want to change and influence? Where is my part in this?

These days, I work at the School for Peace. I found that I want to give even more, to have even more influence, coming from my belief that the SFP with its models and its approach can do even more than what it has already accomplished. There's nothing to prevent a journey like the one I experienced from being available to anyone who seeks to be in touch with the SFP. If the impact on me was so great, there's nothing preventing anyone else who participates in this activity from experiencing that same transformation. These days I'm trying to promote the dissemination of the SFP spirit to many more people and I am working on that very intensively.

My narrative was the narrative of failure, of the victim. Today I have begun to see things differently. Today I don't feel that I'm the victim. I look at things in a completely different way. And I can understand the fear that Jews feel, even though in my narrative they were the aggressors and are still occupiers, but I can connect and can see where it's coming from, this fear they have of losing power. Before my experience with the SFP, I wasn't looking at things that way, and I didn't even let myself think in that way. I was the victim who was paying the price and is still paying the price, and the Jewish side was the side harming me and continuing to harm me. I was living with my injury and preoccupied with how I could protect myself. So it's a different way of looking at things now, of apprehending things.

I think we have a lot of work to do today. We have to enlist a lot more people if, in spite of everything, we want to go on living here and have things be good here. I don't see that either side is going to overcome the other or achieve victory over the other, not any time soon and not later on. The solution is going to be a solution enabling both sides to live together, but the question is how people will live. This subject preoccupies me greatly these days and I presume that we will work on it together—the question of how we want to live here. Do we want to somehow perpetuate the current situation, or do we want to change it so that it will be better? My expectation is that it ought to be better.

Apparently one needs to be very strongly persuaded of the efficacy of this process that people undergo in the groups, as you said, in order to go and persuade other people to participate.

I think that's true. I have a lot of experience now with encouraging colleagues to join the SFP courses, a lot of people across the whole political spectrum and the whole breadth of the social fabric of the Arab population. For most of them who have been through this experience, the outcome has been what I'd call successful. Their conclusions about things changed. The SFP must invest in figuring out how to enlist people to go through this experience. I'm not afraid that people won't be influenced. The problem is how to get them here. I am sure that once they come, and go through this experience, they will change. It will change them.

7 · YOUVAL TAMARI

Educator and Activist

A core studies classroom teacher in a Tel Aviv elementary school, Youval Tamari has also taught at a school with both Arab and Jewish pupils where he led an initiative to introduce greater, more profound equality within the school community. Prior to that he worked as a city planner in Wadi Ara on a cooperative project with Sikkuy involving Jewish and Arab local authorities. He has been active in social change efforts with Zochrot and Hithabrut/Tarabut. He holds a bachelor's degree in Middle East Studies and a master's in urban planning. Youval Tamari took the School for Peace Course for Facilitators of Groups in Conflict in 1996–1997. He was interviewed on December 11, 2007.

> *Everything I do involves the Israeli-Palestinian conflict. It's what defines my work. In practical terms it can be urban planning at one point, at another time education, and at another time politics. The activity and the work are diverse, but the field remains the same field. The way I see it, I am privileged; I do what seems right to me. It's about having a worldview that's somewhat different than the accepted one, but I don't make a big deal out of it.*

For me, the process of change began before I got to the School for Peace, and during the SFP course the process was greatly accelerated.

I grew up in a very Zionist home; my mother is a teacher, my father is in the military. I was an Air Force Intelligence officer [during my compulsory military service] for five and a half years, completing my service in 1996. This was after the Oslo period, and the possibility of peace was very much in the air. I think I was always interested in public issues, so I thought that this would be my vocation and I began studying toward a degree in Middle East history. One of my first insights was that I had never actually met any Palestinian Arabs. I started trying to get acquainted with Arabs, spontaneously at first, and then I chanced on an announcement of the School for Peace course. It seemed like a very good opportunity, and that's how I got to Neve Shalom.

I remember that by the end of the first session, I could already feel a new world opening up. There was the sudden revelation that I'm not the most righteous or most enlightened person or that there's a problem for which I'm not able to see a solution right now, that something is amiss here. There was a very clear feeling that there is a problem here that I'm unable to resolve right now. I remember very clearly the transition from the first session to the second session; it was bothering me that whole week, and I was trying to find a connection between the Zionist outlook and the demand for equality that had arisen, and I couldn't find a solution. I had the feeling that I wouldn't allow myself to show up without an answer, that I had to get this right; that it wasn't ethical, let's say, to let this remain murky. And that I had to decide. And in fact I decided at that point that Zionism was more important, and equality would have to take second place. I wanted to introduce this, not in a nice way. I was aware of the racism involved, and I didn't want to hide; rather, I wanted it to be on the table. That's what seemed right to me.

So I came to the second meeting of the course. I began by saying that I wanted to say something to the Arab group: that in my fantasy, they aren't here. And I didn't think it was going to be very earth-shaking to say that, so when it happened, I think everyone was a little shocked, and this bombshell was hard for them, and the Jewish group's response came in the uni-national session, a few hours later. They strongly attacked me, but it didn't worry me that much. I said, It's better this way than if I hide out and look for all kinds of halfway measures. I think that somehow, something about hearing myself saying this, and hearing the facilitators' response, maybe Rabah's, did something to me. I was left for a long time with a bad feeling. It took me years to arrive at a different choice: around six years, until I decided the opposite. Yes, around the second Intifada. As for conscientious objection, I think the refusers are responsible. From that beginning, until I decided to change my decision, there was a continual process, one step after another, very gradual, and all the time it was somehow undermining the Zionist worldview.

FROM AMBIVALENCE TO CONSCIENTIOUS OBJECTION

For about four years of this cumulative process that took six years in all, my decision seemed clear: I was still a Zionist first and foremost. Then came the Intifada and I got involved, I visited the territories and volunteered with Taa-yush, and then came the encounters at Neve Shalom. My stance started to shake loose, and I made some effort to run away from the question. It wasn't clear anymore whether I was a Zionist or not. I vacillated, I was ambivalent. Becoming a conscientious objector enabled me to make up my mind. I realized that it was an act that seemed right to me; I had the feeling that if I refused to serve, then what that means is: I've decided.

I remember a few other moments in that course. I remember one conversation out in the corridor with Nazih about things he was claiming, about what the Shin Bet does in Arab towns. At first I said it couldn't be and I told myself, but didn't tell him, that it was an exaggeration. And it started to be there in my head, I started to ask myself, why actually couldn't that stuff be true? Maybe it could be, and along with the doubts I was having, I began to understand. I thought about the issue of power relations and suddenly it seemed to me that whoever has power, it's only natural that he'd behave that way. Suddenly I understood that it wasn't unrealistic, that it was very logical that things were like that. I didn't even investigate it, and there wasn't any way to investigate it anyhow. So in the end, I went with a sense that evidently that's how things are. I remember Abeer, this young woman who interested me greatly, she attracted me in some way, with her very harsh responses. On the one hand I had some kind of admiration for her, and on the other hand, I wanted to please her. The most radical people there were really the ones who got me going. In the Jewish group, there was Yoni, who confused me somewhat; at first when they would analyze some point or other, he was ready for some sort of compromise, to relinquish Zionism, nationalism. And then I felt a little threatened, maybe, by this more moral place he had claimed. Suddenly, the longer the workshop went on, it all turned upside down.

I should mention the matter of writing. I think keeping a journal was very important, writing in it periodically; it helped a lot and organized my thoughts. The commitment to write things down was very important. In the second half of the course, we met with a group we had not been with before, at the university, and then I met Nadia, and especially Badriyya, an excellent encounter, in the sense that it really demonstrated the possibility of dialogue with Palestinian women who were not relinquishing their identity, but who didn't feel the need to be aggressive about it, and that option seemed very good. The change was 180 degrees, or maybe 160 degrees. The change was enormous. I came to that encounter very sure of myself, very sure of my ideas, with a very positive self-concept, and left with something fractured, and questioning, with a very strong feeling of something undermined, but a feeling that this was correct. I mean, it was a good thing, the subversion of this somewhat fake confidence that I used to have, at someone else's expense.

Can you talk a little more about this feeling of fracture?

The way my personality is constructed, this fracture wasn't so much on the emotional level, but on the rational level, and it didn't make me feel depressed. I remember conversations with others in the group who had emotional difficulties with the process they were undergoing. Something in me allowed me to take it in a lighter way, to protect myself more; for me it was more intellectual and had to do with action. I immediately channeled it into what I could do with it: OK, something changed in me, so it was important to do something.

First of all, I was studying. I was a university student for two years after I did the Neve Shalom course. My interest in the subject of the conflict kept growing, so I chose courses related to that and was able to add new perspectives about power relations. The insight about power relations was very acute, and I could begin to see this in academia, too, and to observe which articles they were asking me to read, which views emerged, who the more mainstream writers were and, maybe, who were the writers who were offering an alternative. My eyes were opened a little; I looked around more, and found more questions. I had a lot less trust in a lot of things, like texts, lecturers, curricula, media. I went looking for encounters, all kinds of encounter programs. Some kind of ideal was taking hold there, to create connections with Palestinians, and this went on for a fairly long period. And also, I think, in terms of the power dynamics, I started seeing other kinds. Suddenly I had more insight into the issue of Mizrahi Jews, more awareness. I went to meetings of the Mizrahi Rainbow [activist protest movement] and started looking into that, reading, and afterward I studied urban planning, so all my studies were in the context of discrimination, land, and planning. Those were the subjects that preoccupied me. I chose the same perspectives there. I actually did some work for the Rainbow.

I was supposed to write a master plan for the town of Migdal Ha'emek. Each group of students had to choose a point of view from which they were planning, so we took the point of view of the Mizrahi Rainbow. First we learned about what the Rainbow was saying about all kinds of issues relating to planning, and then we built a plan that tried to come from that viewpoint. Later on, we did a seminar project on metropolitan planning for the Nazareth area and the group that was with me defined the plan as an Arab metropolitan area, so there was this ongoing influence on me in terms of my choices in my studies. Power relations in the realm of gender became much more conspicuous for me. I went from a place where I did not recognize or understand things in my own behavior, to a place where I saw more and wasn't as blind.

THE DECISION TO STUDY URBAN PLANNING

My decision to study urban planning came from, I think, a combination of things: I really love this land, and I hike a lot; I love planning in the sense of thinking ahead and trying to shape reality. Something about the combination of factors fascinated me. So I decided to go for a master's, the hastiest decision of my life.

As a child, I read a lot. I read all the Zionist literature about the conquest of the land, the liberation of the land during that era. I connected very much with those values, the love of the land, the love of the homeland, things that were very strong in me. When I came to understand things later, that didn't change. I still love the land very much.

This wasn't a contradiction for me, it just added another layer. Now I love the land that was here before. I got to know Tel Aviv and also Jaffa.

I'm a guy who doesn't like there to be too large a disparity between what he thinks, what he says, and what he does. The disparities were bothering me. I was uncomfortable that I wasn't doing something more active in my life in that direction, and sometime in 2003 I made a decision. I went to live in Jaffa because some kind of goal was coming into focus for me: to be a partner in a binational community. That's how I phrased it, in a very general way. I disqualified Neve Shalom because it's a very closed community, and there's something separate about it. From urban planning, I brought the idea of urbanism. Tel Aviv is my center, and the six months I spent in Haifa was a kind of exile. So Jaffa was the option, and I moved there and lived there for three years. I saw in those three years that I hadn't progressed much toward the goal of being part of a community. My activity was somewhat marginal, in my own view.

THE CHOICE TO BECOME A TEACHER

The significant decision then was to go in for teaching. At some stage I said that my residence wasn't necessarily creating the connection I was looking for. But if I thought about a role in the community, that would be more like it. So that's how I got the idea to go study teaching and when I finished, I went looking for a school where there's an encounter between Jews and Arabs. While already teaching, I did a practicum at Municipal High School Zayin in Jaffa, but I didn't get hired there to teach afterward; there was no position open.

Two years later I had an opportunity to work at an elementary school and I said OK, I'll take what there is. So since last year I've been teaching at the Weizmann School, and I've been given a really good opportunity to get into a process of change there. The current principal, who arrived a year before I did, decided that in a school with an equal number of Arab and Jewish students, we couldn't just go on teaching as if it were a Jewish school in every way. She initiated a process of thinking about what should be done with this insight, and we started in a direction that said, this is a school that still defines itself as Jewish, but acknowledges an Arab identity, gives it scope for expression, acknowledges its Arab students. We quickly realized that the most effective way to move ahead with this was to attain the (formal) status of an experimental school, so we submitted the proposals. Last year, after a long process of defending our idea, we received that status and this September we embarked on a five-year experiment. At this stage, the most conspicuous result is the entry of three Arab teachers (as opposed to only one, as in the past. There is a curriculum that discusses Jewish and Arab heritage and identity; there are a few lessons given separately to Jews and Arabs. We just celebrated the "Holiday of Holidays," instead of Hanukkah. There's a variety of things involved.

Is it mainly you who is introducing these changes?
Are you leading them?

I am the designated leader of the experiment, and the principal is also introducing a lot of things. She is a significant partner in providing leadership for this step. I very much respect this process as one that is being done not in a laboratory but rather in a community, a neighborhood. The area is socioeconomically very modest. One of our challenges is finding out how to promote Jewish-Arab partnership as something that also empowers the Jewish population; this is very important.

In terms of things I took from my training at Neve Shalom that come into what I am doing now at this school, I would cite first of all the notion of the uni-national forum: the importance of being able to give Arabs the chance to run a lesson in Arabic, for example. Also, the project gave me a means of understanding the Arab population better, including what the people do not say, because the Arab population in our school is very silenced, and has made the choice to be somewhat assimilated and not to speak out. Now they have the option to make their voice heard, without the negative ramifications. Sometimes, the greatest opposition to what we have initiated actually comes from the Arab population; they've said, Who asked you to do this? For example, when we began instituting some separate lessons for Jews and Arabs, the Arab parents thought it was the beginning of an attempt to discriminate against their children, as if the separation was coming from a racist place. The purpose wasn't clear to them, and they didn't see why it was good. So there was a little opposition, and [some work on] explaining the processes.

Last year when we were planning these things, I led a group of parents that went through these things as a group, themselves, before the children's turn came. We talked about this issue of separate classes and we reviewed the opposition in a workshop. I am using the facilitation I learned, including with the parents. In my facilitating, I use at least some of the elements of the Neve Shalom model. Empathy for the Jewish group is something I took from that training, in the sense of noticing how I initiate things, remembering that I wear a certain hat and serve a certain community, that there are dynamics of power here, and that I'm in an advantageous position regarding the Jewish community. I aim for things to be done with the least possible feeling of coercion and the most possible dialogue.

What's the hardest thing about this challenge at the school?

There was something really hard: a kind of threat, maybe, that Jewish parents might leave, that the school could actually stop functioning as this kind of school. That's what we anticipated if we hadn't done this intervention, because there had been attrition over the years and registration was declining, as it was for kindergartens in the vicinity. There's a tough moral dilemma involved. One of the components we chose for this experiment, this process—one of the main goals was to provide the Jewish population with a sense of security. We did this in two ways: First was to add lesson plans for learning about Jewish identity, meaning, to enable increased learning about Jewish heritage and holidays; that was the easy part and posed no problems. The second thing we said was that we would try to arrive at an equal number of Jewish and Arab students, but this step could be detrimental to the Arab population if Arab parents wanting to register their children were turned away. We had a lot of ambivalence about this decision, and in the end I decided that it was the right way to go. And when I decide something is right, I work to make it happen. Afterward I tried to work with the municipality and really tried to get an official imprimatur for the project. The various agencies did not want to give it their backing; the city did not want to commit to back it. The city is afraid of being sued. We refused to let it go; we said this is part of the project, we have to get it accepted. So there was ambivalence, a dilemma. No intervention was required this year, because the registration was approximately fifty-fifty, but it's going to come up in the future again.

POLITICAL COURAGE

My connection with Bimkom: Planners for Planning Rights has been more as a workplace, not as a partnership framework. What they are involved in there is very interesting. There was a project to do a planning survey in Arab neighborhoods in Ramle, for example, the goal being to provide a counterweight to the official establishment planning, which does less to address the

Arab point of view. The idea was to try to present some kind of alternative. The way I approached it, perhaps differently than what someone else would have done, was to emphasize giving the residents an opportunity to express what they saw. I convened a whole series of residents' meetings, and the facilitators were Arabs, working very much in the spirit of Neve Shalom.

I was also active with Zochrot. Their mission is to learn about Palestinian communities destroyed in 1948 and bring this knowledge to the Jewish public in Israel and beyond. They use both written sources and oral interviews to get material, and then they produce pamphlets with the information. They also give tours, in and of themselves political acts, to restore a presence to these communities by hanging signs. The Zochrot work involves all the things that interest me: the political aspect, the question of the land, the geography, the history, and the story that is an alternative to Zionism, and also friends, meaning people who are close to me who are doing this. There's a sense of making a statement that blazes a new trail and offers something new. Mainly, I took responsibility for writing reports, like the ones on Sheikh Muwanis and Ramle.

You asked about my conscientious objection. I had an opportunity when a group of draft refusers published a letter in the media, and I hitched a ride with that.

It was during the second Intifada, around the time of the battle in Jenin [in April 2002]. Refusal wasn't something I'd planned; it wasn't something I'd thought about. And it wasn't that significant a question for me, in the sense that I wasn't doing my reserve duty in the territories. So I didn't have that dilemma. Suddenly, the letter came out. It made a political statement of some kind. I was very moved by the courage it took to do that. These things really speak to me. Political courage. I also saw that my cousin had signed, so I had a private opportunity to ask questions and get clarification. There was a certain ambivalence, because I don't go to the territories and the letter, the refusal, was about serving in the territories. I thought maybe it wasn't totally authentic for me. But I thought, and said, that the point for me was also the family aspect, because my father was in the army, and that's the place where I connected. The importance of my signature wasn't in the practical sense of refusing to serve in the territories, but that I was someone whose father was a senior figure in the military, or that's how I understood things. I had some ambivalence about the refusers' leadership. They weren't really looking for people who didn't do reserve duty in the territories, but they understood that my signing might have repercussions, and that seemed right to them, and I thought so, too.

Your father was killed in the army [in a helicopter crash in 1994].
He was head of the Central Command [at the time of his death]. It was complicated. My decision wasn't easy. It was meaningful mainly on the family level, including my desire to be interviewed and my mother's request to be interviewed. It played my political desires against my respect for the family and my wish to protect them. So, again in political terms, somehow when I took that step, something about it was like coming out of the closet. It was public. That also helped me in coping with the Zionist versus not Zionist issue. Apparently I was already no longer a Zionist. I was maybe 60 percent non-Zionist. I don't know if the main thing was the public aspect of it or the decision itself. I didn't see it as a personal step vis-à-vis my parents. Some of the family acknowledged it, some supported it, and I did get some encouragement and reinforcement. There was some opposition, but I didn't see it as significant. I already knew those people weren't in the same place. In fact, I saw it as challenging them by presenting them with this option. For me it was a personal political statement, including to the family. People who were my close friends before that, are still my close friends; in a wider circle, I think that I gained a lot of friends from the political/social aspect of it.

Everything I do involves the Israeli-Palestinian conflict in various ways. It's what defines my work. In practical terms it can be urban planning at one point, at another time education, and at another time politics. The activity and the work are diverse, but the field remains the same field. The way I see it, I am privileged; I do what seems right to me. It's about having a worldview that's somewhat different than the accepted one, but I don't make a big deal out of it. There's a sense that it's a little different. But you could analyze it sociologically and say that it's about privilege: Who can permit himself to focus on this issue? Someone who evidently isn't too worried about basic survival needs. You have to keep it in proportion.

8 · RACHELA YANAY

Organizational Consultant and
Group Facilitator

Rachela Yanay earned her B.A. in psychology from the University of Haifa; her master's is in urban planning from the Technion–Israel Institute of Technology and she wrote her thesis on planning in the Arab sector. She studied organizational consulting at the College of Management in Rishon LeZion. She trained in the facilitation of groups in conflict at the School for Peace and has worked as a facilitator of groups in conflict focusing on Jewish-Arab relations in various forums until 2009. From 2005 till 2009 she worked at Sikkuy—Association for the Advancement of Civic Equality, as codirector of the advocacy section, dealing mainly with government agencies to remove obstacles and reduce disparities between the Jewish and Arab populations in Israel. Rachela Yanay took the course "The Jewish-Arab Conflict in the Mirror of Theory and Practice," a School for Peace course offered by the Department of Psychology, Haifa University, in 1996, and then a School for Peace Workshop on Mizrahi Identity, also in 1996; she took the SFP Course for Facilitators of Groups in Conflict at Wahat al-Salam–Neve Shalom in 1997. She was interviewed on September 14, 2008.

First of all there's my acceptance of the Arab-ness in me; I was more prepared to acknowledge it (after the course). And then there is a different connection to the other place: now it's not off limits, not unacceptable. It is

not the evil enemy who has no connection with me. It is part of who I am.
Denying that they are part of who I am is incomprehensible now. What
were they before? Some kind of group that you designate, they don't
belong and they don't have to belong, and heaven help us if they do belong
because they want to kill me; they want me not to be here.

About the School for Peace course I took at the University of Haifa: that
goes all the way back to 1996. I got into the course with Professor Ramzi Sulei-
man in the social psychology department at the last minute, because I was
an undergraduate at the time and the course is mainly for graduate students.
Ahmad [Hijazi] and Michal [Zak] of the School for Peace were the facilitators
for the experiential component of the course. Afterward, they suggested that
I come and take the Facilitators Training Course at the School for Peace. The
course at the university had been exceptionally good and I decided to go
ahead and register for the facilitator training at Neve Shalom.

Then I began my graduate studies and lost touch with the SFP for a
while. They asked me to facilitate for groups of young people but I had too
little time. When I finished my master's degree, I went back to facilitating for
youth encounters. It was very intensive and meaningful, and I facilitated a lot.
Working with groups of young people, I was learning more about myself
every day. At the Haifa University course, I was very extreme, with very
well-entrenched Zionist positions. I had a lot of questions, yes, but my perspective was Zionist and especially Mizrahi, because that's what I grew up
with. It was the nationalist Mizrahi Jewish Israeli perspective that sees the
Arabs as wanting only to take.

All this is very mixed up with the Palestinian story from 1996 onward. It
was after Oslo, but people were still groping; it was early days for these contacts. Gradually the idea that there has to be a Palestinian state entered the
discourse in a way everyone could accept. Today, if you ask someone on the
street, it's clear that a Palestinian state is acceptable—unless you are asking
someone from the extreme right.

The university course brought me into contact with many sides of myself.
One thing I remember, and I wrote a paper on it, is the issue of social
marginality. There was a young Druze man there who did not fit in too well.
Suddenly I found myself from within Jewish society facing the Arab-ness
inside of me as some kind of marginality. That greatly shaped and directed
most of what I would do later on. Plus the connection between Mizrahi and

Arab was very unacceptable, especially when I tried to take it home to the family. It was very unwelcome then and is still unwelcome there now; they still see me as an extremist.

Later, when I closed that circle and facilitated the university course with Ahmad, I remember the stories the students told and their attempts to take home what was happening in the course and share it with friends and family. Those from the Jewish mainstream had a hard time. It requires breaking through the barriers and going to a place that's not accepted. By the way, Sikkuy (where I am working) actually created a very comfortable frame-work for dealing with these things; when I experience friction over this, it is mostly with people who are more ambivalent. Surrounded as I am by organizations and people who lean in the same direction I do, I don't have to fight about it all the time. At home, well, I downplayed all of this some-what, and anyway they usually know my opinions and they know where I am on the map.

THE LANGUAGE WAS ALWAYS THERE

I grew up mainly with my mother's family, because my father's side was not as close to us. My father is from Yemen and my mother from Libya. I don't know about Yemen, but from the stories they tell I think it was not that hard in terms of being Jewish. But my grandmother's stories about Libya, espe-cially with the establishment of the State of Israel, are stories of persecution and murder. Afterward they came to Israel.

This whole story is engraved in my awareness, a very Zionist story, very patriotic toward the state and the army. I was an officer in the army. I was in the Education Corps, yes, but I was still an army officer and it was clear that this was something that no one in any way objected to—my going to the army and making a contribution there. We pay our debt to the country. My grand-father seemed to feel that he had a debt to the state, every day. As if every morning he got up and had to say thanks to the State of Israel. He was in Rafi and later in Mapai [political parties] through all its gyrations. I have an uncle who was named Rafi, after the party, as a way of honoring Ben Gurion. And the Arabs, that was something totally off limits: The Arabs want to slaughter us—to throw us into the sea. A good Arab is a dead Arab. You turn your back and an Arab will stab you from behind.

Nonetheless my grandfather had business dealings with Arabs. They would show up, all those guys with the alte zachen—the junk collectors. My grandfather was always collecting scrap metal and junk. It was his main business, and most of the people he worked with were Arabs. From the standpoint of language, too, it was easy for me. I grew up with Arabic in the home, North African Arabic, but anyhow the language still sounds good to me. It's not a language I have trouble connecting with. My mother spoke Arabic with my grandmother. The language was always there.

Apart from language, however, Arab culture was not acceptable and did not have a presence in our home. We grew up in a totally Israeli culture; no Arabic music at home, except for my grandmother. She loved Umm Kalthoum. But my mother was only a year old when she arrived in Israel, so as I grew up it was all about Israeli songs, Palmach songs, all of that. Without an accent, without any tinge of the other, and with very substantial reservations about the Arabs.

Arabs, that was something not good. On the other hand, because we live in Kfar Yona, Tulkarm was nearer our village than Netanya, and things were cheaper there. When I was in first grade, they bought me my schoolbag in Tulkarm; I went to a dentist in Tulkarm; we shopped at the market there until the first Intifada broke out, when everything was cut off. Until then, it was a city that people went to. I remember the people who walked around there. I realize it's a stereotype, that we went shopping there and about the Arab merchant and the Arab junk collector and so forth, but that was our experience, really.

Of course, on the other hand, we were a very isolated society because of the education we grew up with. Only one out of thirty children in the classroom was Ashkenazi. We were all Mizrahi at the secular Amal school at Kfar Yona, with maybe four Ashkenazi families there. In the 1970s there was an influx of immigrants from Russia, but some of them went back. So you're growing up in that environment, yet the education is based entirely on Western culture. They are teaching Western literature; the Arabs did not appear in that story anywhere. From our perspective, they did not exist; they were there, and we used them, but they were invisible.

And with all of that baggage, I came to the university, to Ramzi's course. I'd already been in the army and was an officer, I had some sort of Zionist spirit in the sense of this is a Jewish state, period, and nothing else exists here. Now suddenly there's a question, a question about where I had been, all that time. But it involved a lot of denial and repression because, however they tried to categorize me, if they said I was some type of Arab, that wasn't acceptable. Good heavens! Don't call me an Arab. I remember going into the library and the guard at the entrance spoke Arabic to me because he thought I was an Arab. There are a lot of Arab students at Haifa University; there's an Arabic look. I was deeply insulted. It shocked me profoundly. Things came up in the course at the university and suddenly emerged into my awareness, and I struggled with them and turned them into a kind of project.

This brought up Mizrahi identity vis-à-vis Arab-ness and the Arab dimension in it. It posed the issue of how much I had repressed and distanced myself from that experience, and it really reminded me of all kinds of situations I had repressed until then. Like with my grandfather. When I was already at an age to understand things, an adolescent, I would not say hi to him on the street because he looked like an Arab. He embarrassed me. And by the way, my grandfather really looked like a Palestinian Arab although he was from North Africa. He would go around with his ID card in his pocket because they were always stopping him. But from his standpoint it was all OK, because this is the Jewish state, the State of Israel, and whatever they did was OK, he felt, because you have to find the Arab terrorists, so I can pay the price for that. This came up, for the first time, in the course at the university and then it was amplified in the course at Neve Shalom, with even more friction, because the people I met there were coming from a different place. It wasn't just me; I realized that the person standing facing you is going through a process, too.

What was amplified?

First of all, my acceptance of the Arab-ness in me; I was more prepared to acknowledge it. And then, based on that, there is a different connection to the other place. I mean, now it's not off limits, not unacceptable. It is not the evil enemy who has no connection with me. It is part of who I am. Today, tell me what's not clear about Jubran or Nada being people just like me with whom I want to live in full equality. Denying that they are part of who I am is incomprehensible now. What were they before? Some kind of group that you designate, they don't belong and they don't have to belong, and heaven help us if they do belong because they want to kill me; they want me not to be here.

I think that this fear is what drives all of us in the end. It comes and goes, I've found. So I moved closer and moved away again, and there was this dissonance again, and you come back and you examine it again, more deeply, as part of the work the group is doing on these things. And finally the choice is to take it to somewhere that is not merely educational but also activist. That's what I chose when I went to work at Sikkuy. To say there is a situation here that is unacknowledged, that cannot be, there are second-class citizens here, or citizens whose citizenship is conditional all the time and isn't obvious; it's always being kept as a negotiating chip.

The issue of marginality came up very strongly for me in the course in the sense that suddenly I couldn't place myself. I was always so connected to the Western experience, the Israeli experience. That's what there was here: Palmach songs, Israel songs, Independence Day, and suddenly there was a kind of disjunction and a feeling that I belong somewhat to the Arab side; I found myself in some kind of intermediate place. I think that I was the only Mizrachi woman there, and the Druze guy was there, and our reality here in Israel is such that he served in the army. I don't know. I really identified with him because I somehow connected with him, of all people. Not in the discussions within the group, but inside myself.

THE OTHER WHO IS REALLY A PART OF ME

When I went home, I spent some time reflecting and writing about what happened there. We were keeping a journal. So I found myself coming back a lot to that place of the connection to the other who is really a part of me, and again my connection to things Western wasn't too clear. That's the strong marginality I was talking about. All of this opened a lot of windows into what being Mizrahi means and how that is connected with Arab-ness. Is it even connected? Because maybe it's something else; that question also arose. A different kind of Arab; I don't know. Imagine going home with this and dealing with it there, with my statements being so different from the typical statements in the consensus I lived in, and going on with it, choosing to continue . . . and not saying OK, I get it, I'm choosing to go on repressing all this because that's more comfortable.

Until then I had never experienced, certainly not at university although maybe a little in the army, I had not experienced any sort of rejection from Israeli society. I wasn't identified as Mizrahi. I did not have the accent, I behaved like everyone else, I went to a secondary school in Netanya with mostly Ashkenazi children and I was in the best academic tracks there. My family name is Yanay [an Ashkenazi name]. I am light-complexioned except in the summer, so I am classified as half and half and I was comfortable with that. The only place where I felt something wasn't working for me was in the course, in the encounter with the Arabs. Suddenly a picture surfaced from the other side. It made them more human, but it was more about how strongly they reflected back to me the other side of myself that I had always repressed.

You pay a very, very high price in what you are doing day-to-day. If I worked in high tech, none of this would even come up. But I have chosen something more combustible, and I make that choice every day, over and over again, to stick with this work. I suppose at some point I might say: This is too hard for me; I don't want to do this anymore. Sometimes in fact I ask myself: Why do I have to do this work, it takes a lot of energy, it preoccupies me all the time, things happen and you have doubts. Working in Sikkuy, you see the way the regime behaves, and on the other hand you see how the Arabs behave; there's nothing absolutely pure here, you understand that. I ask myself why I need this, when I could switch sides and go to work for some other organization despite their intrigues and problems, but in my experience it's not any cleaner. I could say, well, I'll do something periodically I'll go to a demonstration; but I won't make a career out of it. The moment I chose it as a career, I began dealing with it all the time; it never ends.

I'M A JEW, I'M AN ARAB

After university, I took a year off from studying. I was in Haifa. I facilitated high school encounters with secular Jews and religious Jews there. Then I went to an SFP workshop for Mizrahi participants. It took me right back to the same place. The "uni-ethnic" sessions were the most significant. I sat with Mizrahi women and heard their stories and felt a connection in terms of how my family sees me, their expectations, escaping the boundaries of that, and about marginality and "mixed" identities. The participants with one Ashkenazi parent and one Mizrahi parent, for example; which group did they sit with? Some chose to be with us; others chose to go elsewhere. I could relate to this; who am I? I'm a Jew, I'm an Arab: in Israel this carries a lot of meaning. That was the beginning of my path back to Neve Shalom, coming back to facilitate with groups of young people. I kept in touch, I came to the conferences, and I connected more with other facilitators. I was entering a community, it's really a community, and you meet these colleagues even outside the Neve Shalom encounters; you meet one another in all kinds of places.

I facilitated for about a year and then was offered the chance to coordinate the facilitation for the youth programs. Nada and I did that together. The coordinating role is greater, more meaningful, because you are looking at things from a different angle, and you see the interactions between the facilitators from a different perspective. There can be friction with the management team when they introduce theory on different levels, and then there were all the colloquiums we held, opening up issues in a way that you don't really do as a facilitator.

And there was also the project with Wifaaq, with the Palestinians, which was a different world, a world apart from ours.

Then after dealing with encounters for adults, there was a project with Amjad Musa for teachers. This was fascinating. The group undergoes a lengthy process together: the teacher as change agent. A teacher goes through this process and then you see his outputs. I remember what they said when they brought it to the classroom. They said it was a change in the curriculum, introducing new materials into the curriculum, and that by itself was amazing.

At the same time I was coordinating the youth programs on the one hand, and facilitating for adults, and facilitating a course at Haifa University, the same course I took (years ago): "Closing the Circle" with Ahmad Hijazi. It was a fascinating process to see the students and to see myself there, closing the circle, and to be a facilitator in a place where I had begun my own transformation. I could see different aspects of the processes that I myself had undergone, like going home and having Israeli society give me a hard time.

Talk about your work at Sikkuy.

Sikkuy: The Association for Civic Equality in Israel has three branches: one dealing with Arab and Jewish civic action groups; a second that works with municipalities; and a third that promotes equality in policy at the national and district level of government, with an occasional project involving local councils, too. Sikkuy's position is that the government has to make sure that its citizens will no longer be subject to the kind of broad inequality that has been institutionalized throughout the sixty years of the state's existence; it must take action to eliminate these disparities.

After the widespread protests by Palestinians in Israel in 2000 and the Or Commission report, Sikkuy applied to the European Union to fund a three-year project to monitor implementation of the Or Commission recommendations for change. I came on board with that project. My Arab codirector and I organize and lead all of our department's activities in national and district policy work.

When you go to meet with a bureaucrat or a director-general, do you find all kinds of things emerging from this process of negotiating or from these conversations that you think have some connection with what you did at the School for Peace?

In my opinion, every dialogue I have with government people relating to Arabs is connected, because I can really understand where the directors-general are coming from; I see it with groups. I have a group of Jews, the Group of 120, that works with a parallel Arab group. I was a kind of catalyst or mediator for the process that took place there. This is what Sikkuy is about. I also live this matter of working with groups on a daily basis at Sikkuy because of the composition of the organization: every Sikkuy retreat is a workshop, every staff meeting is a workshop, because the same forces are at work. And every time you find yourself once again a participant; I can see the processes from the outside and yet go inside, too, working both from without and on the inside, I'm always in a game like that. Sometimes I'm aware of particular things happening within the group and can say where I was operating at that point and what happened there. And you see this also in the meetings held by government people with the Arab population. In most cases, they work as a ministry dealing with heads of local councils and there is a lot of mutual recrimination.

Can you give an example of a significant dialogue that you had with someone from the government where you felt that you were really succeeding in moving something forward?

To move something ahead in real time I think is very difficult, but a good example would be Ziona Efrati, head of the Housing Ministry's Program Committee at the time, one of the highest-level divisions in that ministry. Ziona was sitting on the stage at a conference while they showed a film on the Misgav region called *A Different Family,* portraying various Arab families trying to move into communities in that area. The racism you see there is hard to imagine. The local community holds a town meeting and people are filmed sayings things like: "No Arab will live in our community, period. We want our own community, a Jewish community, with our own holidays." It's really blatant racism. Ziona Efrati sat there and said, "I respect every person, no matter who, and he has a right to say what it is that he wants." She said that on the stage. I did not get involved; someone from the audience stood up and said to her, "Do you hear what you are saying? You are the government. The government is saying something very racist here now. In the name of what you call pluralism, you are allowing there to be oppression and racism here."

I had a hard time getting her to the event in the first place. She kept telling me, "What for, we don't work in Tel Aviv, the Housing Ministry works in the north; so bring Uzi Shamir, who's head of the northern district." . . . She did not want to hear that there are matters that are national in scope, and the Jewish-Arab question is not particular to the north and even if it were, it's a discussion that has to happen in Tel Aviv, too. So you tell her: The place where you are, now, has to have this discussion; the people who live in Tel Aviv, the prime movers of this state, have to have it. With all due respect to outlying areas, Tel Aviv is the center and this conversation cannot be conducted only on the periphery. It's always punted to the periphery. I persuaded her and she came.

After the discussion and after what was said to her. . . . Again, the people who show up for this kind of event are a self-selected group. They told her from the audience: "Listen to yourself, this is outright racism, and a government official cannot sit here and say such things." I was sure that that was the end, that we had burnt this connection. Our biggest dilemmas involve how far you can stretch the thread. I have to work with this person the next day; I have to come to their ministry and they have to give me the goods, and she can throw me out in one second because there is nothing forcing her to have me in her ministry. So I'm in this game trying to find the point where there is still pressure but also possibility. I picked up the phone and called her and talked with her and she told me that it did something for her; it took her to a place where she has to think about it. To understand that there's a problem here. Before that, she was talking out of this very clear Zionist ethos about Judaizing the Galilee.

The Ministry of Welfare tells us, in a similar vein: don't touch anything here that has to do with aliya [immigration of Jews to Israel]. We looked into their criteria for allocating human resources such as social workers to the local councils. We discovered that in every community that absorbs aliya, they get special social benefits for that. What happens? Jewish communities that are much better off than the Arab communities, and don't need much welfare assistance, have a lot of social workers; these people can be moved around and need not be utilized solely for new immigrants; they can be used for the entire community. The Arab communities meanwhile have few positions and don't get any more positions this way, because the funding is coming from the system only for aliya-related needs.

We remarked on this to a civil servant sitting with us, and she said, "What do you mean? That's the policy. This is the State of Israel, the Jewish state, and it absorbs immigration, and you can't touch that, ever, period." So we get stuck like that, and when people tell you these things, you can't persuade them of anything. It's as if there is nothing to be done. Meantime we have a saying: a citizen is a citizen is a citizen. We have a long way to go yet before the typical bureaucrat will think that a citizen is a citizen and will make that a priority.

THE ENERGY TO PERSEVERE

I get a lot of energy to keep going from Sikkuy itself as an organization; it's very supportive, like a family. We have small successes; we do. We can go into a ministry and people listen to us. We are viewed as professionals, including by the Arab population. Within the organization there is a lot of learning; your colleagues are your friends and you can really work with them.

Now that this is my main occupation, I feel the price less. My family has their view of me but, even so, I've been through some transformations with the family, and the situation is different today. My sisters understand me better now, and I've taken them to all kinds of events and they were changed. Even my mother talks a little differently now; the dissonance comes and goes. She realizes that what takes place is not OK and that there is oppression and that [Arabs] are citizens like any other citizens, yet the idea of the Jewish state is hard to relinquish because of the fears.

I have learned that people must talk together as equals; this has been very, very essential to my transformation. I had a really hard time with a paternalistic attitude from people trying to make sure I know that they know better than I do. I see that a lot. At a seminar at Aqaba once, there was a big blow-up in the group. I felt that the Jewish participants were terribly condescending, and it made me angry. Meantime, the Arabs took a very belligerent position. They had already been through some empowerment and came on very aggressively, and that aggression repels me too. I'm not prepared for the sides to simply change places. I want something really equitable to emerge here, so that we can engage as equals, and talk together as equals. If we just reverse roles, we're in trouble.

So there's this kind of game going on, all the time, and for me it's very important. I am always saying that I don't want a state in which, after the national question is resolved and everyone accepts the other national group, some other groups will still be unequal. This is one of the hardest things I have to deal with all the time. It's really difficult for me if an Arab tells me, for instance, that we are struggling first of all over the national issue and for equality, but homosexuals and lesbians are not acceptable, or any other kinds of national minorities aren't acceptable. Because from my perspective, it's all one playing field.

9 · NAZIH ANSAARI

Community Development Activist, Educator, Counselor, and Facilitator

Nazih Ansaari was born in Jerusalem in 1970 to a family that traces its historical and religious roots in the city back more than thirteen centuries. He was educated in Jerusalem, graduated from high school during the first Intifada in 1988–89, and completed the SFP Course for Facilitators of Groups in Conflict in 1994–95, facilitating thereafter at both the SPF and Givat Haviva. His B.A. in educational policy and organization and Arabic language and literature is from Tel Aviv University, and his master's in public policy and administration from the Hebrew University in Jerusalem. He also holds a continuing education certificate in organizational consulting from Bar Ilan University. He trained at the Adler Institute and has done extensive group work in parenting, couples and family counseling and with young people and at-risk youth. He developed the city's counseling programs for Palestinians in East Jerusalem to assist distressed populations including women, recovering addicts, and young people, and for over twelve years he ran the A-Tur Community Development Organization promoting community empowerment and awareness while developing social, community, educational, cultural, and physical services and service delivery. Today, A-Tur is the only Arab neighborhood of Jerusalem receiving city funding under the national program for children and youth at risk. Nazih's focus is the pursuit of equality and social justice, and he is among the founders of the Spring of Democratic Education Association, which established, during his tenure, some dozen learning and enrichment centers in disadvantaged neighborhoods of Jerusalem. Nazih Ansaari took the SFP Course for Facilitators of Groups in Conflict in 1994–1995. He was interviewed on October 10, 2012.

> *Because mothers were the dominant force in the neighborhood, I wanted to offer a course at the community center where mothers over age thirty-five would be trained to mentor others. Each trainee was required to adopt seven younger mothers to mentor, with a stipend per hour. When the funding ran out, they asked to keep on working as volunteers.*

I am Nazih Ansaari and I'm from East Jerusalem. In 1994 when I was a student at Tel Aviv University, I heard about the SFP facilitators training course. I have to say that I was uncertain whether or not they would accept me into the course because I wasn't an Israeli; I was a resident of East Jerusalem. In the end, it was decided that I could participate.

I really wanted to get into that field. Not too long before that, I was at an encounter that moved me very much, after the first Intifada in 1988 while I was living in East Jerusalem. It was an encounter of Arabs and Jews and it was my very first exposure to Israeli Jewish society, which I'd always been curious about. I wanted to know more about it, mainly because I wanted to attend a university locally, to get to know both Israeli Jewish society and Arab society inside Israel.

The SFP course really changed a great deal about how I saw things. It changed my prejudices about Jews in general, because unfortunately my first encounter with Jews was during the Intifada. The Jews I'd met were all soldiers who set up a checkpoint near my house or who went looking for me when I came back from work at night. So I had a negative picture overall. My encounter with different Jews in the facilitators course very gradually began to change that picture. It became a more realistic, more diverse picture of reality. I started to understand that Israeli Jews are like any other people, with good and bad, and also extremes.

I BECAME MUCH MORE ACCEPTING

I remember Yossi, a Tel Aviv guy in the course. He introduced himself as a homosexual, and he left a vivid memory for me because he was different than the other Jewish guys in the course, in his thinking, his openness, and his under-

standing of the other. I didn't feel that all the Jews in the course totally understood us as Arabs. They tried to walk in our shoes, they really did. They were well
educated people who were very thoughtful, but with all the effort they made, I
understood that there would always be an obstacle. Yossi particularly surprised
me in all kinds of situations, when I felt that he could identify very well with the
other side. I tried to emulate that, but I was never able to understand the other
side as well as he seemed able to do. Still, I changed a lot on the personal level
and became much more accepting of the other. I committed myself fully.

I met my wife at university. She was half Jewish and half Christian, a new
immigrant. Then came the course and it had an impact on my connection with
her, because we committed ourselves fully and decided to get married and start
a family together. That's on the personal level, about an awareness and understanding of the complexity of the society. For me it was different than for an
Arab Israeli, a Palestinian living inside the State of Israel. And it's still different,
because my demands from the establishment, from the society, are different
than his; he is living in that society and my demands are different today. I am
living in East Jerusalem and for me it is and always will be occupied territory
that someday, in an orderly way, has to be returned to those who must return to
a Palestinian State in the future. So that's another insight the course gave me. At
times, the facilitators probed very deeply and helped me do that, too, looking
inside myself and sometimes finding aspects of my real identity.

This was a major contribution: Who am I? What do I think? What do I
want? There was some confusion there. I was coming from Palestinian Arab
society living under occupation and I integrated into Israeli society which has
Jews and Arabs, and studied within Israeli society in an Israeli institution, at
Tel Aviv University. I also lived in Tel Aviv so I also got to know Israeli society
there. I was afraid of having an identity that was really occupied—how can I
express this?—I was afraid of living with the acceptance of the other, somehow. Even today I make this very fine distinction in accepting the other as a
person even though he is Jewish because it was clear to me that one has to
accept the other everywhere in the world. I lived in Germany and learned
to accept Germans. I traveled to the United States and learned to accept. I
make the distinction between the occupier who is connected to the establishment, and the man who is standing there and working and living with me. In
my own family, I have brothers and sisters who don't make that distinction;
there's a stigma on the Jew, or a prejudice against him, and that's not me. In the
way we educate our children, my wife and I make this distinction, accepting a

person as he is and building a connection with him based on the way he really is and not on what he is as a Jew or as an Arab, but what his nature is.

CRITICAL SELF-SCRUTINY

These questions were always roiling around in my head, all the time, and I was always attempting to look at this even before the SFP course, but a lot more afterward. It greatly affected my behavior, which I started examining from all kinds of angles, to understand why I was behaving that way toward a Jew who was working with me. Sometimes I got furious responses. I had an opportunity to work at the municipality for the first time in an orderly way and some Arabs were angry about it, about the way I was accepting of the Jews there. I was more open and understanding. The Jews didn't like how I was behaving and some called it hypocrisy, as if it weren't the real me, because it was during the suicide attacks in Jerusalem and every time there was an attack, the atmosphere was really tense. They'd say all the Arabs are happy about it and you are, too, but you're not showing it. And all kinds of things like that. So the test was in these situations, to see all the time whether this was part of my identity or not part of my identity. So for example I didn't hesitate to say that I was against every attack that killed innocent people and what does it matter if they were Jews or Arabs. This was coming from a very, very strong place inside me and I didn't hesitate to say this, but it wasn't taken very well by those around me because I also understood that my environment there was very far from being like the one in the course, with all the understanding and containing toward the other that I experienced there. Reality is different: much more powerful than we are. There were very tough moments when I wondered, why don't the two sides accept, the way I do; maybe there's a problem inside me. So all the time I was checking inwardly.

I decided that, if I am who I am and love what I am, I am different from what I was, and I'll keep speaking and behaving the way I really am, and I don't have to cut corners. This was very, very strong, Nava. I came home one day to my neighborhood in Ras El-Amud. There's a pizzeria there and they asked me to bring a pizza home when I came back and it was right then that they had the lynching in Ramallah. So I went in, and it's my neighborhood. I'm one of the more popular people in the neighborhood. There was an argu-ment going on, and I asked them, guys, what you are pleased about, I don't understand, I'm against what you're seeing on television. Meantime every-one was coming in to the pizzeria to see the pictures enthusiastically and I said that I didn't agree with that, which was a shock to the people there except for the pizzeria owner who said it showed us behaving as if we weren't human beings and weren't humane, but that's not really who we are, we are a people who are very humane and just as we are repulsed by what is being done to us, it can't be that we are justifying it when these things are done to them, that's not OK. It was very powerful and I couldn't even eat the pizza, I took some home but I was very preoccupied with what was going on. It did some-thing powerful to me on the inside, something bad, but it turned out to be good. I decided that it was really a kind of test, and that I have to search for the real me and not give up because of the reality that's so powerful out there.

You must have paid a price for this.

Paid a price, yes. There was a period in that neighborhood when I would say hi, how are you to someone and they would pretend they hadn't seen me, and teenagers would say nasty things to me and run away. Even though I was a very dominant presence and very active there and connected with a lot of the young people and was known for it, still, I stuck to my opinion. About four or five months later I met three guys, one of whom said to me, "Ustaaz [teacher]"—because I had been his instructor in a young leadership program—he said that he wanted to apologize to me. He was seventeen. I asked why, and he said because he thought as I did that day in the pizzeria, but had been afraid to say what he thought. I asked him, "Why were you afraid, you belong to a large family in the Hebron hills, why were you afraid to say what you thought? I don't belong to any such large family but I still said what I thought." So he said that it bothered him and he was waiting for the right time to tell me how much it bothered him. So what I told him was, "You have to find out who you really are, because life isn't worthwhile if we don't know who we are, and you have to do what you think is right and believe in the necessity of that and not hesitate."

You've mentioned three things that you took from the course: one thing was figuring out and defining your identity; another was accepting the other; and a third was sticking to your opinion even when those around you disagree, and being courageous and speaking out.

I'm even willing to pay the price. By the way, this influenced me without my realizing it in my professional behavior, too. I always had a very well-defined

position even if it wasn't the most comfortable, like when I left the municipality and went to work in the community center. I was always looking for
justice inside myself; it's that justice that we have to bring out. And it's true
that I have paid a heavy price for this. And by the way, this comes from both
sides; our side also has interested parties who try to achieve things at the
expense of some situation or other. People may accuse me of being a representative of the establishment but when they want something, some service,
they come to me and ask me to help arrange it for them. So it waxes and wanes,
depending.

Some people were angry because I talked about opposing the municipality for holding on to a large piece of land that's supposed to become another
new neighborhood [for Jews] in the middle of a part of [our] neighborhood;
they want this opposition to be attributed to them as PLO people. The committee I'm working with from that neighborhood says, Wait a minute, we are
the ones who did this, our committee, together with this guy who's the director of the community center. So I continue monitoring it, not policing it but
encouraging a dialogue. I invite them to join the committee and work together
even though I know they could be a liability because I have worked hard with
this committee to teach them how to approach things professionally with the
establishment and set aside all our personal considerations and interests. The
people complaining are the same people who are looking to make a buck for
themselves and I'm paying a price on that account, too. So sometimes it's not
the Israeli side deciding I'm doing more harm than good.

It comes from both directions. There's this horrible feeling of being mea-
sured all the time and sometimes feeling helpless. There's nothing I can do
about it, but experience has taught me that if you keep on going and stick to
your course, then that becomes the decisive direction: That's the direction
that can influence those around you with positive rather than negative energy.

So that's an example I lived through at that period, something very close
to home, and I brought it up because it wasn't easy.

CONTRIBUTING TO MY PEOPLE

After I left the School for Peace, I decided I wanted to contribute as much as
I could to my people. That was one of my strongest insights from the course.
And I knew that this contribution would have to be on several planes, not

just one. So I created a course which I called a young leadership course, but it was really about discovering your own identity through life experiences. I gave this course as a volunteer for three years and looked for somewhere to sponsor it. Unfortunately it was the municipality, affiliated with the city, and I didn't hesitate, I knocked on every possible door but they all refused. Some said they wanted to raise money for the course. I said it had to be guaranteed for all the teenage boys and girls in East Jerusalem, and that's a big budget; sometimes I was running a few courses simultaneously because it was in such high demand.

Each course was run for twenty-five young men and women. It was also popular because it was coed, and in our community everything is gender-segregated. But the recruiting was via "bring a friend" so guys brought more guys and girls brought more girls. Today I take pleasure in seeing how they continued with their education; one is a teacher, and another is an engineer. I did a lot of work with them on their future identity, what they want to be, how they can contribute to our society. It really was heartwarming. Once I went to the Bezeq telephone company office on Sallah Eddin Street to arrange an Internet connection for my son and buy a modem and was shocked to discover that three of the people in customer service there were graduates of my course. They fought over who would take care of me, immediately, but I indignantly refused to jump the line and insisted on taking a number like everyone else or else, I told them, it wouldn't be like what we'd learned together. So I resolved it, and it was great moment to see them there, serving the public. The course had talked a lot about circles of identity and life skills, communication, and making a contribution to society as the most important priority.

So there are a few hundred graduates like those.
Hundreds, really hundreds. Wherever I go, I see them. Some worked with me at the community center as youth counselors or course coordinators, because I encouraged them. Some of them liked the facilitating and counseling itself, so afterward we set up a course—the Ministry of Education sponsored it; alas, they were the only ministry to get involved—a course to train program coordinators and counselors for young people who today are working in the neighborhoods. It's really impressive. They're constantly in touch with me. So I was in charge back then of these youth training programs and then became director of the community center, but they are always coming to see me and asking for ideas.

The Ministry of Education course has twenty-four participants now. They are all active in the field. Each of them has their own youth center in a neighborhood where they live. There are various areas and courses they give, but the common denominator is the basic young leadership course with the same complement of content that they themselves went through. Sometimes when I have time and they ask me to, I enjoy giving an identity workshop or a communications workshop. It's great, but it wasn't enough. I got together with one of my good friends, Guy Ehrlich. We met when I was facilitating at Givat Haviva and he brought a group of Jewish young people there and we bonded. He's also a Jerusalemite. Together with another partner, we set up a nonprofit we called The Spring of Democratic Education (*Manbaa al-ta'alim al-democrati* in Arabic; *Maayan hachinuch hademocrati* in Hebrew). We were very enthusiastic; we wanted to teach computer skills and English and provide help with homework and set up computer centers, but in the poorer neighborhoods all over Jerusalem.

So in East Jerusalem we set up four centers like this and in West Jerusalem we set up another five, and it was fantastic to see this in action. Children who didn't know what a computer was were sitting with this instrument and learning and enjoying themselves and discovering that it wasn't just for playing games but also for studying. The whole organization was built on volunteers and we had a lot of volunteers. It was hard for me to recruit volunteers from East Jerusalem but gradually, among the graduates of the young leadership courses, I was able to recruit. I went to Al Quds University in Jerusalem seeking to have them require undergraduate degree candidates to have done some form of volunteer service, depending on what they were studying.

There was a community effort to go into Silwan, one of the poorest neighborhoods in East Jerusalem, and teach there, but these are kids who don't have enough to eat. It was amazing, it was the peak of our activity. There was a summer camp program with culture and identity and then the Hebrew University at Givat Ram agreed to give us extra hours, with organized transportation, and we brought the children from these poor neighborhoods to the university for a long day program that included breakfast and lunch and camp with all the activities for a month. It was very, very tense. I got help from all kinds of group facilitators I knew, both Arabs and Jews, to get the work done, because it was a period with a lot of terror attacks, this was 1998–1999, and it was very hard.

Guy and I directed this project as volunteers, and we had two coordinators and a paid staff, Arabs and Jews. We were able to persuade a few foundations; it was an amazing operation. The summer camp alone cost us hundreds of shekels because there was bus transport and we transported the kids door to door and there were meals.

From my SFP experience, one insight I have down really solid is that in any situation of conflict, there are different ways to conduct things. We have a choice about what to reach for and how we utilize the conflict and external reality. I'm always optimistic by nature. I believe we can change, can have insights, stay optimistic, and that's what I've done. Incidentally, I had a huge argument with Guy about whether to let [Ehud] Olmert visit the summer camp, because Olmert really wanted, as mayor of Jerusalem, to broadcast business as usual in the city. I was very much against it; I was a city employee at the time. Guy said that maybe if he came, we could get funding from the city later. I said it would devalue what we were doing, that for Olmert we were just hired hands and he would want to bring cameras and television and show that we belong to the city and I didn't want that. It was very, very hard. I refused to be part of it. I don't remember now if he came or didn't come but I personally refused to be there. What I remember is that the Arab director was Zuheir Ashkar and that he did a great job.

PROACTIVE ENGAGEMENT WITH CONFLICT SITUATIONS

You asked for examples of operating "in any conflict situation." What I see is that, in critical situations, people tend not to be active but rather to look inward because the atmosphere makes for difficult feelings and motivation is lessened. In the School for Peace course, I found myself doing the obverse: In situations of long silence, with a lot of tension, I wanted to hear from the Jewish guy sitting in the circle that he is really condemning this thing I want him to condemn, or that something is not his but belongs to Palestinians. These recurring silences led me to think to myself: What now? Everything is imploding. So what next? Will we not go on talking, not go on working at this, stop doing this process of working on ourselves and arriving at insights? Each time it was the same; all of this difficulty actually enabled us to continue this dynamic movement.

I learned that this dynamism can be projected onto reality to create a dynamic reality, with all the difficulty that entails, and that's what I did, all the time, I went back to that. I didn't remain silent. When I had no funding for my community center, my attitude was: Well, what could we still do? I ran activities with volunteers, courses that drew dozens of neighborhood children to come and participate. I had no money to pay the basketball coach but I have a guy who's not a star, not a Wingate graduate, not a licensed teacher, but he knows how basketball should be taught, how to run a basketball group. So I brought him in and ran a basketball group. People were always surprised: How was I making this activity happen? I said, "Money isn't everything; you can do a lot with volunteers. It's a value I learned that has long-term impact on a community's resilience. We can create it internally."

After seeing that the mothers were the dominant force in the neighborhood, I wanted to offer a course at the community center where mothers would study and teach other mothers. A lot of them married very young, at seventeen or eighteen. So I thought, OK, I can take mothers who are a little older, say thirty-five years old and up, and who stayed in school for a reasonable period of time, let's say through eighth or ninth grade, and train them intensively and wake them up, with a dynamic course where they'd work on themselves and get themselves established, and then we would give them tools for early childhood education. And in exchange for participating in this very expensive course, I required everyone to teach, to adopt seven younger mothers, visiting them at home and teaching them how to diaper a baby and wash a baby and so forth. The Jerusalem Fund was the only foundation that was excited about the idea but it gave me only limited funding. I managed with that and then the money ran out and we stopped the course. And all the time I was dreaming of how to get it going again. Some of the mothers came and said, "We don't want you to pay us money, if that's the problem"—because we had been paying the mothers by the hour for training the younger mothers.

This gave each woman an income (when there was funding) and helped raise her standard of living, and she's coaching other women. They continued the coaching because they were enthused with the idea. Now, under the national program for children and youth at risk, I've received full funding for this course, and currently it meets every Sunday, a kind of academy for women.

I spent twelve years developing the community center and its work. I really did believe that a dominant presence and dynamism can be created if one wants to, no matter the situation. I always allowed my staff to decide what was good for it. Especially in critical situations, for example when Sheikh Ahmad Yassin was assassinated. All the staff came [and said], "We were at work, and this thing happened. What do you do?" They're looking to me and I said, "Why are you looking at me? Do what you feel is the right thing to do." They were concerned about who might find out. I said, "It doesn't matter, I'll take responsibility for what they know in the municipality or the community centers association; let them find out. I'm responsible, I'm the director of the center."

So then my immediate supervisor, Mr. Tzvika Tchernekhovsky, calls me on the phone and says to me: "What's the situation there in the neighbor-hood?" I said: "We are on strike for three days like all the rest." He said: "Any decision made is OK with me so long as it doesn't endanger human life and doesn't interfere with anything." I said: "We aren't interfering with anything, it's a demonstration, and solidarity won't interfere with anything."

That reflected everyone's feelings and that was the decision. Then after-ward, when we were on strike like everyone else, it was permissible for us to express our feelings, and I said OK, this is the truth, everyone has his truth, it happened, everyone does what he thinks is right to do. The young people wanted to have a conversation around this, shall we do it or not, and the deci-sion was yes, we shall. That's one of the strongest insights from the course, that you always have to have a dialogue and talk things over and put things on the table, and not sweep everything under the rug. I remember my first encounters; all the time I was asking myself whether to say a given thing or not to say it. At the fourth or fifth session it was already very obvious that I was going to say exactly what I was feeling and what I was thinking and noth-ing was going to be swept under the rug.

These days, it only takes half an hour to reach that point. Things are put on the table very fast.

Yes, you're right. Once upon a time, I remember that everything was very delicate and gradual and we thought and apologized before we said anything. I remember at the first session that we insisted, Come on, speak Hebrew. Why would you speak Arabic?! It was Muhammad Marzuk, if you remember, Mervat's husband, who was facilitating, [who encouraged us to speak Ara-bic]. Today with my young leadership trainees working on joint projects, I want them to get to know the other but to do it on an equal basis, not with hostility, not with one group being more dominant. Before I take them out to an encounter like that or to a project like that, I do a lot of prep work. My youth coordinator does a lot of prep with them and everything is put on the table. Then they ask, "So can we tell them this, or not?" I say, "Yes, tell them everything, whatever you are feeling and thinking, that's the way, otherwise there's no point, there's really no point."

When my son Shadi was growing up, he had to do some project at Hand in Hand [bilingual school]—he studied at the Oasis of Peace Primary School [at Wahat al Salam–Neve Shalom] through fourth grade and then at Hand in Hand in Jerusalem. He said, "I want to do something connected with the Palestinian people and identity." It was during the incursion into Gaza, and Ramallah, and all that turmoil. So he said to me, "Why are you keeping silent, why don't you speak?" I told him, "What do you want to do?" He said, "You don't want me to?" I said, "Of course I do, I just want to hear from you first about what you want to do." So he did a Power Point presentation on the history of the Palestinian people and the Nakba. He consulted me all the time about where to find things. Now there's a library at the school and half the books are about the history of the Palestinian people and the conflict. He borrowed books, photocopied and scanned things, and put together a presentation. It was fantastic. So then he said, "Dad, now I want to present this to you and to Mom before I present it at school." I told him, "I have a request." He said, "What?" I said, "Don't show it to us, we want to see it at school." He said, "Why?" I said, "Never mind, just let it be however it is." I went there and Amin Khalaf [director of the Hand in Hand Association] was sitting next to me. He also took the course at Neve Shalom, some years before I did.

So Amin's wife, Ranaa, was sitting there, and me and my wife, Anna, and then it was Shadi's turn, and he made his presentation, and there was complete silence. The Jewish parents are looking at the Arab parents and the Arab parents are looking back at them and Amin whispers to me, jokingly, "What are you evoking for me here, revolution?" I said "No, that's the real Shadi, you know Shadi." His son Sari is in the same class with Shadi, and he said to me, "Nazih, hat's off to you, you went all the way with this." But actually it wasn't me, I told him; it was Shadi. I raised him this way, and he went with it, that's how I taught my children, that they should be real and say what they feel.

Your children feel proud of their identity.

Yes. On more than one occasion, Shadi would tell me about the arguments at school. He wanted to collect clothing and things for needy Palestinians. He brought it up at school and some of the Jewish kids didn't want to be friends with him and there were arguments. I asked Alaa Khatib (the principal of the school) to bring facilitators and do it right, so that the opportunity wouldn't be lost, because otherwise no one would have learned anything from it. So he said that he had directed the teachers to do that; there are Arab and Jewish teachers there.

Shadi was very disappointed. He said that the Jews weren't trying to understand why he was doing what he was doing. I said to him, "But you did try to explain it to them." He said, "Yes, I explained to them that I am part of the Palestinian people and these are my fellow Palestinians. And I went much farther with it," he said; "I told them that if this had happened to Jews, then I would have contributed for the Jews. It doesn't matter, it's a group of people in distress and we have to help them." So this is the education that is important to me that my children be given: You help where help is needed and you help whoever needs help, without looking at the color of their eyes. What does it matter what color their eyes are? If you help them now, then someday when you need their help, they have to help you, too. This was really, really important. I live this; I live this in every sense, and there are always questions and ambivalence and it's not easy.

My wife, Anna, is the director of information systems at Kravitz, the stationery chain. One year a guy from the company invited everyone to his house for Independence Day. I told her, "Anna, you know that I can come, I have no problem with it, but I won't keep quiet. If there's any kind of political argument, you know I'll say what I think." So she said, "No, I want you to come; there won't be political arguments." She really wanted me to get to know the people. So the kids and I went to the barbecue. All the Jewish guys were sitting around; I was the only Arab. The guys were, like, sitting by themselves. I didn't understand why the women were sitting separately. Then the guys started talking and it devolved into a political argument. I said what I thought, and it was very tense. I explained that I say what I feel, and that it's not important to me whether they accept it or not, but that I'll be very glad if they try to understand where the things I say are coming from. The host was trying really hard to change the subject altogether, because it was hard for me. Anna came and gave me a kiss and whispered in my ear that it was unpleasant for her, but the problem wasn't with her, it was with the others. I told her, when you want me to come, I'll come, even though I prefer to mark that day inwardly because, after all, the day has a different meaning for us.

THE NEXT PHASE

I've always dreamed of establishing, together with Palestinian colleagues, an organization specializing in youth, offering services, training, treatment, vocational training and youth empowerment in Palestinian East Jerusalem. That's the next direction I'm thinking about.

Meanwhile, there is another important thing I forgot to mention. When I was first married and we were living with the family, it was a very small house. When Shadi and Sami came along, we had to look for a larger house. I started that journey of looking to buy an apartment or buy a house, but the problem was, there is nowhere in East Jerusalem where you can get a building permit, so you have to buy a house under threat of demolition, meaning, at any time they can come and raze your house.

I really liked the idea of buying a house or a flat in neighborhoods that originally were Arab neighborhoods and had since become Jewish neighborhoods. So I decided to go for it and bought a house in Pisgat Ze'ev, which was a very, very difficult decision. I mean, think of it: to come and live in the middle of this place which for me is a settlement, like Neve Yaacov, although Pisgat Ze'ev is viewed as just another Jerusalem neighborhood. In the end I decided to go for it.

Living in Pisgat Ze'ev, I've seen a different reality, one I don't know, a different lifestyle. There's a lot of racism toward the other, a lot of violence, youths who really whoop it up to high heaven, and lately they built a synagogue so now it's even more festive. On this latest holiday I almost didn't sleep. We're thinking of moving out now.

My son Shadi would go outside to play and there were two or three incidents involving him and his brother, Sami, and some youngsters their age. It wasn't easy. The neighbors once even advertised our flat for sale on the Internet, stating that the reason for the sale was that we had to leave the country. So, it hasn't been easy.

There is so much racism, and the children have to deal with this every day.

I realize that going all the way with these things does sound a little crazy. Meantime, by the way, I discovered that at this point there are a lot of Arab families living in Pisgat Ze'ev and other areas of northern Jerusalem, because

of the housing shortage. That was surprising. Also in Neve Yaacov and northern Pisgat Ze'ev around East Jerusalem. All this really surprised me.

We really want to come here [to Neve Shalom], but things aren't progressing with that. Otherwise, we'll have to look for a house in one of the Arab
neighborhoods. This is the reality for Palestinians in East Jerusalem, and it's
definitely very hard. It's really complicated.

Meanwhile, I registered my kids for the bilingual school in Jerusalem
because I wanted to give them the opportunity that I didn't have, to know
and learn to accept the other from an early age. I got to know Jews only when
I was seventeen or eighteen years old, when I went to work to help my mother,
apart from that soldier I met during the Intifada, and that wasn't adequate;
it didn't reflect the reality. The reality is a lot more complex and diverse. And
where my children's education is concerned, I didn't hesitate. It's not a fore-
gone conclusion in Arab society, not even in education, especially not in education, that you accept the other. It's not something you take for granted. It's
not how children are typically raised or taught, and if they are, then it comes
with conditions. Despite everything, the Hand in Hand experience was worth
it because it gave them a lot in terms of accepting the other and understanding the other. God willing, my children will be continuing on this path, in
this direction.

10 · SEBASTIAN WALLERSTEIN

Planner and Community Activist

Sebastian Wallerstein is director of the Israel Affordable Housing Center, Faculty of Law, Tel Aviv University. Sebastian joined the center after a number of years in the City of Bat Yam's Department of Urban Planning, where he was responsible for promoting urban-renewal plans and housing policies. Wallerstein has a B.A. in economics and political sciences from Tel Aviv University and a M.Sc. in urban and regional planning from the Technion–Israel Institute of Technology. Since 2013 he has been a member of the board of directors of Bimkom–Ianners for Planning Rights. Sebastian Wallerstein took the Change Agents Course for Israeli and Palestinian Planners, Architects and Civil Engineers in 2008–2009 at the School for Peace at Wahat al-Salam–Neve Shalom. He was interviewed on November 11, 2009.

There are elements in this country with racist and oppressive attitudes toward all kinds of populations. This is the milieu we are living in. I have not given up, and for now I'm as deep into this as I can be. There's no choice. The distress, the problems, won't resolve themselves. I know the suffering in Jaffa won't improve by itself.

Mainly what the Neve Shalom course did was to make me more aware, and this greater awareness is always there, helping me assimilate ideas as they come up, like colonialism or oppression. That's the most central thing it did, and I notice this very clearly. It gave me a kind of encoding apparatus that functions during all kinds of meetings and situations when someone speaks in a certain way. Not that it makes things easier, but it helps me to give a name to what I hear and put more of a frame around it.

For example, I am currently part of a process dealing with issues of housing in Jaffa. It's a professional process that also has an element of mediation or consulting, involving the Arab community in Jaffa and all the relevant official agencies, including the Israel Lands Authority, the Housing Ministry, the Tel Aviv municipality, and so forth. When I come to such a meeting with someone in city government, I can't help but notice attitudes that view the Arab population as invasive or criminal, as being involved in illegal building, and always with the same rhetoric of not being OK. The question arises as to why there is such a big increase in illegal construction in a given place. Subconsciously the people from the establishment have the idea that Arabs don't make an effort to behave lawfully. For these officials, a broader and more complex look at the context of this situation is simply not part of their awareness. Whether as a direct outcome of the School for Peace course or not, I don't know for sure, but I am a lot more aware of this dynamic now. It is more likely now to set off a warning signal, like a flashing red light. When you come to a meeting and immediately start hearing these things, you want to say something to change the discourse rather than continuing with this same type of talk that simply perpetuates the status quo.

HOUSING IN JAFFA

Another consultant and I sat with the Jaffa staff of the city's Engineering Department and the Strategic Planning Department to address illegal construction in Jaffa. One woman from the city council was saying, OK it's just that the population there has become accustomed to living in one-story housing and prefers it, and when they see an empty plot they build there, and of course they also benefit from it, another room, that's good. The adviser who is working with me on this consulting project said, "Well, it seems to me that the Jews in Israel also like to live in one-story housing and in larger apartments and if they had a chance to build another room they would also take advantage of that, especially if no one was going to get around to mentioning it for a long time." This is a small example of the sort of thing I'm talking about, and it happens all the time, and that's the reality evidently.

Look, this entire process is, in the end, to find what we have in common and build some kind of consensus, and it's very problematical. I don't always feel, in every setting, that I can allow my emotions to be evident in what I say. Things have to be rephrased constructively so that they can be viewed in a different way without actually pushing something into the corner and pointing at it. So I'll say, We know there's an increase in unlawful construction but it appears to be over and above the desire everyone has to build and expand which apparently exists anywhere, and there are other things that also led to this situation. I need this filtering to be able to work with these people because there's no other choice. In this place where I am now, there's no other choice. If I were in charge of a protest campaign, it would be different.

I'm working in Jaffa with the agency known as Mishlama Jaffa, a corporation under the Tel Aviv municipality, which invited Dr. Emily Silverman and me to take a consulting role to a round table process between the Arab population and the other players involved in housing there, after I wrote a report for them on the subject. One of our recommendations was to bring together all the figures involved with housing-related issues in Jaffa to examine what could be done with more coordination. Each agency had been acting on its own and making life difficult for the others, and things weren't progressing too well. Now the situation has reached an interesting, very complicated juncture. The decision by the director of Mishlama Jaffa to bring us into the process is interesting. He knows we have a longstanding contact with the community. The community's trust in us makes it easier for us to be in the middle but being in the middle is always complicated, and it's the city that hired us and is paying us for our work on the project.

It's very positive that, as a result of the report, they invited us to consult, and that the report isn't just sitting somewhere in a drawer. The process of preparing the report seemed to decrease the distance between positions within the Mishlama itself and bolster the understanding that the way things are conducted could be changed. Meantime, there are also many opposing interests involved and sometimes it's very hard to see the light at the end of the tunnel. I would really love to see an authentic process. The community suspects that it's only another way of stalling and that nothing will really happen; that we will sit down and talk, and people will feel good that something's being done, but that ultimately nothing will happen. This is absolutely a legitimate concern. I think the truth is somewhere in the middle, because among all of the people sitting there,

there's a fairly broad spectrum of positions. There's one representative of the Housing Ministry, one from the Israel Lands Authority, one from Amidar (the state-owned housing company), one from Halamish (a federal/municipal housing company), a few from the Tel Aviv city government and Mishlama, and one from the community: about ten to twelve people in all.

One problem is that these people are not themselves authorized to annul demolition orders. The reps there are civil servants but from a relatively senior level, district directors. My more realistic aspiration is that, if there is something going on within this forum requiring action, everyone there would have to go higher within their organization and demand things and ask for changes. For example, take the statement of the director-general of the Israel Police that apparently if the political map were more favorable, then yes, it would be enough that some minister possessing the will and the commitment would say, we're going to resolve this matter, we'll build such-and-such number of housing units and embark on a campaign of this or that kind to facilitate a solution for the residents, and that would resolve it. That's not the situation today. We are really enormously far from there. So what we're doing is some type of more serious staff work in the hope that the civil service level can move something within the organization. And that's good. By nature I'm an optimist and I do see places where things are moving forward, but it's very sensitive and always on the point of blowing up.

Things are volatile now in the Arab community, too—following the attempt to set up a settlement within Jaffa, a national religious settlement with people from the Hebron settlement and other places. They've taken on the mixed cities as their new flagship expansion project. So right in the heart of Arab Ajami, a historic Jaffa neighborhood where the Arab community has its strongest affinity of anywhere in Jaffa, they've won a tender to build twenty housing units. It was a public, open tender and everyone could submit a bid. Among those who did was the Emunah settlement group, which is building it for them. There was an Arab bid submitted too, with good social objectives, but it lost because it offered less money. Subsequently, the Association for Civil Rights in Israel filed a petition on behalf of local residents and all kinds of other organizations like Bimkom, seeking to get the decision on the winning bid voided on the grounds that the bidder declared that it does not intend to sell apartments to Arabs.

A NEW COMMUNITY COALITION

There's a relatively good chance that the appeal will succeed in doing something. But in the meantime, something else very positive has happened in the Jaffa Arab community, which has long been divided and weakened by internal struggles among its various streams. Now, however, everyone has united because there is a single adversary and they can fight against it together. They've created a new entity called the Coalition of Organizations and Committees for Housing Rights in Jaffa. That forum is now participating in the roundtable process. When I say things are on the edge of exploding, I'm talking about a possible explosion among the various positions within this coalition as well as between the coalition and the process itself.

There was an initial meeting at which there was a declaration of intent and a presentation by each of the organizations describing who is involved. Then Emily and I sat with each participant separately in an effort to draft a consensual document defining the problem of housing in Jaffa. That is no simple thing, but we can work on it and we can move things forward. Some say it is very difficult but, candidly, I'd say that with the exception of a single player in this game (Halamish), all the rest are reasonable. They are prepared to listen and also to act. I think it's good that their perspective is to advance a solution. Each of them also has their own interests. For the city, it's not good when legal disputes drag on for a long time and can't be resolved. So each party to this has their own reasons for wanting to resolve things, although not always coming from the same direction.

In terms of the impact of my Neve Shalom experience, I think maybe it's made me more sensitive. After all, we're two people from abroad—Emily's from the United States and I'm from Uruguay—and we're in contact with a population that was born in Jaffa with a very strong connection to the place. At all the meetings of the coalition, they're speaking Arabic and a lot of what goes on is in Arabic. Emily knows a little Arabic but I'm sorry to say that I don't speak Arabic and it's an obstacle, but it requires me to maintain a certain sensitivity to understand better what each person's position is. It's not easy to get a sense of that from the outside.

It's true that I already had rather good awareness when I began the School for Peace course, but I had never had occasion to talk with Palestinians actually from Palestine in such a forum. That was my first time ever, and the first workshop session was earthshaking. This is strong stuff. It puts you in a place that's not easy. There are questions that you're continually asking yourself. I'd say that it helped me to take the next step. There were things that, before the course, I found more difficult to talk about out loud; now, it's easier to look at things that we do and not mince words in speaking of them. We all know what this is like but it's so hard to acknowledge it. In some way we are partners to this by virtue of our being here; we know there's a problem.

I also find something very funny, or maybe worrisome, happening to me when I go abroad. When I go to visit friends and family abroad, it's a thousand times worse. If I speak out the same way I do here, it's a disaster. I become an ocher Yisrael (someone who brings trouble to Jews); it's about not washing the dirty laundry in public. If you're in some forum with both Jews and non-Jews and you speak critically about Israel, you're more or less considered a traitor.

Mostly people overseas are very set in their opinions about all kinds of things. In this case they say, What, you're coming here to bad-mouth Israel? Aren't there enough people who attack us and hate us? You have to add more hate? I understand that there are people who hate us, but that doesn't mean that we are not doing things that are not good. When I allow myself to express what I think, it's not easy. My friends here share my orientation more. My partner works at the Association for Civil Rights in Israel and we share the same values. In the community there is a spectrum and there are people who will oppose you. Maybe this should be included in the course. If you look at it closely, it involves your workplace, and your friends, and sometimes things are very highly charged and there can be very difficult confrontations. My partner has a friend who was an IDF officer during the war and relating to each other became very hard, almost impossible.

GRASSROOTS CHANGE

Two weeks, ago, I began working with Guri, who was also in the course, doing urban renewal projects. Connections with friends from the group are ongoing; we've been discussing this for over a year and I couldn't do much because I was busy with a lot of bureaucracy and time flew by, but now I've begun working on it. Meanwhile I'm trying to finish my thesis. The report on Jaffa will be part of my thesis. At this point, I want to gain practical experience in the field.

My involvement in grassroots change has been a kind of process under construction. Right around the time I began the Neve Shalom course, I also had the initial contact with the issue of Jaffa housing. Emily approached me, and I was thinking of writing a couple of pages about Jaffa; really, that's how it began. It got underway on parallel tracks like that. Maybe the Neve Shalom course is what gave me the inspiration and determination to develop my interest in this area and go into it in such depth. There's something about these things. . . . When you're actually doing them, there are some very fatiguing, even boring, aspects to the work. The SFP course and the whole environment there helped me to go on and see it on a level that gave it more meaning. I realized that I'm doing more than just going through the motions here; I'm looking into how it would really be possible to improve the situation for home buyers. I mean, at first there was something rather dry that maybe has to do with protected tenancy, but the course allowed me to apprehend the larger dimensions: We're dealing here with the Arab population, a minority, and there is a broader meaning to what's happening with this. Had I not been in the course around that time, I might have found it really difficult to make that distinction. The two processes nourished each other: the course, and my work in Jaffa.

I think at some basic level, I always had the motivation, and I am also active in environmental and other issues. At the same time, I think the course expanded and deepened my commitment to addressing issues around the Arab-Jewish conflict and helped me to see that everyone living in this region is fed up already with this; it's been going on long enough!

Most people are not activists; you went into it very deeply.

It's present in my awareness a lot more. I also think that going back and just forgetting about it is really hard. There's an emotional aspect that enters into it. Today when I look at this society and see Arabs from the community who are angry at the establishment, there's something a whole lot more natural in my identification with that anger. I've seen it and I can't just ignore it now.

As an example, a Committee for Affordable Housing was established in Tel Aviv, headed by a Likud city councilman. This was, incidentally, among the recommendations for providing people with affordable housing. And because Emily was a participant in the Committee for Affordable Housing in Tel Aviv and wanted to raise the issue of Jaffa, they set up a special meeting about Jaffa and invited community members to attend.

At that meeting, the same man was very dismissive in dealing with the issue and toward the Arabs from the community who presented their positions; one of his comments was that there are too few Jews in Jaffa. I remember that I said nothing at the time. It was hard for me there, being so young, and in hindsight I felt that I betrayed the power I had there to speak up. The Arabs responded with restraint and did not get upset, but I went out of there feeling angry and afterward I sat with them. When you come to meetings and see that someone is attacking you in a way that's treated as legitimate, and you're sitting at a table with people from all the political parties, including Meretz, it's as though it is all right in such a forum to say that there are too few Jews in Jaffa. What does that say, that statement? What kind of remark is that? It's treated as legitimate to say it, to listen to it, and not to stand up and slap the guy in the face. Afterward I was angry, not only at myself for not having spoken, but also at everyone else because no one did anything and they (the Arabs) had to sit there and take it, so to speak; they didn't do anything either. It was as if, had they started shouting, they would have been told, "You see, it's impossible to invite you to city hall because all you do is shout, and then nothing need be done in response." So there it was again, this identification with that really difficult situation. Meantime the attorney for the Popular Committee in Jaffa—I had worked with her a lot on the report; I simply put myself in her shoes and wanted to die on the spot—she said to me, "If I yell then I'm a troublemaker and if I keep quiet I'm allowing that guy to humiliate me with a remark like that, to which there's no answer, so it's hard."

Today I feel better able to respond in such situations. This developed very gradually, but it's not always easy even now. I think that this is a challenge that the course addressed less—maybe here and there, when you brought in people who presented dilemmas from the workplace, it touched on this, but I think this is something that really has to be addressed, it has to be opened up and analyzed very thoroughly. It's part of the difficulty because, even when we have the awareness, there's no awareness within these structures. How, within that particular situation, can one say something else? And there are always the risks; so is it better to speak up, or not? So long as this issue isn't central, it's easier. So long as I am there with my principles and my beliefs, it's more comfortable. But part of the point is to build understanding and consensus and to examine how to act. I see that this dilemma is there, within the Arab community: Is now the time for me to come and speak out, and shout: "Listen, for forty years you have done nothing; what do you need data for now? What data do you need? You know what you need to do. If you don't do it, it's because you don't want to. "And so forth. Those things are true. Or is my best route to say, "OK, there's a process underway here, there are new people in the system at city hall, let's give this a chance." So you're always in this situation of choosing the strategy that will be more influential.

Maybe one less positive outcome (of the course) is that I became a little more uncompromising, and every remark sets me off. If it seems at all racist or whatever, it sets me off. I mean here we are, living in this country where there are elements with racist and oppressive attitudes toward all kinds of populations, and I want no part of it, it drains away your desire to act because you're already fed up. I don't know if this is a different subject, but it seems connected; this is the milieu we are living in.

I have not given up and for now I'm as deep into this as can be. I'm always thinking that my generation aspires to something different here. If what I expect is the way things are now, that won't be good. There's no choice. What choice is there? These things won't disappear; all the distress, all the problems, won't resolve themselves. That's the bottom-line belief; I see the suffering in Jaffa, and I know that it won't improve by itself.

MANEUVERING AMONG THE COMPLEXITIES

More attention needs to be given to this place of the dilemma, the complexity, the continual maneuvering between individual beliefs and your prospects to create change. In the end, most of us earn a living with various kinds of Zionist Jewish organizations. It's hard. Maybe it's easier for someone on a grant or with funding from some NGO whose purpose is to advance equality, so then it's very comfortable and you can say stuff and be OK. But otherwise, there are a lot of people for whom it's not always comfortable to push things ahead and it's not even necessarily connected with where the money is coming from, but it's not easy. I've been thinking that it would be good to bring people who are sitting on the fence, who are in the public sector and have a public role and aren't greatly committed to our goal, and ask them what's happening. Maybe create a panel of people with all kinds of jobs and different positions; I don't know. I see this as worthwhile because, down the road, this is the course with the biggest obstacles, insofar as I can see.

Sometimes I do feel alone, apart from a few people with whom I've very close. But even aside from that, it's not a very comfortable feeling because we live and breathe Zionism here. It's not as if we have a choice, and every time you manage to get free of that, there are problems, whatever the issue, and they curse you as a Communist or whatever. Anything perceived as outside the mainstream is problematical. The whole package is problematical.

I feel that we in the LGBT community have lost our way a little bit. . . . Once upon a time there was a genuine battle about equal rights, and there was an authentic discourse about rights, but not today. Not long ago there was this terrible video clip claiming, "We're all the same, down with homophobia," and basically promoting the idea that the gay community is as chauvinist and sexist and militaristic as anyone else. I thought it was awful, repulsive. Now there's so much internal dissension in the community, it's very sad to see the direction things have taken. Still, there are all kinds of voices, of course, and some of them are critical voices.

PART 3 FAMILY AND COMMUNITY MENTAL HEALTH

11 · WASSIM BIROUMI

Clinical and Educational Psychologist

Wassim Biroumi is a clinical and educational psychologist and facilitator for groups in conflict, multicultural encounter, and education for peace. Raised in Acre, he was active with the Sedaka-Reut binational youth movement, where he led an Arab-Jewish collective for two years. He has facilitated tours for Zochrot and has been a member of its board of directors. Biroumi has worked in management at the Causeway Institute for Peacebuilding and Conflict, studying various conflicts around the world, particularly the situation in Ireland, and offering mediation and study tours. He is also active with PsychoActive: Mental Health Professionals for Human Rights. Biroumi speaks Arabic, Hebrew, and English. Biroumi participated in a School for Peace Jewish-Arab encounter workshop in 2001; he took the joint School for Peace university course at the University of Haifa in 2004; and he took the School for Peace Course for Facilitators of Groups in Conflict in 2004 at Wahat al-Salam–Neve Shalom. He was interviewed on June 3, 2010.

When I was growing up, there were things that were forbidden, and things that were self-evident: You are an Israeli Arab, you are not a Palestinian, a Palestinian is someone over there. You are not allowed to stand tall, you must not talk to a soldier; that's frightening. A soldier is an animal, not a human being, and watch out, because the Shabak [General Security Service] is everywhere. The Neve Shalom course simply turned everything upside down. So there's the Shabak, so what, just talk; yes, we can talk about what a Palestinian is, about whether you belong to that or don't belong to that [identity]. This was shocking, and also transformational.

The first course I did at Neve Shalom was in 2001, and then in 2004 I did two at once: one at the University of Haifa, and the School for Peace facilitators course at Neve Shalom. I will explain how and why I got there.

When I met Gharda (who is now my wife), I spoke mainly Hebrew. Here and there I would interpolate a few words of Arabic. Gharda was one of the few people I knew who had a problem with my speaking Hebrew. She recommended the course at Neve Shalom. Before that, I had been in a course on narratives with Dan Bar-On in Beersheba. There it was more about telling stories than about undergoing some kind of process. I felt that I was some kind of instrument: you talk about what you have to say, you tell the story and they listen to it.

Then I got to Neve Shalom, a year or two after the events of October 2000. I knew a few of the people who were killed [during those demonstrations] and I knew what was starting to happen here. The course at Neve Shalom was something of a shock for me, because it was the first time that it was permissible to talk Arabic and it really was open. In all the "coexistence" contexts I had experienced before, there had been much more room for "Let's connect with each other, let's look for the commonalities, let's see what we can do about being together, let's talk about an alternative, instead of dealing with the strenuous disagreements between us." This was always missing, for me. I always thought that not all of the discourse was being tapped.

So I got to Neve Shalom, and here, it was something else. Suddenly Arabic was a very powerful instrument. Palestinian identity was not a disgrace. The space was much more inclusive and open in the sense that one could indeed open up and talk and deliberate about all kinds of issues. From my standpoint, this was a big surprise. My response was also surprising, because I jumped at the opportunity, within only a few months of starting the course. Remember that I did not grow up in a political household. We had neighbors who were very political, very aware, but my parents were very fearful, and my father, in particular, was very much afraid.

After the course at Neve Shalom, I interviewed my father, and the interview was published in Dan Bar-On's last book. My discourse in the book is different than my discourse before the course: I am more audacious, more self-aware, and I know where I am; I am not shy about the fact that I did not come from a politically involved home. My spouse comes from a very political home, hard-core political, but I didn't come from that place. Within the Palestinian discourse, I was ostracized, I was the one who hadn't yet adequately developed, as it were. And hence I was very cautious in my own, Palestinian, society. I opted to stay in the twilight zone. With Jews, I was always the Arab, and with Arabs I was always somehow less.

The course also empowered me in the sense of my political awareness. It empowered me in this sense because it's a natural process we undergo. It's a process, coming from the places we are in, and clearly there is no exclusivity about Palestinian identity, no monopoly. I mean, people can't tell me that I am not Palestinian enough, or not strong enough.

Being enabled to talk about this in the course was transformational. The discourse was very brave, very strong. But mainly what was significant was being exposed to all kinds of dialogue that I had not been exposed to previously. I encountered discourse that was new to me. The course enabled me to hold my head high and feel legitimate doing so. At a certain stage, you feel that some boundary has been crossed, but up to that point it was very relevant and powerful and positive from my standpoint, because I stopped being afraid. It addressed everything that I took from my parents about being afraid— that's dangerous, you'd better not, don't speak out on this or that issue or contradict such and such a figure. The course promoted the opposite stance. It made space for the fears. The facilitator said that, yes, this fear is always around and it has its place, but we are always marked, it doesn't matter what action you take or don't take. The theory part of the course was also an important factor in this. I remember the first time I heard about [Janet] Helms [and her theory of racial identity]; it gave me some kind of framework, some legitimacy for my own place. What the course mainly accomplished for me, in various ways, is that beforehand I was not aware of a lot of things and when I was aware, I had no place to talk about them. A lot of the things I did, I did not do as something political. It was more about repressing parts of myself, about internalizing the oppression (as I can phrase it today), whereas previously I had not seen this. I had felt uncomfortable but had not known why.

After the course I became active. I did three tours with Zochrot in mixed cities: one in Haifa, one in Acre, and one in Ramle. From my standpoint, this meant coming to my society and saying, "I grew up with a certain lack. It's something to be ashamed of, and now the time has come to go ahead and open this up in front of everyone." I wanted to convey that there is another way. In the tour of Acre, my parents did not join me because they were against these activities. They told me, It's very dangerous and Why are you doing these things. After the second SFP course, I already had a better understanding of where my responsibility fits into this, and gradually I stopped being angry at my parents. In the first course I was more aggressive, berating them for having raised me in fear, and so forth.

What made this happen was the talking, the discourse, which enabled the real issues to be raised. Another thing was that legitimacy was accorded to strenuous argument. It's OK to wrangle aggressively; it doesn't mean that I'm calling into question everything I was raised on. And being with other people like me, people who were unaware in the same way I had been—I saw that they, too, were not in the discourse.

GROWING UP IN ACRE

My mother was from Nazareth and my father from Haifa. All my life we lived among Jews. When I was growing up in Acre, many of our neighbors were Jews. I remember that I would go and turn on the hot water heater for one of my neighbors on Shabbat. I did all kinds of errands for her on Shabbat. I know that, for my father, it was very, very important to protect us. The neighbors talked about an incident involving some Communist Party flyers that my brother had. Someone came to my father's workshop and said, "Listen, it's unfortunate about your son, risking imprisonment because he got into politics." And then my father very emphatically put a stop to such political activity for us.

In the family, they made us afraid of everyone around us. That's the definition of terrorism. Like in Soviet Russia, they would tell you to be careful of your neighbor because he could report you, so watch out, and that's what I experienced within my family. I studied at an Arab school, Terra Sancta, and I remember after the (1997) helicopter disaster (in northern Israel), we had one conversation about it and that was that. The children had a lot to say, but the message was that we could vent a bit and that was it. It was a society with hardly any awareness from a nationalist political standpoint.

During my childhood in Acre, there were drug addicts in the neighborhood. What concerned people was having work and putting food on the table. It was actually very easy to control them, and likewise today, but now a little less so. And from there, I got to university, where I was alone facing the Jews. It was very important to me there not to display or express anything nationalist at all. I remember that [activists] would send me emails and I would get really annoyed that they [were] sending me emails about Gaza or about the West Bank. Then I began the course with Dan Bar-On and there they asked me to tell my father's story. So I recounted it in a workshop. They liked the way I had told the story, so they said, without aggression, very gently, in a way they could listen to. And then I met Gharda, and she was very political in her orientation, and in her family, too. It was really nice to meet someone so deeply rooted. She said I ought to go to the course at Neve Shalom, where I could think about, and talk about, these things. So I came for an interview and was accepted.

THE SHOCK OF TRANSITION

I remember my shock at the first session. There was someone there who sat down and said, "I want to speak Arabic," and I remember how that shocked me. My immediate thought was, "Why speak Arabic when we are trying to understand one another?" And in that same moment I understood and I said to myself, "Why not, it's my mother tongue, this is my place and I feel comfortable here." Suddenly, it suddenly seemed a lot less absurd [to speak Arabic]. That's how it started. That it was an open workshop was really good because that shifted me into thinking personally. I remember statements made by Jews there, like, "You have to be loyal," and I remember that I said, "We are not dogs." So on the one hand, it wasn't a nicey-nicey discourse of "Let's all be together" like they conduct elsewhere, and on the other hand it wasn't a political debate about political parties like at Hadash [the Communist Party]; it was a lot more psychological.

After that course, I began to be a whole lot more active and also became interested in other conflicts. It took me out of the egocentric stance. This discourse about oppressor and oppressed, victim and victimizer, about oppression, this also helped me to escape the confines of the Israeli-Palestinian sphere and get to other realms. Right now I'm working with Israelis, Palestinians, and Japanese. I have also worked with Israelis, Germans, and Palestinians.

When you said earlier that the course crossed a boundary, what did you mean?

It was a very substantial crossing of boundaries in terms of the state and of the family. Two years earlier, the state had murdered thirteen Palestinians, and ten years before then, there was an Intifada taking place: I grew up during a very turbulent period. I just have no other way of saying this except to say that there were things that were forbidden and there were things that were self-evident: You are an Israeli Arab, you are not a Palestinian, a Palestinian is someone over there. You are not allowed to stand tall, you must not talk to a soldier; that's frightening. A soldier is an animal, not a human being, and watch out, because the Shabak is everywhere. The course simply turned everything upside down. So there's the Shabak, so what, just talk; yes, we can talk about what a Palestinian is, about whether you belong to that or don't belong to that [identity]. This was shocking from my standpoint because it went over the line very audaciously and rudely. That is, there's a group here that is half and half. Half and half of what? Well, we were always speaking Hebrew and here there is legitimacy for speaking Arabic, and the discourse is open and you can talk about whatever you want. Neve Shalom crossed the boundary, the boundary set by the glass ceiling that I had put in place for myself. That the most I could say was that I am an Arab, whereas here there was something egalitarian, and sometimes a moral superiority because of the situation we are living in. So there's legitimacy, so open it up and talk about it, discuss it. That's what foments change, that the demon is not so terrible. I can open my mouth and not go to jail. I tried this a few times elsewhere, and it worked. Subsequently there were some unpleasant situations but in general, I am still alive, and all of that mortal fear dissipated. Not an existential fear, but the fact that your whole way of classifying things, everything you grew up on, that you tried to build, suddenly goes in the trash if you deal with politics.

Something else I remember liking about the course is about withstanding aggression. When people attacked me personally, the facilitators sat in silence and thereby sent a message that it's OK, we can also fight here (verbally) and it's fine, no one is going to die from that. That broke through boundaries that exist in this state, very clearly: Three years ago when you went out to demonstrate, you could get murdered. Here it was different. So there was this other plane where it was legitimate to check things out. I examined [my] level of nationalism, and the definition of what it is to be a Palestinian. Can there be a Palestinian who is not against the occupation? If I throw stones then I am a Palestinian, and if I don't throw stones I am not a Palestinian? I started to construct a Palestinian identity where before that I was an Israeli Arab.

In tandem with this process of constructing my national identity was the process of developing awareness, to build my responsiveness and to also build it from within. This is what led me to create some disruption between me and other facilitators. When I began facilitating, sometimes I felt that they were "doing a lynch" against the Jewish facilitators (in the staff meetings). And I opposed that, and the Palestinian facilitators really did not like it, and they attacked me for it. That kind of lynching scenario might happen when, say, a Jewish facilitator is sitting in a meeting and they are talking Arabic, and then he asks for a translation and I try to translate for him, and then they start in on him with, "What, you don't know Arabic!" It could be someone saying that [Israeli political dissident] Tali Fahima is a whore even though she paid a very high price for dissenting. Because the Jew never stops being guilty, the Jew will always be the one who is guilty, because there is a dichotomy of victim and victimizer.

The course helped me to see that I can be both a victim and a victimizer. This became a part of my consciousness at some point, that I can be aware of this, and that I can also be someone's boss at work. What moved me to action was ceasing to be afraid. And that happened because of the message I got at Neve Shalom. The School for Peace has been here already for quite a long time, and people have not gone to jail following these discussions that take place here, and it's OK to open your mouth and say critical things.

COMING BACK FOR MORE

I returned for another course at Neve Shalom because I wanted to check out more things; it wasn't enough for me yet. That first process of checking things out gave me a taste of courage, but I had not yet acquired a deeper ability to see the person sitting facing me. I left the course the first time with an ability to confront Zionist Jews and so forth, but it didn't feel finished to me. It didn't adequately explain for me the claims I have against Jews, who sometimes also have their own claims to make. It wasn't working for me, the idea that now I am a strong Palestinian and I stick it to Jews who are nationalist, but meanwhile I am doing the same thing they are. I felt there were some holes in what I was experiencing in that vein.

Another thing, and I also found this on the outside, about Hebrew music that I liked: There is a very active suppression of this music because it's not Palestinian enough. I'm supposed to just adopt customs outright and all kinds of nonsense because I am Palestinian, and all the other parts of me that I grew up with and that are part of my experience, I'm supposed to give them up now to be more Palestinian. This started to bother me at a certain point. Because in the group they expected me to speak only Arabic, and if I spoke another language, then they put me in this slot of, "Oh, you're oppressed, you are internalizing your oppression." I wanted to be in a different seminar group so as to examine this subject in more depth. I was an addict: I got addicted to these workshops. Because anywhere else, on the telephone, on the bus, you are afraid to speak Arabic, so being able to come to a workshop where the platform is open to you, this offers a lot of strength and it feels good to experience that in the group, something I can't do elsewhere. Then when I felt that I was getting addicted to these workshops, I wanted to shift this power gradually beyond the workshop, whether through action or into the discourse in general.

At first it was about getting equipped to cope with the other side, because I would get filled up with rage and then at the workshop I got rid of it all, and then went back to the reality and found that nothing was changed, but at least I could sleep better at night.

And then you wanted to make peace with other parts of yourself?

I didn't grow up in a village nor in a place that was solely Palestinian. In the facilitators group at Neve Shalom, there was no place to say that I am also Israeli; this wasn't legitimate to say there, because right away they tell you that you are internalizing the oppression and it starts to strangle you from the inside. You start to understand that your group does not behave better in how it conducts itself as a group than the other group does. That I love music in Hebrew doesn't make me less Palestinian or a traitor. Yes, I wanted to make peace with parts of my self inside. When I came to the second workshop, I was more confident in my Palestinian-ness, so it was already harder to shake me up, because I already knew who I was. So I felt more comfortable examining other aspects of [myself,] and I was a lot braver in saying, "Yes,

I have aspects like these," and coping with these aspects in the binational context. That's something that has to be dealt with all the time.

I am about to have a child, and we started thinking about a Palestinian-Jewish urban commune, but it started to fall apart because of the situation. People are fed up. And I am aware that on the one hand, the child won't feel comfortable as purely Palestinian or purely Jewish. I wouldn't want to offer him a life in a solely Arab place after so many years, 130 years that we have been living together. We have benefited a lot from each other, and although we aren't prepared to admit it, we are very alike. The conflict and the oppression that exist, function to reinforce the lack of a desire to acknowledge that. Then I joined a third seminar group, out of a desire to take action. Being involved in activism is something that also develops you.

FIGHTING FEAR WITH ACTIVISM

At first it was a lot like the process in the group: going to demonstrations to say, "I am a Palestinian"; to say, "We are here." At a certain point, I began doing talks for Jewish groups about why Palestinians don't want to do national service and what the implications are. Then I started getting into facilitation of groups of Palestinians from Israel; plus facilitating at the School for Peace. At a certain stage, I was active with Sedaka-Re'ut [a binational youth movement]. There I led a Jewish Arab collective for two years. It was ongoing supervision with people who want to be active. It included political discussions, it included discussions on getting out there to do political action that the Palestinians wanted and the Jews were less eager for. It was facilitation with people who are living very closely with each other and continuing to live together after the discussion ends.

I facilitated tours [of destroyed Palestinian communities] with Zochrot and was also on the board of Zochrot. We put together tours of mixed cities. In my activism work, I emphasize mixed cities because I come from a mixed city. Generally when talking about the Nakba or about the years that preceded or followed it, they are talking about villages, and they show people a village woman with her head covered who stands next to an olive tree. My family was not like that.

My grandfather was a school principal in Haifa. In 1948 they threw him out: no school, no nothing. He had a two-story house. He was totally urban.

It was important for me to bring this to the Palestinian discourse. They were on the way to Beirut, to Lebanon, and they put them into boats, the British soldiers started shooting at the boats and the boats anchored at Acre. They disembarked and my uncle was arrested with all the young men. My grandmother said, I'm not going anywhere without my son. I knew nothing of any of this until I asked. And then when I learned about it, it appeared in Dan Bar-On's book and in the Zochrot pamphlet. It was important for me to disseminate this story.

The Zochrot tours were for both Jews and Arabs. Yes, there are a lot of Palestinians who know nothing. It's patronizing to say so, because I didn't know anything either. It's about being in a space and saying what I think and fighting against the fear. In Haifa, there were two police cruisers that went along with us on the tour. In Acre, there was a demonstration against us by the chief rabbi of Acre. I was also afraid in Acre that they would know I was my parents' son. It was one of my fears, because OK, I was prepared to pay the price myself, but not in a way that would harm them.

Now I do other things involving the study of conflicts elsewhere in the world. I joined the management team at the Causeway Institute for Peace-building and Conflict, an organization where they study about other conflicts, mainly Ireland. We registered as a nonprofit organization and we give mediation courses and also take groups to study about the characteristics of the conflict and see what can be learned. This takes us out of our own ethnocentrism a little, since we always think we are the only ones in the world who suffer this way, and studying another conflict elsewhere creates a different discourse of activism and encourages action.

I have a fantasy that in another thirty years I will create a center for victims of terror and of Israeli military actions and Palestinians who were expelled from their homes, a place where they could all come and undergo individual and group therapy, Jews and Arabs. I also participate in Psycho-Active: Mental Health Professionals for Human Rights. I would like to get into a shared urban Jewish-Arab community. I am looking for a house or some way to set up a shared Jewish-Arab community in the city or at Néve Shalom, because there I would not have to get into the basic discourse again, I would not have to explain myself and what I go through. Just knowing that there is such a place helps during these times. If it didn't exist, I might consider emigrating.

12 · YOAV LURIE

Psychotherapist, Occupational Therapist, and Group Facilitator

Today, Yoav Lurie is working as a psychologist and occupational therapist with children, adolescents, and adults in a private practice in Tel Aviv, and conducting two psychotherapy groups for sexually abused gay men and for sexually abused men and women. He is a senior supervisor in the group facilitators program at Tel Aviv University and fieldwork coordinator in mental health in the university's Occupational Therapy Department. He is a candidate for membership in the Israeli Institute for Group Analysis, a board member of the Israeli Association for Group Psychotherapy, and a member of an Arab-Jewish psychotherapists' group investigating the links between psychotherapy and politics. Previously, Lurie was an occupational therapist for eleven years with the Psychiatric Division of the Sheba Medical Center and a clinical psychology intern at the Ramat Aviv Institute for Psychoanalytic Psychotherapy and the Be'eri day care unit at Clalit Health Services. Yoav Lurie took the Change Agents Course for Israeli and Palestinian Mental Health Professionals in 2007–2008 at the School for Peace at Wahat al-Salam–Neve Shalom. He was interviewed on July 30, 2008.

It's very easy to kill off one's political activism because life pulls you toward ordinary pursuits: home, work, friends. In the end, I came to realize that therapeutic and political thinking are connected. I do feel isolated a lot, even at my workplace. But taking the SFP course and having a forum of like-minded people have given me some sort of platform for action that I had previously been missing.

My first experience with the School for Peace was in a weekend workshop. I happened to see an announcement about it in a forum about group therapy. This followed a long period when I had no contact with the Arab-Jewish issue. As a teenager, I was very active in the movement called Youth Sing a Different Song, but life was over-full and I abandoned it. Then I began to miss it, finding no similar platform where I could get involved again. The weekend workshop at the SFP gave me a kind of introduction to the course I took afterward for change agents in mental health professions.

That first weekend, I said almost nothing during the workshop. Mainly I listened. I remember feeling shame and despair at the things that were said there. Just before or after that weekend, I began coming to meetings of PsychoActive. I don't remember exactly when, but it was around that time.

The course I subsequently joined was my first binational encounter, the first time I ever met Palestinians from the territories. It was a different experience from the encounter with '48 Palestinians [Palestinian citizens of Israel] who are, so to speak, living among us, and so there's some kind of acquaintance.

Maybe the hardest thing is to sit facing someone, look him in the eye and listen to his own personal story. I can't decide whether it evokes more guilt or more responsibility. Maybe guilt happens first, and then responsibility toward him, toward a particular person. I remember a specific situation in the binational workshop, when Adnan recounted an experience he had with his mother at a checkpoint. She had had a heart attack and they did not let them cross. This was the situation when I felt that it wasn't someone else doing that to them, it was me, and I was responsible for it. This really subverts things. Saying in self-defense that the army is responsible, or the settlers, or the state—that doesn't come as easily. As if to say, "It's not me."

I am obsessed with wondering how much my being part of this activity is really to make things easier for myself and how significant it is in terms of altering the reality. In the end, I am part of the state, I pay taxes and it's my choice to be an Israeli citizen and so I'm living here, I am part of this, I can't shirk it. To make that sort of distinction and say, "It's the soldier at the checkpoint, it's the settler, it's the government"—I could say that more easily before the workshop. During the workshop it became more and more clear to me that it's an illusion, that it's just something I use to reorganize the reality. Around that time I also realized that joint activity with Palestinians may be the less significant part of all this. Their expectation is that I will go back to where I came from and make change happen there.

What made the binational encounter more difficult? The Palestinian presence? The things they said? The way in which the discussion was conducted?

I think it was my own reflection in their eyes, seeing that in their eyes I am that soldier, even if I don't see it that way. From their standpoint that's how it is. In the group of Israelis, there were three participants presenting positions that we would call more right-wing, and their presence for me was very important because they reinforced the part that supposedly isn't mine. The differences do exist, but the aggression and the desire for revenge are also present in me. It's just convenient for me in my everyday life that aggression and vengefulness are carried by certain segments of the population. Yet the moment I take ownership of this, I can also do something with it. As long as I leave it to the "bad guys," I can sit back at ease and say "tsk, tsk." The moment I see it as part of myself, I have greater responsibility.

Since the course, this realization has influenced me, and I am still working through it. It comes up a lot in conversations I have with people around me who call me, you know, a "bleeding-heart leftist." In those situations, of course, I get into a more defensive place, but inwardly I know that these things are also part of me. In the binational encounters as well, I was astonished at what happened to the aggressive parts of me and how much I deny them. But even when I deny them, the Palestinians don't let me have that option, meaning they don't believe it. I think about Sami and all our conversations. He was able to be skeptical about all that love, peace and happiness stuff in the sense that he got me and knew that there are also other, less pleasant impulses flowing through me.

I've been working as an occupational therapist in psychiatry for nine years. For the last two years, I've headed the occupational therapy service at my location and I am also doing a practicum in clinical psychology somewhere else. Both places where I'm working are very homogeneous from the standpoint of the population served. I can recall just two Arab rehabilitants during the entire nine years I've been working. There are Arab cleaning workers who are more or less invisible and who disappear anyway after a few months because they work for a manpower company and have no job security. There are no Arabs on the professional staff. In other departments there are male nurses who are Arabs, but other than that, no one. Tomorrow I am interviewing an Arab woman who's a candidate for an occupational therapist position, so maybe the situation will change. I'm concerned about what that might give rise to, among the staff. There are a lot of rehabilitants connected with the Ministry of Defense, and I can imagine what that is going to evoke for them.

ACCESS TO LIFE

The course affected me as a therapist first of all by affecting my thinking. The theoretical outlook of occupational therapy is holistic and looks at the person, at what the person does and at the environment. Today one of the hot topics is the whole issue of access. Last summer, at the annual conference of occupational therapists, the main topic was "Access to Life." There were sessions dealing with access to various spheres among all kinds of populations. Some sessions were very impressive and included, in the importance of access, our responsibility as occupational therapists in terms of the social and political plane, and not just within the treatment room: our role in social change and our involvement in the struggles of excluded populations and those to whom access is denied. These sessions dealt with the notion that disability has to do with an inaccessible environment rather than with the person's own disability. I was amazed that no mention whatever was made of the fact that half an hour's drive, or less, from where we were sitting, at Shefayim, there are a million and a half people—Palestinians—whose access to work, education, leisure, social participation—to everything that we as occupational therapists deal with—is either nonexistent or very limited.

So I wrote an article about access to life. I published it in a widely read occupational therapy forum. People responded very harshly to my having even raised this subject in a professional forum, saying it wasn't the place for it and that, so far, they had avoided having such posts and I should not be allowed to ruin that, and that this subject is not a priority—but without addressing the content of what I'd written. There was a general delegitimization of my bringing the issue up altogether, and people said, "First you have to take care of your own"—but I think that right there is the change that happened to me: It's about realizing that therapeutic and political thinking are connected, meaning that now I am less able to make a distinction between the two or to separate them.

After I came back from the second workshop, I ran two seminar sessions, together with Nissim, for students in the clinical psychology practicum. We were invited to talk about the process we had been through. I think that overall it was a very friendly environment. The two seminar instructors were very supportive from the outset, and there was a great deal of curiosity because these subjects are never spoken of in the work context and there's not much that would give rise to addressing them because the place is so "sterile." That sounds awful. There are no Arab clients because of the geographic area.

Five or six years ago I had a client from the Triangle region who was a medical paraprofessional. I imagine that if the treatment were to take place today, it would look entirely different in terms of the difference between us, me as a Jewish therapist and him as an Arab client. This did not come up back then, and it was not addressed, but it was there, absolutely. Today I would not allow that to happen. The same thing applies, by the way, with other clients, not just Arabs. I'm thinking of a Haredi client of mine, and we talk about these issues much more. I also initiate a discussion of politics. It's there and is definitely addressed more than in the past. I can mention a client of mine who's part of the right-wing settlement outpost circles. He takes part in all kinds of activities at every opportunity and we talk about it. Some years ago I had a client who raised dilemmas for me as a therapist. He was schizophrenic and some of the negative symptoms were social withdrawal and lower vocational functioning. He was very active in Kach [the right-wing party subsequently outlawed in Israel], a very extremist organization, and some of the damage he suffered was in his withdrawal from this activity. In the therapy, he talked of his desire to return to activism, and this really posed a major dilemma for me in terms of how much to draw him out regarding his positions. But it did not arise; I managed to remain detached. That would be true much less often today.

It's very easy to kill off one's political activism because life pulls you toward ordinary pursuits: home, work, friends. In the end, I think that taking the SFP course and having a forum of like-minded people have given me some sort of platform for action that I had previously been missing. Even on the simplest level of networking, a social network in which I can operate. I can pick up the phone and consult with you, get information.

ENTRY PERMITS

I'm reminded of a very powerful experience from after the course. We had decided early on that one of us would coordinate the matter of entry permits to Israel for the Palestinian participants, and I volunteered to do it. A few days after the course ended, I suddenly got a phone call from Adnan about a guy from his village who had been arrested at Beit Eba and his family did not know why he had been arrested or where he was taken. Suddenly the discussions and the planning became a reality. He got hold of me while I was at university, and I was thrown into deep water. All at once, I understood the terrible powerlessness of their circumstances. I, even as a Jewish Israeli who speaks the language, I got lost in this swamp of the security system. I called all kinds of liaison people and prisons, and in one fell swoop I realized that you don't really have much chance with this apparatus, that you really can't do much when someone simply disappears one day and no one knows where he is or how to find him. This was a powerful experience both to have, for myself, and because of the responsibility that was suddenly given to me. A few weeks ago there was an in-service training course that we organized, and we tried to get entry permits for the guys from Gaza and I felt that, too. You can get intoxicated by the power that this interaction with them can give you. Suddenly I felt like a warden holding the keys who can decide whether to open the prisoner's cell door or not.

After a great deal of telephoning, I was able to find the guy. It was a whole saga. Finally it turned out that he was at Ofer prison. I was in touch with Adnan all the time. He informed the family. Then there was another saga around the question of legal representation and so forth. At that stage, I felt that his family was withdrawing and that they weren't interested in any more help from me. I felt suspicion and ambivalence on their part.

What did you mean by "the intoxication of power"?

When I leave my house in the morning, I have a choice about whether to deal with the conflict or not. In the workshop, Kristin represented this for me. She leaves the house every morning and does not have that choice, and in that sense I have some kind of intoxication with power. In the sense that I really can use the connections I have, my ability to express myself in Hebrew, and in general, the fact that when I call someone, they treat me differently because I'm a Jew. I can see how easily I arrive at a feeling that I am the landlord and I'll decide how hard I am prepared to exert myself.

CROSS-BORDER TOURS FOR COLLEAGUES

One cannot detach the feeling of crossing the boundary on the emotional-psychological plane from that of the physical plane. The moment I met the Palestinian guys in the workshop at Aqaba, and in Istanbul, I developed a need to cross the physical border, too, because I had actually never been there. It was crossing into the Mountains of Darkness. I am trying to remember. It seems to me that when I was a boy, we went to visit my aunt in Ma'aleh Adumim. I think it was the furthest I had been, and there really was a feeling that this is an area I don't enter, that it's out of bounds because my being there is not legitimate. I suddenly understood that my not being there enables things to happen; it's another kind of denial, that if I don't look, then it isn't happening. This is very infantile.

So I made a connection with someone from Machsom Watch and asked to take part in a tour of the checkpoints. It was a very powerful experience, to go into a no-man's-land where there is no rule of law like here. Suddenly, legality shifts. I joined the tour of the checkpoints around Nablus. After that tour and the meaningful experiences it included, like driving on an apartheid road, I decided that I want to expose more people to this. Because I am also a professional in the mental health field, I thought of connecting the two things and focusing on the population of people with whom I work. With the help of Hagar from Machsom Watch, I contacted a Palestinian therapist she had met one day at a checkpoint, and we met a few times to plan the tour. So far I have organized two tours. The first was for the Therapy Center at Kafr Azzun, which is affiliated with the Palestinian Counseling Center. We were a group of Israeli therapists and we visited the therapy center and heard testimonies from therapists about the impact of the occupation on the reality of everyday life and on their work as therapists.

The most prosaic things are affected. A therapist leaves home in the morning and doesn't know whether he can get to an appointment with a client because he could be delayed in crossing a checkpoint; if the last four numbers of his identity card happen to match the last four numbers of someone wanted by the authorities, he will be detained at the checkpoint. Suddenly all the psychological language that deals with the inner world and emotional space is no longer relevant, because the focus shifts to a person's most basic needs. I saw this clearly in the course in terms of the dilemmas and issues that preoccupied the Israelis compared with the therapeutic work done by the Palestinian guys. For example, a social worker is going to visit some house that has been separated from the entire rest of the village by the Separation Barrier, so she can bring them a goat so that they'll have a livelihood. This is a therapeutic intervention, Palestinian style. The second part of the tour was at the checkpoints around Nablus. The second tour resembled the first, but without a visit to a therapy center, because it had become clear to me that there was some kind of resistance on their part, or among the organization's leadership, regarding the cooperation with us, the Israelis. I hope that next month there will be another tour.

On these tours, what is most conspicuous is how people are surprised and speechless. There's a kind of shock. All sorts of existing defenses fall apart, and then there is really no choice, and some time is needed to digest this and to build something new. The process is powerfully intense. It's an experience that, on the one hand, deconstructs our defenses and, on the other hand, doesn't offer an alternative. After that, the chance to join PsychoActive allows someone to take this experience and do something with it. There are people who came on a tour and subsequently joined PsychoActive. I think that many people have a desire, a need, for a framework, partly due to a sense of being isolated. All in all, we are a tiny minority.

THE FOUNDING OF PSYCHOACTIVE

I do feel isolated a lot. I feel like the eternal party pooper—even at my workplace. When I offered colleagues the opportunity to attend a "therapolitical" workshop, they seemed to wish I hadn't done so. There are workshops all the time on all kinds of subjects, and suddenly I come out with this one. The question is how much energy I have for being the one to ruin the party. I like partying, too.

Of course there are also times when I feel real satisfaction about doing political work. I think I would have to feel that way in order to keep doing it.

The two tours were very successful for the participants and, in that sense, they really did have an impact on people. There was also an impact on the Palestinians who met with us, who felt that they were not forgotten: someone remembers them. The conferences we have organized so far have had a substantial impact. PsychoActive is a group of people that got organized a few years ago in response to the arrest of a clinical psychology intern at a Jaffa medical facility. He was accused of providing information or aiding the enemy. Psychologists who worked with him, along with some other people, organized in his support. That was the first activity.

Since then, PsychoActive has expanded and broadened its reach to encompass other activities. Three conferences were organized with around three hundred participants each. The first was here at Neve Shalom, focusing on psychological obstacles to peace, with lectures by Israelis Jews and Palestinians as well as Palestinians from Palestine. More than two hundred people attended. I think it was a success story in the sense that it exposed therapy practitioners, many for the first time, to a different way of approaching these issues, through our activities. Sessions addressed the impact of the occupation on the psychological health of Palestinians and also on our health, we Israelis. Since then we have held two more conferences dealing with the connection between the therapeutic and the political. These conferences addressed the issues we deal with in our work and allowed participants to see how Palestinians experience life under occupation. There were participants with no previous exposure to this sort of thing, including right-wing therapists, some of them settlers.

There are other projects at PsychoActive, some just coming into being or still under development. One is a training course for Palestinian therapists, with one group meeting in Kafr Azzun and the other in Hebron. We met with a group of Palestinian therapy practitioners to share our experience and knowledge for training purposes with them. This is not at all a simple approach, and all the difficulties and the dilemmas we deal with come up, including the very asymmetrical division of power that exists in this interaction.

Another project I'm involved in is about Kafr Qaddum. The power of such a seminar is in the personal encounter, the exposure to individual people's stories. Adnan related that his village is coping with two main problems that constitute burning issues for them: one was the blocking of the main road that connected Kafr Qaddum and Nablus, which was used for transporting merchandise and commuting to work, traveling to and from school, or getting to the hospital. Once blockaded by the settlers from Kedumim, this access road was closed to Palestinians, creating severe problems for the village's residents—when people were very ill, for instance, or when women were about to give birth, so that not reaching the hospital in time had a very serious impact on people's health and well-being. Some university students have been unable to continue living in the village and have had to rent apartments in Nablus. Businesses have been forced to close. And so forth.

The second issue was the freestanding room that the village constructed to house the connections for electrical power, with aid from a foreign agency, after many years of relying on generators. Once the entire infrastructure was installed, the Civil Administration at Kedumim, which is operated by local settlers, issued a demolition order for the electricity room because it was built in Area C [of the West Bank], if I am remembering correctly. The moment Adnan informed us of this situation, several people in the group organized a study tour to the village, and we were able to recruit MK [member of the Knesset] Yair Tzaban to join us.

On this tour we saw the intolerable situation plaguing the village today. We saw the blockaded road, and we visited the electricity outbuilding, which was already built and awaiting the final stage of the project, now on hold and unable to proceed. So we began working on recruiting MK Chaim Oron to help get the demolition order rescinded. We began an exhausting correspondence with MK Oron, who sent us to the minister of defense. We also wrote three letters of protest to the deputy defense minister.

In the end, they named some kind of committee to discuss the matter and the committee posed certain conditions; if the village fulfilled them all, including demolition of the existing building, the committee would permit the construction of a new electricity room. The village was required to produce all kinds of plans of various kinds and to buy another plot of land, and they performed everything demanded of them. Meanwhile, the Civil Administration tried to hold up the proceedings. Finally the Civil Administration asked the village for a letter explaining why they need an electricity hookup. How weird is that?—For a village of 4,500 people in the year 2007 to be asked to explain why they need electricity. After that, the authorities tried to delay things and there were daily telephone calls to pressure the relevant officials and the electricity officer in the Civil Administration at Beit El. Finally after a long and fatiguing process, the precious permit was obtained in writing. We insisted that they receive something in writing, and now they are finishing

building the new electricity room. Apart from that, two years ago we participated in the olive harvest in the village because of the fear of harassment by
settlers from Kedumim.

STAYING MOTIVATED AND AVOIDING BURNOUT

I think the activity itself is enlivening and gives me a sense of vitality. I don't
surrender to some sort of reality. I do something on my little corner of God's
earth. I am aware that it's one drop in a vast ocean. The more I learn, the more
I discover how much more there is to do. There are more projects, more
thoughts about what can be done together with the Palestinians from Palestine and with Palestinians from '48 [in Israel]. There is a lot more work that
people in the therapeutic professions can do.

There are various projects on the drawing board. There was the matter of
the future vision that we began, the workshop, and there is a lot more to do
on that. All in all, only a very small percentage of the population in Israel
has heard about it or even wants to hear about it. When I talk about it,
people aren't all that eager to find out about it. There are other projects
that are expanding to involve larger segments of our society, other people
who are also excluded. Maybe that's not as relevant to our subject here, but
as I said earlier, it is impossible to work only on that. There's an impact on
how one views other things too, like the asylum seekers arriving from Africa.
We are currently attempting to organize a visit to the Saharonim detention
center in the Negev to observe the situation of the children who are detained
there.

I think it's clear that the course at Neve Shalom was a foundational, formative experience for me. We participated in a demonstration against the
Separation Barrier that was built in East Jerusalem at A-Ram. We were protesting a wall that divided a school on one side from its students on the other
side. I went to the protest with a few friends from PsychoActive. It was a joy-
ful protest with children marching in rows. I walked with the vanguard of
the demonstrators; in front of us stood border police, some of them on
horseback, some in Jeeps. It was a nonviolent demonstration, there were
children there, it was explicitly defined [as nonviolent]. Suddenly the border police began firing stun grenades at us, and teargas. I remember that it took
a few minutes until I was able to open my eyes and see what was happening

around me. The street had completely emptied. In those few minutes, the old distinction between who is against me and who is on my side, what is right and what is not right, was upset in one fell swoop. Soldiers who are, as I said earlier, a part of me or of whom I am a part, were attacking me. I felt that the deck had been reshuffled.

After I was able to open my eyes, I saw that the street had emptied and I realized that I needed to find shelter. I noticed a house alongside the road and I went down toward it. An old woman there invited me to come inside. Everything happened wordlessly. The Palestinian woman gave me an onion [to counteract the tear gas]. Evidently they are already accustomed to this and know that [the onion] eases your breathing. I went inside and the feeling was that now I was in a safe place. Suddenly I saw Muhammad Abu Tir (a Palestinian active with Hamas) standing in front of me. It took me a couple of seconds to grasp that this was him standing there and not Tal Friedman playing him on "Wonderful Country" on television, that this was really the guy himself. Former MK Uri Avnery was there too, evidently having sought to hide and escape the tear gas just as I was doing. So I found myself in a very surreal situation. I found myself hiding, together with a minister from Hamas, while escaping Israeli Border Police. Someone I consider totally demonic, someone I would not want to meet in a dark alley, is hiding with me from soldiers of my country. It was very confusing. I had the sensation of somehow having my eyes opened. Along with that came a feeling that much was being lost, but also a sense of gaining something. Both the course and the activism afterward were eye-opening and brought a lot of pain and sorrow. And yet, at the same time, I was given the opportunity to do things.

It's hard for me to imagine myself in that situation now, but I remember feeling safe: it was a very strong feeling. I felt that I was in good hands. I had a similar experience in Aqaba [in Jordan]. That was actually the first time in my life that I had ever been in an Arab country. In Aqaba I felt that my welfare was being looked after by Arabs; I wasn't in charge there, but instead someone else, someone Arab, was the guarantor of my well-being. It was a very good feeling.

I am convinced that I gain something from my political activism; I've no doubt whatsoever. But it's true that I also lose a lot. Suddenly I make a choice between going to sit in a café on Friday or doing something related to activism. There are periods when I devote a few hours a day to the subject, especially if there's a project that moves center stage. There's a lot of activity that is somewhere in the middle, using the computer, which facilitates communication. And sometimes it creates a lot of tension at home because it comes at the expense of other things.

One question I'm concerned about is to find where the boundaries of my opposition are. Does the fact that I am still a soldier in the reserves, although I don't serve in the territories, have any place in my outlook as of today? When they call me, I go. It happens infrequently but I serve as an occupational therapist and some of the soldiers I treat have been in confrontations with Palestinians. I remember one soldier who told me proudly that he had injured his hand while striking a Palestinian on the Temple Mount. The question of where I locate the boundary concerns me greatly. In the end, it's a question of what price I am willing to pay. I have to say, and it makes me both sad and happy to say it, that although the whole apparatus of denial is working, still when I hear about a child killed in Na'lin, I feel a need to phone the reserve duty coordination officer and tell her that I've decided to hand in my reserve papers. In practice, this has not actually happened. If it and when it does, it would not be in response to a specific event; it would be a specific step, and the result of an inner decision.

13 · DINA ZAREGA

Social Worker

Dina Zarega [a pseudonym] was born in the United States to an ultra-Orthodox Jewish family who moved to Israel when she was five years old. She is a clinical social worker and psychotherapist working in the Jerusalem area in both Hebrew and English with adults. Along with her interest and involvement in the search for reconciliation and justice between Israelis and Palestinians, Zarega's ultra-Orthodox background and religious values, together with her training at the School for Peace, have led her to devote herself to serving as a kind of living bridge between the Jewish religious settler community, secular left-wing Israelis, and Palestinians. Dina Zarega participated in the School for Peace Change Agents Course for Mental Health Professionals at Wahat al-Salam–Neve Shalom. She was interviewed in November 2014.

> I am a bridge between the religious [Jewish] world and the world of secular activism. I don't think we should dismiss the religious settlers. I don't blame the Palestinians for not wanting to talk with them, but Israelis should take responsibility. I want us to draw on Jewish religious sources in these efforts. Everyone knows that Buddhism says these things. I want to make this voice heard from within Judaism.

My name is Dina Zarega. A few years ago, I participated in the Change Agents Course for Mental Health Professionals at Neve Shalom.

I come from a Haredi (strictly religious) American Jewish family. My parents made aliyah to Israel for religious and Zionist reasons when I was very young. The conflict with the Palestinians was rarely evident in the world of my childhood. But later, my high school yearbook dubbed me "the only leftist" in my entire grade. I wondered what they were talking about, and how they had come to that conclusion.

True, I had always assumed I would vote left-wing when the time came. But it wasn't until the School for Peace course that I remembered having participated in an Israeli-Palestinian dialogue program for a few months while at university, when a friend took me with him to the Reform synagogue where it was being held. Otherwise I really had no particular connection to the subject. Traveling in India some time later must have opened my heart to the world. When I returned, someone—I don't even recall who it was—sent me a description of the SFP change agents program. Apparently, the time had come for me to learn why I was a leftist and what that even means. And so I registered for the program, and found it just right for me. It was a formative, eye-opening experience that took me to uncharted territory. It was mind-stretching.

Mind-stretching in what sense?

I wasn't familiar with the Palestinian narrative—neither that of Arab Israelis, nor that of Palestinians over the Green Line. I was a friendly, open person, and I [had] discussed these things before, but in hindsight these were superficial discussions that never really ventured in too deep. I had never experienced this kind of discussion before.

The first session was dramatic. One woman showed up, spoke very angrily in Arabic for a solid hour, and never came back. It was like hearing a song in a foreign language, sensing it expressed a tremendous amount of anger, but having no idea what it was about. That was a preview of sorts. Talking about it now this way feels odd, since it has become so integrated into my own narrative that I no longer differentiate. Back then, between the monthly meetings of the group, I used to talk things over with a friend from the course. From the first session, my stomach was tied in knots from the stress, the pain, the guilt, the fear. The tension was really difficult for both of us. Clearly something very, very important [was] taking place if we felt this way for two weeks out of every month of the program.

The stomach ache was the knowledge we were entering a real encounter, where an unpleasant reflection in the mirror awaited us. Our comfortable, privileged, and normally pleasant lives would suddenly appear less pleasant. It would be painful hearing the testimony of others.

PALESTINIANS FROM HERE AND FROM THERE

The monthly encounters were with Palestinians from Israel, but on several occasions and in other formats we also met with Palestinians from '67, who lived in the Palestinian territories and whose testimonies were very different. During one session in Aqaba, for instance, a Palestinian guy told us that he felt that they were like mice when facing our weapons. My immediate association was the Holocaust, but that's not something you can say or discuss. I don't know if it's comparable, and I don't go there. But that's what I remember from Aqaba. I also remember that it was unpleasant for me to confess it. I think his name was Muhannad.

I am not sure I remember his name correctly, but I do remember his face. This was about six years ago. We, or I, asked him a question and he said, "I'm not at a Shabak interrogation, I don't have to answer your questions about my intentions." And that assertiveness—I guess I'm not accustomed to it, and admitting that here is not pleasant for me. I'm not used to Palestinians having an equal voice and being equally assertive and self-confident. Suddenly, in Aqaba, there was a chance to meet on a completely equal basis, in a neutral location. It was very surprising for me as a therapist. I knew that this is how things ought to be in the world, that this was healthy, even if I found the moment uncomfortable, and even if I somehow profited from the unhealthy aspects of our usual situation. These moments in Aqaba and the encounter with the Palestinians from '67 were fundamental and formative.

Here at home with Palestinians from '48, there were all kinds of meaningful moments. There is one memory in particular I talk about often. A Palestinian participant from Nazareth told us two stories. The first was about going to buy a piano for his house. They went to some Jewish town and he was a little concerned about whether to bring his daughter along or not. I found it strange to hear that Arabs are afraid of Jews: It's supposed to be the other way around: We are afraid of Arabs, they're not supposed to be afraid of us. This was a revelation for me, an unpleasant reflection in the mirror, yet there was no arguing with how he felt. This man is the most credible, friendly, and real guy I know. If he says it's so, I believe him. His other story was about taking his daughter to buy ice cream; we were talking about language issues. He said that Israelis hearing him speaking Arabic with his daughter don't even consider that he's asking her if she wants chocolate or vanilla; they assume that a terror attack is imminent. Looking into that mirror, I saw the veiled and not-so-veiled racism prevalent even among leftists—thinking that it is natural that we fear them but that they don't fear us. We have all kinds of notions to protect ourselves, but these are often false. The program tells us to live in a world where one can lay these things out on the table very simply; it alters one's consciousness.

Do you remember at one point referring to this as "coming out of the closet"? As a leftist who understands where Arabs are coming from— something like that.

Now that you remind me, yes. I remember saying it. The course gave me the words for many things. Even though I thought of myself as a leftist, I couldn't explain why, not in any depth. I thought: peace is good. But I didn't know how to articulate this or argue terribly well, or how to speak from the Palestinian perspective when they weren't there to speak for themselves. I developed a stronger voice during the program. I felt that the course, the participants, and the SFP facilitators were my back-up in coming out of the closet, as it were. I could speak out about these things more clearly and confidently. So when I say, "I believe that the Arabs think . . .", "I believe that the Arabs feel . . ."—I have support for it, I have testimony, I have heard these things myself firsthand. It isn't just empty talk, I'm not just saying what I like to think is true.

Some arguments I'd like to use don't reflect the way Arabs may think about a particular issue. Or maybe other Arabs do, but not the Arabs sitting in the group at Neve Shalom. So it depended on whom you wanted to quote, really. I also think the encounter had more credibility because the discussion wasn't always that pleasant; it wasn't about "Let's get acquainted, let's get along, let's be nice to each other." The feeling was that people say everything on their mind— or nearly everything, in any event. It wasn't a conversation just with those who want to get along happily in Israel and who wish people would leave them in peace and stop reminding them that they're Arab; there were also people who felt that their Arab identity was important to them and wanted to express it. It related to that sense of coming out of the closet, maybe—the idea that we were acquiring a more credible foundation for our attitudes.

FRICTION WITH FAMILY AND FRIENDS

I have always been an individualist, and have never had the urge to conform. Otherwise, I may not have signed up for the SFP course to begin with. Maybe the email about it would not even have reached my in-box. I still can't remember who sent it to me.

But there's also an answer from before Operation Cast Lead (December 2008–January 2009), and a different answer after it. After the course and before Cast Lead, I didn't feel that my opinions were causing any serious friction with my own circles. I'm sufficiently grounded in both the religious world and the world of secular activism. A leftist, yes, but also someone who bridges gracefully between those worlds. Cast Lead was the first time that there was a rift, and it seemed very, very deep, as though my thoughts and feelings were genuinely bothering people, threatening people, infuriating them—including my friends and family.

I think that all leftists who were outspoken during that war met with tough responses. I did, too. I was condemned and denounced on Facebook, with comments like "Go burn," "Go live in Gaza." When you post something on Facebook, it reaches the whole world and comes back at you. I'm prepared to admit that the war so revolted me that I was a little less preoccupied with the nasty things people were saying. What's going on here is very worrying, socially and politically, but it's OK if they curse me. In the midst of the bombings, Gazans and the Israelis in the south have it far worse than the leftists in other places who endured some cursing on the streets.

With my own friends, other things happened. There were tough, painful, probing discussions. I got a grip on myself then. During the war, people felt helpless. Things seemed to be happening at a different level and there appeared to be nothing we could do. One can go to demonstrations, but most of them were on the Sabbath. I felt that I had undertaken the task of insisting on talking about it with my friends. One of my girlfriends is a settler. I'm very fond of her, and I admit it. My background enables me to be in touch with these people, and I still love them. I don't visit their homes because I don't like going to the territories. But I've stayed in touch with this friend while insisting on explaining my opinions to her, using the language she is accustomed to. In the lexicon of religious people, I talk about human beings who were born in the image of Elohim, whose purpose could not have been to create people who would kill each other: I don't believe that. This is both a religious and psychological way of seeing it. I don't believe that there are bad people and good people. No one is born evil. I believe that if people behave violently, there must be a reason, and we must address that reason. If we listen, perhaps it will evoke change, spark tikkun [repair]. Coming from this place with these opinions forms a bridge. It enables dialogue, rather than arguing. I try very hard. I want to be a bridge between these worlds, and to be better at it than I have been so far. This is very important to me.

Also during that war, I heard that my beloved Arabic teacher was collecting medicine and basic necessities for Gazans. He has a relative who's a doctor in Gaza and is known here too; he's wonderful. So I got involved. I said I'd collect things myself and bring them to the collection point at Notre Dame in Jerusalem. I posted it on Facebook. It was Tisha B'Av, which was very symbolic. I said I was collecting basic necessities, and that this was an opportunity to help the needy. People were suffering from common things like eye infections. There were reports of a need for salves and aspirin because of the heat. There was a shortage in water and people were suffering headaches. This was really about bringing in some basic humanity. Of course this met with considerable objection but really, how much can anyone object to helping people obtain eye ointment and aspirin?

And people contributed. All day long people knocked on my door to give—friends, friends of friends, and others. They donated wonderful care packages. You could tell people went to the supermarket and had given careful thought to what they bought. They didn't know that afterwards their things would be sorted into categories. People took a tote bag and put in a baby blanket, a baby bottle, aspirin, eye ointment, and sanitary napkins. Religious men came too. For me, this was the most amazing thing in the world. It was a moment of sanity and benevolence in the middle of this terrible war

These are people you could argue with, for hours, about politics—and still they showed up.

I wouldn't put it that way. People listened from the sidelines and wished me success—or not—but I think the ones who came were from leftist circles.

Although there are not many and we hear little of them, there are, in fact, some leftists among the religious public. Think about it: we hear little about the left in general, so the religious left is entirely swallowed up. But they do exist, however small their ranks. I think they welcomed the chance to sound their voice in this way.

Every day of the war involved major drama. I wasn't sleeping. I would get up several times during the night to read the news online and see what was happening. It was a complicated month and a half. One day a guy from Beit El, I don't remember his name, posted that he wasn't a leftist and in fact votes for [Naftali] Bennett, but that he was going to annoy his friends, and wrote that what we were doing in Gaza was immoral. He also said that the racist behavior on the streets in Israel was broadening to target leftist Jews as well as Arabs who happened to be passing by. Then he mentioned the Holocaust. So I thought I should share his post because it was someone from Beit El. It was as though he was saying those things, not my leftist friends. So I posted it.

Here's another example. A guy wrote something about Palestinian "barbarism" in relation to the vandalizing of the Jerusalem tram. He said we should stop providing tram services to residents of East Jerusalem. So I wrote to remind him that there was a context to the destruction. He had made it sound like they just destroyed property because they felt like it.

This sparked a whole debate. One woman wrote that the Arabs should grow up and admit that they lost the wars and come to terms with that; she said we are providing services to this population and that they have privileges that we ourselves don't have. I told her that [East] Jerusalem residents suffer a maddening lack of privileges because they fall between the cracks in the system, and neither side looks after them. They can't freely fly abroad, for example—something she did not know. These discussions are ongoing, but I still feel a rift.

MONITORING MY FACEBOOK PAGE

The discourse about Palestinians as barbaric simply must stop. So now I don't allow such discourse on my Facebook wall to go unanswered. It comes with an emotional price. It's draining, it wears me out. And sometimes the effort gets undermined, such as when ISIS suddenly publish their accursed

photos, and you lose some of your credit and strength. When Hamas exe-
cutes suspected collaborators in the street, that's also brutal. I thought: what
lousy timing. I don't know. It wasn't easy during that war to always be pointing out the Hamas perspective on the justice of military actions, but it was
important that religious people and right-wing people know there are others
among them, people they know and love, who talk to Palestinians and who
feel and think very, very differently.

Some of these religious people probably think I'm nuts. I don't have a good
counterargument. But others think I'm very compassionate, and they can at
least identify with that aspect. Regrettably, there's difficulty in the discourse
with settlers, for whom living in dignity and safety is now part of being a Jew
or of being religious. It's become a moral value in its own right. Jewish scrip-
ture posits no value in Jewish people living safely at the expense of others in
this land, but these people sanctify specific excerpts to back their position.
I challenge them. I find that charity and peace are actually more prominent
in Jewish texts than national independence—and I tell them so.

Something else changed for me during that war. It used to be terribly easy
for me to be angry with settlers who consider themselves peace workers. Talking about making peace while living in settlements: I mean, what is that?
However, during this last war I came to feel that these voices are significant
too, and that it's good they exist. If we allow them, maybe even support and
strengthen them, they'll reach out to their friends in the settlements more
easily than you or I could do, even though I'm somewhat connected there.

If Bibi [Netanyahu] had been able to achieve a fair pact with the Palestinians, I would have been glad for Bibi: We have to support every voice trying
to do something. Unfortunately Bibi was totally unsuccessful. But at one
point I thought, wow, let him bring peace; I'm ready for him to bring us an
agreement. I do sometimes get tired of how the left acts so self-righteous and
superior, as if they're the sole custodians of the truth. I'm glad if anyone can
contribute to sanity here, and I don't much care which direction it's coming
from. That was something else that changed for me.

*Would you like to elaborate a little more about the role that you took on,
of bridging between these worlds?*

It's a tough job, especially because I'm not all that successful at it, being
an individualist. Although I am religious, I'm very, very liberal, and I am

not well-rooted in a community. I began responding to posts by some of my rabbis from the past. Just before Rosh Hashana, for instance, a well-known rabbi from the national religious community posted that he was greatly moved when, after the murder of the three boys, Israeli security forces were able to liquidate the two who abducted and murdered them. I wrote and told him it was a very depressing post for the eve of Rosh Hashana.

Mostly people didn't respond to my replies to their posts. But it was nice to see dozens of other replies posted by religious people who said, "You shall not rejoice when an enemy falls," or some such quote. Or "Have a little compassion for human life." It was really interesting to read these and be part of this community, to participate in it and tell myself that I was speaking out so that these other voices will not be met by silence.

So you're always responding, you're not giving up on the religious Jewish population but instead seeking ways to hold on to them.
Very much so. I love that community. That's the thing—I wasn't able to find friends at Neve Shalom who saw this the way I do, and likewise at PsychoActive, where I am active. I couldn't find friends who thought as I do. Some of the most kind-hearted people I know live in settlements. The dissonance is great. It sounds odd, illogical even—but I'd be lying if I said otherwise. So how can one do something with this? Despite everything, I'm optimistic about this because if all settlers were evil or haters, we'd be in serious trouble.

But this is not the case. I simply know it. So that gives me hope. If not for this political conflict—you know, these are people who always stand with the weaker side when there is a conflict in some other country. Something has happened here involving a problematical religious discourse, and there's also a historical political situation. We sent people to live in certain places and now we're trying to tell them, "Uh, time's up, that's it, come back." Meantime they built themselves, not only nice houses, but also an ideology and self-respect, and they have a narrative they feel comfortable with. Somehow deconstructing that narrative is a worthwhile cause. I don't think we should dismiss it altogether because we may be losing more than we gain. Not that I blame the Palestinians for not wanting to talk with them, but I think that Israelis should take responsibility and not dismiss them up front.

SHOOTING BACK

The Neve Shalom course was certainly a formative event in my life. I'll probably still be saying so when I'm eighty, depending on what else happens in the meantime.

As a therapist, I think I can say that the biggest change was internal. Even during the course itself I said that I was sitting differently in my chair as an individual, and as part of this world. I have become someone who knows her neighbors, loves them, and feels compassion towards them. I want to create a different reality, I understand that a different reality will influence my own reality. I think that the most life-altering places are the spiritual ones.

Sitting differently in your chair? How were you sitting before that?

There was a time when I was blind, especially toward the Palestinians. I've always loved foreign identities, particularly Oriental ones, because they interested me. It began as "hummus Orientalism." I can't quite distinguish where that phase ended and the other era began. I still love Palestinian embroidery. I'm more connected to all parts of the society I live in now, and better acquainted with them. I pay more attention and I see more, all the time. It's a different life.

What was going on? Why didn't you see all of that before?

I think it was racism. This has been the most interesting journey, and the most important one. I see the extent to which Palestinians live here as second-class citizens, and how they have to fight to belong. You can be the most accomplished person in the world but as a Palestinian, you are still an inferior citizen in this society. I see the serious implications that this has, how you start internalizing it. Fanon was right. The oppressed internalize what the oppressors project onto them. I don't agree with his support of violent revolution to achieve liberation. But I do see how this affects people's self-image, both collectively and individually. In practical terms, I've done all kinds of things over the last seven years. For the past five years I [have been] a member of PsychoActive, which emerged from the SFP courses for mental health professionals. Once a month I go to Hebron, where I have a very deep emotional connection with two Palestinian families and in general with the community, with what has happened there.

A few years ago, PsychoActive began a project with B"Tselem called Shooting Back, distributing cameras to Palestinians to use as alternative weapons, so to speak, so that when violence occurs, they can document and publicize it. This produced several very important testimonies that were broadcast in prime-time in Israel, including a famous clip that went viral with a [Jewish] settler calling a Palestinian woman *sharmouta* [a whore]. One reason that PsychoActive was invited there was because it's frightening to face soldiers with a camera. Where do they find the courage to do that? Where do they find the strength? Meantime it also involved the families in all kinds of issues, like gender. Can women do this filming, or only men? Who will do this work? They invited us to support the families in addressing these issues. Gradually a few people began using the cameras, but this has become somewhat marginal to our project. I feel that the primary thing is to cross the boundaries: to go to Palestine, visit Palestinian families, hear of their experiences, and witness what they go through. Also to make ourselves heard as a society within Israel that does not agree with the occupation and does not identify with the violence, humiliation and racism that they experience. This is very important to me. It seems that I go mainly for myself, in order to feel in touch with what goes on there, which otherwise I have no connection to. In the five years that I have been going once a month, I have forged some very strong connections.

What about when there's a war going on?
We had been invited to the first night of Ramadan. Clearly they very much want this contact, to feel that we do not hate or fear them;, to know that we take them into account, and also that they too have something to give to us in this process of communication. Then the war broke out. We went downstairs to the car and saw soldiers everywhere and understood that something was going on. My friend checked her Facebook and saw that there had been a kidnapping. This was the day the three youths had been abducted. So we didn't go that night because this was where they were searching, in Hebron. We kept saying we would come, but Ramadan came and went, and then the war expanded. Only one of us went to visit her families. We were afraid of being on the road more than of Tel Rumeida, where it was reportedly relatively quiet.

After the war, we went back. We were there about ten days ago, maybe two weeks. It was painful, very moving, to see friends we had not seen for so long.

We talked about the war, about how it had been for them, and how it had been for us. I was very worried that they would feel that as soon as there's a war, we see them as the enemy. But our not going wasn't about that; it didn't come from that place.

The women we visit speak in Arabic and I understand a lot, but don't speak that well. I speak a little in Arabic, mixed with gestures, a little English and a little Hebrew. I had studied Arabic for a few years and picked up some more Arabic in Hebron—enough to help someone on the street with a question, but there's room for improvement.

This connection is my main activity with PsychoActive. I'm a member and sometimes have the energy to participate in discussions, but don't always make it to the meetings because most of them are on the Sabbath when I don't travel.

CREATING SHARED CEREMONIES

I'm also active in other ways. I was active with a research group with various colleagues working on developing nonviolent communication, mainly within Israeli society. We met every two or three weeks for a few years to think about this project, but currently I'm less involved there. For a while I was doing shared Memorial Days with Palestinians and Israelis.

The year I was at Neve Shalom, I didn't want to celebrate Independence Day. I went to something called Independence/Nakba with a group of activists situated on the boundary between leftist activism and spirituality— people who came out of Tamera, in Portugal. They've been doing this for a few years. Over two days, there's a lecture on historical perspectives by Hillel Cohen and some other historians, and a sharing circle so that people can talk about their experiences. It wasn't a celebration but more like spending two days together and dealing with this stuff. After a few years, we started holding Memorial Days in various cities in order to reach a wider audience. I joined a group that held a shared memorial ceremony at the YMCA in Jerusalem for three years.

We created a ceremony. It was quite complicated and included staged segments and sets of testimonies each with a bereaved Israeli and a bereaved Palestinian. Some of the Palestinians lived in Israel, some in the West Bank. It was not easy for the Palestinians; Memorial Day is something Israeli. The project itself is not easy or simple. But every year we presented something different. Sometimes it [is] about '48 refugees, sometimes it features someone from the Bereaved Families' Forum to put the bereavement on an equal basis. There was singing in both Hebrew and Arabic, and not a political but rather spiritual atmosphere. There were sharing circles where people shared their reasons for attending the ceremony, and related what they felt on Memorial Day or Independence Day or Nakba Day. There was a candle-lighting ceremony, which people could dedicate to their loved ones who had died, or to peace and such. I found it extremely moving. Fewer Arabs attended than Jews, of course, but I began to understand that it doesn't matter so much. The hall was full to bursting. It grew from around eighty people originally to over a hundred, and then to over two hundred. The most important for me is that as Jews, we have an alternative place with room for our ideas, where we are not part of the discourse about God's vengeance, the Holocaust, and so forth.

EMPATHY AND COMPASSION

As a therapist, this work involves a worldview and values that I agree with, from the work of [Heinz] Kohut, who puts tremendous emphasis on empathy and compassion. I see these concepts as relevant in one-on-one encounters, as well as encounters between groups or between nations. Whatever fears may be driving us, if Israelis and Palestinians can sit down and talk with mutual empathy, I think this will lessen the demonization and dehumanization. . It will make it possible to say You are a human being and there are reasons why you behave the way you do. So that's one thing that is developing for me in my clinical work.

Generally, I believe empathy is the key to understanding every idea, although I must admit that I am finding ISIS a challenge to my faith in this at the moment. Perhaps one day someone will figure out a way to understand where this came from too, and do something about it. Still, this is what I believe.

Now, several years since I took the SFP course, I can surely say that it has been among the major influences in my life. Sometimes the impact is evident in a series of small, simple things.

Here is another little story. Just about the time the course ended, a woman friend and I traveled to India. We were sitting on the plane and for some reason I turned to my friend—a psychologist who also attended the course—and said: "You know what? I think I'm the most racist person in the world." I said, "I'm a Jew and I'm religious and Ashkenazi and I grew up in a National Religious home. Take me to meet Obama, and although I'll be very excited and will be a little in awe of him, part of me feels superior to him." I remember telling her this. Thank goodness this tendency of mine is latent and not full-blown. Maybe it had to do with preparing to visit India, where we roam around feeling like Whites—something in me that I very much want to challenge. If Neve Shalom hadn't exposed me to this, I couldn't have confronted this because I wouldn't even have known it was there. I'm amazed by how I've managed to challenge it in ways that surprise even myself. I don't feel now as I did back then. I don't feel that way toward people who are far less distinguished than Obama. When you hear yourself saying something like that, something cracks open on the spot. You hear the words coming out of your mouth and instantly understand how ridiculous it is, and can't believe in it anymore. It comes from being raised in a home with good intentions and good deeds. My family clearly wants to feel that they are liberal, but maybe they weren't all that liberal after all. We were raised as the Chosen People, in an environment in which Ashkenazi people were a little more respected than Sephardic people, and religious people were a lot more respected than secular people, and men were more respected than women. That's the world I'm from. Perhaps this is why I can hear these things and see how all issues, including gender, are interrelated.

I want to portray how life-changing this is. I no longer see the same world before your eyes. That's one thing. A second thing is that I'm aware of how modest my role is, in terms of my exposure as a human being. My life is very private, the clinic is private, these things are not happening publicly, and I'm not a public figure—perhaps regrettably. Yet I do see how a different voice can gradually make itself heard and have an impact, even if in small, quiet measures. I'll give an example from before Rosh Hashana. My brothers and sisters are all ultra-Orthodox and politically right-wing, and their children grow up that way. When they say racist things, I take it up with them. They're young children, four or five years old. They've heard it, so they repeat it. I explain to them that we don't talk that way.

That's on a small scale. I feel that in order to maintain the connection with my family, I sometimes have to restrain myself. I have to find the right doses for things. This was difficult during the war. The young children [in Israel] are afraid. They go to the shelter when an alert sounds, and it's not easy to explain to them that the Arabs are now launching missiles at us because there's a siege on Gaza.

Before Rosh Hashana one of my nieces had stolen some Bamba [a snack] from her brother. I told her jokingly it was the eve of Rosh Hashana and "Thou shalt not steal." And I told her that stealing is rather serious and soon we'd be getting to "Thou shalt not kill." She said to me, "No, only the soldiers this year have to repent about killing." I looked at her and she said, "They killed people." For me, this was amazing. My voice had penetrated after all. She didn't mean they had committed murder or were at fault, she only noted the fact that there were soldiers who had killed people, without getting into the circumstances. Suddenly you see the importance of a voice, no matter how small. Hearing such things is terribly interesting and very moving.

You've been going to Hebron for five years; that's a long time.
What next? Do you have more plans?

I very much want to create a dialogue within the religious world. I have a hard time making it happen because this demands a tremendous expenditure of energy, and you have to go against the current. In Hebron, though, it wasn't going against the current—they really wanted us to come, and we really wanted to. It was hard. You have to travel. Sometimes being on the road is frightening, but on the whole it's OK. I don't know what will happen with this, but I still want to do it. That's one direction that interests me. I also want to continue to develop this connection between empathy and compassion in the clinical setting and beyond, in wider groups. I would like to write more about this, or find additional ways of advancing this. I also have a fantasy about incorporating the religious discourse in this, and find a way to use Jewish religious sources so that it won't be just Buddhism saying it. Everyone knows that Buddhism says these things. I want to make this voice heard from within Judaism.

14 · SLIEMAN HALABI

Cognitive Psychologist, Group Facilitator, and University Research Associate

Slieman Halabi was born in a Druze village in the Galilee. After high school, Halabi moved to Ariel to study behavioral sciences. He earned his master's degree in cognitive psychology at Tel Aviv University (TAU) in 2014 and currently lives in Berlin, working as a research associate at Jacobs University Bremen. During his master's studies in Tel Aviv, he participated in 2012 in the SFP-designed course at TAU called "The Arab-Jewish Conflict in the Mirror of Theory and Practice," which in hindsight he views as a turning point in his life that shaped his political identity. Thereafter, he studied the facilitation of groups in conflict at the School for Peace and worked there and in other organizations dealing with dialogue between Israelis and Palestinians. Halabi is also an activist and a member of the Salaam-Schalom Initiative in Berlin, a community group focusing on minority-majority issues. He plans to continue his research and earn a Ph.D. Slieman Halabi is a 2012 graduate of the SFP Course for Facilitators of Groups in Conflict. He was interviewed in September 2014.

I thought of myself as Druze. I wasn't an Arab but I wasn't an Israeli, and I didn't know who I was. At a certain point I started calling myself Palestinian, but it took time to get friendly with the term. I did not want to become estranged from any of the identities I have inside me. I learned that identity is like a spiral, and that you are always encountering many identities within yourself, depending on the circumstances and the people you meet. Your Druze identity will come up, and your Arab identity will come up, and all the other identities, too. That has proven to be a memorable clarification for me. I really wish everyone would attend a workshop like this.

I have been doing group facilitating while working on a master's degree in cognitive psychology. Two years ago, in 2011–2012, I took the SFP-Tel Aviv University course on the Jewish-Arab conflict, for which the experiential sessions were facilitated by you [Nava Sonnenschein] and Maya [Rabia]. I didn't connect with it and I wasn't going to take it, but the departmental secretary highly recommended it. The subject frightened me. She persevered, however; apparently they needed more Arab students for the course. She got some doctoral student to talk to me about it, and in the end I went ahead and registered for it.

Tell me about your experience at the course.

I had a very hard time there at first. With all those Arabs and their yelling, I felt like I had no place. I felt OK coming to talk to you about it because apparently I had an issue with identity. I didn't know if I was an Arab or a Jew, or maybe I felt more Israeli. I didn't know what I was doing there. I've always had some place—I remember I'd always go to my mother to talk, when I came back to the village, not often, but I would tell her about important experiences I'd had. What they were saying at the course was extremely interesting, but a lot of the time I didn't believe them, and sometimes I said so. I enjoyed that. Eventually, when I started reading, the penny dropped for me. During that entire period, I was at the peak of figuring out who I was, investigating my identity, and reading more. It motivated me greatly to read more about Druze identity. I was caught between two very frustrating things. On the one hand, the Palestinian Arab group was saying a lot of harsh things, and I listened but didn't exactly understand where I fit into all that. There was always this sticking point, like a compass point setting my direction, because I hadn't experienced a Nakba: If going through a Nakba is being Palestinian, where did I fit into that story? It took me some time and a lot of reading to understand where I fit into this thing.

I must say, though, that if the Palestinian group there had not embraced me, I think I would have gotten lost. That group had good people who were really there for me. They said: We aren't asking you to be part of us, but you have to know your history and who you really are and how Israel has manipulated you into becoming who you are today. Together with the agenda of the facilitation, this built something. Meanwhile Maya was there reminding me that denying my own identity was not what I was there to do. Evidently I was feeling guilty about who I was or feeling bad about the complexity of the identities inside me. I can still hear her telling me that identity is like a spiral, and you are always encountering many identities within yourself, depending on the circumstances and the people you meet in this or that situation; your Druze identity will come up, and your Arab identity will come up, and all the other identities, too. That has proven to be a memorable clarification for me.

MY INTRODUCTION TO THE NAKBA

I had done my undergraduate degree at Ariel College, which was the first time I studied about the Nakba. I went there due to various constraints and didn't really know what the place was. I didn't realize where I was going. I'll tell you about an experience that will speak to identity. I don't think I was a hundred percent connected to my Arab identity, at least not while I studied at Ariel. I lived in our house in the village until I was eighteen, and then went to study. That was my first encounter with Israelis. I didn't know what settlers were, didn't know who these people were at all. They were ambivalent toward me and I've never understood it, nor do I now. It didn't occur to me that it was because I'm an Arab; I didn't conceive of myself as Arab. I thought of myself as Druze and didn't want people to see the Arabness in me. I cultivated this Israeli accent over time, and it was better when I was a student in Ariel because I didn't want anyone to hear any Arabness. It was a secret and I didn't want anyone to see me even as a Mizrahi [Jew]. I didn't even want to get suntanned. I wanted to be seen as some type of Ashkenazi, and I didn't know why. I've never told anyone that, but evidently it was important to me.

I had no notion of an Arab identity and thought of myself as completely Israeli. I got a Zionist education but it wasn't very political. I went to a Druze private school for the sciences. The principal strongly promoted the atmosphere of joining the army; it was a very Israeli atmosphere. At home, it really wasn't like that. We don't talk politics at all, it doesn't interest us, we never fly a flag outside, neither Israel's nor Brazil's [for soccer]. My father hated these things, and we kids never tried that stuff. But certainly there was always something in the educational ambience suggesting that Arabs were something frightening and that they hate us. And that Israelis are better and we have to stay as far away as possible from Arabs. My family didn't have many Arab friends. But it wasn't particularly at home, it was my whole education. Plus the religious education in the Druze heritage suggests that the Arabs betrayed us all the time and killed us a thousand years ago because we left Islam, and that whole narrative. So I'm saying that there's also a Druze narrative that's interesting and should be looked into. It's a distorted narrative.

By the time I started my master's program at Tel Aviv University, I was in a different place; I understood that I wasn't an Arab but also that I wasn't an Israeli, and I didn't know who I was. I wanted to be a researcher, a self-actualizing person who wasn't involved with all of that stuff. I wanted to be a good citizen and become a researcher. I had no awareness of the obstacles that awaited me on that path because of my identity, because of who I am. I thought I was someone who was entitled. Although it was an illusion, being in that situation was fine. If we're talking about the "law of attraction," it leads to a lot of good things because you feel that you're a good person and entitled to have it all. You're not living in any kind of victimhood. Then the course at TAU confronted me with the whole concept of who I was and what my identity was.

When we divided into the uni-national forums, did you have a dilemma?
I don't recall that I had a dilemma, but about a month ago Miyada, one of the participants in the course, recalled that I wanted to go with the Jews. I truly don't remember that. It may have happened but I don't recall having a dilemma about going with the Jews. I wasn't thinking about nationality. I wasn't thinking about Arabs. I went with the people who speak my language. I get together with Maya occasionally and when I last saw her, I asked her to tell me how I was then, what I went through, as she saw me from a distance. She said that mine was a very humane voice saying that there seems to be an inhuman attitude towards one another among the participants, and her impression was that this was important to me. I do remember that someone spoke about the Holocaust and I said: "Why are they [the Arabs] reacting that way? Maybe it's a very difficult personal story." Now I understand better.

That period was quite frustrating, a period of depression. I couldn't focus on much. I couldn't think at all about writing a thesis. I sat around for a year, by the way, because of you folks, because of that course, not doing anything. An entire year, I did nothing. I couldn't concentrate on anything and couldn't think about anything interesting apart from this story. Other than that, I didn't attend university for a year because I was in a world of facilitation. I desperately wanted to get deeper into that. I wanted to move ahead and my university studies didn't interest me very much.

THE EVOLUTION OF IDENTITY

I had come to feel that I had no identity after reading a few books on the history of what the Druze went through in Israel. It was always about how the Druze were treated, because my center is with Israel, with Palestine, from whatever angle you view it. That was always the place I went through to understand myself. So I read about Nabih al-Qasem, for example, the story that he tells in his book about the Druze in Israel, a very significant book for me; and also Rabah (Halabi), and I also read a little about the history of 1948, what happened, where the Druze were then, and it was very important to me to understand that.

Then I realized: "Hey, what is this nonsense, the Druze? I mean, we are Arabs, part of the Palestinians, and yes, maybe our relations weren't the best. Among the Arabs, there were always relations that weren't so great; that's very clear, even self-evident." I always had this question; that's how it all started for me, with this question. But I did not define myself as Palestinian until I met people from the West Bank who called me that. I said to them: "Why are you calling me that, I didn't go through a Nakba?" I asked the question just that way from a guy from Bethlehem. He said, "You don't have to go through a Nakba; that has nothing to do with it. You're part of the history of the people who were here, with Palestinian leaders and Palestinian culture. It doesn't depend on whether you became a victim of the Nakba or not. And secondly, you're still a victim because a lot of things have happened to you [Druze] in the sixty years since the state was founded, right through the present day." So then I really started calling myself Palestinian, but it took time to get friendly with the term.

It was the Neve Shalom course that ignited my interest in identity. There was a segment addressing the relations between Jews and Arabs, and they mentioned the Nakba. My first encounter with the subject of the Nakba was during my BA studies in Ariel with Moshe Levy. After going through the process, you go back and take a look at what happened in your life, when you suffered racism. I hadn't been aware of this at a very basic level. I did suffer from racism more than once. At the university, for example, our lecturer on punishment law—I studied a little criminology—presented some kind of study on crimes by Jews and crimes by Arabs and the percentages attributed to each side. He said: "Why do you think that Arabs are charged with more crimes than Jews?" One of the students sitting next to me said: "Because they are idiots"—right in the middle of the lesson, as if it's totally legitimate. I wasn't thinking of myself at all, I just said to myself:" How dare you talk that way about Arabs." Not thinking of myself. I had cut myself off but I still cared on the level of human morality. Maybe at that stage I had already realized that I am an Arab, so somewhere in there, after Moshe Levy's lecture, I understood that being Israeli isn't me; being Israeli will really never be me. It was acutely frustrating, when I understood from a sociological standpoint that it would never happen.

And another time I had a course at Ariel on the heritage of Israel. You have to do twelve credits in that. One of the courses I took was about Zionist content in Hebrew poetry. I don't connect with it at all and I don't understand any of it. My Hebrew isn't good enough to read literature, but I asked the lecturer whether she could make allowances for me because my mother tongue wasn't Hebrew. She said, "OK, make a note of it on your first paper," and she gave me a grade of 80-something. On the second paper, when I wrote her the same comment at the top, that my mother tongue wasn't Hebrew but Arabic and I'd be glad if she considered that, or something like that, she gave me a 53. The second paper was critiqued much more because it was evaluated by a graduate student in Hebrew literature. That was one area where I felt I suffered from racism. There were others.

It was frustrating and depressing, because I felt that I was, in some sense, giving up my privileged position, but that's also an illusion. As if being Druze gives you some kind of privileged position. It came out in terms of how I introduce myself to people. When I meet an Israeli Jewish woman, will I say I'm Arab or I'm Druze? I felt that if I said I'm Arab, I'd be giving up a certain privilege, because clearly she would like it better if I were Druze. At that time, I was working in a shop in Tel Aviv, and I'm still working there; and people ask me, based on my accent, if I'm French. Something about my accent is subtle, and so they think I'm French. I reply that my mother tongue is Arabic, and then they say, "Oh, an Arab." I remember that before the SFP course, I would have said I was Druze; afterward, I would say I was Arab. From a conceptual standpoint there was also the question, Why be part of a victimized group that suffers from something—but I felt that I had no other option. I'm part of that. I began to understand that we [as Druze] suffer terribly from racism, and also from land confiscations and underfunded budgets. We serve in the army, but afterward people treat Druze veterans just like other Arabs [who don't serve]; there's no difference. We aren't privileged in any way whatever. Maybe only at the airport they are a little nicer to me because I'm Druze, and they don't check me; maybe that's the only privilege we have. Or maybe also on the human level, in the attitudes that people [Jews] have, knowing that Druze are trustworthy and loyal to the state.

Letting go of that imagined privilege was very empowering. I think that the process is linked closely to psychological measures of anxiety and self-confidence and very sensitive things, and I think the process boosted my self-confidence very significantly. If I'd done a check on my self-confidence before and after [the course], I think I [would have found that I] got a very serious boost. And now it's not just a process, but I'm also working as a facilitator.

THE SFP FACILITATORS COURSE

After I finished the Neve Shalom course at the university, I began the SFP facilitators course right away—on your recommendation, of course, because you and Maya said that I have a good grasp of processes, so I said, "OK, that sounds cool, facilitating groups, it's a prestigious vocation and will mean that I continue with the dialogue," because it was really hard for me when the process just stopped. I very much wanted to continue with it, because my story didn't fully have closure. It never does, for someone in the course. So I needed more. I remember that my focus in getting to know people was with people from the West Bank. I started to build ties. Arabs became the majority of my friends and I wanted to proceed with my dialogue and with the process and not have it stop. So I came to the facilitators course.

As the course got underway, I felt suddenly that I was coming there with a lot of experience. I don't know why, but that's how I felt. Apparently the [previous] experience had been significant. I think I expressed myself in the facilitators course as if I were observing from the sidelines. I understand what happens between the groups, because I'd done the work in the intergroup dialogue course, so my voice was more critical than just a participant's voice. But it did challenge me. I think that in that group, I was the Arab participant. I no longer spoke in a Druze voice very meaningfully.

My voice was a Palestinian voice within the encounter group that opposed and persevered and struggled and didn't give up. That's how it feels to me.

In the continuing process of formulating my identity, it wasn't just the course that was significant; it was also getting to know Palestinians. The course wasn't like a university experience, because of the participants. The university participants were very strong. In the facilitators course, it wasn't that way. The statement I made was: "Be stronger, be Palestinians, I'm sick of hearing your voice. I am coming with a strong Palestinian identity and you aren't." Maybe at that point they were already beyond all that, post-nationalist, I don't know what, and I respect that. But for me at that time it was hard because I wanted them to be like me.

You've never mentioned having been angry about the way you had been before; were you not angry?

I wasn't angry about having been educated the way I was, or about this or that knowledge having been concealed from me. I felt that I was on my own, reading, and suffering from the things that I wasn't told about. I didn't know whom to blame, the primary school that I hated or the high school that had educated me in that way, or the Druze educators who had taught me that way. Later I really wanted to know about how it works, this story with minorities, and what we are as a minority for Israel: nothing. There was nothing like that in school.

It's interesting that your anger was directed at school and not at home.

No, because at home there wasn't anything very deep. My parents are always nice to everyone. They never said things like the Arabs have betrayed us on the national level; I never heard that at home. I grew up in a very humane household, I think. My mother was very nice to everyone and will always do good things for everyone. And remember that we grew up in a village; there are no Arabs there who aren't Druze: no Muslims and no Christians. I went to Ariel [at that time it was a college] to study because I wasn't accepted at the universities, and it was also an economic decision. People told me it was in the territories, but I didn't understand much about it. The first time I went there, there was this kind of wire on the road. And on the first day of classes, I heard that there was a terror attack at the entrance to Ariel, and then the penny dropped in terms of where I was, not at that precise moment, it took me maybe a year to look at a map and to see and understand. To pick apart this very Israeli conception that Ariel and all the settlements are part of Israel. You don't understand where you are. I don't know exactly how I thought back then. I think my brain maybe could not comprehend that all around there were Arabs who were worse enemies than the Arabs in Israel. I didn't know exactly what that was. Then I understood that Nablus was very close by. And I remembered during the Intifada how we would see this on television all the time, but it hadn't really gotten into my head. It took years until that happened for me. So actually I really only understood it after the whole process was done.

In the middle of this process, I had to go back to Ariel because I had to get out of a flat in Tel Aviv and I didn't know where to go, so I went back to Ariel right in the middle of the whole process. It was really hard. It was December 28th, right near the end of the training. It was really, really hard to go back there, because by then I understood what Nablus was and what Ramallah was and where I was and what a settlement was, and I asked and I clarified things for myself. Miada (one of the Arab women in the group) was very supportive and embracing and she explained a lot of things to me about what the settlements were, and after that I finally grasped all the complexity. If not for that process, I would have remained blind to so many issues and understood nothing.

What really struck me was that all of us had to undergo something like this in order to understand through dialogue, with people that could motivate you politically, and in terms of identity, of course. Otherwise, I wouldn't have done it. It changed my entire life and made me what I am today. I could no longer go on with my illusions, with that dream of being a good Israeli whom the state would embrace and accept as I am, allowing me to advance in life and in my career. Maybe the shift is not all positive, because it brings you down to reality and you stop dreaming. But it can't be helped. It's better to be aware and to know that people's attitude toward you is based on what you are and isn't about your maybe not acting nice when you were talking with someone.

PURSUING DIFFERENT DREAMS

At some point I stopped dreaming about being a good Israeli, and being successful. I stopped dreaming that rosy dream of being accepted at university to work as a researcher. What I dream about has also undergone a transformation, and now it's about social change. I dream about what I want to change; that's a lot more meaningful for me now. It's about my summoning up the energy and motivation, and it means more to me to create the change coming from this place than from some naïve place. I have a lot of dreams, but now they're all about change.

What are you doing to foster social change now?

Well, since the course, and of course thanks also to Neve Shalom and their contacts, I went to Givat Haviva (Kibbutz Artzi Seminar Center) and worked there for a couple of years in their youth encounter program, Mifgashim. They wouldn't have taken me on if I hadn't been through the SFP facilitators training. Looking critically at the facilitators as I'd been trained to do at Neve Shalom, and not just looking at what the group is going through, does a lot more to develop the quality of the facilitation. When I went there, I asked myself how I wanted to implement the things I learned here in terms of facilitation; how to bring the change I underwent into the group and to make change there, too. Undoubtedly there was a setting and a program there, but it was all tinged by what I learned here, what good reflection is, how to talk about it and connect the micro with the macro, and all the foundations of facilitation that we learned here. At first it was hard there with the insecurity that comes with any new workplace you go into, but afterward, of course, I became (if I may say so myself, humbly) an excellent facilitator, and everyone there wanted to facilitate with me and I accomplished meaningful things there.

This past year has been earthshaking for me as I developed this inner dialogue about whether I want to be a nationalist Palestinian or a post-nationalist and stop with all this harsh criticism, not that I'm harshly critical, but deciding to stop being a nationalist. I don't want to be in this place, being a nationalist, it's not healthy for me. It affected the groups. So my boss came and said to me, I understand that you think a certain way, but if you want to work in facilitation, the group will demand that you be Palestinian, look Palestinian, talk like a Palestinian and have a Palestinian identity. You can't be a post-nationalist now, the group has demands, they are undergoing a process. So I understood that a national identity serves something in the process and isn't necessarily important [per se], because maybe my dream for the future is not to be in a place where we have two nationalisms seriously critical of each other but just have normal human rights, where we can just be regular citizens, not Palestinian or Israeli, or whatever. But apparently it serves something needful in the group, and over time I came to understand that. So however much I didn't want to be in that place, it pursued me.

The work I was doing there with teenagers was important even though it was only a two-day workshop. The short time frame is frustrating, but you do see some results, because through the encounter people leave with a tiny crack having opened somewhere. They're young, I don't know, but maybe something small. There were better groups and less good groups. But the groups that were more open to listening, and also Palestinian groups that were strong, this was helpful in getting that crack that we want to see opening.

That's the Jews. What process did the Palestinians undergo?

The first time you are able to make your voice heard in the presence of the Jewish group is terribly significant and empowering, very empowering. This is also thanks to the facilitation, which empowers and supports them [the Palestinians] and makes space for this to happen. Even if what they say isn't entirely correct, you emphasize that it's important that they speak out. Even if the content isn't right, it's about what they are feeling and want to express, and you always have to support them in that until they get to the moment when they can be self-critical as well. With this unpleasant situation looming over them, the Palestinians need a lot of reinforcement to be able to inform the Jews about the injustice they are perpetrating.

And what's this shift you spoke about the Jews undergoing?

It's about opening their eyes and seeing what the Palestinian minority living within Israel is going through. It's about changing the stereotypes they cling to as a support system for all their racism toward the Palestinians. There are many layers to this. It's about understanding their responsibility in this thing, especially when shortly they're going to join the army. What do they want to do, exactly? We don't always accomplish all our goals. What happens there in these small moments is about people's uncertainties and people's frustration. In the unit on "The Conflict and Me," for example, when there is discussion of the Nakba, and the facilitators reflect this back to the group, and they work on it, something happens to them. It saddens me that it's of such short duration.

Meantime, since the facilitators course, I have facilitated here at the SFP, and now I'm also facilitating a group of students at the David Yellin College of Education. Each meeting is four hours. The first part is a lecture; the second part is discussion. This has also increased my confidence as a facilitator. I'm working with Michal Levine, who is wonderful and whose work is excellent, and also with Revital Yanai, our supervisor. I'm much more aware of the quality of my work there than in the youth programs. The work is much more challenging, and you see the results—I'm not sure if you see them more clearly than with the young people, because young people are a lot more transparent. But you feel that you are doing something more serious and you don't have to waste most of your time on the setting.

It is absolutely clear to me that I will be working in this profession. My thesis also deals with this. My adviser is Professor Yechiel (Hilik) Klar. Hilik studies how people conceive of the conflict using a measure called FENCE. We talked about how to develop this research, and I said that relying on one such measure is not enough; it measures how leftist or rightist people are, but there are many other measures, of identity, for example. There was a problem in that he did not see that there are Arabs with a low FENCE score, with a commitment to their narrative that could be low. I told him to check the Druze. I, for example, feel that with the complexity of my identity, I won't have a high FENCE score. So the research was formulated to also investigate identity and the integration between people's [identities], and to look at who you identify with more.

My thesis investigates which variables lead you to a fuller picture of the conflict: variables involving identity, identification with certain groups, and the integration between identities, as well as the FENCE measure. FENCE is commitment to a narrative, like rightist or leftist, but not precisely. It's about someone being able to say, My people are right about everything they say. If someone from my group criticizes my people, that would weaken us. There's a validated questionnaire, and they also look at the Druze, finally, which is a very interesting group to look at now for the first time and see what its attitudes toward the conflict are. We also took the questionnaire to Palestinian colleges like Al Qasemi (in Israel), which is ostensibly not a Zionist institution, to assess how they feel there. I imagine we'll find that people have trouble integrating identities. I see this among the facilitators, by the way. I have a pretty good integration myself, although I didn't complete a questionnaire, but I suppose I've achieved a fairly good balance between all the identities—Israeli, Druze, Arab, and Palestinian.

How do you achieve this balance?

I don't know. I didn't want to become estranged from any of the identities I have inside me. I wanted to give each of them legitimacy. The statement that I always remember is that we are all a product of this reality and it's impossible now to blame ourselves and say this isn't good, or this is bad, what I have within me. No. This is how I was educated. The things I got from Israelis also have a lot of good in them, really; a lot of good. I can't say that the entire Israeli education I received, including at university and in other places, is bad. It's not. I got a lot of good things from it. And even parts of my identity, my behavior, that are Israeli, are not necessarily bad. I see the advantage (of the process I've been though) in how I relate to people, now; I don't look at them by their labels. In a way, this brings me back to the innocent and humane picture I used to have, a long time ago. Through integration (of all your identities), there's a human world that you can see is complex, rather than seeing it simply as a dichotomy. If something is Israeli, that doesn't mean that you have to see it, or see them, as inhuman. Do you get what I mean?

You're containing more complexity within yourself, in fact.

I think so. Maybe at first it was harder because I wanted to disconnect the Israeliness in me and not deal with it, and say, I'm not Israeli, call me a Palestinian. So OK, but eventually I realized that no, there's a balance, I have all of that in me, the plane of identity has many components and it's great. I'm glad. One need not cling to something small. Plus remember that I wasn't educated to be Palestinian. I won't be like a Palestinian who was thoroughly educated in a Palestinian home and has these roots in the most fundamental way. It's there, of course, and I carry it with me everywhere, but that's not exactly the same thing. Nor was Israeliness fully present at home. It was a mixture of everything.

I haven't been active politically. I wasn't connected with anything political; I used to go to demonstrations but it wasn't something I connected very well to. And I wasn't in the army. I saw it as a very violent environment, so I pulled together all the health-related things I could and received an exemption on health grounds; I was really lucky.

GETTING INSIDE THE DISCOURSE

I recommend that everyone, in any society, undergo a process like the one that the SFP course offers. It's not about being Israeli or Palestinian. It brings you into a social discourse and an awareness through that discourse rather than through the media or through books; you are simply inside the discourse.

I very highly recommend this for Druze people especially, because they live in such a closed world that is so hard to get out of. Plus I realized that my being

Druze brought me to a very deep change which I attribute to this identity, and its complexity, and to the facilitation in the course. I really wish everyone would attend a workshop like this.

I would also add that good facilitation is very important; without that, one can too easily miss a lot. I worked in one very bad organization and had difficulty watching what goes on there. Good facilitation is a necessity. A good facilitator can look at a dynamic and articulate what's going on during the process and consider what best serves the two groups involved so as to move the process forward. A good facilitator also understands where he is in the process and what he himself is undergoing in a process parallel to that experienced by the group. He can make sure that both groups are present in the dialogue and participating in an authentic and candid way while he maintains a level of professionalism that places him outside the process enough to allow him a degree of objectivity.

It may be that this peace you made among all the identities also helps you to contain people who are in different places.

Yes, I see this at work when I'm co-facilitating. Working with the co-facilitator approach, you often encounter facilitators who are very angry at everything that is happening. I am not angry because I see that it's a process and I see things that have to be taken apart. My inner peace, as it were, really helps me both to be with the group peacefully and not to be angry at the group. And even when we are angry at ourselves, when you hear Jewish voices you can be angry not at them but about the fact that you are distressed or dealing with something terribly sensitive. The way I experience this, I'm able to contain it, but inwardly I'm asking myself after these years of working in facilitation, whether the time has come to understand that it's a process. After all, you see the changes. You understand that very frequently we manipulate things in order for something to happen there. About the changes, I'm the kind of person who doesn't look at it too much, I just enjoy those moments when there is a change. My approach to facilitation, by the way, is very much in the Bion mode: I tell the group at the end, "Hey, this is yours, you did this, I just brought you here. I'm not totally happy, and not totally sad. I know that I've done my work and now it's up to you."

PART 4

UNIVERSITY TEACHING AND RESEARCH

15 · NORMA MUSIH

Curator, Scholar, and Activist

Norma Musih was born in Buenos Aires, Argentina, and grew up in Israel. She studied Fine Arts at the Bezalel Academy of Arts and Design and completed her M.A. at the Hebrew University in Jerusalem. In 2002 she co-founded the nonprofit organization Zochrot with Eitan Bronstein Aparicio. At Zochrot she held different positions: director of the education department, curator of the gallery, an editorial board member for the journal *Sedek,* and associate director and then executive director of Zochrot. Today Musih lives with her partner and their daughters in the United States, where she is pursuing her Ph.D. at Indiana University. Her research focuses on the intersection between photography and citizenship in Palestine-Israel; her work draws from her curatorial experience and her activist engagement in Zochrot. Norma Musih took the School for Peace Course for Facilitators of Groups in Conflict in 1997 at Wahat al-Salam–Neve Shalom. She was interviewed in November 2007.

I came out of the SFP course with the feeling, which I still have, that if I remain here, I have to work on all kinds of things. If I'm here, then I can't be here without acting. I can't just be here and hide out. If I'm not doing something concrete, then I become even more part of what's happening here.

Thinking back to your experience with intergroup encounter, the main component of which was the facilitators course at Neve Shalom, tell me in what way this has influenced your life.

I was very young, and it was my first serious experience, dealing in such depth with political issues. I was twenty-one. It was exactly ten years ago, right after I finished my army service. It really shook me up and the imprint is still with me today. It was some kind of turning point, a milestone. Something happened to me there. People ask me how I've become the way I am; they find it very hard to understand Jews who work with issues of the Nakba and the [Palestinian] right of return. So Neve Shalom was the turning point.

Before that, I'd had all kinds of intuitions that I hadn't been able to crack open. I did not grow up in this country. I came at the age of fourteen and then lived on a Hashomer Hatzair kibbutz, Zionism at its best, but there were a lot of things I was uncomfortable with that I couldn't articulate. I felt intuitively all kinds of things that I didn't know what to do with, ideas I had no idea how to defend or even to talk about or explain to myself. I remember having trouble the first time I voted in an election, and that was even before the course. The whole kibbutz voted Meretz [a leftist Zionist party], but I knew that I couldn't vote Meretz, and in the end I voted Hadash [the communist party]. Afterward I had all kinds of conversations about it and had to explain my choice and stand behind it, which was hard. Because on the one hand, I had those demographic fears, and on the other hand, that didn't fit with my value system. Later, at the School for Peace, I suddenly found words to articulate a lot of these feelings, and I could explain them and also allow the Zionist parts of me to be expressed. It was coming from both directions.

I remember feeling as though the pennies were dropping for me, so to speak, one after another. Take that whole demographic approach, for example, the demographic threat. I began to understand the terrible things embodied in that, the terrible fear concealed in that. From our side, I of course understood this. I once brought something to the course concerning demography and Ahmad [Ahmad Hijazi, the facilitator] cleared up for me something about the size of the population in Gaza and the crowding there. I remember that it bothered me very much, and I understood something there myself, because I find it threatening, too. I also remember very powerfully this thing about hearing Arabic spoken, because on the one hand I wanted to hear Arabic, and on the other hand I was very afraid to hear Arabic. So first of all, the process allowed me to understand that fear, to call it by its name, and to look at it—and, after that, to stop it. Not right away, but yes, to give it legitimacy, to understand it, to know that it existed. If you can call things by their name, you can express them, explain them, and of course afterward think about them. If you can give them a name then you can understand them.

Why, for example, Zionism? Why did I come here? Why am I staying here? These questions actually somewhat abated, too. I also remember something like this directed at me: I wasn't even born here, so what is my role? The Jews who were born here, "OK [they said], but you have another passport and you could live somewhere else." The truth is that this matter wasn't resolved for me during the course; that began a little later on. In the course itself, I didn't learn exactly why I'm here and what I'm doing here, but I ended with the feeling, which I still have, that if I remain here, I have to work on all kinds of things. If I'm here, then I can't be here without acting. I can't just be here and hide out.

THE QUESTION IS WHAT ROLE I CHOOSE

What drove me was hearing what we are doing, and understanding that we are doing it, and that I'm part of it. If I'm not doing something against it, then I'm even more part of it. In either case I'm still part of it, but the question is what role I choose to play. This question of what to be working on is always changing. Later on, when I was at Bezalel [art school] I felt a huge chasm between my experience at Neve Shalom and being a student at Bezalel. It was simply the complete opposite. I found it very difficult to bridge that gap.

At Bezalel, I found out what happens when you don't act. It was terribly autistic, detached from reality, something that deals totally with itself, with what is going on in New York at the galleries, not what is happening here. From the cafeteria at Bezalel, which faces in the direction of Issawiya, I actually witnessed people's houses being demolished there. You can see the dust it raises. That I am sitting at Bezalel drinking my espresso, talking about conceptual art and seeing the demolitions in real time at Issawiya, this chasm was simply too hard for me. My attempt to do things at Bezalel involving political art did not go well, both because it wasn't fashionable and because I didn't find anyone to work with on it. Then I met Oren, from B'Tselem, who was also in the course at Neve Shalom, and together we tried to establish a group of students to support Issawiya and create some kind of connection between the Bezalel students and Issawiya residents, so that the students could see the home demolitions and the people and feel an obligation. But it didn't work, and what I hoped to create didn't happen in the end.

I don't know why. I seem to remember the residents of the village telling us not to come there and show off. It just didn't work. But by going down there to the village, the path there had already become much easier. I used to go every Sunday. After that I began working in a residence for pregnant women and girls. That was a different direction in my work, not related to the conflict, but there were also Palestinian girls in distress there.

I tried all the time to bring things from one realm to the other. Doing political art at Bezalel didn't work, and going with students to work in Issawiya didn't work either. In the shelter for pregnant young women I saw all kinds of things about the power relations among the residents [the pregnant young women]; not between Israelis and Palestinians. I started to become more aware of these relations also in Israeli society. I remember talking about this in guidance discussions. That tool of analyzing power relations and understanding the social and political context, was always there, to analyze what was happening, to what extent and why. I took that from the facilitators course, and now I can't help but relate to this, between men and women too; it changes and develops. But I think that the first awareness was at Neve Shalom.

POLITICAL CURATING

I taught political curating last year with Ariella Azoulay at the Minshar School of Art. As a final project of the course, we planned with the students an exhibition using photographs dealing with the occupation. In that context I was able to make the connection between art and politics and do things I wasn't able to do at Bezalel. The idea was that the exhibition would combine elements of an approach from the art world that makes any photograph legitimate for an exhibition whether it's an art photograph or a journalist's photograph. The question is, What is done with these photographs?

That was the course. They had to bring photographs to every class session. The idea was to build a kind of photography exhibition. Each student brought photographs and had to explain what he or she saw in them and why they had brought them. Each student chose a question that interested them. Someone took the issue of children in the territories; someone else took the question of soldiers. They each found themselves a niche and asked questions about it. Together, we addressed ourselves to this space, the territories.

Together with the students we thought a lot about the occupied territories. We thought about the spaces in the territories as a fenced-in space, divided up, parceled out: What's going on there? What is happening to us? What is happening to the Palestinians? Who is being portrayed? When? Who is photographing them? Who is looking at whom? What kinds of relations are occurring there? We learned a lot from the photographs.

Talk about your work with Zochrot.
My role at Zochrot is changing. I began with the educational phase at Zochrot. We started with groups of teachers. In the first year, there was one group; in the second year, two; and this year we have three groups of teachers, who learn how to teach about the Nakba in Jewish schools. I'm developing this program and have also been leading the groups. This year we began developing an educational kit. The activities are being written for the teachers, and the pedagogical and theoretical background laid out. The pedagogy covers how and what to teach, while the theoretical background lays down the wider questions that a specific activity is addressing.

There is a lot of resistance to this, but it's also really fun, because you can see the change. You can see the process as it happens. It's a little like what happened to me at Neve Shalom: understanding things we are keeping inside of us; understanding our difficulty in saying the word "Nakba" for example, even though my encounter with the "Nakba" didn't really happen in the course. The course was the beginning, and although it didn't particularly address the events of 1948, my questions were certainly formulated there. I didn't find answers, or maybe I wasn't ready.

Now, with the teachers, I feel the shame that I had also felt myself. This understanding is about the gap we have inside ourselves between what we think about ourselves and what we are doing. If we think of ourselves as open, liberal people, then how are we not prepared or able to talk about or acknowledge the Nakba? How, if history is so important to us, are we so quick to erase the Palestinian history of 1948? If memory is so terribly essential to Israeli society, how can we erase the Palestinian memory? I feel all of these questions strongly again now with the teachers. The moment they start visualizing this gap, the moment they confront it, something very powerful happens.

Last year there were two women in the teacher's group. These women were powerfully transformed and eventually began volunteering with Machsom Watch. They were the salt of the earth of Israeli women. One was married to a pilot, and her children were all pilots, too. During the study unit on the right of return, she began to cry. She said, "I can't. I can't respond to this. She said, "They were right, and I can't say that." I felt how she was being torn apart inside—torn between something she grew up with and was educated in and then taught to children, and the understanding that there is something real here that ought to be, that morally should be, acknowledged. It's amazing to watch that happening. It was very moving.

There are difficult moments all the time, because I have no answers. People confront these gaps between the traditional curriculum and what they are learning in the program, and the dissonance just grows and grows. This often leads to problems with their principals, with other teachers, and even with the students in their classes and with the student's parents. There are many questions I can't adequately respond to. The teachers often say that when you start to talk about the Nakba and about 1948 all kinds of truths are discovered that weren't evident before, there are problems: Either they feel that they're lying to their students now when they don't teach this material, or they feel that they've already lied to their students in the past when they didn't teach it. How are they supposed to deal with this?

My answer to the teachers is that it doesn't have to be all or nothing; they don't suddenly have to change everything they do with their students. They can always pose questions challenging their students to think. One of the teachers, for instance, who is now leading one of the groups in Jerusalem, told about how, a year or two ago, he went with students for a trip to Kibbutz Netiv HaLamed-Heh, and the whole time, while hearing the Zionist story being told to his students, kept wanting to say something and wasn't able to. In the end, after they had toured around the area and seen a lot of sabra cactus [which rural Palestinians traditionally used as fencing to demarcate fields and yards], he asked the students something about the cactus, and in that way he was able to pose some kind of question. Even if it wasn't answered and even if he hadn't told the whole story, from my standpoint it was already a success in that someone was looking at the place and asking a question.

*In these courses that you gave at Zochrot, did you use things that you
learned in that course ten years ago? Did that first course give you tools
and a way to work with them?*

Yes, certainly. I knew nothing about facilitating groups before the facilitation
training I did at Neve Shalom, and subsequently I went on and learned a lot
more. I got more experience at IPCRI when I facilitated groups of teachers
and school principals, and also with students later at Givat Haviva. The facilitation I learned at Neve Shalom, I did not learn anywhere else: how to sit with
a group, how to talk, how to work with them, it's from that course at Neve
Shalom. In terms of content, there are a lot of things I still use, like power relations, as I mentioned, and racism, things that really came from Neve Shalom.
Some things came later in my work in Zochrot. In many senses Zochrot grew
from the School for Peace. It's not a coincidence that Eitan [Bronstein,
Zochrot co-founder] spent a lot of time there, and that I was there taking that
course, as were other people who became the core of Zochrot. Zochrot is a
kind of continuation; the course opened up many questions, and afterward we
had to somehow find the answers that we hadn't found at the time.

My feeling is that, from the moment you first put on these lenses, you
can't really take them off again, and they become part of the way you see. It's
impossible now for me to decide that I won't look critically at things anymore. When you consider the Palestinians as an occupied people, using
these lenses, you see the occupation everywhere.

After October 2000, I was living in Abu Tor [in Jerusalem] when the Intifada started. It was very interesting there. Half the neighborhood is very
wealthy Jews and half is very poor Palestinians. The house I lived in was at
the very end of the Jewish side, in what was formerly Jordanian territory; it
was a kind of lookout spot, a multistory building used by drug dealers because
it was on the border. One tenant living next door was a drug addict, the
woman upstairs was a prostitute, and across the street started the Palestinian street. In the building I was living there were Jews and Palestinians, and
when the attacks began by the border police, I found border policemen load-
ing ammunition cartridges in my yard. I really couldn't stand it. I would call
the police and complain; it was really terrible, but they told me to just stay
inside.

I was constantly seeing border policemen arresting Palestinians, in Jerusalem and the vicinity. I wanted to intervene every time, and a couple of times
I really did intervene. Watching what was happening, it felt like a knife in my

belly. I just couldn't look at it, and I felt like I wasn't doing anything, and I felt guilty, and somehow impotent, which is also hard. One time when I intervened it was also hard to be shouted at by the border policemen. I couldn't tell if the Palestinian they had arrested even understood what it I was trying to do. I moved to Tel Aviv. Maybe that was escapism, but I couldn't watch what was happening in Jerusalem any more.

I DON'T THINK OF MYSELF AS SOMEONE VERY RADICAL

I used to find it hard to say that I supported the [Palestinian] right of return at the beginning, to say it outright, to make that statement out there. But the clearer things became to me, the easier it has become to say it. I am less afraid. Saying everything outright somehow also neutralizes the fear on the other side. They sense that you've said it all and that there's nothing more. You start with the Nakba and end with the right of return, so from the start I've been saying that I support the right of return and there's nothing else coming to be frightened of because it's already been said, and that's liberating.

The last time I went to the United States, I took materials with me. They took me aside at the airport for special treatment. They took my passport and opened my suitcase and called someone and then called somebody else, going one step further each time. It was very humiliating. I thought about how Arabs go through this all the time and realized that my feeling of insult had something racist about it, like: How dare you! I was insulted. They had no problem with that; they actually saw me as some kind of threat. That's hard. I don't remember ever having felt that way before. I don't think of myself as someone very radical; my parents are fairly bourgeois. Knowing that I'm crossing some kind of red line here that puts me on the outside, as if now I no longer belong—that is a difficult feeling. Both personally and with Zochrot, I am stubborn about insisting that I belong, that I'm not going to let you exclude me, I'm part of what is happening here, and Zochrot is part of what is happening in Israeli society. We are not extreme; we are right here in the middle. I want to feel part of Israeli society. It's very easy to say, all right, I'm part of Palestinian society, I also speak Palestinian, there's no difference, but I'm not like a Palestinian, and I'm not saying the things I say from the same place a Palestinian speaks from. I think I have to contend with a lot from the people around me, and in my studies.

CULTURAL CREATIVITY FOR POLITICAL CHANGE

With any political change, a lot has to take place through cultural contexts, and there I really feel that I can do something in spite of the situation, and that it's crucial. A change in the culture could bring political change. I am more able to accomplish things through this medium, and I can relate to it more.

For example, *Sedek* [the journal published by Zochrot; the names means "crack" or "fissure"] deals with cultural issues and the Nakba, which is a very major change here in the field of Israeli culture: speaking about the Nakba in Hebrew, using the Arabic word as part of the Hebrew language, that's already a change.

The third issue of Sedek dealt with the right of return, and in that issue we saw more Arabic in the Hebrew. That's what I want to see happen to Hebrew, that it will also include Arabic, that it will develop, that there will be cracks in it . . . that Arabic will be in Hebrew and also in Israeli culture generally. It's still hard now because Sedek and the gallery at Zochrot are both still in their first stages. I hope to have the time to develop that work more. Thinking about all this through culture should lead to the next project, while expanding our ideas about politics.

Sedek, the journal, deals with the Nakba here and now, with the attempt to write about it and to think about it. What I'm trying to do in the gallery is an integration of thinking and creating. The more thought and cultural creativity there is about this subject, the more tools we will have to think about it. And with more tools, something else will develop; a different language. So we are creating this toolbox for ourselves and for others. It's very challenging. For example, in the gallery at Zochrot I am working on an exhibition that will address what can be seen today in the places that used to be Palestinians villages. The villages were destroyed after 1948, but every destruction leaves traces. And we can train ourselves to see these traces through photographs, for example. This connection between the written and the visual is very important to me. I also think it's very powerful—like that teacher who pointed out the sabra cactus to the students, because otherwise perhaps they, and even he, might not have seen. This link between what is said and what is seen is very strong. I don't believe that a picture is worth a thousand words: you must speak [at least]) a thousand words to understand a picture. Moreover, everyone will have a different thousand words for the same picture. One must simply create the talk about what is seen. What people see and how they see it is what opens new opportunities: seeing, being able to see, and training the eye to see different things. This training is extremely important for us. It allows us the space to see together these photographs of 1948.

These days, I'm studying with Ariella Azoulay and working on my doctorate under her guidance. Working with her has helped me a lot to make this connection between art and politics. I am writing about women "martyrs." I intend to look at them as a cultural phenomenon. To look at the videos they leave behind. In watching their videos, I'm also trying to see them, to listen to them, to listen to what they are saying. At the same time I am looking at works of art that deal with female terrorists: films, literary works, etcetera, in order to understand them together, as part of the same culture.

16 · ROI SILBERBERG

Political Educator

Roi Silberberg describes himself as a political educator. He researches and works in the field of education for peace. In 2006, he completed the SFP group facilitators training course at Neve Shalom, and he has since initiated and worked with educational projects in various settings, including the Peres Center for Peace, the Israel Association for Civil Rights, and Zochrot. In 2009, Zilberberg founded Amal: The Association for the Advancement of Spoken Arabic, which promotes the teaching of Arabic in Jewish schools, and he has published several articles addressing this subject. He completed his doctorate in 2015 on the philosophical problems in peace education. Roi Silberberg took the joint School for Peace university course at Tel Aviv University, "The Jewish-Arab Conflict as Reflected in Theory and Practice," in 2005; the SFP Course for Facilitators of Groups in Conflict in 2006 at Wahat al-Salam–Neve Shalom; and the SFP Change Agents Course for Mental Health Workers in 2008. He was interviewed on December 13, 2011.

The SFP dialogue course taught me about my responsibility and about where I wanted to take responsibility in my society. At a certain point I realized that I was needed. It was a call to action: to do something to address how important it is for people who live here to speak Arabic.

I'll start with the path I followed to get to Neve Shalom and the School for Peace.

I came to this field more or less accidently. I began a course in gender identity with Prof. Ariella Friedman, which turned out to be very powerful and
beneficial for me and helped me to understand a lot of things. The course
was said to be utilizing the School for Peace working model, which incorpo-
rates work with Jews and Palestinians. It was just a casual remark, and I didn't
even ask why this was significant. The next year suddenly I noticed, in the
same course catalog, a course about the Jewish-Arab conflict, and I knew I
wanted to register. I won't say that all the changes I underwent came out of
that course, as if I'd been totally blind beforehand, but afterward I began
taking the study of Arabic more seriously, for example, though I'd been
studying Arabic already.

The dialogue course that you [Nava Sonnenschein] facilitated, by the way,
I experienced as something social to do. I signed up along with some friends,
people I worked with in my biology lab courses. Later I was the only one from
that group who went on with it. I remember telling my Arabic teacher that
maybe she should come along too. In that course, I understood a lot of
things—about my responsibility and about where I wanted to take responsibility in my society. At a certain point I realized that I was needed precisely
because I understand what other people don't understand. This added something new, inside me, and turned me into someone better. That feeling was a
call to action, and it gave me a place and gave me a lot of other things.

FEELING THE CALL

It was a call toward some kind of goal. I thought it was an important goal, to
do something for my society, to ameliorate its blindness, its lack of awareness, the violence, the racism. I definitely felt called to this. My studies are
about continually reformulating for myself what exactly is not OK in this society and to understand exactly what happens when something changes.
Now, in hindsight, I can't recall just how I formulated this awareness at the
time, at age twenty-four, but I had a very strong picture in my head. I realized that I wanted my children to live in a different society, a better society,
closer to the kind of society I seek. Today, I want my children not to blame
me for the society I brought them into. This developed through some sort
of process; I didn't feel the same way six years ago. It's self-defense, somehow. Evidently reality hasn't changed drastically thanks to my efforts, but at

least I want to take a position where I have done what I could to be able to justify myself to my own children.

So I really felt a strong sense of being called to this thing. During the dialogue course, you asked me about taking the facilitators course next. The question came out of nowhere, it seemed, although in my family it's very strong: my mother is an organizational consultant and facilitates a lot of groups and teaches group facilitation. This had never seemed to me like something I wanted to do. I don't think it's about the politics so much; it's more about my changing, at that point, the work I wanted to do in life. I wanted to get into doing more social things, get out of the laboratory and get into other things with people, and have an impact.

It's hard for me to attribute this shift directly to the dialogue course. I was beginning to feel that if I were to write an article about cancer, it could help the world, but that wasn't the influence I wanted to have. To publish an article or lecture to students wasn't what interested me and the work itself was really impossible; even the product wasn't right for me. So, in short, it seemed really silly to go on with it. I kept on with my master's in biochemistry but alongside that I did the dialogue course, and looked for some way out. I seem to be very fortunate, in that the facilitators course gave me another profession. Really: another profession.

My path, what I can do really well, is to learn. I knew that the best entrée for me into this field would be through studying. Being a project director or something like that would be much less helpful for me. I had an opportunity to do a one-year master's in human rights in a program with Arab students, which struck me as the chance of a lifetime. I would be very strong in this subject and would have a lot more opportunities and possibilities. The week after I finished my master's in biology, I started a second master's in human rights.

FROM BIOLOGY TO HUMAN RIGHTS TO SPOKEN ARABIC

Human rights law is developing very intensively. This program was in the law faculty at the University of Malta. The degree itself was interdisciplinary. Most of the people there had a bachelor's degree in humanist studies, or literature, those kinds of things. I felt that I had a profession as a group facilitator that was very relevant to the world of human rights and, as a facilitator, I worked with Arabs. Almost all the students were Arabs. I was very happy to be coming into that situation. I might not even have been accepted otherwise, if I had applied just as a scientist. On the other hand, I realized that group facilitation is very nice but that what was very important to me was education and that I can view group facilitating as part of educating. I underwent a very powerful, personal experience there. I think that the process I had been through here, learning the theoretical side of Jewish-Arab relations, had given me a way into relationships with Palestinians in particular, but also with the Arabs from elsewhere who were there. I have a very good friend, a woman I met there in that program; we're still friends. The whole first month there we spent talking together, late into the night, about the conflict, and crying; dealing with it was very complicated.

When I was done there and came back, I did two things. I signed up for the Change Agents Course for Mental Health Workers at Neve Shalom, and I solidified my own identity as an educator. I became a teacher, a science teacher. I earned a teaching certificate and then very quickly realized that the formal education system is not for me. That was very difficult for me, and also for the school. I've since discovered that most young teachers don't survive their first year in the system. Meanwhile I was in the change agents course, for nearly a year. The issue of language emerged very strongly there. That same year, I was also studying Arabic four or five times a week. I learned Arabic because evidently I had realized, back in Malta, that Arabic is very important. In Malta they offered only literary Arabic. When I came back here, I got into spoken Arabic very intensively. And I brought it very strongly into the change agents group in the course at Neve Shalom. I came to see how important it is for people who live here to speak Arabic.

How did you come to arrive at that understanding?

I think I experienced both positive and negative reinforcement. A lot of people emphasize the negative reinforcement. Arabs like to get angry and shout about how Jews don't know Arabic. I think that the positive reinforcement for me, from people I work with, was very strong: from good friends, and from people with whom I had almost no real communication apart from a few sentences. I have two examples in my head, Rabah and Ranin. When Ranin participated, when she came to the first few meetings of the group, and Rabah was walking around the School for Peace and talking to us in Arabic, when I answered them in Arabic it was amazing how much my responding in

Arabic neutralized something in them. They still weren't able to be pleasant, at least not to me, and I can't generalize about other situations with other people. But though it didn't change their attitude toward me, it did neutralize something in their hostility. Once I had spoken to them in Arabic, they had to summon up something else in order to go on in the same way. This is a very strong example. But with people I have good communication with, people who are friends, whom I love as friends, the reinforcements are verbal.

I'm someone who works a lot with feelings, someone who, when there's no communication, feels it very strongly. When I took on a project that I was offered with the Youth Parliament of the Citizens' Accord Forum, I had to figure out how I might be able to get into a long-term project when it did not include the study of Arabic. Something was missing. I'm really ambivalent about how to deal with this. I'm coming in as a facilitator, but that's not the most important thing that needs doing.

So I studied a lot of Arabic that year and meantime it also came up a lot in the group in the change agents course for mental health professionals. The group undertook to study Arabic—especially Tamar [a participant], who also took responsibility for organizing it. The study group, with six or seven people, wanted a lot of sessions. I think they had at least twenty sessions; that's when I understood the power of this. There can be difficulties but, when I was trying to study Arabic and there wasn't anywhere to do it, I didn't view that as a difficulty. During that phase it seemed only natural to me that I'd be doing whatever was necessary. I would telephone people I thought might be suitable and propose that they study Arabic, maybe start a course. In the end I filled up my calendar. There was no problem and I didn't feel overly burdened by it. I felt simply that if I had a Monday free, I had to find an Arabic lesson.

But when that change agents course group wanted to study, I realized that if Tamar hadn't been supervising it personally, it wouldn't have happened. She said that if there was nowhere to hold a class it didn't matter; they could study at her house. Or if not, they'd find somewhere else. Worst case, they'd invade some house. Without this sort of strength, it doesn't happen. So I understood that there is a really huge need, and I decided to get into this. I didn't know how. Meantime I said that optimally maybe we should set up a nonprofit association for this. It took me two years to get it registered, and along the way something was coming into being, the beginning of a project that would fit right in. The association's bank account was opened just two weeks ago, by the way. Getting these things done here is really, really hard.

THE BIRTH OF AMAL

I decided to call it Amal: the Association for the Advancement of Spoken Arabic. The Change Agents Course for Mental Health Workers ended with a call to activism. We did a small project against the war on Gaza and said maybe we'd do other things. That was all I knew about getting into activism. I hadn't a clue about the world of fundraising, for example; I knew very little about the New Israel Fund and Shatil and so forth. I'm learning now. I did a training program with Shatil for community organizers; the eventual goal was getting to action. I did a course at the British Council called Intercultural Navigators. I took it with a predefined goal of utilizing it to initiate projects. During that whole period I went to seminars abroad to initiate projects for cooperation with overseas partners, through EuroMed.

I met folks who were thinking along the same lines as I was, and we decided we wanted to get into the matter of Arabic. We had a few meetings about how to promote spoken Arabic. I said a school would be a good way. Ismail, a guy in the group, once worked at Perach [the tutoring project for disadvantaged youth], and he still has very good connections there. I told him I'd come to a meeting. They suggested to him that we take four university students, and that's how it started. They said the students would have to work with children. We said, "We can't, we have no groups of children. Our modus operandi is to get into the schools." So again, we went back to Perach and informally, through their connections, people called us from schools. We interviewed the university students and matched each one to a school. We had realized that Arab university students don't know how to teach Arabic. We told them that we knew they didn't know how to teach Arabic, but that it would be OK. Last year, we finished the program with six Arab students working in three schools. In each school there were two students, and at the end of the year they knew how to teach Arabic. Now it's the second year, and it's clear that there are students who know how to teach and students who don't. These are Arab university students studying in various fields, from medicine to literature, and we had one doing African and Ethiopian Studies. They are teaching Arabic in Jewish elementary schools for students from fourth grade to sixth grade.

Our concept is to link what the Perach student wants with what the school wants. We are very flexible with the student as to what he or she will teach the children, and very flexible with the school in terms of the conditions. We aren't willing to leave a school because the hours don't fit or the classes don't fit. Last year we had three schools, and in each school we had fifth and sixth grades, with two classes per grade, which comes to four classes in each school and eleven classes total, with 360 children in all. This year we have more children and more university students. We're up to 390 children.

Working via the formal education system is a kind of trick. It's a factory for children; they have to be there. The classes are large, so we divide them. In big classes, we divide them into three groups of maybe ten children each. Now there's New Horizon. If you manage to get into the New Horizon program, you can really utilize the school system. With New Horizon, there are a lot of small groups and a lot of individual instruction. It's meant to continue until late in the day. The name "Amal" is an acronym in Hebrew that stands for *aravit meduberet lekulam* ("spoken Arabic for everyone").

Can you tell me a few things you learned at Neve Shalom that you are implementing at Amal?

The key point that I always introduce is to talk about political things. We do this in the teacher training at all levels. I brought in that video clip *Nakba Charta* ("Nakba Nonsense") [a video provocation by the far-right Im Tirtzu organization]. Training the Arab university students to be able to teach Arabic in a Jewish elementary school is a two-day program. Some of the students find it shocking at first; they have never heard of Amal, and they don't know how to teach Arabic. I decided that on the second day, for an hour, they would have to raise political issues, including how a class behaves when confronted with your Arab identity in a Jewish school. I said that the best demonstration is to show the Nakba Charta clip. They had a really hard time with that, and my partners have a hard time with it, and the students didn't know how to assimilate all this.

So one thing you've taken from the Neve Shalom model is that the teachers solidify their political awareness so they can do something with it when they work with the children.

I wouldn't presume to claim that much. The thing is to bring up politics. The subject has to be opened. You naturally begin with a discussion and see that their political awareness is not very well developed. You say OK, we'll do empowerment in this realm here, too. But you don't need a sophisticated political awareness in order not to be afraid to say what you think. It's a matter of confidence, on both sides. My Jewish partners also don't want to bring this up because they're afraid.

From the first School for Peace course I took, when I was thinking about my own children all the time, I realized that this thing is always there. I'm always thinking about my children. I often tell the teachers, so how do you want your own children to grow up? And in my first meeting with the principal, I always ask that. "Let's say that now your child is coming to first grade: How do you want him to be?"

That is part of what happened to me in the SFP courses. It was a very profound process for me, and I don't remember all of it. But I do remember a lot of moments with the group. I also felt, during my stint as a formal observer of the group process in that SFP course, that things were happening to me. This was a hot topic in the change agents course I was in. I am sure that this contributed. It gives you confidence to deal with this stuff. There was a personal connection. In Malta, too, I had this, thanks to the group, and later on even more so. People are always wondering what might happen. I saw this working as a facilitator, especially in schools, when you're working with children; there are a few projects doing encounters between children in elementary schools. You'd think an experienced teacher would be much better equipped and trained to handle encounter sessions for young children than a facilitator would, but the teacher's afraid. She has a lot more tools and abilities and a lot more of the emotional preparedness, which cannot be taught, and more experience, but she can't do it. The fact is that no one considers having the teachers do this themselves.

What you're saying is that you took, from the SFP courses, the confidence to do these things. That it's possible to do the impossible?
That the sky won't fall, even if we disagree a little.

At the beginning, you said that the course took away your blindness. What did you mean by that?
I'm not like a lot of Jews who say that they weren't political, or that they don't know about a lot of things. That really wasn't me. I remember that even as a very young child, I would ask questions all the time and I would get answers. And I remember that at my house, they would say, "That's unjust"

or "Things shouldn't be that way." As an older child, I was very political. On the knowledge level, I made sure to know everything there was to know. And before I was conscripted to the army, it was very important to me to clarify all these issues. I also read a lot and had in-depth conversations with friends until very late at night about the army and the army's role and about what is right and what is not right, and we would get more information from the newspaper and we would compare notes. It wasn't on the level of consciously knowing, but on other levels. Awareness is first of all on the emotional level. Plus, as a male who is being groomed for the army on that level, I found that somehow that part is always marginalized. But it's very important. Now there was a much stronger feeling of urgency. Suddenly it seems to me much more important.

I can look back to a point, even before the SFP courses, when my awareness began to change. I was in Germany for four months at a biology lab doing my bachelor's degree. It was the nicest time in my life, and all my life I hadn't known where I would live. I thought I'd learn another language. I wanted to be a world citizen with my future wide open. At some point I realized that I wanted to come back to Israel and I told myself, "Wait a minute: How could that be? How does that fit?" Then I told myself that if I wanted to go back to Israel, if I was giving up this opportunity [in Germany], then evidently I felt that I had deep roots back in Israel; more than likely I'd stay in Israel and spend most of my life there. And then I decided that I would have to deal with the things that are happening here. I can't just be doing universal, cosmopolitan things here. This has not yet taken me away from the sciences, but meantime it has turned me into someone with an obligation to get socially involved. So I started to take all the other courses. For someone who decides that his life is here, that decision may be the most important fact about his life. Not just for me; for anyone: this reality of the two cultures, or more than two cultures, or the multiculturalism, or the multilingual reality, it doesn't matter.

This centers your life around this subject; that's major. Otherwise you might have been sitting in some genetics lab today.

Yes. It's major. I'm always meeting people from that period of my life. They're all doing post-doctoral work abroad. They all came back for Christmas. I'm in a different place, and it's just fine. Well, I can't blame my profession. But beyond the uncertainty and instability, the world I'm in now has a lot of different things in it, work and a livelihood and people and friends.

COMMITMENT AND CONSCIENCE

This choice also created commitment. I have the feeling that I have understood a lot about where things are heading. I'm someone who really likes to think ahead and predict where things are going. Not only have I thought about how my children might judge me when that day comes, but I've realized that the day is not far off; it's a day we can think about concretely, and there will be a process. We'll get there gradually, eventually, to a situation when the value of things will be seen. The price we are paying today will be seen: let's say, the price for the army and for participating in wars. I think that the day will come when I will be very, very sorry that I served in the army, even more than I am sorry now about it. So I refuse to do it anymore. I didn't refuse with any kind of formal letter. I refused in conversations. They said, "What will we do with you?"; they said, "The army has conscience committees." So I was interviewed to be permitted to go before a conscience committee of the army, and I passed that interview, and they haven't called me again; it's been a year and a half. Possibly one day they will call me to the conscience committee, or maybe not, but it doesn't matter to me. I've already had my say. Meanwhile, I've written it down for myself. So if I have to, I'll have a letter ready. From my standpoint, I have it covered. I was really stressed about how I'd say these things, but I already have it straight, in my head. It's something I came to understand in the encounter groups, that I anticipate that it [my army service] will be judged as something negative or that it was unfortunate that it happened, and even if they don't say anything bad about you because everyone served, still it will be unfortunate that it happened.

This is a very profound understanding about responsibility. Most people say "I refused, I didn't do that; it was the [national] group, it wasn't me," while you are saying that your group did this but you are still responsible.

Yes, I went quite a distance with this, because I said that when the day for judgment comes, it won't be superficial judgment. Just as I ask my parents:

"Where were you and how did you allow the situation to deteriorate?" I grew up in a certain way because of how you behaved and how you chose to live. I don't say this to cast blame, but rather because I want to understand. At the point when understanding comes, people will want to understand who I was and why I did what I did. It's not just my children, who will love me, and who will want to understand me and to understand themselves, but everyone. I think that people are seeking. . . . I'm working from an ideal that sometimes I oversimplify. I oversimplify to make it purer and more comprehensible.

There is a price to pay, more than one, for the path you have chosen.
The Citizens Accord Forum offered me facilitation work twice a week, facilitating with the Youth Parliament in Jaffa and in Acre. It's a half-time position, and I think I'll take it because it will enable me to stop living at my parents' house and to pay rent. So there is a price I pay, but it's hard for me to lay blame for this because maybe it's part of my character and there are a lot of people working in this field who do pay rent. It doesn't have to be the way I'm doing it. I didn't want to give up my doctorate; I said I had to do my doctorate, too. My thesis topic was the post-modern challenges in peace education. I'm not willing to give that up.

I think the shift I've undergone, and the path I've chosen, are also about the kind of person I am, as well as what happened in the three Neve Shalom groups I was in. I remember that one of the participants in the Palestinian groups afterward also became a facilitator. He was the only one of the Palestinian participants who talked, and at some point there was an incident that was kind of threatening: He said, "We will become the majority and then you will have to be careful, you ought to think about that now," and all kinds of stuff like that. I thought about my children and wondered what would happen to them if they [were] living in "a state of all its citizens" and going to a shared kindergarten; maybe there would be violence done to them because they are Jews: all kinds of things like that. Meanwhile I looked at that thought, wondering where these fears were coming from. What reason do I have to think that, in a state of all its citizens, they'll beat up my daughter at kindergarten because she's mine? Right then and there, I decided to set that thought aside. It was a feeling that I always have with me. It was a very significant moment and I talked about it in the group, but I said it in such a confused way that no one understood.

I think it's about understanding the fear: understanding that the fear is baseless, just as our hope may have been baseless. Right now we're talking about the fear, and the fear is baseless, so then what do you have left to hold onto? What is our reason for thinking they will beat up on us? We are talking now about a state of all its citizens and about the occupation and we are thinking that they'll beat up our child in kindergarten.

The fact that the Arabs talk passionately and firmly, that certainly does something. It makes you think that maybe things will really change. It makes you think that there's power there. Sometimes it's threatening, but even if it's not threatening, it makes you think again.

That's why I said that deconstructing the fear is an additional challenge; I don't know how. But for me it's important because I like making predictions. I said that I'm counting on the fact that one day, my children or my society will judge me differently than is the case now. What allowed me to see a different reality was when the Arabs talked with passion and firmness in the group. As to deconstructing the fear, I don't know what to do.

THE EXISTENTIAL ANXIETIES OF THE OTHER GROUP

In terms of other important formative moments, I was strongly affected when there was an incident where they thought someone [Arab] had intentionally run over [Jewish] people, and so they shot the driver even though it wasn't clear if he'd had a problem driving or done it intentionally as terrorism. Never mind, they shot him. In the group, one of the Arab women talked about how she was afraid to drive on the roads because she was afraid they would shoot her.

The authenticity of that moment made me understand the existential anxieties of the Arabs. Today when I'm working with Arab university students, I understand this very well. There's nothing I can do, but I understand it very well. This is what guides the dialogue. That they are passionate and firm doesn't have to mislead us; their strongest driving energy in every interaction with Jews is their existential anxiety.

Sometimes this can make me feel powerless. I find myself in the meetings, talking, explaining, we're doing something and I'm saying, "I would like you to feel safe to express yourselves but we can try again in the next session." It's pretentious. If I come to a training session and I say I want them to talk candidly about their place in this society, that's pretentious. It happens with Arab friends of mine too, but it's rare. It's that culture clash—because when Jews say something, it has certain subtexts, but for Arabs it has other subtexts. So self-expression involves what the implications are and what this means.

I'm trying to think of an example from the 2006 SFP facilitators course. For a while I was feeling very drawn to Arab women, and since then I've discovered that it's something that a lot of men who get into this field experience. I felt it very strongly during the course. There was a young woman from East Jerusalem in the group. Without our having spoken beforehand about it, she said: "The fact that there's a sexual attraction between us doesn't mean that you don't have to listen to me now." We hadn't talked previously, and this statement really shocked me. That these issues are so important and yet hardly talked about is something I realized in hindsight. But my shock at that moment was about how she was capable of saying something like that. First of all, she felt this: she knew things about me without my having said anything. Secondly, she herself also felt something. Thirdly, I don't know, I couldn't get my mind to think beyond that point; she was challenging me politically. We don't really deal with these things.

That you felt a sexual attraction to an Arab woman went way beyond some kind of obstacle posed by racism.

Yes. For me, yes. There are some guys who have an Orientalist attraction that I don't permit myself. We went ahead in the group and no one responded to this. I understood how central it is in our lives, the issue of an interpersonal attraction (across national boundaries). All kinds of philosophers have taken this in various directions, the eroticism of the conflict. This is an important part of life when you are interacting with other people.

It's part of the deconstruction of the dehumanization that people go through—the ability to simply relate to one another as equal human beings.

The dialogue group in its focus on the conflict between Palestinians and Jews found it very hard to address these gray areas involving situations of blurred identities. An overly close relationship leads to a blurring of identities. This disturbs the established setting, in which it's very difficult to relate to the possibility of hybridization. Just expanding our boundaries is already something.

I'll elaborate a bit here and try to understand what caused what. These days, theorists in the philosophy of education are trying to get past the stage of this pretension in thinking that a certain lesson in class can teach a particular thing: the pretension that anyone is capable of knowing what really happens in a child's head in the classroom. The attempt to track the educational influence, to discover which strands are more influential, is meaningless. An educational experience means that something has happened to you in your life, you've experienced it, and you've accorded it a certain meaning, and there were other people doing that with you. To try to understand what happened there and where it led to, that attempt is legitimate, but what you can get from the attempt is already a different question, i.e., what the conclusions are. I think that the attempt through this interview to see what our experience in School for Peace courses did for us is addressing an important question: It's to understand the significance. When I look back now, first of all I feel a lot of gratitude: I'm deeply grateful to the other people involved, to myself, and to the world out there for having led me, or caused me to be led, to choose this path.

Another thing that looking back does for me is that I understand that often it is hard for me, hard for us, to know why we do things, what hidden factor might be involved, what covert motivation. Often I tell myself that maybe it's my personality or maybe it is these people I talked about, people I met along the way, people I very much admire. Either way, I am reminded to keep looking at how I am living my life.

17 · NADA MATTA

Scholar and Feminist

Nada Matta is a Ph.D. candidate in the sociology department at New York University. Her research interests are political sociology, labor and social movements, class analysis and capitalism, and Palestine studies. Before moving to New York to pursue her Ph.D., Matta was involved in political activism in Palestine/Israel. She is currently writing her dissertation on labor and youth movements in the 2011 Egyptian revolution. She hopes to contribute in her future academic work and political activism to social justice and equality. Nada Matta took "The Jewish Arab Conflict in Theory and Practice," the joint School for Peace–university course at Tel Aviv University, in 2004–2005, and the SFP Course for Facilitators of Groups in Conflict in 2007 at Wahat al-Salam–Neve Shalom. She was interviewed on July 14, 2009.

> *There's something about the School for Peace. . . . You learn these things there and then you begin to act. It's important for people to understand what's going on and understand that it's necessary to do something about it. That's what seems important to me about that whole experience. After being there, I increasingly felt that I wanted to be part of grassroots activism.*

I actually did two Neve Shalom courses. I did the first one at Tel Aviv University in 2004–2005 during my third year as an undergraduate in psychology. I don't remember who told me about it. A few of us signed up, including a friend of mine who was also a psych major. It may have actually been my first such meeting with a Jewish group. I was already fairly politically aware when I got to university, but not very politically active. I'd participate in political activities but passively; I wasn't organizing anything. In any case the course that had the greater impact on me was the subsequent one, the School for Peace facilitators course at Neve Shalom. I remember how significant it was and how much it influenced me. Doubtless the two courses are connected but this is what I remember.

All of the politics concerning these kinds of encounters also come into it, but speaking from a personal standpoint I feel that, if one is talking about empowerment, the entire experience was very empowering for me personally. It was also empowering politically for the Arab participants to deal as a group with the Jews and speak our minds candidly. The School for Peace approach to facilitation is empowering for the Arabs. The assumption is, and it's correct, that there are clear power relations reflected in the group as a whole; speaking candidly and to the point imparts a lot of power. There's a feeling that's connected with our conflict and that whole issue of which group has more justice on its side. The Jews in the group had, insofar as I recall, a difficult experience emotionally because of guilt, something the Arabs don't feel in that context. On the contrary, I felt that we were saying things that the other side did not know. I think the Jews get more new information than we do from this course, because we Arabs already have some contact with Israeli society. But in this course, acquiring information is not the main focus; the main thing is really how to cope with things. That's what is really empowering from both a personal and a group standpoint. In terms of politics, everything we went through there is political education.

It's very hard in retrospect to distinguish one thing from another because, since that time, I've developed a lot politically after coming from a small village where I did not encounter Jews at all and growing up in a household that wasn't very political. And I wasn't politically active in the village. So the School for Peace was important in my political education. I'm trying to think about the transition. There's something about the School for Peace. . . . You learn these things there and then you begin to act. It's important for people to understand what's going on and understand that it's necessary to do something about it. That's what seems important to me about that whole experience. After being there, I increasingly felt that I wanted to be part of grassroots activism.

BECOMING EMPOWERED

That happened, I think, as part of becoming empowered: understanding that power exists. When you reach the point of action, and the people around you are supportive, both the Arab group and the Jewish group, that's very significant. I'm thinking of Zochrot, for instance, which emerged from there. All the work with that kind of very progressive Jewish group is significant.

You spoke of realizing that the Arab group's speaking out there has power in it, that there is power in the influence they bring to bear. Can you be more specific?

You feel this power to influence the Jews because it does have an impact in terms of the ability to create change. The Arabs' experience of changing is more about empowerment and less about learning new things. For the Jews, it seems to me that it's very meaningful to learn new things they didn't know before or now feel differently about. Making that kind of change happen is very empowering. But there's also a feeling of doing things together and that also empowers the Arabs, because it's hard to deal with these things alone. It's important that there are Jewish partners in the political activity, and that's a product of the encounter. Most of the Jewish participants in the encounter, more so than among the Arab participants, are political activists.

My home wasn't political in the sense that they weren't political activists. It wasn't that we didn't discuss politics or didn't care about politics; the family cared, but they were not party members. Although my parents vote and talk politics like everyone else, they aren't involved. They were also stressed somewhat by my political activism. Their generation is a little different in terms of their attitude toward the Jews and the State. Like many Arab parents, before I went to university, they told me not to get involved in politics. It didn't help, but they tried.

I'd like to understand this process of empowerment in more depth. You say that you came from a home that didn't push you in that direction much, but you mentioned two things about your experience in these courses: One, the ability to speak out and say what you wanted to, and secondly, that there were people there who were ready to be influenced.

Well, nothing much would have come out of it if the people we met there had been less accepting, had shared less, had not become afterward real friends and comrades for action—it would have been something else. So it's very meaningful that there was change evident on the other side. One arrives initially with a lot of doubts about what the Jews are or are not prepared to do. Accepting is one thing, but then came a different phase: moving on to action, becoming active in the struggle together—that's something different, something else.

Was I surprised, in some sense, by that? I don't remember what I was feeling at the outset, but as you get to know the people, there are surprises sometimes, yes. When I think about some of the people and consider their background, a very militarized background, and things like that—I'm thinking of a couple of the Jewish guys in particular—where they got to [in the course] was significant and I really respect them for it. After all, they belong to the majority. The majority doesn't have to do anything. It can live just fine without doing anything. It really is very different from our situation.

Why did I come back to do a second course? Well, I remember that I didn't talk that much at the university course. And you urged me to come, and my friend Ulla was coming, and then Rabah interviewed me and insisted that I come to the facilitators course. I was curious, and I enjoyed facilitating. And as I've said, the experience for the Arab group was positive overall, and especially in terms of that feeling of empowerment. The uni-national forum also was very interesting and gave us a lot of strength. So it was Ulla's coming along with me, and your encouragement, and also I was simply attracted to it— that's my recollection.

You haven't talked about identity.
Is this empowerment part of formulating one's identity?
I would call it political awareness more than identity. I remember that at school, and at home, too, I knew that I was Palestinian, so that wasn't new to me, but the feeling that there was more to it—yes, that was significant. To understand that you are part of a group gives you a better understanding of what identity and belonging are. I knew I was Palestinian, but in a more theoretical way; without really feeling it. In the village, you don't have that feeling of a Palestinian identity. It got stronger at university, and in the group, too. There are other people with you, it's a shared experience and specifically from a political standpoint with the Jews.

THE OBLIGATION TO ACT

I'm trying to think back to what may have changed, in terms of identity. Really the feeling of translating it into action, that's what you feel (in the course), that you belong and you want to do something, you have a moral obligation—and this has stayed with me. I feel that I can't leave it. In New York now, I'm active. I organize things that I initiated. At first it wasn't about Palestinians; then this year, I organized things about Palestinians. It's part of the obligation, morally as well—that feeling of concern about what's happening in the territories and all that.

This wasn't from a young age, as I said: I felt that I belonged and like a lot of other Arabs I felt a solidarity with the Palestinians in the territories. But the feeling of obligation became more and more a part of my life. It's on my mind all the time. And I'm increasingly taking an interest globally; it's beyond the national. I have become more and more leftist now, in general, in the global sense of a moral obligation toward all the struggles taking place, not just the Palestinian. There's a lot out there. It came up a bit at first in Tel Aviv when I became very interested in social power relations overall, between workers and employers and all kinds of relations of exploitation that are not necessarily national, they're international, and they exist here too. This has an increasing share of my interest. I see Palestine as part of that whole story of American imperialism.

Awareness—that is, real empowerment—to be aware and want to learn more, that's where it leads. And I'm in a place now in New York where I'm very exposed to left thinking in general, and I'm very drawn to it. It interests me greatly right now. For instance, I want to do a doctorate, and I might do it on Egypt, maybe on the relation between the state and workers or on Egyptian politics. The work on Egypt is also related somehow to Israel. American imperialism in the Middle East is inseparable from Egypt and Israel. Dictatorships in the Arab world are as bad as Israel. And they have a similar impact on the national Palestinian struggle.

So this is an obligation to the oppressed everywhere?

Yes, although I won't say that the emotional impact on me is the same as with Palestine. I was in New York and didn't get here for Christmas. I had a terrible month. I was having nightmares about what was happening in Gaza.

I cried, and it was hard because I was also alone. Emotionally, what Palestine does to me Venezuela doesn't do, but I care and hope that the socialist experiment in Venezuela succeeds. I follow what's happening and it interests me. I get up in the morning in New York and read *Pal Today* and I read the Palestinian newspapers; so, it's different. My interest is very global and I stay informed globally; I think it's all connected. They are not separate struggles; the one here is undoubtedly more national in nature. Some people on the left think that the conflict in Israel Palestine is a class struggle. But I don't think that's very precise. The struggle here is more a national one and less a class struggle. The Palestinians are in a very difficult situation, it seems to me, and it's even more difficult than South Africa. It is worse because Palestinians are excluded from Israel, they have no leverage, no structural leverage to bring to bear as South Africans did. The Africans were able to pressure the regime because the regime was dependent on them. For Israelis, Palestinians are simply redundant, peripheral, because they aren't important and again they have no power, and of course the armed struggle is not between parties of equal power; it won't succeed, it will simply fail. If the Israelis needed Arabs as workers, it would be different; Palestinians would have had more power.

AFTER THE FACILITATORS COURSE

Afterward I worked at Neve Shalom, first as a facilitator and then as a coordinator of youth encounter groups. I was responsible, together with a Jewish coordinator, for organizing which schools would be participating. I made arrangements with a school and did preparatory work with the children, the teacher, and the principal, and later on they would come to the School for Peace [for the encounter workshop]. At that point I was facilitating, not with the young people but with the facilitators, and writing a report on the workshop afterward. During the workshop itself, I provided support to the facilitators in dealing with the problems that the children had. It was a significant learning experience for me. Facilitation is group work, and I learned a lot about the national and the political, but also in terms of interpersonal relations and group work. It was significant for my own learning to be working with such experienced facilitators. That work specifically was very challenging—the coordination and working with a Jewish coordinator and organizing things together.

The relations in the Jewish and Arab groups are not easy. There's also an interpersonal dimension. I had to be the Arab coordinator and be responsible for the national aspect for the Arabs. There are expectations of the Arab facilitators, that you will respect the lines, preserve Arab nationality, and support the needs of the Arabs. I had these expectations of myself, and so did the Arab facilitators doing the workshops. Plus there was the connection with the Jewish coordinator, and you're facilitating for everyone, which is very different than when someone is facilitating you. There's an overall responsibility that complicates things in terms of the connection. And there are the Arab facilitators; they have their needs, and sometimes there are things I don't agree with, let's say things that were said, or opposition that was expressed, not greatly to my taste. So it's hard when you're in that place where you have first of all to accept and also to offer criticism, delicately.

I remember once regarding the subject of women, which is a very sensitive subject with the Jews. By the way I don't much like to get into that, because the Jews love to latch onto it as a weak spot (of the Arab group). On the other hand, things must be addressed candidly. I remember on one occasion, something about the hijab, I think. Taking a position that is farther removed from Arab culture is not easy, and some issues are more sensitive than others. Today I find all this much easier, and politically I find it easier to make distinctions. I have no problem being very critical of Arab society, for example; I was critical in those days, too, but now I'm even more critical about things that don't seem right to me. The encounter with the Jews makes it a little harder; talking about these things is easier in the uni-national forum. That's the kind of thing I found challenging.

Or take the whole thing about language, for instance: there were facilitators who insisted on not speaking a single word in Hebrew. There were long-time facilitators who didn't want to speak Hebrew. So OK, there were times when it didn't sit well with me because I felt we'd already gone beyond that. And if someone feels that it's not appropriate to work with Jews and I can totally understand it, then you don't have to, without coming to Neve Shalom and acting out about it. But as coordinator, it's not possible; I have to accept it and work with it. It's not the same as being someone in the group who can simply say, that doesn't sit well with me. So that's the sort of thing I recall having found challenging.

That's the clash between nationalism and feminism.

These things are difficult in front of the Jews in the encounter, because I know how they exploit this to accumulate power. And it really is a weak spot in Arab society.

Again, these days I find such conflicts easier to deal with. There's a political maturation. And also things are clearer to me now in terms of where I stand about them. I'm very secular; I have no connection to religion. But I don't like people who disrespect religion. A lot of the religious people are also poor. And sometimes Arab liberals can be disrespectful and elitist when it comes to religion. On the other hand, I am very clear on what status religion should have in society. For example, the state, and the laws, and all social rights should be based on civil law and not religion. Religion should remain in the private sphere.

You mean, not to use the issue in a manipulative way.

Yes, and not to be elitist, as in, I know what's good and what's not. There are social causes for the kind of religiosity we have in our society.

Could this have to do with your identity being in a more open, more aware place?

Yes. At university I work with a radical supervisor and I am part of a radical group of students. It is also related to my feminism. Unfortunately, feminists in academia are more involved in gender studies. I don't connect too well with American feminism in general or to gender studies specifically. What does it have to do with me? Feminism has been taken to a place where it's not the feminism I want it to be.

I understand feminism first of all as political and against all oppression. It can't be feminism to want equality with men but not care about the occupation or exploitation. I don't get that. The picture is a bit complicated when one needs to prioritize struggles. Given where Palestine is, I don't think that we ought to concede the feminist struggle now at all, and that's my problem with the Islamic movement or Fateh. Sometimes, yes, priorities are made: When people are being killed on a daily basis, it's impossible to think about what's being done to women. But I don't think that we should give up and give total priority to the national struggle; not at all.

SIKKUY, RESEARCH, ACTIVISM

At a certain stage I did not want to work in facilitating any longer because all the political talk along with the facilitation was emotionally exhausting. Moreover, things had begun to repeat themselves and I felt that I had gotten everything I could from that realm, and I also wanted to move to Haifa. So I went to work for Sikkuy, in the north.

I also have something to say about facilitation in general, about all of these projects. I have a problem with them today. Even back then, I began to critically think about this work. A lot of money is spent on these kinds of workshops. I always distinguished between what Neve Shalom is doing and what they're doing elsewhere. There is a lot of money invested in encounters and, given how they are typically conducted elsewhere, I felt that all the international money spent on encounters could be going to more important things. I sort of rethought the whole thing. Not every place is Neve Shalom, where the group became a leftist hub where Jews and Arabs can come and learn from one another and afterward become activists. To me, that's the strength of the place, along with the contact with Palestinians in the West Bank. I think about all these other projects and the many organizations doing them—this is not about normalization or Israelification or any of that—and I wonder what the real utility is and why so much money flows to it. It's a question that needs to be asked. Why is there so much money coming to this and not to other things? If these projects were a serious threat to the status quo, they would not have gotten that much international support. But at the time that I stopped facilitating, it was because I felt that I had gotten tired; the work wasn't easy, and it takes a lot of your energy personally. Facilitation isn't easy. So I went to work at something completely different at Sikkuy. I worked there for a year, writing reports on discrimination in budget allocations between Arab and Jewish localities.

The transition from Neve Shalom to working with other Jewish-Arab organizations later on was hard, including from the standpoint of the Jewish colleagues in some other places. Certainly my experience at Neve Shalom helped a lot. Once at another organization, I was working on a report with a senior Jewish woman colleague. When she changed some of what I'd written, my reaction wasn't typical of who I thought I was. I am still uncomfortable remembering that it took me a while to ask her to restore the things I had chosen to say, in the words I had chosen. There was some kind of deep and ongoing inner process involved.

I worked hard at Neve Shalom all the time, going to schools. . . . At Sikkuy, when I was working half-time, I got some rest and enjoyed being in Haifa. Then, after Sikkuy, I began thinking again (not for the first time) about continuing to study, and I wanted to study in New York. I don't know why; I had always wanted to study in New York, because I love big cities. I thought it would be the best place for me. I tried to set that up a couple of times but wasn't able to, and then I was accepted for a Fulbright fellowship and went to San Diego and then I transferred to New York.

My application was to study about Israelis, the Israeli left actually. I was in England first for a year. Before I came to Neve Shalom to be a coordinator and after I finished my B.A. in Tel Aviv, I went to the University of London and did a master's degree in Communication, Culture and Society in the department of sociology. My thesis was about the post-Zionist discourse in the journal *Critical Theory* (*Teoria VeBikoret*). I was critical of the post-modern discourse dominating post-Zionism and the Israeli left. I then started doing my Ph.D. on the Israeli left under the supervision of Nur Masalha in England. I started doing it from Palestine because I had no money. I started developing a topic about the Israeli left. What potential does the Israeli left have; what doesn't it have? I began formulating the idea.

I chose that subject because I thought that if the Israeli left were to develop and be a real left, I don't mean [that of the] Meretz [Party], it could really create change.

So you had some kind of hope for a change like that?

I don't know if it was hope; I thought the left was too small. Maybe Zochrot and what they were doing had something to do with this, for me. I was critical, and I also found hope in these little places, Anarchists against the Wall and all that, but it was so small that I realized that it's impossible to research it, it's not big enough to be meaningful. Sadly, as a social phenomenon it's not very significant. After that, from talking to people and thinking about doing a project like that, I understood that it was important, but if they are marginal, and they really are marginal, there's no reason to invest so much effort; if it were part of a broader project, then, yes.

But in general, I've distanced myself now from the idea of doing a research project about Palestine. I'm very emotionally involved with that subject and I thought it might be preferable for me to do my doctorate on something a little more remote; and also because of the change I mentioned earlier in my political thinking. I'm more interested now in studying the Middle East, the relations between the United States and the Middle East and Egypt, for example. International relations, and what happens in Egypt, are no less important than what happens within Israel and Palestine. The Palestinian problem has always been connected to the Arab world and is still inseparable from the broader picture.

I don't know yet where I will end up. I'm always saying how much I love Haifa and want to live there. I'm always saying I'll be back. People are always telling me to think about what's going to happen, when I'm studying and investing so much, because with my political views, my options to work afterward in Israel at an Israeli university will be very limited. Even for left-wing Jews, there already isn't much room in Israel. So I don't know what will happen. In principle, I want to come back; it's about my personal life and my political life, and what I love here, not about my career. I don't feel very attached to New York. I feel more comfortable living in Haifa, and it is more fun to be in an Arab environment, but I don't know what will happen.

What about things you've organized in New York?

There's a group of young people I've worked with at NYU since my first year there. We run a Radical Film and Lecture Series program; we invite students and screen films. We try to attract B.A. students, and we show films that have a radical take on political and social problems from all over the world. We also do events on Palestine. We invite speakers. On Gaza, for example, I organized something very big and 150 people attended, which is quite major compared with what we usually do. There were two speakers talking about Gaza and its significance. We're also organizing a lot of events about the economic crisis. We do a lot of really interesting events. I don't have a lot of time and political activism is taking a lot of my time. But this year we set up something called the Palestinian Solidarity Coalition. The initiative came from undergraduate students. This coalition did a lot of activities and made a lot of noise. Even Ynet wrote about it, about what was happening at NYU. We held a demonstration against the assault on Gaza and NYU is a very Zionist place. There were counterdemonstrations and there was some action; it was right around Israel's Independence Day. We demonstrated, and they demonstrated against us, and all of Washington Square was watching.

The political activism, the research, the educational work, they are all connected. I don't find meaning in other things. There are two interconnected aspects to this work: personally I find satisfaction in it, and politically this is what interests me. I am morally committed, but it's also part of what interests me. I want to do it, and I think it ought to be done. I have the ability to do it and the privilege to do it. There are people who can't engage politically, not because they don't want to, but because they don't have time, whereas I can afford this. So for that reason, too, I feel that I have to do it.

Certainly, I also get things from it. I'm not learning about Palestine through the activism at NYU, but I [do] learn how to organize for Palestine in an American context. The assault on Gaza made it impossible to remain silent. It was on my mind all the time. And I felt that people were looking at me, that I had to be there; there are expectations of me as a Palestinian. The problem sometimes in activism around Palestine is that the American left takes ultra-left positions. For example, at one of the demonstrations we did, I said in the flyer, "End the Occupation." They didn't like that and wanted me to say: "One-State Solution, End Apartheid." So if you say "End the Occupation" you're considered not radical; it's sort of naïve. In New York, in my opinion, "End the Occupation" is something very important. People first have to understand that there is an occupation and that it has to be ended before we can talk about one state or two states. The political debate on Palestine is dominated by the one state–two state debate, and it did not make sense to me. Americans did not have to take a position on this. In the West, they should be fighting to end the occupation. If we get that far, we'll already be in a good place. But I learn a lot from the other activism I do. I'm learning about the whole world, and that gives me a different perspective on things. I'm moving away a little from a more rigid nationalism; I have a hard time with it. There's something about nationalism I don't like: rightist, aggressive, not progressive. I don't like that very much. I'm nationalist only because there's a specific national struggle. If I weren't a Palestinian, I wouldn't be a nationalist.

Is there anything else, now as you look back, that you want to add that relates to your experience at the School for Peace and what you did afterward?

I'm thinking about connections with Jews. If I had not been at Neve Shalom, I don't think I would have had connections with Jews, because I had cut my ties with the Jews I knew at university. My connections with Jews now are very important; otherwise I'd be completely cut off from Israeli society. And the only connections are the ones from Neve Shalom that have remained; they are important to me personally, but from the standpoint of what this picture says about where the country is now, where the people are, it's frightening. In the assault on Gaza, I was very depressed, seeing what Israelis were saying. I followed it on Ynet and *Haaretz*. I was really depressed by the racism, pure and simple. Places like Zochrot and Neve Shalom are important; they help maintain a little sanity.

It's a scrap of something to hold on to.

Yes. In human terms, it helps to feel that things aren't lost entirely.

18 · SARAB ABU-RABIA-QUEDER

Sociologist and Activist

Sarab Abu-Rabia-Queder is a senior lecturer at Ben-Gurion University Institute for Desert Research and a feminist activist in Bedouin women's organizations in the Negev. Her field of study focuses on the sociology of gender and education, identity, and work among the Palestinian minority in Israel. She has published three books, the latest (which she co-edited) titled, *Naqab Bedouin and Colonialism: New Perspectives* (2015). Abu-Rabia-Queder took the School for Peace Course for university students at Ben-Gurion University in 1996, and in 1997 she participated in a Jewish-Palestinian student delegation to Germany. She took the SFP Course for Facilitators of Groups in Conflict in 1999–2000 at Wahat al-Salam–Neve Shalom. Sarab Abu-Rabia-Queder was interviewed on December 3, 2009.

You don't have to be in a nonprofit organization to create social change. There are a lot of nonprofits out there but not a lot of studies [of social change among the Bedouin] and no women doing them. Among Negev Bedouin women, I am the first Ph.D. and the first to be hired as a faculty researcher. So I'm exploiting this mandate in order to expose things. That's a form of social change. First you expose taboos, and then you challenge them.

The Neve Shalom course seemed appropriate for me because it was a very special opportunity to meet with Jews and talk about myself as an Arab woman. I wanted to tell my story, as a Muslim Arab woman who grew up in

Beersheba, who attended first a Bedouin school and then a Jewish high school. I thought the course would offer a good platform to share these things and articulate them for the other side, and then it also changed a lot of things for me about my conception of the other.

I studied in a Jewish high school beginning in the ninth grade, and I was there during the first Intifada when there were suicide bombings. I remember, in 1988 and 1989, I'd sit in the schoolyard at recess and people would sit down in front of me and say, "There was a suicide bombing. What do you think about that?" They were giving me a loyalty test. It really bothered me that I had to prove myself, prove my loyalty, prove what I was thinking. Sometimes they also wanted me to explain the other side and why they commit bombings. Where is that coming from? And you still weren't OK. Being the only Arab student in a Jewish school was very hard. I can't say that I suffered discrimination in my life because I don't see myself as someone who suffered discrimination personally, but as part of a minority living in Beersheba I see it. I do see it. I see that I did suffer discrimination: There is no Arab school and I had to attend a Jewish school. Now I have children, and we have the bilingual kindergarten, which is the only place I could send my children, both to learn the language and to get to know the other.

So the SFP course was a platform where I could come and give voice to the pain that I couldn't express during high school; maybe I'd be able to do that in a group of "peers" (I say it in quotation marks) with both Jewish and Arab students. Then suddenly you discover that the Arab group is not homogeneous, but actually very heterogeneous, and there are different voices. I recall that there were radical voices on both sides and also some in the middle but, relatively speaking, as a group it was rather radical. When someone risked expressing a moderate voice, they weren't excluded but were rebuked. In these group encounters, people are initially swayed by the group and can get carried away, but the extremism gradually loses its edge. Then the individual voices begin to be heard, and cracks appear.

A UNIQUE VOICE

I was in the middle; not one of the radicals. Afterward we traveled to Germany and talked about the Holocaust. To see those scenes was very painful for me, as a human being. I remember saying: We are all human beings and we have to understand one another. I connected there, not politically, but from a human place of pain. Some of my Arab friends and colleagues laughed at me.

In the discussions later, we did ask at one point whether the Jews learned anything from the Holocaust about their attitude toward the Arabs. The question evoked a huge storm. Because what does that mean, that we are all human beings? No. They are Jews and they did what they did to us and we have to see the victims of the Holocaust as those who are hurting us today. I was somewhere in the middle, seeing both sides, because I had experienced being on both sides. In my Arab primary school I was an alien, because I lived in the city and I did not look like a Bedouin. Some people even thought of me as Christian and said so. Then, in the Jewish high school, I was an alien again because I was an Arab. I was always an alien, and I'm accustomed to speaking in this exceptional voice and getting rebuked for it. It's an exceptional voice in Palestinian society, too, but it's a voice that is also new to the Jews in Israeli society.

It's good when you speak out among Jews who don't know Arabs and who think all Arabs are terrorists and primitive and all that. Suddenly they see that Arabs are intelligent people who can speak, who have an agenda, who can even argue intelligently. That accomplishes something positive; you change the perception of the Arab that we see in the media. People may be astounded but that's fine, because it also creates a type of friendly social connection you didn't think would occur. I've always had connections with Jewish friends; growing up, the group I hung out with was mostly Jews, because I lived in that kind of environment. Only at university did I connect more with Arabs and with Arab society, and then as a married adult with children. But the experience of my adolescence was an Israeli experience, so I wasn't conscious of the discrimination I ought to have been, so to speak, conscious of. I did not come to the course as someone feeling discriminated against or lacking or unequal. What I wanted there was to speak out about people refraining from looking at me as an Arab woman who isn't normal. Speaking out that way on the Arab side, what does that do? It was very hard. Their attitude is: "Where do you come off saying such things? Who are you to say people should be seeing them as human beings?" That was very hard.

You were able to make your voice heard as a Bedouin woman speaking to the other Arabs in the group.

The truth is that I don't remember any more if the emphasis was on being a Muslim Arab woman or a Bedouin. I think the Bedouin thing came up more with Amal [Amal Elsana Alh'jooj] because she was from a village, whereas less so with me because I didn't live in a village and I wasn't living the Bedouin life. So for me, that didn't arise.

I think that, ultimately, you aren't empowered unless you experience a crisis. How was I able to be empowered? By crises I went through, and heaven knows I went through a lot of crises in life. Walid and I were the only two Arabs in the group who had attended Jewish high schools and knew about what it's like to be alien, what it's like to be exceptional in the dominant [Jewish] group's setting. People see you as different, and it's that way every day. It's not like being unable to find a job; that's a different kind of discrimination. It's not ordinary discrimination as in, "We won't accept you." They accepted me, and I am an Arab woman, and they accepted me at a Jewish school. But I was alien, and I was exceptional, and sometimes they also called me derogatory names: little black Arab girl, dirty Arab. I had stories like that, but the educational setting in general embraced me and defended me, and punished the people who called me names. It was a very leftist and understanding environment. That's empowering because you learn to make your different voice heard even in an environment that is very dominant [Jewish], and gradually you learn that it's toughening you up for adult life afterward. When we were married, we went to live in an apartment building where all the other tenants were very religious Jews. We were Bedouins living in the sixteenth-floor penthouse, its first owners. The next day they wrote in the elevator, "Beware, Hamas is here." So we laughed, because I was already used to that sort of response. Or someone would say to me, "But you don't look like an Arab." You know those getting-acquainted processes in the group where they go around the circle and get to know each other; in real life you encounter the same thing. So you don't get excited by it. I already know what to expect from these people. It doesn't hurt anymore and we don't get upset the way we used to, once upon a time. So in a certain sense, it's empowering.

Your encounter with the other Arabs in the group—how did that affect you?

I saw that there are other voices, even within my own society. Moreover the mainstream Arab experience here is to be discriminated against, to live in a village; that's the discrimination we are accustomed to, living in an unrecognized village with no infrastructure, or an Arab or Bedouin village that has no educational system or employment and [the] father would be unemployed. But I came from a family that was very well educated and financially comfortable, not the wealthiest, but both parents worked and I didn't lack for anything as a child. It's hard to come off as the Arab who's discriminated against. It's as if you have to work hard to show that you are in fact a victim and do encounter discrimination. The Arab group, the minority to which I belong, did not see that in me; they saw me as alien because I don't have the normative characteristics of discrimination and victimhood. I don't have that. No one did me any favors to enable me to go on to university. I had no problem studying, I had no language issues, I did it all myself because I have a very supportive home. These conditions are not all that normal. So it was as if I had to prove that I am discriminated against, to prove that I'm a victim. Suddenly you see this. As if to be accepted into your own group, you have to be discriminated against and if you aren't, then you aren't part of the group.

Did this reinforce your sense of belonging as a Palestinian?

I always had that sense of belonging because we come from a very strong family. That I did not live under difficult circumstances doesn't mean that I don't belong—as if saying I'm a victim makes me Palestinian. There is no axiom like that. What's axiomatic is that the Jews decided that they want to see us that way, and unfortunately some of Bedouin society, men and women both, have adopted this image of being the victim in order to be accepted by Jewish society. You may be an authentic leader, but you can't be an authentic leader if you're not that poor Arab. No! I can be authentic even if I'm not the poor Arab. On the contrary, I can lead from a place of strength; I'm not running away from that place.

The part that came later, when some of us went on a delegation to Germany, was the biggest shock, the strongest aspect of the encounter. The group sessions at the university were not my first such experience with Jewish society. I had already had more difficult encounters, and in the course it also had a virtual aspect because, after all, there were people observing it. And it's not the most authentic because we are swept along by the group voice rather than being moved by the individual voice. I think that the real stories, and the growing closer, come later—in the individual conversations in the corridor. By the way, I'm not saying that these groups cause only radicalization; on the contrary, they often bring people closer.

In Germany it was very group-oriented; you really wanted to make your group's voice heard, because there we encountered the Holocaust, which colored the sessions with the group voice—the national voice, the national voice of the Jews and the Palestinians, of the victim—and we had to prove that we are also a victim, and it was a group effort. There's no space there for the individual voice or narrative. It was a place for the dominant group narrative because of the meeting with the Germans. This reinforced the nationalism and being part of Palestinian-ness. For me it also brought into sharper focus things I wasn't particularly aware of, such as when you want to talk about being a Palestinian woman, you want to talk about your own special experiences as a Palestinian. My unique voice actually did find a place there. It cast light on the added aspect of discrimination because I studied in a Jewish school as a disadvantaged minority, and that voice was apparent, that power, whereas it didn't have much space here in Israel in the sessions at the university. Maybe that's because the entire meeting here is with the dominant Jew, whereas there the meeting was with the Jew as victim. Every story of the victim served to reinforce our victimhood as Palestinians, as opposed to the victimhood of Jews in the Holocaust, something very difficult to compete with. As Arabs, we did connect with each other very powerfully there; we did unite. For me the experience was very empowering because I had never had that connection with the Arab group. We were walking along and suddenly we were singing in Arabic on the streets of Germany. I was empowered as a Palestinian who suddenly is not being seen as alien. Suddenly they were seeing me as part of the "Us," all of us together.

BREAKING THROUGH BARRIERS

I was finishing my undergraduate degree when I did the course with the group here at the university, and I was finishing my master's program two years later when we were in Germany. Then I came back and got very connected. The Arab group stayed friends after we came back, and I also had a good friend in the Jewish group until eventually we drifted apart and went our separate ways. Then there was the whole story of my struggle over my choice of a husband. I finished my master's degree and started my doctorate. But my work changed direction during that period; I started my volunteer work with non-profits. I was the first coordinator of the Association for Bedouin Women's Education in the Negev. I was one of the association's founders and I established the first group of young women. I launched volunteering in Bedouin society.

You termed it a change in direction, but doesn't it also seem to you to be a continuation?

I'm not sure that I'd connect that later work to the course; I don't know that what I began doing after my master's was coming from my experience with the group. I volunteered with the association, and I was very, very active in enlisting young women to continue studying after high school. I was active in opening the first college preparatory program for Bedouin women here. I initiated all that activity with civil society and volunteer activism in the community. We set up the Negev Bedouin Women's Forum—I and Amal [Amal Elsana Alh'jooj] and a few other women—and I was the coordinator for two years. I was very, very, very strongly active in the community with grassroots women's organizations. We held conferences, training workshops, group forums, seminars. We were running north and south to meetings with women's groups. On Saturdays we were heading out at five in the morning. There was a lot of energy and a lot of activity alongside my studies. I was also exercising and I had a lot on my mind, and then I met my husband toward the end of my studies. When I began my doctorate, I began doing less with the community activism and got more into the academic aspect.

A TABOO MARRIAGE

The story of how I met my husband Hassan is that it was forbidden. I didn't know that this was a taboo marriage. I came from a tribe that is considered "authentic" and he came from a tribe that is considered "not authentic." Such a marriage is outside the tribal boundaries permitted me. I was living in Beersheba and suddenly, boom! My Bedouin identity falls apart right in front of me. It's not an economic matter. It's about Bedouin history, about who came to the Negev first, who owned the land, and who was landless. He's a wonderful guy; I met him through community activism and a month later we decided that we wanted to marry. I told him that he had to speak with my father, so he talked with my father and then the struggle started. My father didn't know how to deal with it. Hassan came and went for nine months, talking with my father, just to get his permission. There were battles at home, and my father didn't know how to come to terms with it because he knew that such a marriage was problematical. There had been cases of young women receiving a contract, with their father's permission, but when the tribe heard of it, they compelled the couples to divorce. My father didn't want me to go through all that trauma. So we thought about what to do. He agreed but we kept it secret. We said we'd do the marriage itself in secret and they'd only find out afterward. Of course there is no such thing as secrecy, and the whole thing exploded on us, and we fought for two years to persuade my uncles and the family and the tribe, and in the end we married, thankfully with everyone's blessing.

All of that spurred me to write my doctoral thesis on this subject of what happens to educated Bedouin women once they've completed their studies. Education is certainly advancement, but does it actually allow them to control their own lives in terms of choosing their partners? After that everything was much easier. So that's what I did, and it was a major struggle.

How I'd link all of that to the group [at the SFP course], I don't really know. Maybe if you interview me in another five years, I'll be able to look again and tell you that yes, it's connected. But the power of struggling to make a different voice heard, that's something that has been with me a long time. Even when I needed to attend a Jewish high school, it was a battle. I had to recruit one of my uncles and my mother to foment a revolution at home in order to get anywhere with that. That, of course, paved the way for my younger sisters. But my whole life was full of struggles like that, which is why I say that struggle is normal. I've always had that, but the Palestinian-ness got stronger in those encounters in Germany. At the Jewish high school we always learned about the Holocaust, but we never studied the Palestinian narrative. I think the encounters here at the School for Peace gave me an opportunity to say that. At a Jewish school you've living with it. You aren't all that aware that you have to speak up and say, Teach me about my own narrative. You are there to study and get a diploma, some kind of certificate for a good life or something like that. At home they taught me that education is what brings advancement. If you want to get ahead, you have to study; there's no middle ground. So I always looked at the Jewish high school as a type of springboard for my self-actualization. I came for the matriculation certificate, because in the Beersheba area I had nowhere else to get one: I couldn't have studied in Tel Sheva because the level of education there is very low. The Jewish high school was my only option. My father's only condition for agreeing was that I would not attend parties or go on school trips; for two years, not to behave as the Jewish girls did. So I was always a minority.

Something about making your voice heard goes with
you to other places, too.

The awareness I developed in three very intensive group settings over a period of months—the group at university, then the facilitators course and then the encounters in Germany—that awareness is always with me; always. It's always with me because it opened my eyes. Because I had always lived in the Israeli mainstream, and knew nothing of such encounters, when I found myself a participant in those groups, everything came into sharper focus— in Germany, too. And the effect has been permanent. When you sit down in such groups, or even just in your departmental meetings, and you see how people relate to Zionism, for example, or how they relate to Arabs, you have this awareness, it's there, in everything.

Here's a good example: they put an Arab woman in the prime minister's office, and you realize—that's how they shut us up. This same woman calls me and says she wants to do a one-day training workshop for pioneering Bedouin women. I ask what the purpose is, and is there funding? She tells me, no. I ask why she wants me. She says she spoke with a few Bedouin women about the date. There wasn't any content; she isn't describing any. She is bringing a Jewish lecturer to speak about leadership and propose ways of getting ahead based on the life story of a successful Arab woman from the north. As though there aren't enough success stories from the Negev, or as though there aren't enough Arab women lecturers from the Negev, she wants to help us advance via Jews and Arabs from the north. I explain to her that perhaps she should plan this together with us, to see what we'd like to do with the day. She tells me that I sound hostile to her. She is certainly hearing hostility, and she wants me to apologize for having said that she ought to involve us in the planning. Her approach is totally top-down. When you're sitting in a government ministry, you have the power to come and decide for us; you can decide what the content of a program will be. So I asked her: "Why don't you involve us and treat me as an equal? I'm prepared to absent myself from the seminar because of this attitude, and if it goes on this way, I'm prepared to write a letter to the Office for the Advancement of the Status of Women in the prime minister's office about this attitude, about how they relate to us. So I won't be there."—So, yes, that's part of the awareness that is certainly with me; it's always there. You notice how people are relating to you, or to others. And you hand this on to your children.

BILINGUAL INITIATIVE

I have three children, two of them already speaking, and the third an infant six months old. As Arabs in Beersheba, we suffer a lot here from a lack of appropriate educational frameworks. Until I had children, OK, I managed. I attended an Arab school through the ninth grade and learned reading, writing, and speaking in Arabic, but I am missing a lot of things, like poetry, and a deeper understanding of Arabic literature. But now that I have children and want my children to study these things, but there's no such schooling for them here. The eldest attended a Jewish kindergarten where they continually studied about the Jewish holidays and learned Jewish songs. I kept saying to myself, "Wait a minute, where are the Arabs? What about my religion? What about our culture? Where is our identity? How will I instill all that in my son?" I live in Beersheba and my life is conducted entirely in Hebrew. At home we speak Arabic, and on weekends at my parents' house or my husband's family's home in a village, there we fit in and they see their identity and all that, but how can I teach them?

I worried about this until finally there was an initiative, in which I participated, to set up a bilingual kindergarten, and now we have a bilingual class. I was among the first people in Beersheba to join the founding group. At first when we approached the Beersheba municipality, they refused to give us this. For thirty years here already very senior people like my father have been trying to get some kind of educational framework for Arab children and the city has refused, but when we came with the idea of Jewish-Arab and bilingual, suddenly they agreed. We have a mosque that's been here a million years that they don't want to give back to us. Today they've made it into a museum because they are afraid of Islamic terrorism. Do you understand? This is how they see these things.

So today, my son is in this new framework. He's encountering Jewish children every day, and you have to see the Jewish children speaking Arabic.

It's not just a matter of language and culture; it's also about children being given the strong self-confidence to speak in their own language. My son, when we go downstairs to play, talks to the Jewish children in Arabic. Do you realize what kind of confidence that is? He feels no lack or inferiority because he's Arab, and my little one, who's four, is the same way. And the Jews meanwhile are learning to connect with Arabs as human beings. The Jewish child isn't looking at Arabs through nationalist or political lenses, but strictly through a human lens. I think that if the day-to-day interactions or the workshops you run at universities can finally teach the Jew and the Arab to look at one another through the lens of humanity without ignoring the discrimination and the pain that each side feels, I think it could lead to cooperation. And I don't say this as a cliché. I say it because I see how my children are living it.

BEDOUIN WOMEN BREAK FREE

For me, my doctorate was the closing of a circle. I wanted to give exposure to Bedouin society, to the pain that educated Bedouin women experience. In the thesis I mainly wanted to tell the love stories and the struggles of Bedouin women; to let that side be heard. There hasn't been much written on it, and I was very interested in the whole struggle of getting this out. Those who had written on the subject previously said that education is a way for women to advance; they get out, they get to a university with values of liberalism and individualism; the university liberates them because suddenly they are free and they think about themselves and become aware and start to do battle, because the university is an empowering space.

Meantime, these researchers were ignoring the pain that goes with exposure to that space. I wanted to reveal the pain and the cry of the Bedouin Arab woman in that space. It was a therapeutic and healing process for me and for other women. There was this encounter with women who talked about their pain. It came out as a book about a year ago under the title *Excluded and Loved*. I feel liberated for having published it. It's also about liberation through my own personal struggle, with all the bad stuff and all the pain it involved for me. I wouldn't wish that situation on any other woman in the world—that suddenly tribal forces are deciding for you whether you are allowed to marry or not, and there's a lot of pain with that. I really wouldn't wish that on anyone, but it was simply a liberation. For the women I interviewed, it was also a type of liberation. We have no legitimate settings where we can tell this story. We can't go anywhere and talk freely about love, about what I call forbidden love in Bedouin society. This encounter with a researcher who has sailed on the same craft as the woman she is interviewing—suddenly they become two women telling each other about their pain, and the opportunity for that encounter is empowering to both of us.

Today I'm a lecturer in the faculty of the Institute for Desert Research at Sde Boker. It's a dream come true but it's a long road, because now the pressure has started. All my research relates to my own individual story and to processes happening in Bedouin society that are not seen in mainstream research. I'm working now on a research proposal about the whole subject of economic development among Bedouin village women: informal economic participation compared with formal economic participation, addressing the things that have to be taken into account in the job market. The aim is to identify things that aren't visible in the job market and make them visible. For example, consider poor women who have no money, ranging from illiterate women to those with a ninth grade education. They have no money. So every month, each of them from her child allowance money pays in 100 shekels; they call this jama'iya [gathering], and they collect in the aggregate, say, 4,000 or 5,000 shekels a month. At a certain point the following year, while continuing to pay in, each of them receives this sum back in one payment. It's a type of economic participation that first of all helps the household. It also challenges the traditional gender role, because suddenly the woman is bringing in money, and it has nothing to do with the men, so she is helping. What do you do with 5,000 shekels? That's a lot of money for a woman in those circumstances. So she buys things for her children; she helps her husband pay down debts. Now there are women who are reaching sums in the tens of thousands of shekels; a woman can use this to buy gold jewelry for herself. So that's one example.

I'm working on another study now with a partner here in the economics department; from my standpoint, this is a continuation of my doctorate. We will look more closely at the connection between education, social opportunity and social mobility in Bedouin society. Has education for Bedouin women who acquired it at various intervals actually had an impact for them in the job market and in various types of employment? I see myself going on with research and I view research as a type of social change. You don't have to be in a nonprofit organization in order to create social change. There are a lot of nonprofits out there but not a lot of studies [of social change among Bedouin] and no women doing them. Among Bedouin women in the Negev, I am the first to receive a doctorate and the first to be hired as an academic faculty researcher. So I'm exploiting this mandate in order to expose things. That's a form of social change. First you expose taboos, and then you challenge them.

I've read a lot of studies in the general areas I'm working on but all the researchers, whether Jewish or Arab, are studying the Palestinian mainstream, which means the Palestinian Arab mainstream in the Galilee, from the center of the country north. There's almost nothing done with the Negev, not just Bedouin. I read recently a study where they did a comprehensive survey but because Bedouin society is nomadic and segregated and has certain cultural characteristics, it was hard for them to gain access. This was very painful for me as a Bedouin woman. Bedouin in the Negev also have their own characteristics. For example, the Central Bureau of Statistics has not one single statistic that addresses the recognized and unrecognized villages in the Negev. What, are we not to be considered a part of the Arab mainstream? We are. The field here still has a lot missing and doesn't adequately address the Bedouin in the Negev. I see myself as a kind of social change agent in this realm.

And in my work as a lecturer, when I give a course, it's very important to me always to connect the issue of the Bedouin, not to detach it from the context. I link it to what is happening in the Middle East. There's a course I teach to students from abroad called marginal education, about the education among minorities in the Middle East, not just Bedouin. I give examples I'm familiar with from daily life, but I'm always comparing them to what is happening in Saudi Arabia and Jordan. A lot of students from abroad, Israelis and non-Israelis, say to me: "Wait a second, as a woman you would not have had the option in an Arab country to get ahead; here, it's a modern state and those are primitive countries." I tell them: "On the contrary, if you look at the statistics for 2009, there is one Bedouin woman doctor in Israel. Go to Jordan and see how many Bedouin women are at university, and how many women are managers, whereas here it's maybe two or three." I do blame the state, because the historical political processes here were delayed. Here [for Arab communities] there was a military regime from 1948 till 1967, and people did not go out to study. So the whole situation regarding higher education is a product of the last thirty years; it's all new. Whereas Palestinians expelled to Arab counties [in 1948] were educated by UNRWA or the countries that absorbed them, here no one was concerned about them, so everything began much later. I want my courses to raise awareness of these things, by raising the issues and addressing the aspects that people know nothing of.

I took the American students on a tour to an unrecognized village to see what a school looks like there. The university and the security office in particular did not want to approve it. It was during the period when Qassam rockets were falling, but only in Sderot, and the war hadn't yet begun. The security department gave me a hard time and I told them it was an unrecognized village, it wasn't Gaza. I asked a colleague familiar with the security department to help me. So he told them, it's next to Moshav Nevatim [a Jewish community] and they said, Ah, next to Moshav Nevatim, OK then, and they approved it. The American students were amazed to see that the running water there is not provided by the state and the electricity is from a generator. Just because there's a school doesn't mean there's electricity.

You are a tireless change agent in the way you live your daily life.

I don't know if I can connect this to those courses I took. The awareness, yes, it was made much more acute in the aftermath of that series of encounters. What is awareness? It's something you already had but suddenly it jumps to the fore. And when it does, you take it to all kinds of places, but it will always be there in your head. You take it with you, it's always there. Sometimes when I am sitting in meetings and I see how people are relating to Arabs . . . once I would have jumped up immediately and created a provocation, but I've learned to be more moderate and let time do its work.

19 · MARAM MASARWI

Sociologist, Educator,
Dean of Faculty, and Feminist

Maram Masarwi is currently the dean of the Faculty of Education at Al Qasemi College of Education in Israel and a lecturer in the faculty of Education at the David Yellin College. Masarwi earned her Ph.D. in the Department of Social Work at the Hebrew University; her dissertation was titled, "Gender Differences in Bereavement and Trauma among Palestinian Parents Who Lost Their Children in the al-Aqsa Intifada." Masarwi also holds an M.A. in education from Lesley University–Cambridge and a B.A. in occupational therapy from Hebrew University. She is a twenty-one-year resident of Neve Shalom–Wahat Al-Salam (Oasis of Peace), a binational intentional community of Jews and Palestinian Arabs of Israeli citizenship engaged in educational work for peace, equality, and understanding between the two peoples. Masarwi is the author of the book *Politireligization of Bereavement in Palestinian Society: Gender, Religion and Nationality* (Hebrew, 2016; English, 2019). Maram Masarwi took a Neve Shalom Encounter workshop for young people as a high school student and later took the School for Peace Course for Facilitators of Groups in Conflict in 1993 at Wahat al-Salam–Neve Shalom. She was interviewed in June 2014.

One of the most important and meaningful things in the SFP course for facilitating groups in conflict is that it gives you tools for your whole life.... As soon as you begin this process, it's as though you're beginning to see past your blindness. Then no one can tell you not to see, because you are already seeing. And you also find that you are dealing with yourself through the way you are dealing with the other. I think that facilitating groups has been not only about making a living, but also has offered something that renewed my spirit, shall we say, each time, and let it grow. I'd even say that it often allowed me to stretch the boundaries of my spirit.

I did the School for Peace facilitators course just after I came to Neve Shalom. Ahmad and I came to live here in 1992 and I did the course in 1993. It became one of the turning points in my life in terms of awareness; it shaped my consciousness.

When I was fifteen years old, I participated in workshops for young people at the School for Peace, so the facilitators course wasn't my first exposure to Jewish-Arab discourse and the dialogue with the other side was familiar. I had been through it and was fairly experienced at it. But the SFP facilitators course brought my awareness into sharper focus and reshaped it. For the first time I was suddenly exposed to the theoretical awareness that I could connect what happens in the group with the macro, with what goes on outside—connecting the micro and the macro. I think it was also my introduction to the theories of Paolo Freire. We heard about him as a person, we heard his views, and gradually I began thinking in the terms he used, and realizing how all his terminology really speaks to us, talking about our day-to-day lives. That was the beginning of awareness, and of course there was a process involved. There's something about human consciousness: As soon as you begin this process, it's as though you're beginning to see past your blindness. Then no one can tell you not to see, because you are already seeing.

BEYOND A COMFORTABLE BLINDNESS

I think that all of us frequently find it more comfortable not to see things. As psychological self-defense, it's part of human nature to push things aside rather than contend with them or understand them, especially when you're in the place of—I don't like to use these terms today—the victim and the person who is causing the suffering. These days, on the one hand, I think that reality is a somewhat complicated. On the other hand, there's also the truth; there are several truths, but there's still one truth. So then I think that somehow it would be very comfortable not to see things because, as soon as you don't see them, you can't take responsibility—not for yourself, not for the place where you are, not for your life, not for your conduct in that life.

Although it was a long time ago, can you remember various points in the process you underwent during the facilitators course that offered a way out of that blindness?

Rather than specific points, I'd say it was about the process. The entire course was a kind of turning point in my life. And let's not forget that it caught me at a specific time in my life.

I was twenty-three and had just gotten pregnant and was beginning my life here [as a member of the Neve Shalom community]. I was transitioning from being a young woman to being a mother; from Maram the student living in Jerusalem to Maram the resident of Neve Shalom–Wahat al Salam. So there were some very critical moments in my life at that period, and the course was part of a profound and lengthy process. And it also exposed me to relationships with people I'm still in contact with today. One of my best friends was in that facilitators course. There was Orly, and Daisy, and Amnon. . . . Yaeli and I haven't kept in touch that much recently but for some years, we did.

So relationships, and opening your eyes, and what else?

And tools. I mean, I think that one of the most important and meaningful things in the course on facilitating groups in conflict is that it gives you tools for your whole life. It's amazing, this ability to read a group's dynamics; to understand how a group conducts itself, the conduct of the people in the group, how groups can interact with one another, how your behavior can vary from one group to another and from one period of time to another. It was an amazing tool to acquire. I have continued working with it; I still carry it around with me in my portfolio of tools, my tool kit, so to speak.

I've made use of this tool kit in educational settings, mainly, and also in gender contexts when I have worked with women and with students; it's been very, very helpful. When I started working, not so much in doing therapy but more when I started facilitating with students of education: Suddenly I would go into a lecture and I'd see that there was some kind of dynamic within the group, in the classroom. [I used these tools] in dealing with that, in how I related to each young woman and young man in the group, and in relating to the group itself. This has consistently lent added value to my teaching and in the way I work with people generally. In my lectures, it wasn't like when the lecturer comes in, talks, distributes material, and leaves. OK, that's my role as a lecturer, I come and I teach, but there wasn't anything very meaningful in that. When you can see the dynamic of the group of people, the students, it's different. You have something to add there. Moreover this happens all over again, every time I teach. I'm not supposed to be teaching facilitation in teaching, or facilitation with students, but often I can give them tips that they can use later, in living their lives. It's something that's remembered forever. So very often I tell them, Come let's think about a class as a group; let's think about the different characters in a classroom and about the behavior of the students in the class. There's the leader and the clown; there's the victim, or the group's philosopher. And suddenly I see how my students' eyes are opened, because they themselves first of all begin to understand this better. They understand the dynamic in which they find themselves in my class and they can also understand more about the dynamics they may encounter in the future.

Now this doesn't turn them into facilitators; it really doesn't. But it's another alternative reading, I'd call it, that really adds something. It adds to your overall ability as an educator to understand the dynamic you are looking at; your ability to deal with the characters you face; your ability to manage, sometimes, this dynamic. So I think that these tools that the course gave me are very, very significant, both to analyze the group's dynamic, and also to be able to reflect on certain processes that are occurring within the group; to conceptualize this reflection, to articulate it, to convey it to others. I think it's an art, a permanent skill that you continue to develop over time.

I must add that, subsequently, I did two additional facilitation courses that were very different, each with a different focus, and that I learned a lot from them. Yet if I had to point to a very serious turning point in my professional and personal life, it would be the SFP course, undoubtedly.

I also catch myself quoting from it, both in my own studies in facilitation and in my work in general. It's a source, a bible that you go back to all the time. Nostalgia comes into it, too. It's not just the knowledge it gave me. For me, at least, there was something about the SFP course that evoked nostalgia for something that, over time, becomes very valuable. The real value is in the emotional experience we bring with us to certain things. The emotional experience I took away with me from the facilitators course is a very interesting one, something almost "holy"—in the sense of an experience that had a tremendous influence in shaping something foundational.

THE ABILITY TO BE SELF-CRITICAL

In terms of what changed, emotionally, I'd say the ability to be self-critical, to see my own behavior in the group, the way I deal with the group, my difficulties with the group, my comfort level with the group, how I deal with things within the group. I mean, at the level of my own individual awareness. This is an amazing thing.

And of course an aspect of this change was in Jewish-Arab terms as well. My first such experience was in tenth and eleventh grade in Jewish-Arab encounter workshops. We were part of a long-term project, a whole year of encounters with Jewish youth from kibbutzim. It was on the level of "Oh how lovely, this is nice." On the level of, "OK, we'll have some hummus, cool, everything's great, everything's fine." Suddenly, in the facilitators course, it was challenging on several levels and in different realms: On the personal level, on the national level in the uni-national forum, and then facing the other.

The thing that was most empowering and interesting and moving and difficult, and sometimes also disheartening and even shattering, was to find that you are dealing with yourself through the way you are dealing with the other. As if you are supposed to relate the other and suddenly you're not exactly relating to the other; you suddenly discover your own weaknesses and your own misery and your own lack of awareness and your own issues. And it's not limited to the individual level, not just about Maram, as if the package altogether involves only one person's human confusion, but rather there's a more collective experience and it's about what belongs to me in this collective baggage, what I've chosen to keep and what I've chosen to throw out.

And in terms of identity?

Yes, I think somewhere there it forced me [to address that]. As an example, even though I was aware that mine is a displaced family, with all the ramifications of that story, of our having been uprooted and our history as a family right through the present time—the facilitators course was the first time I really was forced to face all of that on the emotional level, I think. I had to cope with the anger that suddenly began poking its way out, because until that course, everything was cool, everything was fine with the other side, it was all OK and I had friends here and friends there. In addition, I grew up in a very complicated and involved reality if I take into account that my dad was himself a graduate of a Jewish high school.

My grandfather and grandmother didn't talk much about the past. I remember that my father's two best friends both married Jewish women, one not long after the other. That was the atmosphere in our home while I was growing up. Nechama used to give me supper sometimes and we were in their home and I'd hear his friends, my dad talking with his friends in Hebrew at our house. This was part of our everyday experience in Taibe. I remember Judith, the mother of a childhood friend of mine, lighting Hanukkah candles in the middle of Taibe in the 1970s. It was a weird reality, totally weird. I never felt the connection to the heritage, the roots, in the conventional way, but it was an alternative reality in terms of Jewish-Arab relations within Taibe. Yet my grandparents' silence continued to resonate inside me; I know it's a displaced family. At some stage I was curious, in adolescence, and I investigated my grandparents a little, but it was more comfortable for me just to say, OK, all right, so that happened, and I'm moving on now.

There was something in that course forcing people to deal with this reality and then the anger started poking out and then there were the ramifications of this anger within the group. I remember we were telling a lot of jokes in the uni-national session. We had Mahmoud (an Arab participant) in the course with us and he was really pro-Israel. I thought I'd been corrupted, but there was Mahmoud was on the level of Everything's fine, it's all fine, it's all cool, everything. In the uni-national session we pounced on him and I still remember how angry we were at him, like, How could you say this? How could you say that? Daisy and I still laugh about it, about that experience. So that's one of the things that really and truly had a formative influence.

Were you also angry at your family, and angry at yourself for not knowing?

I don't think I was really able to interpret my anger. I mean, sometimes this was terrible for me, that I didn't know what I was angry about. Often my rational mind said one thing and my emotional world said something else, because sometimes there's no logic in the emotional world. Yes, there was a period when I was very angry at my parents and I rebelled very strongly. There was also a period when I wasn't angry, and I blush to say it today, but there was a time I dismissed my grandparents as weak. Today, not only do I not have that anger; I also have great admiration for them.

I remember once asking my grandfather about hate, about this hate thing, and he said to me, Why hate? What for? Hatred is an enemy that you point at yourself. Why do that? That's what he said, and then I asked him, But what about what they took from you? And he said, OK, everyone takes; you think I'm not angry at the Arabs? And you think I'm not angry about this? And he told me then about the 1936 rebellion and how he ran away from the English to the revolution and then had to run away again. I didn't really understand at the time, I listened, but I was twenty, so what kind of deep insight could I have had about life at that age? Today, I really admire my grandparents.

They were from Sidna Ali. My grandmother was originally from Ijzim, near Haifa, and my grandfather from Sidna Ali [on the coast, near what is today Herzliya]. They have some very hard stories. My grandmother's village was the only one bombed, there and Tantura, it was one of the villages on the seafront. So, yes, there are some very difficult stories.

Sidna Ali was a very sophisticated expulsion. In the Shubaki family there, one night they took away ten men, all from the same family, and stood them in the village square and shot them, and then the whole village packed up to leave. My grandfather stayed behind. There's a dimension to the family stories that there aren't any good guys and bad guys in my family story. That is, we were expelled by Jews and a Jew rescued us. Right from the outset there's an a priori dimension that things were not black and white. A friend of mine and I are always laughing about this. He tells me, My grandmother is a laundress and she's always saying, 'Allah will take the Jews,' but I don't get what that has to do with laundry now, the things that happened then? And he says, It doesn't matter, and we laugh. He often brings this up as if to demonstrate how the conflict sometimes gets into our veins, even into his grandmother's laundry.

I imagine that the influence of Israeli-ness on your identity was not negligible, and then suddenly you were dealing with the more nationalism-oriented parts of yourself that challenged the other side and weren't as pleasant for the other side.

In the Triangle area around Taibe in general, a national consciousness did exist, but it was among a certain group of people, Al Ard ("the Land") movement and what was at that time Rakach (the Communist party). Otherwise awareness at that time was fairly low because the Nakba in most cases was in the Galilee and not in the Triangle, although there were refugees who ended up in the Triangle area. In fact, I come from a displaced family. It was absurd. In Taibe there are two major displaced families, the one we belong to and one other, and that's it. I think that in Tira [the neighboring village], there's only one extended family; only one. There are not that many refugees really in the Triangle area, and that had an influence in shaping our collective identity in the Triangle. In the 1970s and 1980s, especially the earlier part of that period, this kind of awareness didn't have all that much of an impact.

MY TWO PARALLEL TRACKS: ACADEMIA AND GROUP FACILITATION

In the years since I took the facilitators course, I've had two parallel tracks: academia, and group facilitation. I think that facilitating groups was not only about making a living at a certain stage of my life, but also offered something that renewed my spirit, shall we say, each time, and let it grow. I'd even say that it often allowed me to stretch the boundaries of my spirit. Each new experience in facilitation, each new attempt, had some very significant learning for me in it. And again, I'm not using this phrase lightly when I talk about stretching my spirit; it really did that. But it also enabled me to understand reality through other, additional lenses. This was built up in layers, in strata; it's not something that just happens. I always say that the human spirit is so complex, it's layered, like an onion. Every time you think that you have arrived at some kind of insight, you peel away another layer and say, Ooops! Where were you? And then you peel another layer and you say, What? This is one type of experience I got, along with these tools from the facilitators course, tools for facilitation and being able to read a group, and reflective ability, and the ability to look at a dynamic and draw conclusions of one sort or another based on that dynamic.

Understanding the link between the intragroup and the extragroup allowed me first of all to understand different dynamics in our lives, and then gave me a better understanding of, say, the politics of power. What is it to be weak? What is power? What power do the weak have, and what weakness is there in the cards held by someone who thinks he has the power, and what is the dialectic between these? Gradually I learned more and more about that, and understood how much this politics of power has implications for our choices in life and the places where we are in life and our levels of awareness. I also have to say that, at some stage, my gender awareness—which anyway was there when I was quite young, in comparison to, say, my national aware-ness—my gender awareness became more acute. In that realm, too, in the politics of gender, suddenly to see things through these other lenses made a big contribution.

And power relations?

Power relations, of course, made another contribution to my understanding of social processes, sociopolitical processes, or sociopolitical-gender pro-cesses that occur. And I should add that, even more so in recent years, the gender dimension of the conflict has emerged as another layer, another com-ponent in this journey. I have made use of this in facilitation, in my work with my students, in guidance and instruction.

In the last seventeen years, I have worked with students at David Yellin College of Education, at Achva College, and now at Al-Qasemi College of Education. The work is really fascinating and I love it; it is one of the things I'm very attached to. I really love my students; that's how it is. This is always my foundational point of departure and, even more than that, it's an emo-tional state for me.

The students I work with are mostly very young adults. I also teach gradu-ate students but my experience with graduate students is very different than with undergraduates. Generally the undergraduates have just finished high school and may not have made the most correct choice in coming to Al-Qasemi but there they are. It's a default choice for those who weren't accepted to university and had to choose between discontinuing their stud-ies or attending a college. At Al-Qasemi I also see outstanding women stu-dents who easily could have been admitted to a major university but who are at Al-Qasemi College instead due to parental pressure. All kinds of dreams crash that way. Suddenly someone will have forgotten why she wanted to be a photographer, after her dream is shattered because her family tells her there's no way on earth that she is going to be a photojournalist, so she becomes a wedding photographer in their family business while completing her stud-ies. That's the type of thing I address with them all the time. It reaches the stage where you see that these students are not emotionally available for studying; they come and register for the course because it's expected of them. I talk with them a lot and we laugh together.

When my students don't seem emotionally available for studying, in order to make them emotionally available I will often work with them individually. They need to understand who they are and what they are; to ask themselves these questions. Sometimes I come into a classroom of girls and tell them something like, "Today I'm going a little further with this: What are your dreams?" And they all look at me as if I'd arrived here from some other planet: "What do you want from us? What dreams are you talking about?" Because, when something severs us from our dreams, we say, "What are you talking about?" This just reinforces my inclination and determination to work with them. I can offer them processes to go through that prompt the reemergence of these wishes on the individual level, wishes that address their reality, their ambivalence, the difficulties and the challenges. I find myself doing wonderful work because there are women there who are very strongly aware, and who have learned one or two things about life, just a little, and they are more motivated and more conscious. One can do a lot of work with that, but mainly I use it to clarify things with the students. I often see that I am able to counter some of these complexities, clean up the errors and sweep them aside, out of their emotional world—and then the students are more available for studying. So that's one modality where I'm using my tool kit, to understand these students and their situation and to help them. How do I analyze reality? How do I judge it? How do I make things clear to these young women students?

THE AMERICAN MOM IN THE SUPERMARKET

In my work in instruction and guidance, in teaching, I never teach about anything without connecting it to the here and now of our reality, our lives, to sociopolitical or gender processes that we go through. I'll give you an example that happened not long ago and that I've used quite a lot. I'm fond of this series of steps and always use it. Not long ago I went to a supermarket nearby, full of families with children. Someone came in, an American mother with what seemed like a whole tribe of children, maybe eight children. She paused near the checkout at the supermarket entrance. So I say to myself, it'll be interesting to see what she does now with this squad of eight children she's brought with her to the supermarket. I loiter briefly nearby with my cart to hear what she's going to say because it really interested me. So she says to them, in an American accent, she tells the eldest child, "You will be responsible for these two siblings," and she gave him a list and said, "You three will bring the items on this list, I'll bring the rest, and we'll meet next to the cashier in twenty minutes." When I heard this, Nava, I'm telling you, I thought: I can't be hearing this, it's impossible. I saw, I began to see, and my grocery shopping didn't interest me any longer.

I followed the children with the cart and I saw the dynamic among them, I saw what they did. I saw how the eldest boy immediately gave out tasks: You watch your brother and we'll meet back here. I started to analyze these children's skills, everything they have to do so that in twenty minutes they'll all be at the cashier's up front, and it was about *orientation* and *language skills* and *classification* and *discipline* and *cooperation* among themselves. I'm standing there analyzing this in my head and admiring them; I'm observing them and I'm trembling all over and I want to run after their mother and tell her, That's really fabulous, really fabulous how you are raising them. Then I tell myself, this whole thing is amazing, that I can learn from this because I could come into the supermarket, see this, and learn from it. But I didn't make do just with that.

I'm currently teaching a course on group language skills to parents of young children. So I come into the classroom that week and tell them, Listen, I have a story to tell you. I tell them this story and invite them to analyze it together and to think about the kinds of skills these children need at the supermarket. The kinds of things I'm thinking about are, for instance, the ability to look at reality and to analyze it. Metaphorically it's like having a camera attached to my head, a camera I'm always pointing at things, I'm zooming in on all kinds of realities and checking them out, and learning from them, and bringing them for analysis, and they turn into helpful adjuncts to my work with my young women students.

This approach, I think, from what I'm hearing from you, is about the ability to empower them, so that they don't get stuck at the ceiling their parents set for them, and also the ability to connect this to the reality of their lives and to use something Freirean, to use the knowledge that they bring with them. Do you think your choice to go into education was influenced by the facilitators course or is it something you always dreamed of?

What I always dreamed about was academia. I'd go even farther and say something that might make you laugh. In my family, everyone on my mother's

side is a teacher or a school principal; her grandfather was a school principal, her father was a school principal. For three generations my family
are teachers, all my uncles are teachers and two of them are principals. It's
like the Ministry of Education expanded into my family [laughing], and I
swore that never in my life would I be a teacher! I told myself there was just
no way I'd go there. Meantime today I wouldn't trade this profession for any
other. I have worked as a therapist and I loved it, working as an occupational
therapist, but still. I love the realm of education so much and I believe in it. I
think that if we are to have possibility and to have hope in this world, the
only way forward is going to be through how we educate. I don't believe in
bombastic things. I believe in the tremendous power of education to have
an influence, bit by bit, delicately, slowly, on the coming generations, and
this has proven itself; it proves itself completely.

You haven't said anything about your political activity.
Do you want to talk about that? Is it important to you?
It's not a matter of important or unimportant. I can't describe myself as an
activist; I'm really not. I'm really far from being an activist; I am more involved
with the politics of humanity, which I find more interesting.

I can't describe myself as one of those people waving flags at protest
demonstrations and shouting. That's not me; I've chosen other routes. My
political activism is in very human and delicate doses. I'll give you an example. A lot of people have asked me why I translated that poem by Mahmoud
Darwish recently and emailed it to people, when I'm not coming from a literary genre myself, so why did I do that? For me, that was my activism; I
mean, my activism is when I can connect people, when I can open their eyes
to specific points regarding certain things, information, experiences. That's
more my activism, and I love to work in that arena.

BEREAVEMENT AND GENDER

As you know, my doctoral work dealt with the gender differences in the
bereavement and mourning processes of Palestinian parents who lost their
children in the Intifada. And again, as I mentioned to you, we are always going
on journeys, and that was another journey in my life. I went to interview families, fathers and mothers. I examined the differences between fathers and

mothers in their coping with the loss and the bereavement. In addition to addressing gender differences and the different modes of coping as between women and men, and there are differences there, I also found myself dealing with areas that I hadn't intended to investigate because the nature of qualitative research is such that often it gives you gifts along the way that you didn't really intend to receive. And truly I think that this is one of the most amazing things that happened to me, and in hindsight one of the most ironic, but amazing in the sense that it opened up an entire world, a world I think that people are afraid to touch, of bereavement. I remember, for example, one exchange that will be with me forever. When I had just returned from discussing the findings from my doctoral research with my colleagues, and I was driving down from Jerusalem with a friend who had studied with me at the Mandel Institute, he said to me, How is it that you [who subsequently lost her husband and younger son to a car accident] chose this sort of subject? Isn't it strange that somehow only bereaved families, people coming from bereavement themselves, are addressing this subject? Sometimes I even think that maybe, in some sense, I tempted fate concerning bereavement [when I chose my thesis topic]. But, as difficult as I thought it would be for me, I wanted to touch this field. And then one of the unanticipated things that occurred along the way was the connection between our political reality, the conflict, and the gender issue, which suddenly became deeper and more powerful for me and I had very, very authentic and profound insights into this thing.

In the context of these different patterns, the gender division and the connection between nationality, religion, and gender, there is a place where we as women find ourselves in this reality we inhabit, this saga of conflicts. We may be more accustomed to this place, we may sacrifice more, we may be more able to accept it. As a Palestinian woman who isn't exactly from either of the sides, I think I was privileged in that I did not have to make the sacrifice or face the threat of having to send my son to the army or sending him to participate in the struggle and suddenly losing him to the conflict that way.

The understanding dawns suddenly not only that you are a part of this, but also that you are an instrument to provide combatants for this struggle. There is a lot in that, even though I'm already critiquing myself for having said it, because that understanding makes us automatically helpless, it places us among the have-nots, finally. That is where we are, Nava. I look at the whole process of decision making in this world of diplomacy and politics, and I see how many women are suffering from this, and how little they influence this, and how little are they partners to it, and yet they are a part of these processes.

I think the influence women wield has been very minor; I don't want to say that women have zero influence, but they have very little influence. My findings brought this into sharper focus, and suddenly I saw these connections, and on a more profound level, but also on a very critical level. And I was often left with very existential questions on the philosophical level, to which I'm not sure I have answers: questions about the nature of the human spirit. Why do we do this to one another? Why do we do this to ourselves? And sometimes you have answers, I mean, sometimes you have answers for parts of the picture, for bits of the puzzle. One can talk about the politics of power, about economics, about the dynamics of gender, about faith and the sacred. It's always possible to add another dimension, and another, but it still doesn't give a complete and whole picture and there are not always answers.

Is there something else you need to say that we haven't touched on or that you didn't talk about? You're going away for a post-doc now.

Yes, first I must say that because Ahmad [Ahmad Hijazi, Maram's deceased husband] was responsible for the facilitators course for so many years, it left me with a kind of warm corner in my heart for the School for Peace. The other thing I meant to say is that our elder son, Esam, has just embarked on this path; there was this course you just had at the SFP, and another that they are planning here now with Wassim and Yonatan. I went to Esam and told him, "OK, go on, do this, go on, do it." It's very important. I have this deep desire to pass this gift on to him. I wanted to say to him, "You have no idea what a gift this is for life. Go participate in these workshops, go and be part of this, go be part of this dynamic." Because I know that this is going to change a lot for him—a lot about his understanding of reality, about his conception of life, his desire to work at his future career, and his understanding of himself.

PART 5 PIONEERING NEW ORGANIZATIONS

20 · EITAN BRONSTEIN

Political Educator

Eitan Bronstein, who describes himself today as a political educator, was born in Argentina. At the age of five, when he moved with his family
to live at Kibbutz Bachan, he changed his name from Claudio to Eitan. At
eighteen, with no qualms, he enlisted in the Israeli army; today, he notes, he
would not have done so. His two older sons refused to be drafted. For Bronstein, the violence against Palestinians in Israel and the West Bank were his
final crisis over Zionism. In 2001, he founded Zochrot, which works to raise
awareness in Israel of the Nakba and Palestinian refugees' right of return.
He remained with Zochrot (as its director during the first decade) through the
end of 2014. In March 2015 he founded De-Colonizer, a research and art laboratory for social change, which develops materials and methods for challenging the colonialist character of the Israeli regime. Eitan Bronstein took
the School for Peace Course for Facilitators of Groups in Conflict in 1991 at
Wahat al-Salam–Neve Shalom. He was interviewed on December 24, 2008.

> *The most significant outcome of the course for me was this very important
> understanding that I still carry with me, which remains the subject of fairly
> bitter arguments with many of my closest friends, on the left in general and at
> Zochrot specifically, about the extent to which we Jewish Israelis are part-
> ners in this whole Zionist project. That we criticize it and work against it,
> that's of course very important, it's crucial, and it's commendable ... but we
> are still and will always be a part of this. My understanding of this came*

from very emotional places more than from intellectual places. And then I understood that we have to do whatever possible to struggle against these exclusivist components of Zionism.

I heard about the community of Neve Shalom before I heard about the School for Peace there. I visited the village and somehow heard about the course, and signed up. At that point I had already been involved in political education for many years, as a counselor in the Ratz party's youth movement and later with Meretz Youth. The Nahal pre-army groups from Meretz Youth were very political and we dealt with a lot of political situations. I also did political work elsewhere. So the subject of the conflict, of course, wasn't new to me and I wasn't making my first contact with it there at the School for Peace. It wasn't my first time meeting Palestinians, either. But it was my first chance at such an intensive encounter for dialogue with relatively well-educated, interesting people from both sides. A small group with two co-facilitators offered the opportunity for a much more in-depth encounter than I'd had previously.

I think that what I learned most clearly, the most meaningful experience I had in that course was to understand my role, my partnership, as a Jew in this conflict. Let's say for the sake of argument that my politics did not change at all between the start and the end of that course; the course itself had no significant impact on my political opinions. I had other opportunities for that. The most significant outcome was this very important understanding that I still carry with me, which remains the subject of fairly bitter arguments with many of my closest friends, on the left in general and at Zochrot specifically, about the extent to which we are partners in this, we Jewish Israelis, totally partners in this whole project, this Zionist project. That we criticize it and work against it, that's of course very important, it's crucial, and it's commendable . . . and all the other positive things I can mention—but we are still and will always be a part of this. I hope that maybe in another few generations, people will be able to say that they weren't a part of this, which we who are here today cannot say. In the broad philosophical sense I think that the Arabs also have their share in this, but that interests me less and for me it's marginal. Palestinians must draw up their own accounting. When I do mine, I absolutely understand that I am a part of this thing. My understanding of this came from very emotional places more than from intellectual places.

There's one specific experience I recall from the SFP course that was riveting for me. You may remember that I told a story about a dream I had once that there would be no more Arabs here. Between one dialogue and the next, the entire week between those two sessions, I was thinking very intensively about this and dreaming about it, too. I still remember: I dreamed that I was walking in Tel Aviv. I was walking down Ben Zion Boulevard toward the center of town. Walking along, I saw some street cleaners, the ones who have a wheeled trash bin. The cleaners were Arabs. There are no Arab street cleaners now, but back then the street cleaners were Arabs. It was during the first Intifada when there was a fair number of incidents in which Arabs, all kinds of Arabs, whether workers or otherwise, it makes no difference, attacked people, mainly with knives. At the time there were a lot of knife attacks, not bombings. There were attacks by Palestinians on Jews in all kinds of places. At the bus station in Jerusalem there was a terrible attack in which someone managed to murder several people. Arabs could move around here relatively freely; we didn't have all the walls and closures. Although the number of cases wasn't huge, the dimensions were enough to frighten us all, because we Jews are afraid when we see an Arab.

OUR FEAR OF ARABS

I remember that in the dream, I see this man and I'm afraid of him, that is, it immediately occurs to me that he could take out a knife and attack me. The really hard part of this experience for me was that I was afraid of an Arab, but never mind that. I understood that, in principle, I am afraid of every Arab, including my fellow participants in the course. In practice, though, very quickly you exclude the people in the course because you're with them and you aren't afraid because you know them. But I understood right away that they, and all of the Arabs around me, are perceived as potentially wielding a knife, including people who are talking to me now in the room . . . people with whom I'm more or less aligned politically . . . For me this was a very important revelation, clarifying for me that I am in fact a part of this thing. For me, this is about a task we have, certainly since 1948 but maybe even before, since Zionism came into being. . . . There's a very substantial task to be rid of this colonizing component in our personalities and our identity, and it's something I can't be rid of, but I can deal with it, I can assimilate it. I can reinvent myself, I can work toward marking the destroyed villages in Tel Aviv and have it still be Tel Aviv. I write in Hebrew, which is the language of Zionism but not in the way Zionism tells us, that it's a renewal of the language. Mainly it's the invention of a language. Meaning, I am working from the assumption that everything was built here by this project and it's totally colonialist. So this insight really helps to think all the time about how we can challenge this, dismantle it and rebuild it. Not, of course, by erasing everything that's here, and not by destroying and expelling and all of that, not through new oppression—but rather to always be thinking of how we can rid ourselves of the problematic components, or deal with them, and try to bring out other things that are a part of our identities.

During the course, I remember that it was—I don't know, amazing, surprising, a kind of shock. I used to think that we were all on the same side, and that there's another side which is the bad side that one has to struggle against. Although in hindsight, possibly I was more on the side that has to be struggled against, back then. For example, I didn't think then that one should not join the army, and all kinds of other things that I think today. But, crucially, I suddenly realized that my identity has components that a Palestinian does not have. He is of course influenced by them. I am talking about the occupier parts. Maybe he can identify with it, envy me for having this power, but the respective situations are different. I live here as a Jew, I live on a kibbutz, I served in the army, etcetera. Some components of my identity as a Jewish Israeli are very hard. In parts of myself I am an oppressor, I was born to automatically be a soldier, and so on and so forth. That was a surprising experience for me. I didn't anticipate it at all and it was earthshaking.

Do you think that this shapes, or shaped, a lot of things that you did afterwards?

Yes, undoubtedly. I think that my founding of Zochrot was clearly a continuation that followed on from the work at the School for Peace. Even as it recedes in time, I am still talking about the story that way. Zochrot began there with the tours of Canada Park [built in 1967 on the remains of three Palestinian villages, Imwas (Emmaus), Yalu, and Beit Nuba]. We are still working there, and the work will apparently never end. Certainly this idea that we must make a significant change in our identity, as Israelis and as Jews, here, and that the Jewish public must change fundamentally in order to live in this land—that is precisely the part that continues on from the SFP course. This element is so significant that it's fair to say that, to a great extent, it was at the SFP that I got the bang, the shock, the shaking up, and that to some extent at Zochrot I am trying to see the possibilities for remediation, egress, hope. I'm trying to see how a new identity can be built. How do we rebuild it when, again, we don't want to annul it. We cannot annul the occupation-related components of our identity, but we can understand nonetheless that they exist, and see what that implies.

Tel Aviv, from my standpoint, is an occupied place like Ariel or Kedumim. That's how I apprehend it; for me, the occupation begins in 1948. The violent conquest and expulsion at that time was a lot more violent than in 1967, and for me, Tel Aviv is Kedumim in principle, not from the standpoint of an overall resolution to the conflict. In principle, it's the same occupation. Now, what does that mean? I'm in Tel Aviv, and I can go to villages, Palestinian villages, I can look at them, I can do things in the surrounding area. . . . I can think about what it means if refugees were to be in Tel Aviv, or if refugees wanted to return to Tel Aviv, or whether they'd have a right to return to Tel Aviv. These are things that definitely came out of that workshop. It's impossible to begin this process without understanding that we are a part of this thing. And in my opinion, someone who doesn't feel that he's a part of this thing is in a very problematical situation, because he cannot understand this colonialist component in our identity. I think that we have to understand it. I think that, as an occupier, I am here to take some useful step that might create some kind of discussion with the Jewish public. We are the ones who have to change it. There are also people who were not born or raised as Zionists here, who grew up in Matzpen families or the equivalent and who did not serve in the army: such people see this from the outside and, to some extent, they really are outside. I don't think that they are without responsibility; they can't divorce themselves from responsibility. But they see it from the outside, and therefore their ability to make change here is, I think, problematical and limited. Change must come from those of us who grew up within this reality, and I mean Israelis, Jews, "normal" people who were raised here, served in the army, are living here, do not deny that they are a part of this place. People like us are the ones who can take responsibility and try to think about creative ways to challenge these parts of ourselves.

THE EXCLUSIVIST FOUNDATION OF ZIONISM

The second Intifada was a very important breaking point, and its impact on me was influenced a lot by the School for Peace. The second Intifada really shook us up. We were very confused, and it was very painful. I remember that I couldn't go to work. I went to Umm al-Fahm, to demonstrations. There I was, and it was a very difficult and frightening experience. After that Intifada, after it started, after some time went by, I understood that the problem we have here in Israel, with the oppression of the Arabs within Israel, and maybe in the territories too, is not a problem of more equality or less equality; it's not a problem of, Come on, we'll allocate more resources, we'll allow more freedom of movement—that's not the problem. The problem we have here is a lot deeper. It's about how we were born, how this place was born, how it came into existence. And at that point I think I really began to see. I mean, I understood that there's something in the foundation created here that's distorted. Then, after the second Intifada broke out, I increasingly understood that Zionism—the exclusive foundation of Zionism, holding that this place belongs only to us, that the memories are only ours, that the language is only ours, that the land is only ours, etcetera—that this basic place of Zionism is the problem. And then I understood that we have to do whatever possible to struggle against these exclusivist components of Zionism.

As for the army itself, my attitude shifted as my son approached the age when he began the process of preparing to join the army. I had never refused to do military service. In 1982 I was jailed three times for refusing to serve in Lebanon as a reserve soldier. Later, in the first Intifada, I was jailed twice for refusing to serve in the territories during the Intifada. But after that, in the second Intifada, I was a type of soldier [in the reserves]. I visited bereaved families [on behalf of the army]. So I wasn't a real soldier. Thus the issue of serving in the army or not had not been a question for me. I would spend two or three days a year in the Tel Aviv area and Givatayyim visiting bereaved families. But when my son got to that age, the question began to bother me, and then he came to me one day and told me, Look, I'm not going into the army. I was surprised, and it was a kind of revelation too, and I wasn't prepared for it at all. After he began the process of refusing to enlist, I of course supported him strongly and through him I was also getting strength myself. At some point the army asked me to sign a form saying I'd continue on a volunteer basis, because I'd gotten to the age when I could stop going.

They told me that everyone in the unit was a volunteer, with people sixty or sixty-five years old who kept on doing reserve service. I'd become friendly with these people and I found it interesting to encounter people around the question of bereavement. From the families I learned some very fascinating things germane to our subject: about Zionism, and why they had come to the country, and all kinds of interesting stories. But when they asked me to sign for another two years, I realized that it was a little peculiar for me to volunteer while my son was refusing to go. So I just explained it to the commander, she understood, and I was done. They separated me from the reserves. I wasn't really in the situation of refusing outright, of saying, "No, I'm not going to the army any more." I never got to that point, alas.

Your son, in some sense, is carrying on along that road.

Yes. Not only is he carrying on, he's also embarking on his path from a point of departure much more advanced than mine was. When he told me he would refuse conscription, while I was still in the army [reserves], he beat me to it. He suddenly opened up something for me. I wasn't suggesting that he refuse induction; I wasn't yet talking that way. And if he had gone, in the end, to the army, then probably I would have found myself some other text; I would have been describing it differently; I wouldn't have been as certain as I am today that one should really not join the army. So he liberated me, he beat me to it, but he also learned things from me.

I always brought my children with me to demonstrations; he was always there. At a certain point, and I still feel it, both my two older sons started behaving as if, Well, OK, we understand; we're in; but we also have our own place; we're not with you on everything, automatically, we're really not. And at a certain point he really did want to stop coming to demonstrations. In some sense it was a kind of compensation for me; I understood then that a lot of things are so clear as to be taken for granted, even if he didn't always show me this explicitly. The step he took had even more long-term ramifications than I'd expected. We talked about it at the time and his mother and I were both definitely in favor of his not joining the army. I said that I would prefer that he not go but I was still his father, and if he had decided to go I would still have been his father. So for me, suddenly to see him take a step like that, independently, to fight for it—that was intense. I wrote him a letter about it. I explained that this had given me a chance to think retrospectively about myself, about how I saw things, how I understood them, and a little bit about what it's like to be a father in this context. All this business about being part of the occupation also touches very powerfully on questions about how we educate our children. To have children in a place like this, to raise them in a place like this, is very problematical. So for me, it was a type of compensation, a certain validation that at least I had done something well.

Many of the SFP course graduates I've interviewed have said that this subject became the central axis of their lives; is that true for you, too?

Yes, it's true, but it didn't happen immediately. After the course, I did all kinds of things. I spent a year in Brazil. And then at some point I went to work at the School for Peace for a few years, and subsequently this has been what I do. From there, I went on to Zochrot, which is mostly what I've done since then. And from my position today, because I have a lot of connections developed mainly through Zochrot, here and there I might touch on something that's not connected with Zochrot itself, but nearly everything has to do with the conflict. I don't really know how to explain, or justify, my choices.

My studies were, in general, interpretive and critical. But the idea of continuing this work was there. The original research proposal for my doctorate, for example, which I never finished, was to write an interpretation of the construction of the landscape in Israel, in the context of the destruction of the Palestinian villages in 1948. I was already very interested in the Nakba. My academic writing, some of it published and some not, was all in that field. After the outbreak of the second Intifada, I wrote about the murder of Asel Asleh, who was at the School for Peace. That text was published later on. I even visited his parents. And we did a simulation about the Intifada, remember? At the SFP, after the second Intifada began, we were pondering how to do educational work with that, mainly about uni-national seminars for Jews. I looked into everything that was happening and I read a tremendous amount. Adalah, for example, published a very harsh report about those events. I used the material to develop a simulation, a kind of investigation or encounter between different witnesses, different pairings of people involved in the event. All the characters were based on real stories: a young man who was protesting; a soldier whose comrade in the unit had shot someone; a Jewish woman whose car was torched; Shlomo Ben Ami, who was the Minister of Police. The simulation was very interesting and we used it lots of times. Later I also wrote a text for my thesis at university. The one about Asel was published.

You've been involved in the educational aspect of this thing for a good many years, in facilitating groups, coordinating projects, building programs. Would you like to say something about that period?

That's true. At Zochrot we also place a lot of importance on education. Certainly; we deal with that. And if you view it broadly, everything we do is actually a type of education, or reeducation, but we also do education in the more traditional sense of the term. To enable someone to arrive suddenly at a different understanding of the conflict, of the other, involves education, learning, reeducation. The task was to try to endow the experience with all kinds of different forms, mainly for Jews. I can't overemphasize the importance of learning that we, as Jews, have a part in this matter, and therefore the responsibility is also ours.

I love this place, and I'm not yet completely alienated. Many young people are leaving the country. It's quite amazing to me that young activists suddenly decide one fine day just to leave. But there are also people who say, OK, my project has become completely political, I want to change that. Maybe because I also have children, who still have a great many years ahead of them, I have a great commitment to this thing about education. It's very precious to me. I'm working at this all the time, trying to see how a person can learn this place anew. Educational work is a very significant element at Zochrot, too. We ponder how to make the educational work very strongly ethical, and also responsible, systematic, professional. I have no option of going somewhere else. However difficult, I choose to love the place and the people here, and I do what I do from love.

COMING FROM COMPASSION

I often see that Jews respond to the things we do at Zochrot, or to such work in general, mainly with fear or hostility or shock. Sometimes they have very harsh responses and even make threats; at times, their responses are violent— not physically violent, but verbally violent. To that sort of thing, my response mostly tends to be compassion. I think about this all the time. If someone has been raised from birth to understand that this place, in all kinds of ways, belongs only to him, he's grown up within a very ethnocentric experience. Any time someone harms what he thinks of as his side, he can't see anything beyond that. Let's say there's a terrible attack on Gaza. What

Israelis are counting here is how many Qassam rockets fell [on Israel], and whether a school was hit, and are people suffering from shock, or was anyone injured or, as happens in a few cases, killed. Meantime it's as if the other side doesn't even exist. This isn't happening merely because someone is hiding [the facts]; there are reports all the time from Gaza. People are killed there all the time, and the reports talk about "people who participated in the hostilities." This is part of our identity, it's how we're built: not perceiving that this other reality exists. There's some kind of very severe blindness, a very serious obstacle, that doesn't permit us to see the other side at all, because we understood with Zionism right from its inception that we were building something that is only for us, and we were building it ourselves, from nothing.

I would mention two texts here. One will be appearing in the next issue of *Sedek*, the journal published by Zochrot: an analysis by Sharon Rothbard of the "Tower and Stockade" phenomenon. Think about this, about this image of the kibbutzim founded via the tower and stockade. Every single kibbutz, right up to the present time, is a closed place. I lived from birth within a closed kibbutz. There are armed guards at night. What is that? The whole experience is of growing up within an armed camp. Have you had a chance yet to see the amazing film by Ran Tal [on the history of the kibbutz] that they are talking about lately, *Children of the Sun*? I want to write about this and make the connection to our issues. In my opinion, it's an amazing connection that has gone unnoticed. I also read a long article about it in *Haaretz*—it's just amazing— about the implications of this amazing phenomenon of how we grew up on kibbutzim. The film is very powerful, it's done with a lot of compassion and love, but it takes a sober look at collective child-rearing practices. Suddenly I understand these connections. When you've grown up here from birth within closed places, and all around you are Arabs living in open places. . . . Zionism was built with this iron wall. Even Jabotinsky, the most important Zionist thinker eighty years ago, wrote that we would have to be living here behind an iron wall. So you grow up in this kind of situation. It evokes compassion because the situation is so distorted. We are distorted; it's a type of disability. We have something problematic about our way of being with the world.

In what way are we disabled?
It's something we had built into us; it was forced on us. It's a whole discourse of some kind, with a million practices, things we do and things that are done

to us, that make us this way. Not because we were born that way. Why am I saying all this? Because I think that our response comes from that place. It's clear to me that most people's response to activities like ours at Zochrot, for example, comes from that place. And I understand it as a response coming from weakness, from fear, real terror—What would happen here if the Arabs really returned? The fear is that you'll be open to the space out there, which is the normal situation if we want to live as normal people in this space, but for us it's a type of distortion. It is we who are distorted, I think, because of this identity that closes up into itself, frightened and confused. Hence I think that people's response is not because they are that way originally, because they are Israelis or Zionists. Even Zionists are not bad people originally. If I thought they were born bad, I would be doing something else. Sometimes I see people who are exposed to the things that we do, who say, I didn't know, I didn't think, I didn't hear about that, I didn't understand that it was that way. We need to get down to the roots of this. At the School for Peace in that course we went all the way to the roots, mainly the roots of this identity, to be able to understand: I am part of this side [in the conflict]. We at Zochrot are addressing this matter of how being this way was built into us here, and trying to understand why we are this way, and trying to work against that. And there are more people now who understand that maybe there's a way out of this thing.

The solution that makes sense to me is that we have to let go. Now, at Zochrot, we are doing a lot with the issue of return [of refugees]. We are working now to gather information about one state, about return. We don't need to be thinking about the right of return but rather about return itself. A good friend of mine suggested that we don't need to be thinking about return, that the right of return and return are not what we should be focusing on. I say that's the idiom people use when they are really saying that they want to live here in peace. But what's behind it is getting rid of this insanity of ours. That's the problem. The problem is for us to stop being colonizers. Otherwise, we won't resolve it. First comes the understanding that you and I and the person who is a refugee or a resident all have the same rights. Once you get that far, things can be resolved. The political discourse calls this the right of return, but that's really incorrect, because that's not really the problem. The solution is to realize that we have a choice. We can be in this space as a minority, since we are already a minority anyway, or we can accept the fact that all of us want to live in this country in peace, all the people who are here and also the refugees.

One state seems like the best possible option for getting out of this situation . . . one state that enables national expression, of course, national and cultural expression. And clearly it has to be a democratic state . . . one state with national and cultural expression for everyone living here. How exactly this will happen is a very big question. We spend a lot of time addressing this now; fantasizing about it, and trying to invent this new thinking that doesn't even exist yet. It's quite amazing really, that there are no texts, nothing at all. Maybe the best text is "Altneuland"; we have to go back to Herzl and read how he imagined the Jewish State. It's just amazing. So we're trying to do something a little bit like "Altneuland" now . . . to think about it. Because there's nothing here now, nothing for the Palestinians. Nothing; nothing. For us, it's not credible. . . . They have been shouting this, for years now, at all the conferences—the right of return, the right of return. . . . It will be OK. There are progressives at these conferences who talk about one state—Palestinians, and Jews; but no one says what that means here. What is that, Tel Aviv and one state? Jerusalem and one state? We have some work ahead of us with Jerusalem, as a capital for two peoples. But yes, we have to start inventing this, whatever it is . . . I'm glad that I'm beginning to be able to persuade more and more people, including Palestinians, that the time has come to begin thinking about this, and maybe if the time has come to start thinking about this, maybe that means that the time is ripe for it. It's somewhat amazing that it hasn't happened already. As to precisely how, well, with the situation we have now, it's obviously going to take a few generations—this fantasy that, yes, we will be able to live in this space.

21 · AMIN KHALAF

Social Entrepreneur

Amin Khalaf, a social entrepreneur and strategic and educational consultant, today leads the East and West Center for language study in Jerusalem (www.ewjerusalem.com) founded in 2014. His proudest achievement in recent years was the establishment of the Hand in Hand Association for Bilingual Education. Under his leadership, the association founded four joint schools for Jewish and Arab children, today serving over 900 students. Hand in Hand has received accolades both in Israel and abroad while it has developed unique new curricula and produced the first-ever multicultural school calendar in this country. Khalaf holds a master's degree in Islamic and Middle East Studies and an M.B.A. After completing his education, he worked as a journalist and taught in Arab and Jewish schools and at the David Yellin College of Education while also working in various settings promoting cooperation between Jews and Arabs. Amin Khalaf took the School for Peace Course for Facilitators of Groups in Conflict in 1991 at Wahat al-Salam–Neve Shalom. He was interviewed on October 12, 2008.

A lot of the worldview that we took from Neve Shalom might be obvious at Neve Shalom but not for a lot of other people, even today. Take the whole issue of equality. It was at Neve Shalom that I first heard someone say that, even when there's numerical parity in a classroom, for example, a Jewish child in the group will still feel like the majority. That's difficult to explain and hard for people to absorb. But we learned to put everything on the table, not to be afraid even if it created an uproar, that was OK, we knew we just had to keep the process going. I believe that every aspect of Jewish-Arab relations in this country is really all one ongoing process, all the time.

Nearly twenty years have passed since I participated in the School for Peace Course for Facilitators of Groups in Conflict. Maybe it's only natural that this period of someone's life is the most intensive: fifteen years of a career, marriage, family, children. About the course I can say, without exaggeration, that it changed my life—in many respects. The timing, in terms of where I was in my own life then, was also important.

I was twenty-six or twenty-seven. It was a turning point in that I dealt intensively, for the first time in my life, with Jewish-Arab relations. Until then, it hadn't interested me much; to phrase it positively, I can say that the first time I dealt with the conflict was at the Neve Shalom course. The course itself was a significant experience. It was my first such workshop of any kind.

I was a student and also ran the office of *Al-Ittihad*, the newspaper, in Jerusalem. At first I was active at the Hebrew University, but in the Arab Students Council and not with the campus movement. I thought then, and still think, that it's easier to be active on the Arab side, to be the minority, than to deal all the time with Jewish-Arab relations, which is exhausting and difficult. It's difficult and exhausting because you are trying to create something new. It's the truth, not just a slogan. Sometimes people say it but don't really understand how hard it is to swim against the current. It's doubly tiring.

So the course was definitely a turning point in my life, for two reasons. I began dealing with Jewish-Arab relations in the State of Israel and I am still doing so: a very significant change for me. Second, after the course I was a part-time teacher in the (binational) primary school at Neve Shalom. I did some facilitation work for the School for Peace and in other programs outside Neve Shalom: the Van Lear Institute, Children of Peace, David Yellin College—a lot of places, doing different kinds of facilitation. During all the intervening years, the worldview that you delineated in that course is the one I retained, and still do, and the experience has stayed with me. We learned to put everything on the table, not to be afraid to put it all out there even if it created an uproar, that was OK, we knew we just had to keep the process going. I believe that every aspect of Jewish-Arab relations in this country is really all one ongoing process, all the time. Sometimes the process is tiring because it means always working with the other, along with the inner process which really is not easy, how we live together, the shared meaning, what our prospects are or are not: It's not simple. Later on I was a teacher in Beit Safafa and continued doing group facilitation with Children of Peace, Van Lear, and elsewhere.

There are different working concepts that evolved in different places in the country. I'm still a believer in the Neve Shalom approach; that's where I belong: with the continuing aspiration to touch on the most difficult points and create from that something that aspires to something egalitarian, while dealing with all the power relations. For example, at Hand in Hand [Association for Bilingual Education in Israel], language is really the foundation, all the time. I believed in that, even before the Neve Shalom course. But Neve Shalom also helped us. Two things I think are unique about how Hand in Hand views language. I always say it's a tool, it's an identity, but it also reflects the power relations. And also, when I talk about the Hand in Hand multicultural model, I say multicultural in the structural sense, that is, it involves the power relations within the organization. I believed these things prior to the Neve Shalom course but Neve Shalom reinforced it, and I'm continuing to work that way because that's my worldview. That's how I'm built.

REMEMBERING THE SFP COURSE

It may be surprising how much I remember from that SFP course: the getting-acquainted exercises at the beginning; the amazing and beautiful group cohesion. It was a fairly unified group. We spent every evening together; we went out together to cultural things. I also felt that I could be myself there: truly I was saying exactly what I thought, from my own personal viewpoint. So that's how the course changed me. I felt that everyone paid attention; it was pretty good material. And we were able to create a lot of tension without having it all fall apart; that gave me confidence. And you and Rabah [Halabi] taught us: "Speak up, put it out there, the world won't disintegrate." That's something I still carry with me. There were fascinating scenes in the life of the group. Once, one of the women didn't show up, so everyone went out looking for her in Jerusalem; really lovely things like that. I personally was very influenced by the farewell process there; it was very reinforcing. Even now if I looked, at home, I'd still find all the notes people wrote at the end, and the flowers and drawings we gave each other at the final session.

People said all kinds of positive things, exchanged things, and I've kept every-thing people gave me.

The course also contributed to my own development as a person. Some-how I had never really expressed myself, never talked about myself or talked about things from my own individual viewpoint; in the course, I did that. The feedback I received in the group was encouraging; people were, like, "Do it! Go ahead!" And I made friends there, maybe not friendships that lasted forever, but people I stayed in touch with [for some time].

That course gave me the model, the direction, a way of looking at language, and we are trying to develop that at Hand in Hand. It was a basic tenet at Hand in Hand right from the outset. A lot of the time when people ask me about our concepts and say that they're very advanced, I say that they were inspired in no small measure by Neve Shalom. It shaped my worldview: the unceas-ing quest for equality. A lot of the worldview that we took from Neve Shalom might be obvious at Neve Shalom but not for a lot of other people, even today. Take the whole issue of equality. Even when there's numerical parity, for example, half Jews and half Arabs, I always said that one of the things I'd heard from someone who worked at Neve Shalom was that even in that situation, a Jewish child in the group will feel like the majority; that's where I heard it. But explaining that is really difficult and it's hard for people to absorb. Equality, from the standpoint of the experience at Neve Shalom, [can be elusive]. Even though Hand in Hand has a different discourse, undoubtedly the way Hand in Hand has been built is due in part to what Neve Shalom was doing.

Speaking as president of the association, how would you say that this expresses the language issue, for instance? We know that the language question is very hard, and that even with 50 percent Hebrew and 50 percent Arabic spoken at school, equality is still not attained.

Take the forum of the principals of our four schools, for instance. When Hand in Hand was getting started, we dealt a lot with the issue of language, from a belief that when we aspire to equality without having parity in the matter of language, we won't get close to equality. Even you and I, now, didn't hesitate as to which language I would speak, and I began speaking Hebrew. So Hand in Hand is continuing along the path. The association's original name (Center for Bilingual Education in Israel) showed that bilingualism was the cornerstone of our activity. We have developed a model and are continu-ing to develop it, and we wrote a book about this bilingual model, and we

are continuing to address it. The first item on the agenda for the principals'
forum was bilingualism. We've had some success, but it's not easy. With the
Jewish children we've had some success in this regard, but it hasn't reached
the level we wanted to see, whereby a Jewish child could finish third grade
and be able to read, write and speak Arabic. We aren't there yet, despite all
our efforts. The basic model as we first developed it was to have two teachers in the classroom [an Arabic speaker and a Hebrew speaker], and they
weren't translating; the children worked with bilingual teachers because it's
the only way to succeed, and we also work with the parents, because after
school the child goes home. That's the basic model.

But then we saw that, outside the classroom or the school setting, one
[language] still imposes itself on the other, [affecting] the power relations
on the inside, and so forth; what could we do? So we developed and built up
the bilingual model that defines some circles we can have an influence on:
the child, the teacher, the educational environment, the curriculum. We
worked on this for two years. We set up a forum on bilingualism to see how
to promote these things. At first, in our school, the children were not separated for even a single hour of the day; they were always together. So a model
evolved in which there is some separation, but in a very carefully controlled
way, not like at the Neve Shalom primary school where there is quite a lot of
time spent separately; I think at Hand in Hand, it is less. Today one of the
association's tasks is to strengthen this tension between day-to-day life and
the vision. The vision is that we must aspire to bilingualism. Meaning what?
It's not easy; we cannot just give in and go with the flow. You take a deep
breath. So our task is always to bring people back to the vision. It's tiring, but
that's our destiny, to keep swimming against the stream. Bilingualism means
that the Jewish child, parent, and teacher will speak Arabic too.

You have, for instance, a policy regarding the hiring of new
Jewish teachers who are bilingual.

You know, we let ourselves off the hook on that a little. We say it's preferred, and if you say that, you've already compromised the principle. Yes;
we have to make it a model. I remember that at Neve Shalom at one point it
was decided that if we really believe in bilingualism, a bilingual teacher should
get additional compensation. We were thinking of doing that in our schools.
I must confess that even we sometimes get tired. It went away, for various
reasons, and we ought to raise it again. Because sometimes we do give up;

we get tired. It's not working, so we say let's look at what works and go with the flow. The challenge of the high school, for example: I know it's hard, it's hard from every standpoint, but the question is do we give up or do we push ahead. We have a tenth grade now in the Jerusalem school, an Arabic-only class. The challenges are always hard and always tiring. Once the principals told me, just the fact that you get there in the morning and walk into a Jewish-Arab environment that promotes equality, just for that you need a 50 percent bonus every month. I haven't thought enough about how hard and tiring it is.

THE PROCESS IS TIRING

Dealing with this issue is difficult. In a uni-national association things are easier for me; personally; the Jewish-Arab partnership is very difficult. The process in that environment feels tiring.

To begin with, you are working with yourself and with the other side; explaining about your awareness, your worldview, your ideology. You go through a process and start to feel some kind of change, and the first difficulties you feel are your own. But for a member of the minority, again, it's always easier. Do you really believe in this path; is this the way? You are asking others, and they are asking you. But you also feel how hard it is when the other side has to gradually begin, very slowly, to relinquish the power, to begin very slowly to cross the line. In terms of how the Neve Shalom course posed this, is the Jewish participant crossing a red line? Is he still a good enough Jew? In building this partnership, to know what is permitted and what is forbidden is very difficult. What I find very frustrating and difficult is that, in so much of Jewish-Arab relations, this is not on the conscious level. I feel it because I have so much experience with this, and sometimes it's hard to explain.

One beautiful thing about Neve Shalom, despite the difficulties, is in looking at who holds positions of power or influence within the community. Neve Shalom made quite good progress in that regard. But in a lot of other places, it's almost nonexistent. A lot of people, if you broach the idea that it might be hard that the person at the top of the pyramid is an Arab, they'll say, "What are you babbling about? There is no such thing." Clearly there is such a thing, but that's the behavior apparently. So even though you want to believe in people and respect them, you'll see opposition: Someone is really unaware, or really doesn't think he is racist, and has trouble with the idea of Arabs leading or being at the top of the pyramid, yet he's not aware of it, and that's frustrating. Everywhere, within the organization and across the country, this is what's accepted today.

Where in this country today would we find places, even just a few places, where an Arab is in charge? Azmi Bishara, in his day, announced his candidacy to challenge the usual thinking. Are we really prepared today to have an Arab prime minister for the State of Israel? People say, "Yes, yes, what's the problem?" There are a lot of problems. The question of whether we are really prepared for an Arab minister is not so simple. Maybe a minister whose picture is hung on the wall of the ministry, sure; but one who really has an impact and makes decisions and tells us [Jews], the hegemonic majority in the State of Israel, what's right and what's not—no one is ready for that. When I read the debate surrounding the appointment of Ghaleb Majadele [as minister without portfolio], not that I really went into it in great depth, but you really felt the covert racism. The covert racism is many times greater than the overt racism and much harder to cope with.

Could you give an example from the story of Hand in Hand of how you coped with such racism?

Well, nothing comes to mind at the moment; I think there's an inner resistance to discussing this. But there have been a good many examples. Take the opposition we have today to the idea of a high school due to lack of numerical parity. Instead of appreciating the people who came and worked with us all along the way, [people say that] if there's no Jewish-Arab parity [due to oversubscription by Arab families and undersubscription by Jewish families they're not in favor of having a high school. There are also sensitive issues in terms of funding; some feel that funding must come equally from both Jewish and Palestinian sources. In this context an emphasis on symmetry is problematical. Equality between majority and minority is not necessarily based on having parity in sources of support. The needs and the way of conceiving the situation on the two sides are different.

They say, for example, that Arab families come to a Hand in Hand school because they want a good education for their child, whereas Jews come because of their ideology. In my ten years of working with Hand in Hand, I've been unable to persuade people [that this is imprecise]. My view is that when you ask an Arab what he's seeking here, he says, "A school"; and the

Jew says, "I believe in this path." Fine, but what does that say about the conceptual outlook of the majority and the minority? The Arab parent accepts the ideology a priori; he is willing to live together and wants to live with Jews, so he feels less of a need to declare it; his need is for what he lacks, which may well be a good school for his children. But he accepts the ideology; if he weren't willing to live with Jews, he'd go to some other school. So in his conceptual outlook, the educational factor is emphasized. The Jewish parent, who has a great many schools to choose from, comes to Hand in Hand because, despite everything, he feels that this partnership is important for him, and he says so. It goes without saying that his child will get a good education here and if that weren't so, he wouldn't come to Hand in Hand just for the ideology. So each is presenting things a little differently and then people start making a big deal out of it. There is a power issue hiding behind this, too. Behind the scenes, Jews are saying, "We are more humanistic, more ideological. These things are more important to us. The Arabs are basically just opportunists looking for a good education for their kids." Go explain all this to people. It's not simple; it's complicated.

I understand from what you've been saying that sometimes, because of the asymmetry, it's necessary to provide reinforcement to one side at the expense of the other side.

No. We really do have a policy. Our point of departure is symmetry from a numerical standpoint between the Jewish and Arab children. I'll give you an example, call it an advanced discourse. We always have to ask the minority partner the extent to which we won't dance to the majority's tune. I say that today, if someone wants to claim that there's no money to teach Arabic in order to improve the level of the Jewish child's Arabic, you'll find the money. Whereas if there's a need that's essentially the minority's need, raising the money will be hard. So one could ask, how equal is the provision of resources for the needs of the respective sides. It's really important to be aware of these things and to get real, and not to just go with the flow and stay tied to your own side.

I'd say that my aspiration now, after so many years of effort in this field, is how we can change the reality. One thing that has frustrated me in the encounters that are held is that while improving our understanding, they don't really create something new. The question is how to create something new, and we need to find out if it's even possible. There are very few models of

Jews and Arabs trying to live together and provide models of what living together on an equal basis might look like and how it could work. Out there in the real world, I think the creation of Hand in Hand was also an attempt to answer this question of whether it is even possible and, if so, how it can be done. So we developed this model, and our aim was to promote egalitarian cooperation. The emphasis has been and will continue to be on egalitarian sharing in education. The association itself was founded in 1997 and the first schools opened in September 1998, one in the Galilee and another in Jerusalem. We have three foundational tenets: First, bilingualism, on which we have a worldview fairly similar to that of Neve Shalom, wherein language is not just a communication tool but also an important component of identity and a reflection of the power relations in the society.

The second component is the multiculturalism; from an ideological standpoint we say that it's good, that it adds something and diminishes nothing. While the demography is half and half, the most important from a structural standpoint is a fair division of power within the organization. The two cultures both have a place, and the important thing is the binationalism, so that both narratives have an equal place in what is done at the school. And I think that mostly we have succeeded. It's a real challenge. As you know, there's a narrative of the strong, and there's also a narrative that is silenced and has to be afforded space, with the boundaries delineated. Today we have 900 students at Hand in Hand, in four schools: Jerusalem, Misgav in the Galilee, Kufr Qar'e in Wadi Ara, and Beersheba. The Beersheba school is run in partnership with a local organization, Hagar. The Galilee has grades one to nine, with 200 students. In Kufr Qar'e there is something lovely, another step toward equal relations, in that a Jewish-Arab school was opened in an Arab village. That school has 200 children through the seventh grade. And in Jerusalem, there are 460 children from compulsory prekindergarten through tenth grade. In Beersheba, there are two kindergartens with two grades, preschool and regular kindergarten. All the schools are flourishing. In Jerusalem, the intent is possibly to establish a joint Jewish-Arab community high school that could accept children from all the existing [bilingual and binational] frameworks, including Neve Shalom.

Can you say something more about swimming against the stream?
My critical approach began early, around seventh grade, when they started building a moshav [a Jewish semirural community] next door to us. I was a

child, and I looked at this and wondered why they had good roads, and nice houses, and we didn't. What was that about? We even had a principal who taught us, for about the first third of the year when I was in seventh grade, that there really is no such thing as a Palestinian people. I remember thinking that it was pure foolishness, that he didn't know anything, and that he was talking nonsense. Around the same time, I think when I was in eighth grade, every kid I knew had a dream to raise a [Palestinian] flag on Independence Day. I don't know how I dared, but it was unplanned. An eighth grade teacher came and said, "Let's start decorating the classroom for Independence Day," but I said, "A fourteen-year-old boy doesn't do decorating." The teacher made a mistake by saying whoever didn't want to could go out to the schoolyard. So our whole class went out to the yard, leaving only two girls to help the teacher decorate. I went on like that in high school and then at university. In high school it was an incident with Bassam Shakaa and Karim Khalaf [West Bank mayors severely injured in an assassination attempt by Jewish underground terrorists.]. In the high school I attended, they spent two hours one morning talking about this, and it was an important milestone in my life. Later, the Neve Shalom course was another important milestone in my life, an important influence on me.

Perhaps because you went in the direction of bilingual education, it capped your rebelliousness, because if you had gone in a more political direction, your rebellion might have been more pronounced?

Well, yes, I used to tell myself the same thing. And my political inclinations are toward the Arab parties, the Arab nonprofit organizations where I was, where I lived. Even today I feel that that was more comfortable for me, and maybe that's part of the fatigue factor.

PARTNERSHIP IS NOT EASY

Having chosen partnership, the question is where am I contributing more, and which is really the right path to take us in a broader direction, whether toward equality in a state defined as a state of all its citizens, or toward something more autonomous; and which of these is better for the Arab population. So what I've been doing for the last fifteen years or so: what does it mean? We've all been raised on the idea of equality for the Arab citizens of Israel, but how? Everything I've been doing has been an attempt to answer this question of how. What is equality? And I think it's also about this dream I have, in the context of Hand in Hand, about a center for knowledge about bilingualism: What is bilingualism? Does all of Israel in fact have to be bilingual, or is there an intermediate possibility there somewhere, between the situation we have now and a situation in which every citizen has to be bilingual. While it's clear to me that Hand in Hand won't be able to change the State of Israel, it can make a contribution, or offer a paper saying this is the direction, and someone afterwards has to make it happen. But equality, in terms of how to make it happen, equality is the way.

Partnership is not easy; it's a burden, it obliges you to do a lot more coping, and it's no less of a contribution; on the contrary. Partnership for me, from a personal standpoint, has not been easy. Sometimes I also think that an Arab can only go so far. An Arab can be a member of Knesset here which is pretty respectable, but to dream of being prime minister—you're overdoing it. At Hand in Hand, I'm the association's president and Sam is the director-general, and our hierarchy is always in flux—the CEO is Jewish, the president is Arab, and both of us report to the board. In general, I deal with education and he deals with administration. Our schools have two principals each, and a complicated allocation of roles. I believe in the direction, but it's complicated. Still, there's no other way. My worldview, which few people will understand, is that if we aspire to equality, there has to be an Arab principal and the default mode, maybe that's not the right term but that's the direction, is that there shouldn't be a Jewish principal. It's caused considerable problems. If the default mode is this direction, then we have to learn how to live with it. Policy is set jointly, responsibility for implementation is one person's, with maximum information sharing, but the responsibility is that person's. That's the best description I can give of our direction. I don't see any other possible way. I was always looking for how equality could be possible in general, and it was the question that always bothered me and still does, even now.

22 · MAYA MUKAMEL

Psychologist and Activist

Maya Mukamel, a clinical psychologist in Tel Aviv, writes and lectures on the interconnection of the therapeutic and the political, trauma theory and treatment, the history of psychoanalytic ideas, and psychology and gender. She teaches at Haifa University School for Art Therapy and the Bar Ilan University Gender Studies Program. She is a steering committee member for the Politically Sensitive Therapy training conducted by Psycho-Active: Mental Health Professionals for Human Rights. Mukamel and colleagues from PsychoActive and Social Workers for Peace address the military interrogation and detention of Palestinian children and youth and the impact on the individual, the family and the society. The group has trained several dozen volunteer professionals who observe Ofer military court proceedings, interview detained minors, and write expert opinions for defense attorneys. (Participants include Ruth Ben Asher, Manal Abu Haq, Sunny Gordon-Bar, Dov Bernstein, Laila Baranse and Michal Fruchtman; Rivka Warshawsky, who initiated the visits to Ofer military court, also initiated the PsychoActive training in Politically Sensitive Therapy.) In 2015 Mukamel participated in a forensic documentation training project initiated by the Public Committee Against Torture in Israel based on the Istanbul Protocol, providing a handbook for professionals conducting physical and mental evaluations of torture survivors. Maya Mukamel took the joint School for Peace–university course at Hebrew University in 1997–1998 and the SFP

Course for Facilitators of Groups in Conflict in 1998–1999 at Wahat al-Salam–Neve Shalom. She was interviewed on January 15, 2008.

> *The course was a very significant hallmark for me. Acknowledging and dealing with racism has been my preoccupation ever since. With Machsom Watch, I wanted to understand how the Israeli soldiers are able to do what they do at the checkpoints. At first the soldiers may try to connect with the Palestinians, explain, provide information. Soon, though, the soldier no longer even looks directly at the people. . . . If I were there as a soldier myself, that might also happen to me. In any case, I think that the encounter with my Mizrahi-ness in the SFP course awakened in me a strong identification with the Arab group.*

I took the Neve Shalom course at Hebrew University in Jerusalem in 1997–1998, my last year as an undergraduate in psychology. You and Ahmad [Hijazi] facilitated it, Professor Charlie Greenbaum coordinated the course for the university, and Michal Zak was observing the group. For me, it was a truly fascinating year. I think it was the first time in my academic studies that I experienced an integration that combined an experiential process with theoretical study. This integrative approach has stayed with me ever since as a powerful and effective way of learning. From the standpoint of the group encounter, the course caught me at a good time; I was ready for it. I had felt a need, although I couldn't articulate it, for something that was missing during my studies, and in hindsight I can say that I was really waiting for an opportunity like that course: to have contact with issues not as texts, but as something experienced that becomes part of life and encompasses subjects so relevant to daily living.

I've always been interested in the encounter with people and in addressing materials like these. When I entered university, I was waiting for that kind of experiential learning opportunity and was surprised that it didn't materialize; my psychology studies often seemed very detached from life, particularly life in Israel. Before the Neve Shalom course, I had been in a few youth encounter groups, but those involved no continuity or study. The Neve Shalom course, then, was my first in-depth experience of that kind.

I remember that the initial group experience was very turbulent. Someone in the group launched an "Intifada," that is, vented a lot of anger that bordered on threats against the Jewish participants. He was at the first meeting and did not return, but it was an earthshaking provocation and a little shocking: a hard way to begin. I think the entire process was affected by that beginning, mainly the fact that the talk in the group was moderate and restrained, even when tough things were said. Maybe from the shock, there was something quiet and reserved about the group, as if nothing very dramatic was going on, which allowed for the development of a process that was more delicate and involved less of the uncontained intensity that so often characterizes encounters of this kind.

What was the most significant thing you took from the SFP course?

Perhaps the most significant thing I took away with me from the course was some kind of awareness of the interaction between identities, between types of awareness, both mine and others'. This was something I hadn't met with previously in the same way. In the group I came to grips with the fact of my being Jewish, Ashkenazi, Mizrahi, a woman—all these components that I was paying attention to for the first time. One of the more memorable experiences for me was actually in the uni-national forum. The first time I've ever dealt with the fact of being Mizrahi was when the ethnic conflicts came up in that uni-national group. One of the Mizrahi women talked about her family's experience of humiliation when they immigrated to Israel, and the ongoing experience of oppression. In response, one of the Ashkenazi women told her: "What's the whining about? You people have the legitimacy to say whatever you want . . ." And when she said "you"—in the plural—suddenly I felt it, that feeling that someone is relating to you disparagingly because of your background, that people think certain things about you and see you in a certain way, because of the color of your skin, without knowing you. They see themselves as the ones granting you the legitimacy to speak up. It was an experience that maybe I would not have had any other way. It was mortifying, and somehow disappointing . . . and it stayed with me.

In general I felt pretty OK with what I was feeling and thinking. Prior to that, I hadn't felt that anything inside me would cause people to define me in a certain way or ascribe all kinds of things to me—at least not openly—and it was my first encounter with a situation like that, in such a harsh way. Throughout the whole process, I was surprised at how much people see one another in stereotyped ways. Yet at the same time, I appreciated the fact that the participants were able to scrutinize themselves and deal with the stereo-typed view. But clearly the things said were not always from a place of dia-logue. Sometimes they signaled superiority, or power, and only made the superiority more present and more powerful. In any case, I think that the encounter with my Mizrahiness awakened in me a strong identification with the Arab group.

There was this feeling that things are not self-evident, that you think you're in a certain place and that it's yours—it's your home, your society, but then that's not exactly how things are, it turns out. And there are all kinds of things you haven't noticed day by day but that can be decisive concerning the sta-tus you'll have in certain places.

And what happened with that? Did you protest, did you stay silent, did you respond?

I didn't respond. I was hurt, and I think I was simply in shock. Apparently my defenses were good enough that I could tell myself, when that particular woman spoke, "Who does that woman think she is, speaking that way?" But in the end, what she said is what I remember the best from that entire year. Encountering that labeling and facing the question of whether I was speak-ing because she "was giving me legitimacy"? The condescension! All of that continued to preoccupy me, and still does.

It definitely connects with what the Jews do to the Arabs in the group. There's a very basic connection that's not even consciously made. Suddenly I discover that I'm part of the Jewish group that is doing this to others. I'm labeled by the Jews and I'm also part of those who are oppressing and label-ing the Arabs. So being in that group meant always being divided in those ways, and there's something very troubling and sometimes even paralyzing about it. The way the map of power divides into branches within my iden-tity was sometimes too much. And suddenly it seems that there's no place that's free of that, suddenly I'm both here and there, yet not really in either of those places. I don't feel oppressed, but I did become very aware of people behaving oppressively toward me. That's not something I really absorbed at home. On the contrary, at home being Mizrahi meant a certain kind of pride.

My mother is Polish and my father is Iraqi. My friends are mostly Ashke-nazi; I grew up with no awareness of ethnicity. Even now, looking at people and at the relations between people, it's hard for me and seems wrong to me to say of certain people, they're Ashkenazim, or they're Mizrahim.

LIBERATING MY ARABNESS

Since that course, there has been almost no year in which I have not been intensively engaged with the Jewish-Arab conflict, in all kinds of ways. I'm still looking for precisely how and where it's most suited to me to work on this. I think that my biggest insight has been about how complex this subject is, and how difficult the situation is, because the most difficult things, I think, remain unseen. Racism, in its most profound meaning, isn't seen.

I remember my encounter with my own racism, which was rather amazing. Some of the course was held at Neve Shalom, and included a simulation exercise for finding a political solution to the conflict. We divided into mixed [Arab and Jewish] work groups and each group worked on one topic—education, culture, etcetera. The committees' conclusions were presented by representatives of the groups in the plenum, with everyone present. The committee representatives sat on the stage, with signs in front of them indicating the names of the committees to which they belonged. The signs were written in three languages—Arabic, English and Hebrew—and the Arabic was first, at the top. Suddenly I realized that the fact that the Arabic appeared first bothered me a lot, and was somehow threatening to me. I remember that at that point, I tried to suppress the threat and told myself, "OK, OK, what's wrong with you, why does this bother you so much." It was hard.

I also felt the connection between this and the Mizrahi/Ashkenazi issue. For example, my unconscious attitude to Arabic as a threatening language, on the one hand, and on the other hand the fact that it's a forgotten language for me, because Arabic was spoken in my father's house but became lost to me. I felt how unfortunate it was that I didn't know Arabic, that I hadn't learned it from my father and my grandfather and grandmother. Partly because it's the language of a part of my family, it's not a language I can really reject. I often found myself understanding what was said, even though I didn't know I could understand it.

And alongside very strong processes of repression of the Arabness of Mizrahim in Israel, there were also very strong processes of repression of Yiddish. My mother has a Yiddish library at home and there won't be anyone to read those books. It seems to me that if in my generation these cultures of Arabic-speaking and Yiddish-speaking Jews are not preserved, then they will be entirely forgotten. It would require someone who cares that something has been forgotten in these people's transition to Israel. But in spite of this commonalty, clearly the case of Arabic is different than that of Yiddish, because Arabic remains a language identified with "the enemy."

My father and I never discussed this connection to Arabic; he died when I was beginning my undergraduate studies. It's something I think about a lot, especially given that my grandfather, my father's father, died recently. It was a lost opportunity, and I hope I won't lose the chance to talk with my uncles about it.

THE SFP FACILITATORS COURSE

When the SFP course at the university ended, I wanted more. I wanted to go deeper into it and create continuity that would become part of my life and would not end with the academic year. So the following year I entered the course for group facilitators at the School for Peace at Neve Shalom, and I did some work facilitating groups in conflict. I was glad to have the opportunity to continue with the process in that way and found that, as a facilitator for groups of young people, the experience of the complexity of touching on this subject only intensified. Suddenly I had a lot of questions about facilitating group processes like those: which age group is it best to work with, and when, and with what model. Some of these subjects came up in staff discussions, as a result of the encounter itself.

A little later on I began to be active in Machsom Watch. I was active for about three years, every Tuesday. At five in the morning we would leave the house, and at quarter to six we met at one of the checkpoints—Qalqiliya, Tulkarm, or Nablus.

To do that for three years every Tuesday at five in the morning . . . you need a lot of inner strength.

I see it as being drawn to a traumatic place, something that cannot be ended and you can't let it go. The checkpoints have tremendous drawing power for me. It was astounding to see that whole system being built. When I began going out to checkpoints, the construction was more or less just beginning, and it got more and more sophisticated as time went on. To watch it happening week by week was something I found very hard, and still do.

Most Israelis don't do this. What impelled you to do it?
I don't know. Maybe the feeling of powerlessness, the sense that there's nothing to be done. OK, maybe as you say it's a type of action, but it's still a very limited action. A group of women who see, document, and make sure these things reach the media.

While at the checkpoints, we had interactions with soldiers, and we had interactions with Palestinians. At first I intervened more in the soldiers' behavior, and over time came the realization that sometimes this is harmful to Palestinians at the checkpoints, and sometimes it just doesn't help. So it's a very wearying activity. But above all I wanted to understand what the soldiers are doing, and how they are able to do what they do. I saw that when a soldier is stationed at a checkpoint, at first sometimes there's an effort to maintain an unmediated connection with the Palestinians, to explain, to provide information. And I saw how, after not very much time spent serving at a checkpoint, the soldier no longer looks directly at the people, and from week to week a kind of screen drops in front of his face. I tried to understand this. It's very possible that if I were there as a soldier myself, it would also happen to me.

After about three years of this, during the last part of my work with Machsom Watch, and then subsequently, I was a partner in an independent group of a few mental health professionals in Jerusalem that was seeking a way to create a connection with Palestinian colleagues. The group included Sarah Kalai, Sarah Metzer, Danny Eisner, Tristan Troudart and me. We discovered that when people try to organize such encounters in a more established way, with a lot of Jewish-Israeli participants, with a lot of preparation and with long-term plans—the attempts fail, for all kinds of reasons. So instead we tried to create a few personal connections and build trust, and through these connections to try to see where we might be able to develop it. And in fact, through a connection with the people at S.O.S. in Bethlehem, a program was developed for a professional education seminar for Palestinian staff, and it was done successfully. We went to Bethlehem once a month for nine months and gave workshops. On the way there, we crossed checkpoints, with all that that entails. We came as members of Physicians for Human Rights; if the organization had not assumed ideological and logistical sponsorship, I don't think we could have done it. Since that intensive year, in fact, we have initiated an annual project of greater or lesser scope, with professional training for Palestinian staffs. We have worked with additional volunteers, professionals from Israel. We planned and implemented three other courses, each of which was conducted over long weekends, for several months. The teamwork was very moving for me, and I enjoyed participating very much. It doesn't just take energy, it also energizes . . . unlike going to the checkpoints.

THE FOUNDING OF PSYCHOACTIVE

After that I was one of the founders of PsychoActive. This is a group of mental health professionals, men and women, each of whom has some interest in the connection between psychology and the Israeli-Palestinian conflict. Aligning with the various interests of the members, PsychoActive focuses its work on several areas. Although each member is coming from a different place, from the outset there was a shared momentum around what happened to Majd Canaaneh. Majd is a Palestinian psychologist who had done his residency in Jaffa. He was accused and tried for harming state security and sentenced to ten and a half years' imprisonment. A few women in the group—one was his supervisor, another his colleague and a third was doing her residency under the same supervisor—were witnesses to the way he just suddenly disappeared from work one day. They looked for him and waited for him, and his patients came and waited for him, but he didn't show up. After a few days, when they were able to make contact with his family, they learned that he was under arrest. Their shock at the attitude of others at his workplace, and the disparity between the man they knew personally and the man who appeared in the indictment—all of that prompted the beginning of action. There were attempts to be in touch with his attorney, and a close tie grew with his family; these friends followed his trial and have been corresponding with him for a long time. I think that the group came into being with that as one of its focal points.

Another focus of activism by PsychoActive, at least from my standpoint, was the attempt to broaden the work of the group that had organized the workshops and professional education seminars. More and more people expressed interest, and over time the groups of organizers and lecturers multiplied.

Another source of strength nourishing the establishment of PsychoActive was people who had been through the School for Peace course on change agents in mental health fields. Many graduates of that course expressed interest in continuing to be active. Another source that energized the founding of the group was the academic activity of people who wrote master's and doctoral theses in psychology dealing with related subjects.

With PsychoActive, apart from my activity in the field, I think I also contribute in terms of forging connections between people and institutions. I've made all kinds of connections, through personal acquaintance, with Palestinian therapists from Palestine, in mental health circles, with leftist activists who are not mental health professionals, and in academic circles. I stand at a kind of intersection where it's easy to make connections, and that is important because people need one another to do this work. That's how I see my place. In recent years, I've been writing a lot and spending time on the computer, so I'm exposed to the emails and the internet—creating easy access for the group's communications network. It's a bit hard for me to talk about the organization as a hierarchy with a center and leadership, and so forth. But I do feel that I have a role.

Did your master's thesis or your doctoral dissertation deal with this area?
My doctoral dissertation deals with it somewhat indirectly. It's a theoretical study that addresses the concept of Gvul, which is both "limit" and "border," in three disciplines: psychoanalysis, philosophy and political philosophy. It is connected with the notion of boundaries—the boundaries of identities, political borders, and the boundaries of awareness or consciousness. I try, inter alia, to examine how and when awareness comes to have boundaries, where awareness stops, how blockages of awareness are created so that one is unable to grasp what is "beyond." . . . I try to ask how these places could be made more flexible, thinking about human consciousness and human interactions that would make less coercive use of concepts and ideas related to boundaries. So, yes, one could say that matters of identity and conflicts between identities have entered very deeply into my academic work.

PsychoActive (the full name is PsychoActive: Mental Health Professionals for Human Rights) is actually a listserv. Some members are more passive recipients of emails, some take part in the correspondence, and others are more active and initiate, rather spontaneously, all kinds of projects. An initiative goes out to the network and a core group then forms around the idea— based on the interests of the men and women themselves or prior acquaintance among them or the area where they live, and so forth. Thus far, a number of such action groups have coalesced, and they are fairly autonomous, with each group communicating internally about their activity so as not to overload the entire list. Sometimes there are questions for discussion or updates on the general list. At any given time several activities are happening in parallel among PsychoActive members, and the activity is quite diverse.

Apart from the activity in support of Majd, other action initiatives that have garnered momentum involve meetings with Palestinian colleagues. Although the activities we've done in the small groups I described took place before the founding of PsychoActive as such, it seems to me that they gave direction to the activity of training professional staffs. Other groups from PsychoActive have initiated large, impressive study projects, planning a full academic year of learning. We, members of one small action group, have continued to meet through the years with Palestinian colleagues to expand our activity with Palestinian mental health centers, and we try to maintain a good connection. We owe a lot to the resources allocated to us by Physicians for Human Rights. I understand that there was a period of time when forty percent of the PHR budget for professional continuing education was allocated to fund our activities. Our people work on a volunteer basis—all the organizers, of course, and all the lecturers, too.

Another of PsychoActive's main activities is organizing training seminars addressing the connection between psychology and politics. We hope to launch a tradition of conferences, the first of which, called "Psychological Obstacles to Peace," was held here with you at Neve Shalom. It was a very successful conference in terms of the content, the impact it made and the number of people attending. Jews from Israel and Arabs from Israel and from Palestine talked about checkpoints, from a professional standpoint. Professor Jessica Benjamin was a guest lecturer. The second such seminar now [2008] being planned is called "Therapolitical," expressing our orientation to the interface of therapy and politics. Psychologists identified with the political right wing were also invited. What we added for this seminar, which I believe is excellent, is a series of discussion groups where participants will think about and analyze what was conveyed in the lectures. One of the invited lecturers is from the management of the Gaza Mental Health Center. His presentation is certain to be interesting and challenging. He has told me about the situation in Gaza under the siege. He doesn't receive emails because they have no electricity, they have no generator, they have no heat in the cold weather. We are trying to work together and cooperate so as to help promote some kind of change in this situation. If he is unable to get a permit to enter Israel to speak in person, we hope to hear his talk by telephone.

It seems fair to say, in summary, that the School for Peace courses marked a significant milestone in your life.

Very much so. Certainly, the course was a very significant hallmark for me. I think that acknowledging racism, and dealing with racism, have been my preoccupation ever since, in various ways. That was not the case prior to the course. In PsychoActive, too, it's not easy to keep on dealing with racism in the broad sense. The PsychoActive group did not begin as a human rights organization; the intent was social/political activism—and also, from my standpoint, feminist activism, but somehow that has shrunk. There was an attempt to inject gender issues, as part of the spectrum of social issues involved in the activity, but it's not easy. It will be interesting to see how this develops. Sometimes people are prepared to mount the barricades for a particular issue, while some other issues may not merely be sidelined—sidelined, I would understand, because it's impossible to address everything, and everyone has to choose what he or she wishes to deal with—but may actually fail to earn acknowledgement and understanding. Activism in Psycho-Active, as with the course at Neve Shalom, raises more questions for me than it answers. As I continue dealing with these issues, that's what I feel. They are hard questions.

23 · BADRIA BIROMI

Environmental Educator,
Group Facilitator, and Urban Planner

Badria Biromi earned a B.A. in psychology and education from the Hebrew University in Jerusalem and a master's degree in urban and regional planning from the Technion. Her dissertation, "Planning Factors Influencing the Employment of Arab Women in Nazareth," won an award for excellence. Biromi has served for five years as director of Link, a Jewish-Arab environmental organization in the Galilee that has mounted numerous projects shared by both communities. In one such project, Biromi persuaded 150 garage owners to recycle engine oil waste by selling it to factories that use it for heating. Biromi has also worked as an urban planner at the Arab Center for Alternative Planning in Eilabun, where her projects included advocacy for the establishment of new Arab communities; as northern region director for an educational nonprofit, A New Way; for the City of Nazareth, as an urban and regional planner; and for the School for Peace at Neve Shalom as a regional project coordinator and a facilitator of groups in conflict. Badria Biromi took the School for Peace Course at Hebrew University in 1996; the School for Peace Course for Facilitators of Groups in Conflict in 1996–1997; and the SFP Change Agent Course for Environmental Justice in 2011–2012 at Wahat al-Salam–Neve Shalom. She was interviewed on September 17, 2008.

I deal a lot with environmental justice. I don't refer to it as political or Jewish-Arab work, but that's where it's coming from. The SFP course gave me the background, the knowledge, and a lot of power. I don't have to justify myself any more, or speak a lot about myself. I'm very committed now to empowering the local leadership. People think maybe someone else should speak for them, but I don't see that as the right approach at all.

I did the SFP course for university students in my third year at the Hebrew University. You [Nava Sonnenschein] and Ahmad Hijazi were the facilitators for our cohort. I really fell in love with the facilitation process in that course because it was my first experience with this very interesting approach to working with groups, and I'm not saying that just to be complimentary. You two had fabulous chemistry and the subject was fascinating, and my experience there was terribly important for me, even though I've been involved in other Jewish-Arab activities all my life because I grew up in Acre.

Later, after the course, some of us signed up for the SFP facilitators course at Neve Shalom and I fell in love with facilitation again. I haven't had much chance to practice it. I remember facilitating students in a joint Jewish-Palestinian project at some point. I continued to find facilitation very interesting. In 1998–99 I worked in Tel Aviv on a women's project, another very interesting experience.

In 1996–97 while I was in the SFP facilitators course I was working toward my master's degree in urban planning at the Technion. Toward the end of that winter there was that disaster with the two army helicopters that crashed in northern Israel, and in the course we had no idea how to deal with it. The Jewish participants took it very hard that we didn't immediately identify with what they were going through; that was very tough for me. What had we been working on that entire year if not to understand the other and where he was coming from? Why do we need all those meetings, then? As if at a certain point there's a sense of lack of trust. But from a personal level, I persevered with it.

I always have the SFP courses on my CV. It's very important to me, and it's added value. I'm always influenced by the courses I take—but the SFP courses, addressing the Jewish-Arab conflict and dealing with facilitation, were particularly important. I moved ahead with these. They were a formative experience.

LINK FOR THE ENVIRONMENT

After I left Jerusalem, I joined a nonprofit called Nisan–Young Women's Leadership. It's a Jewish-Arab organization working with young women and dealing with feminist issues. It gave me a way forward that was more positive. Not so much regarding politics, though. As I went from one workplace to another, I felt that politics wasn't the focus. I felt that I could make change with small projects, and bring in the Jewish-Arab issues, without having to introduce big political issues all the time. Where I am now, I deal a lot with environmental justice, though I don't refer to it as political or Jewish-Arab work, but that's where it's coming from. The course gave me the background, the knowledge; it was formative, and gave me a lot of power. Sometimes now there are discussions that come up in which I feel that I'm already beyond that stage. I don't have to justify myself any more, or speak a lot about myself, I can just address the issue from a very strong and decisive point of departure.

In the environmental organization I direct now, Link for the Environment, the Jewish-Arab issue is not center stage, but everything I was doing at Neve Shalom I can still do in the current setting. Right now we are involved in a Jewish-Arab project but the basis for it is environmental. As director, I'm always injecting my perspective on where we should be working. For example, next to Deir al-Asad there's a kibbutz, Tuval; we do an educational and community project there, with ecological construction and study tours in the field. Each of the activities is small, but when you look at the whole big picture, you find that it's actually extremely influential, which I'm pleased about. People from these two neighboring communities meet in the afternoons. One Saturday morning there was an activity for children; they used green building techniques to construct a bench and they cleaned up the campus of their school. The people are able to meet and do things together now, without the intervention of my staff.

Another thing that I think comes from my experience at Neve Shalom is the idea of taking responsibility for a given group. Let's say, for example, a group of people could meet even without Link, but Link provides a kind of home, or an umbrella, for people to come together. The [Arab] mayor of the village and the [Jewish] head of the regional council can get together in any case and exchange a few words, but when we bring them together in one room with the community activists from the field and the children who are involved in the project, it creates a different atmosphere and gives them a kind of push—so they realize that talking is fine but why not also do something together? My main purpose is not just for people to meet. I'm more interested in having them pursue a shared goal together. Environmental justice is an area that I include in all kinds of grant requests I write. Everyone talks about it, even in government, but in fact not much is done about it. Some of the issues are very delicate and intertwined. There is still a minority that is discriminated against and doesn't get its fair share of funding, of justice, of land, of anything whatever—and it's still important to me to do something about developing of my own society.

Could you say more about being decisive and working on the things you believe in?

If you don't insist on something, it's not going to happen by itself. If we didn't physically assemble the people from Deir al-Asad and Tuval together in one room, nothing would happen. The secretary-general of Kibbutz Tuval came to see me right after I took this job to tell me about his vision; he spoke about big ideas and he brought notebooks and maps but, to tell the truth, I don't think his constituents felt any of this in the field. It wasn't concrete. The project, by the way, is called "The road to good neighborly relations." It was already in place when I came to Link. So I don't think that, today, the relations between the Jews and the Arabs in the Misgav region are better as a result of this very lovely project we have invested so much in. On the other hand, we have done concrete things. I remember attaching a picture of an activity in the field with children clearing a path and collecting small stones to surface it with. There's a group of Jewish and Arab women who go walking together using that path now. These things were there, but no one was providing a framework. No one was giving them the relevant expression.

There's something else important. We're always talking about the intra-group work, the uni-national forum as the course called it. I think that with Link activities, this dimension is there. We have a great many projects or activities that are solely for the Arab population, and we aren't shy about saying so. For example, there are several schools, Arab schools, where we decided in 2008–2009 to invest tremendous resources and staff time, because the staff and I believed that there were things waiting to be expressed there, in an intra-group spirit. When I approached the Jewish schools, they declined to participate because they are already so overloaded with programming. So we try to direct as many resources as possible in terms of money, and equipment, to the Arab population. Quite often there is equipment left over from an activity, so we donate it to a school. If you ask me, I don't think that this damages the Jewish-Arab identity of what we're doing, because it is being sustained and is moving ahead, even if expressed perhaps in a different way.

The two main channels for our work are the Jewish-Arab dimension and the environmental dimension. The organization was founded in 1995 by Stephanie Feitelson. I joined in 2005. It's not a large organization; we have five or six people and an annual budget of less than $200,000.

You mentioned the power of working in a group: what's that about?
At the SFP course, I fell in love with this whole subject of group work, of pursuing certain goals within a group. Today this element is generally a prominent part of most of my projects. As an example, we currently have municipal forums that work on environmental goals in their town. The community project I mentioned earlier, even though it's smaller, also has this element.

About five years ago, we succeeded in opening a second-hand shop in Tivon called "On Second Thought." It's based on principles of community building, recycling, contributing something to the community. People bring things they don't need to the shop instead of throwing them away. The Tivon shop is already independent and no longer requires the connection with Link.

In a nonprofit with Jews and Arabs on staff, how are you received as an Arab woman director?
It's fine, no problems whatever; the people I'm working with are very open and tolerant and try to be super-accepting, learning Arabic and integrating into the city's atmosphere. Our office in Nazareth is very visually prominent. In the nonprofit sphere, there aren't any problems with my role either. And there are other Arab women serving as directors of environmental organizations and Jewish-Arab organizations. I believe in certain ideas. I think people accept me as I am, as I present myself. I've never encountered anyone who seems skeptical about my leadership role, and even if they are surprised, it's in a positive sense. It's a professional work environment, in the end.

Before I joined Link, I worked as an urban planner at the Arab Center for Alternative Planning in Ramle for five years, from 2001 to 2005. They work mostly on planning issues in the Arab sector, seeking alternative solutions, especially in the Arab communities in the north, but we also worked in the

Negev and in the mixed cities. Youval Tamari and I worked together on a project in Ramle. The work I did there encouraged me to continue in this direction. I loved the work, it's my profession, it allowed me to have an influence. I found the issues very interesting from several perspectives: in terms of the planning issues and the politics with Jews and Arabs and the whole history of Palestinians in Israel, all that highly charged material—and there were also successes. The center implemented all kinds of small projects successfully and I felt I was making a contribution to the community through this work.

AN ALTERNATIVE PLAN

Here's an interesting example involving the environment. We did an alternative plan for the Dar El-Hanun area. In the Triangle vicinity there's a forest near Dar El-Hanun. Six or seven years ago, the Jewish National Fund and the Society for the Projection of Nature in Israel and all those green organizations wanted to have the area declared a green zone to protect it from development, and we got into it with the argument that it wasn't justified from an environmental standpoint. We had to prove our contention and it was a very difficult process. At the time I was at the most intense point in my one-year Heschel fellowship course and I had to decide which way to go: to agree with the environmental people and say the area should be preserved on environmental grounds, saving the trees, the hiking areas, the clean air, and so forth, but at the same time there was a community there prior to 1948 which was a hundred or even a couple hundred years old. It was a community, not a few tents in the wilderness. I decided to go in the direction of environmental justice, and the Greens didn't look favorably on that. I'm sure you know [former member of the Knesset] Hana Sweid, and the Arab Center for Alternative Planning has a certain image. We said that the people in Dar El-Hanun, a community whose existence there predated the founding of the state, should be left where they were and not relocated. It made headlines. I don't remember the details, but it was about not allowing Umm al Fahm or Baqa al-Gharbiyye to develop. The Greens said whoever was living there should live there but if someone wanted to add another story on his house for his son, he wouldn't be able to. This was an aspect of advocating all the time for the "weaker population" of Arabs that I didn't enjoy all that much, but OK, it's about environmental justice from my perspective.

On this specific plan, when we were opposed to it, I didn't like having to choose between the environment and justice for the disadvantaged. At Link, the keynote is being proactive: being constructive and taking the initiative. We work a lot with people and with groups. In my previous position I had to write a lot of official letters with maps. Now it's more focused: we go to some park and clean it up, or do something with parents and children; the main thing is that we actively do something. At the center, there was always a much longer drawn-out process. In a project we did in Sakhnin, for example, we were always waiting for the next scheduled meeting of the district planning commission and it took forever to get anything approved. I'm a bit hyperactive and I have to see results with my own eyes.

CREATING AN INTEGRATIVE COALITION

I worked with the plan for Sakhnin for about a year, I guess, and I dealt with the mayor and the city engineer on the environmental justice aspect. I set up a coalition of Jewish and Arab organizations from the Galilee and we encouraged the city to address this; we put out a pamphlet with our positions. We advocated for expanding the jurisdictional area of Sakhnin, even at the expense of the Misgav regional jurisdiction. We have a plan for Hurfeish that I consider, even with all the contradictions involved, the height of environmental justice. There's an Arab community there, a Druze community but in my view it's an Arab community, surrounded by a tremendous amount of green-designated areas and nature preserves. We are helping them, not with legal steps but just through action, to assert their ownership over that land. We have photos, too—children at the riverside, and prominent figures from the community who come and say they want to see what Link can tell them that they don't already know. It's been a very fruitful cooperation with the city, the residents, and the community center, cleaning up this nature preserve. We organize people to go hiking there and we have a group of old-timers who tell stories to the children. It is another way to implement our policy of environmental education that integrates with the Jewish-Arab aspect.

In terms of having the tools I need to represent Arab communities before the district planning commission, I prefer to be able to submit things in writing but that's not always possible. When I have the city engineer with me, he can do the talking. He does all the mapping and the needs assessment, and

I'm there to help out in case something isn't clear. I'm very committed to empowering the local leadership, which is an essential aspect of the project. I view it as a type of leadership education: getting someone to see that they have the background and the education, so why shouldn't they speak at a meeting, even if the district director for the entire northern region is sitting there, even if it's a little intimidating. People think maybe someone else should speak for them, but I don't see that as the right approach at all.

24 · AVI LEVI

Political Educator and
Environmental Activist

Avi Levi began his political and community activism in 1997 at the School for Peace facilitators course. The ideas and partners he encountered there kindled his enthusiasm to join the effort to create positive change in Israeli society and its relations with its neighbors. He went on to work for many years as a facilitator of youth encounters at the SFP and with the Reut-Sedaka youth movement, where he was also a member of the executive board. Levi subsequently was director of Green Action, promoting the idea that protection of an environment must encompass fruitful cooperation with, and respect for, the people who live there, irrespective of religion, race, or gender. He became a leading partner in several projects designed to advance these ideas, including the Activism Festival, held in Israel for several years starting in 2002 to encourage cooperation among activists from different spheres and sectors, and the Sacha fair trade campaign, which featured local Palestinian organic products and sought to raise awareness of the damage caused by Israel's Separation Barrier to the environment, to Palestinians, and to the pursuit of cooperation between the two peoples. Levi and his family are now living in Leeds (UK), where they moved after he was awarded a Rotary Peace Fellowship to pursue a master's degree in peace studies. Avi Levi took the School for Peace Course for Facilitators of Groups in Conflict given at the Open House, Ramle, in 1997. He was interviewed on September 9, 2008.

I began that course as a 'passivist' and was transformed into an activist. Before, I didn't think it was possible to make change, to have an influence, to actually do something. Now I live in a world of social change; the course put me into that world. I've been an activist for fifteen or twenty years, and I think there's a feeling of rebellion that you can't squelch. People try to suppress it, but that can change as soon as you give them tools. This spirit is one of the most significant things that a political activist has. I think everyone has this spark of natural rebellion against injustice, whether environmental, political, or human. Looking back, it's hard to differentiate between my experience in that course and things that have happened since then. Opening my eyes was a process, learning to understand the other, discovering that the information that we, the public, receive, is mistaken and that our connection to reality is very flimsy in the best case.

The School for Peace facilitators course was undoubtedly one of the courses that most influenced my life, among all the various seminars, workshops and other things that have had very broad impact for me. The SFP training really changed my life, as exaggerated as that may sound; I don't know how other people have framed this in talking to you, but for me, it truly changed my life.

The course I participated in was held in the 1990s sometime. It wasn't even in your regular program of course offerings. I did the SFP course that was given at the Open House in Ramle. I got there purely by accident through a friend of Michael Rafael's, and Michael and I did the course together.

Michael told me that a course was opening in Ramle, that there was a group of Arab participants but the Jewish group was way too small and needed more men. I was living in Tel Aviv but I really wanted to do a group facilitation course. I wasn't thinking so much about facilitating groups of Jews and Arabs, but I said OK, I'll go and do this one, and the fee was subsidized by the Open House, so I signed on.

I think what the course mainly did for me was to transform me from being a "passivist" to being an activist. Up until then, I had what I thought of as the correct views: I was a leftist, I was against the occupation, I was against the oppression of minorities of any kind in this country or anywhere, but I was very passive. I kind of roamed around the university as a student. I also worked doing therapy with special-needs children at Alin [the Israeli Society for Disabled Children] and in all kinds of other settings.

NETWORKING WITH JEWS AND ARABS

The experience of the course itself, plus the connection with the various participants outside the sessions, and certainly the work afterward at the School for Peace—during two or three years at differing levels of intensity, when I was working as a facilitator in SFP courses at Neve Shalom—the experience of the course brought me totally into this world of the relations between the two national groups in Israel and beyond the Green Line.

I had absolutely not been part of that world before then. Absolutely not. Again, if you had asked me, I would have said all the right things, more or less the same things I'd say now, but I didn't think it was possible to make change, to have an influence, to actually do something. It didn't seem relevant to my own life or connected with me in any way. But ever since that course I have lived in a world of social change; simply put, the course put me into that world.

The whole set of relationships there was complicated. It's not as though what I learned there turned me immediately into some kind of true believer. I had a lot of criticisms. I had a lot of arguments with participants and staff members and with friends. Even things that I didn't much like, though, were instructive later on, in hindsight: Since they hadn't worked well during the course, in retrospect I could say to myself, OK, I will do things differently.

And today I am in the world of the market, very close to the world of commerce, the material world, much less in the world of talking, much less in the world of change by means of ideas and discussions and encounters, but rather change by means of the material; this is also partly because of what I learned back then. Many things have happened in the interim. And these aren't the only things I've done. I've tried in various other places to change things using action that was more, I don't know if I want to make fun of it, but I could say luft geschäft [literally, air business]—that is, by talking, meeting, seeing and hearing. But today what I do, in a minute I'll expand on this, does more to enable people to live, that is, it gives them the basic requirements of life, deals with the basic needs of life, but it's still the same realm of relations between Jews and Arabs.

Along with the content of what I got from the SFP course, there's also the level of connections. I'm still connected with people I met there, both Jews and Arabs. Each of them is in some different world. For example, Badria and I are connected these days through her environmental work as the director of Link for the Environment and, in between, we were also in contact in various other ways. With Michael and Noah who were also with me in the course, I have a much more intensive connection, but all of these contacts have been important. Later on I also initiated activities of the same kind·while working in other frameworks, like Reut-Sedaka—including the Reut-Sedaka Village. Independently, in all kinds of other settings, I initiated things of this type, and my connections via the School for Peace provided the reservoir of contacts for finding facilitators and coordinators.

Can you point to what it was about the course that really may have changed you from passive in this field to active, to a social activist, as you termed it?

I don't think that there is any one thing. I think it's all the circumstances taken together.

I was in a certain place in my life at the time. I was ready for a change, after seven years of working in various capacities with the disabled, from being a helper for people with disabilities, to being coordinator of a program, to running a sheltered living facility. At some point I had gotten all that I could from that, and I traveled in Africa, and then came back, but I didn't know yet exactly what I wanted to do. I did the SFP course when I was around thirty, after a mini-career in a different field. Personal circumstances and personal connections, like getting to know Michael just as he was leaving his position as director of Green Action, made it convenient for me to integrate there.

Another thing was this eye-opening experience. I sat there and suddenly I think I got into a place that had been blocked to me before. I had been what is called an "armchair leftist," one of those people who think that the people living on the other side of the border are human beings, who say that Arabs are human beings and deserve to be treated with respect—but they sit in their armchairs in Tel Aviv and go to their offices in military enclaves like Ramat Hachayal and come home again. That's not enough to recognize the reality we are living in; but now I can.

Eye-opening? I want to understand this better.

Take, for example, when the last Lebanon War happened. Suddenly the entire nation was enlisted for an attack, and there was this aggressiveness everywhere. People you knew, the people around you, whom you knew as leftists and humanists, suddenly displayed this urge to attack. I think that most people I know who have been through encounter experiences like the SFP course just did not go there at all; they just did not get to that place at all.

Being in a framework like the SFP course is one of those things that makes a difference, because it integrates the ideological, the political, and the social, and frequently also the personal and the emotional. The very profound emotional experience you undergo is addressed, and you have an experience that changes your ability to relate to people, both Jews and Palestinians.

I did the course a long time ago and it's hard now to differentiate between my experience in that course and things that have happened since then. Opening my eyes was a process, and I think the course was one of the sparks that ignited it. I'm not sure that everything happened in that same moment, but it ignited the spark, and that became the direction. Opening my eyes does relate to my understanding of the other, yes, and of course to my understanding of the information that we, the public, receive; our connection to reality is very flimsy in the best case and of course mistaken. This knowledge that the world is not as it seems is a way of connecting with an entirely different world. It requires understanding all the social and political process that occur here, in more depth; understanding the people and what they experience.

The two or three years that I worked at Neve Shalom after the course were in some ways an earthshaking experience. I mean, I started out very enthusiastically and optimistically, and ended up very uncertain, feeling that it wasn't possible to really make change. I saw that bringing young people together for three days, in the way these weekend youth encounters are done, may not be enough to change things, or may create change but not the change we sought. On the one hand, it was clear to me that some of the participants experienced something eye-opening, as I had. But the political conclusions that this leads them to draw are not under our control. Sometimes they decide that yes, "they" are human too, with aspirations and needs and abilities like ours, and so we'll remain enemies because we have a disagreement and this disagreement will not be easily resolved. Of course, some of the young people went away euphoric, like: We're all brothers and sisters. In hindsight, probably the most significant thing I did is bring people to an experience resembling what I went through, an eye-opening experience, a kind of awakening, if we can use that term.

PEACE NOW, GREEN ACTION, SINGLE PARENTHOOD

Since around 1998, I have worked as the youth coordinator at Peace Now. I went a long way with the connections and the knowledge I gained at the SFP course. I also have done encounters involving Palestinian youth. I initiated this kind of activity because I had the relevant experience and information and acquaintance and encouragement to do it.

Regarding my activism, I was the director of Green Action during the movement's most active period in 1996–1998. This involved organizing direct action with other young people, climbing trees, chaining ourselves to tractors and bulldozers to stop them from working, things like that. It was a very stormy period. Then I directed the Peace Now youth movement for about two years, and then I didn't work for almost two years because I went on a sort of parental leave to take care of my son.

Ending up a full-time parent was a process for me. When my son was born, I was still at Peace Now coordinating their young people's program and working intensively for ten or twelve hours a day, with a lot of responsibilities. Suddenly at some point I realized that I had had a child but didn't have time to be with him; I was going to miss experiencing his childhood. I was always taking him to my mother, his grandmother, his aunt, and had no time to be with him myself. A child is an experience that requires time and attention in an intensive way and he also gives all of that back to you.

So then as an experiment, my partner and I left the city, I left my job, and we went to live at Hatzeva in the Arava, where life was much less expensive and much easier. She had a job and I was supposed to be initiating a few things in order to bring in money, but we also wanted to have time with our son. This experiment didn't work out, and my partner and I separated.

Alone with my son, I returned to the center of the country but decided to continue staying home with him, partly because it was very hard to find work. It's a very strange experience, suddenly to be a single parent and understand what single mothers in Israel are up against. Job hunting, you may come with some kind of managerial experience, with knowledge, abilities, and talents, yet the only work they are going to offer you is to do telemarketing for Bank Hapoalim. That's what they deem suitable. And if your object is to be part of the management at some nonprofit, people are very concerned about what would happen if they need you in the evening or early in the morning or at odd hours, and who will look after you child if he gets sick.

So I stayed home with him for nearly two years, until he went to preschool. It was a very instructive experience. Then I went back to running Green Action, which had nearly fallen apart and was in a bad way. I resurrected it and we initiated some new things. One was an activism festival that ran for four years. The idea was good and the first three years were amazingly successful. Each time more and more people came. I think that the initiative for that activism festival was also something I'd taken from Neve Shalom.

Talk about the activism festival.

The idea was to put people into a shared experience for three days, giving them a platform to walk on, to march on. You don't just lecture at them or tell them stuff. It's not like at school where you are teaching them. You're not teaching; you're giving them a convenient base to walk along on, to meet one another, see one another, get to know one another. You arrange some formal settings where they get acquainted and also nonformal settings where they are together around a campfire, at meals, and at evening performances. This event was quite sizable, with 3,500 people and something like ninety organizations represented. There were segments of ten workshops simultaneously, with four such segments each day, two in the morning and two in the evening. Each time there were a lot of workshops and at all of these sessions people were meeting. They were preparing the food together in the shared kitchen. We arranged for people to have many unstructured opportunities to get to know each other, as we did at Neve Shalom, believing that the connections made during something like that are connections of a different kind. At first everyone is trying to show off, then later they start to talk with one another. They talk about their families and friends. I think there's a connection between these models somewhere.

FAIR TRADE WITH PALESTINIAN FARMERS

Now I am director of the organization, but it is very small and I direct a small staff of just three people. Our activity right now is about fair trade and we focus mainly on working with Palestinian farmers and producers, including Palestinian women. Green Action has worked a lot on globalization issues. It has addressed the consumer culture around issues of social justice and globalization, but in an activist way, using protest demonstrations and what's known as action against: against the World Bank, against global trade, against the International Monetary Fund. At some point, I began to feel uncomfortable only working against things, because you aren't offering any alternative. People don't know what to do even if they agree with you; they don't know how to behave differently.

When the idea of fair trade arrived here, we were very enthusiastic. This is a way to circumvent the capitalist commerce of large corporations. We created a fair trade center that focuses on human beings. That is, we take care that anyone producing the products that you consume will be fairly paid for it. Gender equality in the production process was important to us; making sure there was no child labor was important to us. The compensation must be adequate to provide producers with health care, decent housing, and education for their children. This whole idea came here from Europe, where it focuses mainly on the third world. It's a type of alternative path, to help the third world, Africa and South America. Here we saw that although we want to help the third world, the third world is only a few minutes' drive from some of our own homes. It's impossible to ignore this fact, and we decided to connect the two things. We bring coffee from South America so that people can consume fair trade coffee, the flagship product in the fair trade movement. Meantime, there were Palestinian farmers with whom we had demonstrated against the Separation Wall, against the environmental impact of the Separation Wall and the human impact of the Wall and the damage it does. The Wall makes it almost impossible for Palestinians to earn a living producing olive oil, because there's no one for them to sell it to.

We decided to buy from Palestinian producers and sell in Israel. We focused on the quality of the end product and the packaging and on locating the responsibility with the producers. The idea was to give them the opportunity to produce high-quality products and move the production capacity to them. So we began with these yellow containers and ended up with very lovely packaging. Products include olive oil, zaatar, and grape honey, the latter a Palestinian product unknown in Israel. The farmers get a lot from this, both in terms of professional expertise and improved product quality and, in the last analysis, also a lot of money. A whole lot of money comes to them through us from the Israeli consumers. We work with a few central locations in Beit Ummar, Wadi Fuqin, and the Salfit area. Relatively speaking we are not a large organization. We market to shops in Tel Aviv, to natural food stores, to organic products stores and among a lot of private individuals who sell to stores outside of Tel Aviv. The tote bags we sell are sewn by mothers and grandmothers at the Hand in Hand bilingual school in Kufr Qar'e; they were shown in the film *Bridge across the Wadi*. The nonprofit doing this fair trade work is called Saha. The tote bag production involves the entire school: the children, the teachers, the parents, the grandmothers, everyone together, using fabric scraps collected from factories. All the income goes to the school.

So actually your work is an integrative effort involving both green activism and the Israeli-Palestinian conflict.

Yes, that's exactly right. I worked for many years in the environmental world, the world of environmental organizations. One of the main problems there was a relative lack of connection between real life and the ideology. The discourse in the organizations was very high-level, but what does that amount to? There were all kinds of struggles against the damage done by air pollution, pollution of the sea and of the land. But after work, people go to malls and buy more products. They are struggling against it while believing that it's possible to produce more and more and more, and to consume more and more and more, yet the factory should be nonpolluting. There are still a lot of people who believe that.

I think that we will have to reduce consumption very significantly, not only with recycling and not only by using recyclable plastic or recyclable glass, but simply by producing less. The production process itself pollutes. It does damage. It's not just the production process in isolation, but also the transportation, the consumption, and what happens to the product after the consumer is done with it. This issue, the consumption cycle, meaning production and consumption, is the one factor we can point to as having brought us to the present situation, in environmental terms.

So the central way to address this must be to change our consumption habits completely. That means, first of all, consuming a whole lot less. It means focusing on local consumption, and not consuming products produced half a world away.

One of the loveliest stories I know about the olive oil is this: There's a delicatessen in Ramat Hachayal where they sell a lot of Italian delicacies, including Italian olive oil and a lot of other Italian imports. One day the owner came to me sort of in shock and said: "Listen, I'm out of Italian olive oil. I tasted your olive oil at a friend's place and it's exactly the same as the best Italian olive oil I was importing. Let me have a few crates of that." Since then he has been selling it in quantity. It's an Italian delicatessen selling Palestinian olive oil, and this is the process I want to achieve. Instead of people buying olive oil from southern Italy, because of the brand, they'll understand that the same thing is happening here but it doesn't have to be flown from one side of the planet to the other.

What is it like, working cooperatively with
Palestinians within a reality of occupier and occupied?

I have Palestinian partners. In every such group, there's someone who is more dominant. It's very complicated and difficult, there are problems, and in each place it works a little differently and has different problems. Clearly if the partner on the other end is in some ways "Israeli," if he speaks Hebrew and has spent some time here, then it's easier. I don't speak Arabic. I have tried to learn, starting when I was in the SFP course, but I don't learn languages very easily, and in the end I let it go. So I always bring a translator or someone who can talk [for me]. A week ago I was at an Israeli factory that bottles olive oil. Sitting with me there, the owner of the factory sort of leaned back in his director's chair, heard that I pay the Palestinian farmers 23 shekels per liter of oil, looked at me and said, What kind of fair trade is that? I pay as little as I can, that's fair trade, what do I care, I pay 15 shekels a liter instead of the 23 shekels you pay. From a commercial standpoint what do I care if it's not fair. Let them deal with it. What's it to me? If I can get it for 15 shekels, then 15, and if I can get it for 14, then 14. That approach repulses me, it's exactly the attitude I'm trying to combat. So behind every bottle of olive oil is a bottler: someone who filled it with oil, sealed it and put the label on.

I adopted an approach from the outset of working with people as equals. We are doing the same work. I get there and if the goods I'm supposed to pick up aren't ready, I sit down with everyone else and work on the goods, bottling and sealing.

THE DYNAMICS OF MEETING AS EQUALS

At the SFP course, I had my first encounter with people who weren't Jewish. Maybe it's hard to grasp this, but at the age of thirty I had never once met Arabs. I saw them the way everyone else does, as construction workers on the building next door. As the hewers of wood and drawers of water. I had no communication with these people. The first time I sat and talked with Arabs face to face, eye to eye, was at the course. In a certain sense my way of communicating with them was fixed there, and this influences and directs all my work with Palestinians now. I mean, if something like this had happened to me before I turned thirty, I would have been speaking as a humanist. Later I could see what humanists are; I have met a lot of humanists who are patronizing. A friend of mine, for example, asked me for someone who does home renovations and I immediately thought of one friend of mine but he said, No thanks, he's an Arab. That's a very common attitude.

Maybe because the SFP course was one of my first encounters with Palestinians face to face, I don't see them in that stereotyped way, I just don't think like that. I think it's one of the amazing things that happened to me in that course, along with giving me the opportunity now to go through this spiritual learning process. Ahmad [the late Ahmad Hijazi] and Michal [Zak] were the facilitators in the course. Before that I was studying psychology at university, and what I wanted was to take a group facilitators' course and the one at Bar Ilan University didn't suit me. I wanted to go in the direction of group dynamics and the SFP course included that. It wasn't just a sociopolitical encounter, but a dynamic encounter, there was a dimension of interpersonal dynamics, and it dealt with those dynamics and there was space to express them. It was an experiment in relating to dynamic processes within the group. This truly gave me space and allowed me to go through a process.

Then afterward when I went to work in other places, it was really hard for me when I saw that an encounter included only political discussion and conclusions; I was outraged, and I couldn't work that way. Every time, I tried to turn it around. I think it gave me legitimacy in incorporating interpersonal dynamics into all my encounters with Arabs, as well as with Jews, but also with Arabs. I mean, the encounter is not just political; the encounter always has a dynamic interpersonal dimension and afterward there is the political dimension.

This also creates problems when, for example, leftists come to assist a certain farmer and suggest that we start selling that farmer's products. It aligns with my principles, but maybe I have met with this person five times and am trying to work with him, yet something in the dynamics is not working right and I can't work with this guy any longer. Meanwhile, I see that people continue to work with this farmer based on the politics, based on the social dimension, because he's disadvantaged, he's one of the have-nots, so they feel they have to help him, and it doesn't matter if he's being less than honest. I can't adopt this generosity of spirit and simultaneously this patronizing attitude that says, we'll help them because they're have-nots. People may be have-nots but they have to be human beings, too. I have a feeling that I acquired legitimation for this attitude of mine at the SFP course, and it's a very important component of my relations with the Palestinians. It's not a marginal thing.

So that may be one thing. Sometimes it's hard in hindsight to figure out the influence that different things had, but the course was clearly a watershed for me, because from there on, my life changed greatly and if I hadn't done the course, my life would have been very different.

What are the things central to the soul of an activist, in your opinion?

I've been an activist now for fifteen or twenty years. I think there's a feeling of rebellion, a sort of mechanism of rebellion that you can't squelch. An awful lot of people I know who are not political activists have acquired, somewhere along the way, an excellent system for suppressing the natural rebellion that they feel. At the first spark of rebellion, they are trained to respond with Let it be, what's the difference, there are more important things. But that can change as soon as you give them a way. You tell them: "This is a tool I use to live in this world with that spark of rebellion, so that you don't ignore it and don't suppress it." I can't always implement it or express it, but it's legitimate and I make room for it. I think this spirit is one of the most significant things that a political activist has, because in my opinion everyone has this spark of natural rebellion against injustice in all kinds of contexts, whether environmental, political, or human, and for me this is definitely the central thing.

Many people suppress this part of themselves and a few are able somehow not to suppress it. Is there some sort of optimism that aids this?

Not necessarily. I'm not an especially optimistic person; in fact, I'm fairly pessimistic and I can't suppress that. I don't think optimism is required. I look at a lot of people who are bigger activists than I am, someone like Yishai Menuhin, say, or Yoav Hess, all kinds of people I'd really consider teachers in the realm of political activism, and they're no different, really, but they are essentially optimistic people who believe that everything we do makes a difference and has an impact and that reality changes for the better. I'm not naturally an optimist, but I'm still an activist.

I AM ALREADY THE CHANGE

You are reminding me now of one of the things I got from the SFP course that turned me into an activist. When I started that course, I always drove from Tel Aviv with Michael and Noah and we would argue the whole way. Michael is an activist with the soul of an optimist, an irrepressible optimist. He was always sure that everything would be OK and he would do the things that would change things for the better. And there I was, this sort of "passivist," you know, like "What's the point, what for?" We argued the whole way in the car. I would say, "What are we going there for? We're going for nothing. We'll go in, sit there for a while, talk a little, and I'll go home and you'll go home and that's it. What could that do?"

At a certain stage I suddenly had this revelation that I am already the change. I mean, the fact that I'm going there and participating in this seminar, that's already a change, one level of change has already happened. I'm a person in this world, the world was one way when I was in this place, and now the world is different because of my being in a different place. That's already a change in the world. That's already a change that has its space in the world, with due respect, beyond the fact that everything I do is in addition to the change that has already happened. As soon as I became an activist with awareness, as soon as I started doing things to change things, the outcomes of what I do are value being added by my changing, which is the first step; the first step happened at that seminar. Just participating in that encounter, just my meeting with the people and going through the process I underwent there, that's the basis for change. I can use this seed in all kinds of ways, and if it works, I've gained something, and if it doesn't work, I've gained less but I haven't lost. This was a very significant realization that I found there and took away with me: that a change in me is a change in the real world. After that I did a lot of work with young people, addressing the environment and political and social issues.

I think now as we are talking, I realize that the SFP course was influential for me in this particular regard too, in realizing that as I change, the world changes. Coming from that course, I got to being director of Green Action which started me off in the environmental movement. But I got into it from that course: from the realization that the environment is the place where people are living. And people are human beings. Protecting the olive tree isn't enough; we also have to protect the Bedouin who is sitting under the olive tree.

25 · AMAL ELSANA ALH'JOOJ

Activist and Advocate for Bedouin Women's Issues

Amal Elsana Alh'jooj, founder of AJEEC (the Arab-Jewish Center for Equality, Empowerment and Cooperation), is executive director of the International Community Action Network at McGill University (ICAN-McGill). At the age of seventeen, Elsana Alh'jooj established the first Bedouin women's organization in the country. She became a leader in the Arab Bedouin community in Israel and a key figure in sustainable community development, as well as an influential shaper of public opinion. A graduate of Ben-Gurion University of the Negev (Israel) with a Ph.D. from McGill, she has earned numerous awards and honors in Israel and abroad and was named one of the "101 most influential people in Israel" in 2010 by the Israeli financial newspaper *The Marker*. Elsana Alh'jooj took the joint School for Peace–university course at Ben-Gurion University in 1996, and in 1997 she participated in a Jewish-Palestinian student delegation to Germany. She took the SFP Course for Facilitators of Groups in Conflict in 1999–2000 at Wahat al-Salam–Neve Shalom. Amal Elsana Alh'jooj was interviewed on December 3, 2009.

AJEEC is an Arab-Jewish organization which is 90 percent about action in Pal-
estinian society. You can't talk about partnership and creating partnership
if the Palestinian population is not empowered. You can't talk about being
empowered without seeing that translated into the language of rights and

equality in the State of Israel. Thus we as an organization focus a lot on empowering the Palestinian minority. At the same time, I don't see Arab-Jewish partnership as optional; it's a must.

Whew, this takes me back.

I had two rounds with Wahat al-Salam–Neve Shalom. The first was the seminar given at Ben-Gurion University, at that time facilitated by Rabah Halabi and Michal Zak of the School for Peace. As part of that course, the group took a trip to Germany. And then there was the School for Peace facilitators course.

The facilitators course was in 1999–2000, ten years ago now, and the earlier seminar was in 1996, so there was some kind of process. I think that often when people talk about this kind of seminar or about Jewish-Arab encounter in general and about dealing with the conflict itself, the issue of identity sits very squarely in the middle. Some people arrive at the discussion with a well-established identity, and others are still looking for theirs. Of the people with an established identity, some are unwilling to reexamine it whereas others are open to reexamining it. There are all kinds of patterns.

A DYNAMIC, LONG-TERM PROCESS

I can only look at my own life. For me, there was no singular, crucial, identifiable point in time in this whole process of mine with Neve Shalom. I can only talk about a long-term process that is still ongoing and still dynamic; it is still being constructed, still enriching and still being nourished by all the projects I'm working on now.

I speak as a child who grew up in a very politically solid reality. I was raised on the songs of Marcel Khalife, in Lakiya in the Negev. I've been in jail and I've been very politically active. The first stage of my connection with Neve Shalom was the BGU seminar. I came to it with very definite views. One of the students filmed the entire course in 1996, the whole process, which really helped me: I watched it a couple times and heard myself. I heard a young woman who generally listens to herself, who was very assertive and determined, who tries her utmost to see that her position is the right one, that it reflects the truth very clearly, who demands of the interlocutor: How can you not understand, how can you be unable to understand this? So the process for me began as a young woman who brings her truth and thinks that only her own truth is the truth.

In hindsight, when in those days I listened to the other side, I was listening in order to respond, not in order to understand. So we finished that course and I felt that I was getting farther away instead of closer to the conversation. I felt: OK, now I really know who the Jews are; they aren't ready to understand me and even when I bring my truth, they're not interested. Then I flew to Canada to do my master's degree. That experience took me far away from the source of the conflict and the daily encounter with Jews, who for me had symbolized oppression, the olive tree uprooted, the [Bedouin] village unrecognized, all those things. Until my first workshop, pretty much my only contact with Jews was of that kind.

The university in Beersheba had given me this space, the space where my professor was; I had positive experiences with my professors. They changed the image that had become familiar to me of who a Jew is in my life. But now when I had that distance, in Canada, suddenly I found myself standing up to talk about the seminar I'd been in [at BGU]. Whenever the Canadians talked about the conflict in Quebec, the conflict over language, immediately I went back to that place of the seminar, and my perspective was: Why are you unable to talk? We've managed to talk. I brought this to the group in Canada: See, where I come from we are prepared to listen, we are prepared to talk, yes. So the perspective of distance showed me not to make it a war, but to try to understand.

Maybe in Canada I was also helped by the people's personalities there; which particular people you are encountering at certain stages in life can be very important. In Canada I met very significant Jewish figures and indeed, they were to have a meaningful impact on my professional career. Meantime I began to wonder: It's not possible that these Jews are so much better than the Jews in Israel. It can't be that there's no place in Israel like this place here where you can create this connection. Does it depend on me or on the other side? And then when I came back home, the first thing I wanted to do was to pursue this. I'm not sure but I suppose it was a desire to continue the process I had begun at Neve Shalom, or to relearn it, or to re-experience it with new insights. In 1999–2000 I entered the facilitators course. I really wanted very much to understand where I fit into all this, and I wanted to listen, and not just to come there with my one and only truth.

THE MICRO, THE MACRO, AND ME

The course at Ben-Gurion University offered a kind of microcosm. In the sessions there, I could play the role of the minority and be a fighter, and then away from the course suddenly feel liberated to be myself. That's really what happened. There was a learning process: I learned what happens when I represent the voice of a minority, and that was a really strong thread in the course: that there we are really playing out a microcosm of the reality of the Jewish-Arab conflict. That frame helped me to see when am I saying something because they are expecting me to talk that way or are expecting me to behave that way, as opposed to saying what I believe in.

If you look at the process over time, yes, at first I always took care to stay within the consensus of the Arab group; that changed, and I was ready to fight for my position. And fighting for my position was actually from a woman's standpoint, because the women's and men's issues did arise there. So assuming I am determined to stick to my position as a feminist woman who sees things in a certain way, why can't I fight for my position if I see things differently than my Arab Palestinian colleagues see them? The workshop helped me develop this capacity to say what I have to say, rather than having to present one particular opinion.

It enabled you to speak in your own unique voice as a Bedouin Arab woman.

As a Palestinian Arab woman, but also as a woman, period. I actually found it easy to connect with this place of, on the one hand, feeling that yes, I represent my group, but meantime in many cases being able respectfully to say no: No, thank you. In a particular case, with its specifics, I have my own position. And then gradually when I accumulated the strength to articulate my position, I could also talk about my position in a national context, so it was coming from there. If I'm strong enough to talk about these women's issues, and everyone says OK, that's clear—because it's very easy to present your position as a woman on the women's struggle when you're in a Jewish-Arab group—then it helps you when you get to the more difficult national issues around the Nakba, the right of return, the right of the Jewish people to also have a state and whether I do or do not acknowledge this right.

To present myself as a woman, as part of something universal, helped enable me to see myself in terms of universal principles. If I claim this right for myself, who am I to reject it vis-a-vis others. I remember that back in 1996, I completely rejected it, I wasn't prepared to think about you, the Jews, having a state at my expense. I wasn't prepared to talk in terms of: Yes, you should have a state, let's talk about how to do that. This "let's think about how" was not in my lexicon. I saw my own victimhood much more strongly. I think that this reflection by the facilitators in the course was often about Paolo Freire. There was a lot of discussion about understanding my place as a victim and as oppressed, and also about how I internalize this place. And there's a statement, or question, engraved on my mind, I take it with me wherever I go, and now in my day-to-day work I ask this kind of question of the staff. I remember not only this specific sentence, but also Rabah's hands gesturing in the workshop when he said it: "OK people, here there is power for the minority; the majority has conceded. Notice that the majority has conceded and the power is now there, and you aren't taking it, so what's going on here?"

TAKING THE POWER THAT IS THERE

Since then, I have founded an Arab-Jewish organization, and I didn't just get up one day and do that because I felt like it. I really invested in thinking about it, in depth: Is this what I really want to do? Is this the place where I want to make my contribution? Is this where I want to invest myself? It would be easier for me to establish a Palestinian organization here; that way, you'll always stay within the consensus, and you'll always provide that feeling of national affinity that everyone wants to feel. From a place of awareness, I went in this other direction. And very often today I look at the discussion on Jewish-Arab relations within the organization. We're not just an Arab-Jewish organization that does projects in the field, but an Arab-Jewish organization that I was determined would create an internal dynamic of Jewish-Arab relations among the staff, too. And I frequently say to myself: Did you notice that you're the head of this program and Sarit [a Jew] is just the secretary and yet you wait for Sarit to tell you what needs to be done; where is this coming from? You are the program's director, so lead the program. What are you waiting for? Or in some other situation a Jew is a coordinator and you are his director and you suddenly wait for the Jew to tell you what needs to be done. Where is this coming from? I think my awareness of this is something I learned during the facilitators course, maybe at some strategic moment, and it has stayed with me all through my work in directing my organization, in all the projects that we have initiated, Jewish-Arab projects. I'm always with the insight of, OK, what's happening here, how are we building this project, what discourse are we bringing to the Arab-Jewish partnership? What kind of Arab-Jewish partnership are we creating? Are we creating something that brings in two narratives? Or is there one narrative that everyone interprets from his own perspective?

I have never seen all these insights in play anywhere else. I can only connect it with the process I went through [at the School for Peace and afterward], and I can also give myself some credit for it because I am a person who learns. I have learned, and then I have continued to follow up, and then the book Identities in Dialogue was published. I think that the first day that book was in the shops, I was the first person who began reading it to see how it would connect for me. And to this day when I say to staff: "This is the approach Neve Shalom uses; other places have their own approach," I immediately add, "So, people, we can always say there are other approaches, but I want you to do it this way and after that while you're working, you can start to build your own approach." If you look around today, most of the staffs that deal with facilitation and not just Arab-Jewish facilitation but facilitation in general, are using the Neve Shalom approach—and not by accident. This is apropos of what it did for me.

Another area where the course at Neve Shalom gave me insights was the Arab-Jewish question as a whole—along with my experiences in Canada, seeing the conflict from a distance, and along with what happened during October 2000, which was really strong. So you say OK, sixty years of coexistence, or sixty years of illusion, or sixty years of capitulation—what was it? I have insights coming from that place. I thought that I knew how I wanted the Arab-Jewish issue to be seen in Israel, so I wanted to set up an organization that will deal not just with dialogue and not just with being, but really with doing. I wanted to do it from a stance of joint action; I'm a woman of action. I don't see myself as someone who can live as a facilitator, but really as someone who knows how to do things; nonetheless, within this life of action, I wasn't prepared to relinquish these aspects of being. The Arab and the Jew can go learn about active citizenship as interns at a Bedouin village like Hashem Zaneh and if they discuss this charged subject of citizenship, so OK, we have the facilitators who can guide them through this process. So I integrated the doing with the being, between the Arab-Jewish conversation and what we bring from a place of learning/study and from a place of insight and also joint action. So, I don't want to exaggerate, but maybe—I can't say with certainty, but maybe—if I had not gone to this place of learning about groups in conflict and also had not spent time in Canada, I could have been a person very, very strongly oriented to the idea that I'm not interested in the majority and don't want to even see them. I could easily have ended up there, because that's how I grew up.

GROWING UP WITH JUST ONE NARRATIVE

I grew up in a household where my grandmother would say Palestine, and did not say Israel, and we were Palestinians. My father is from the generation that lived under a military administration [until 1966 in most Arab communities in Israel] and he almost never said anything either way. My grandfather and grandmother were very outspoken. In fact my grandfather was very outspoken in 1947 about what was going on. My grandmother's father was a sheikh who struggled against the idea of the founding of Israel. That was the environment I was raised in: We were the only ones with rights, and I wasn't prepared to discuss anything else. I was also raised on nationalist songs and poems that presented only the Palestinian narrative, and any other narrative was delegitimized.

This was in Lakiya, where I was born. We even had a Lakiya clubhouse, and my uncle was active there. He was jailed for seven years and joined the PLO. That was my reality. By fourth grade, I was drawing the Palestinian flag. It was during the first Lebanon war; I painted a Palestinian flag the size of an entire wall. We had a white-painted wall outside, the first time we had one, and I painted a huge Palestinian flag on it. The police came and arrested my father, because I was only in third grade. Lots of people said it was my fault that my dad was in jail, but other people said I was a hero. I enjoyed the attention. I started doing things; I burned tires on Land Day. I burned one on a hill and saw the police come so I went and burned another one somewhere else; it was a game for me.

Then I got a little older. I saw the soldiers come into the village, eighteen-year-olds doing orienteering training. I would act mean and hide their designated targets and tell myself, let them look all day, what do I care? So that was my childhood, that's the background. And I was also in jail. In ninth grade, I was in jail during the first Intifada. When Abu Jihad was killed, I said that Israel had murdered him. I took my whole class outside and we boarded an Egged bus and tore it apart. We waved Palestinian flags out the windows. They arrested us at the Shoket junction. So that was my youth. I remember that the commander at the police station told my father that he was insane for letting me run around that way and do the things I was doing. So my father looked at him and said, "She's an adolescent, she has to have an outlet for her strength and her energy somewhere. I'd rather she do it this way, with you, than with something involving family honor." So that was how he saw it, and he gave me the space to act, when he himself could not have done those things as a young man growing up under a military administration. So he gave me legitimacy to be that person. When I entered university I was very extremist, it was a war, and I was on the Arab Students Council.

I'm trying to remember why I went to that university seminar with Dan Bar-On and Neve Shalom. Maybe it was an open course and I needed the credits; I can't really remember. But it had nothing to do with any insight on my part about going to that place, as far as I remember. Maybe some of my friends were taking it so I went, too. But I know why I went for the facilitators course at the School for Peace. That had to do with my childhood.

Wait a minute. You've said that at the course at the university you could say all those things to Jews, do battle with them, challenge them to hear your voice.

Hurt them, take out all my anger on them! Before that, every time I saw a soldier I was frustrated, helpless, but now there was this room that gave me a safe space so I could dish it out to them for a change. I saw every Jew in the course as a punching bag for years of accumulated anger. I remember I really did hurt people, sometimes they cried, and when I thought maybe I should ease up a little, the Arab group would tell me, no, they deserve it. So maybe I was coming from this place of, I'll show them! I just don't remember for sure how I decided to do that course. For sure it was my first-ever opportunity to sit with Jews on an equal basis and tell them everything I was feeling, without fear. Sometimes I'd even exaggerate a little to make them feel how guilty they were. I'd express my victimhood very thoroughly to prove to them that they are the victimizer and I, the victim, and I didn't want to hear about their suffering. The more I am a victim, the less I can see them as unfortunate, and connect with them. As if the more I invested in this stance, the less I could see them as anything but victimizers.

The things you mentioned, like talking on an equal basis, which is very empowering, these are substantial reasons. There aren't many opportunities like that. The question is, Why did you go for it again? You said it was to find yourself. What were you looking to find out about yourself?

Right after that I flew to Canada and there was an incident on a bus that made me stop and think. It was when they gave me the address of a battered women's shelter to visit, as part of my fieldwork practicum. I got on the bus and asked the driver in English and he told me that he didn't speak English, and I told him that I don't speak French, so he told me that he couldn't help me. Suddenly I heard a woman speaking with her daughter in Hebrew, and immediately, without stopping to think about it, I felt very confident. I felt secure, as if I were at home. The thing that all my life represented the ultimate insecurity, that did not belong to me, that didn't let me feel at home, suddenly it was familiar. So I went over to her and started speaking Hebrew with her. I was proud of myself for knowing Hebrew, whereas in Israel I was embarrassed to know Hebrew, as if knowing the enemy's language means you want to belong to them. Now suddenly I was proud: Hey, I also know Hebrew. So I asked her and she began explaining about the conflict over languages in Quebec and I said what a fool, like he's not prepared even to talk with me or listen to me. I took a look at myself and asked myself, In what way do I resemble that bus driver? In the context of the Palestinian-Israeli conflict, How am I like that guy who won't even engage? And I saw the implication right away, how I'm not willing to listen to the other side. He wasn't willing to listen to English. Then in a more aware way, from within this experience, I began to think: I'm alone here, suddenly I hear Hebrew, and how did that affect me?

READY TO BE MORE VULNERABLE

Another thing was that my adviser there was a Jewish woman. Suddenly I'm looking at this person who is looking at me and listening to me. Not that they didn't see me and listen to me at Ben-Gurion University, but there was a wall there, a huge wall between me and the lecturer, like, talk to me about the subject but I'm not interested in hearing anything else. But in Quebec I was ready, maybe because I was alone and needed confidence, I was ready to be more vulnerable and be myself, and it wasn't all on them anymore, aleyhum, aleyhum. You can't be sticking it to them when your friends aren't there, anyway. It may have been about this feeling of confidence I was looking for. And so gradually, because I was ready to open up, be vulnerable, and show myself and talk about Amal and her feelings, suddenly little by little I began to connect with the French people there who talked about the English language and how if you spoke English you would pay a price because you were acting superior. And suddenly I was exposed to this other conflict in the world.

So I was asking myself, well why don't they talk, it's about language, it's about identity. So why don't they talk? Don't they have to talk? So I connected with it, and then we had a course on this subject, and a meeting with groups of Indians in Canada, so there I was in that place again. When they began talking from a stance of victimhood, I got angry, I got angry at them and said: "Get a grip on yourselves and say what you need to say, say how you see things differently, and take the initiative." Ahh! That's exactly what I tell myself. It was hard for me to connect with the discourse of victimhood, I connected with them but then said, "OK, I hear you; next!"

I had already been in that group for four months and suddenly they are talking about this, and when you hear it from the outside, you project it onto yourself. So I thought, Well, when I go home I'm not going to continue talking [this way] anymore because I'll sound just that way. What do I want? OK, there was a Nakba, and it was at the expense of the Palestinians; everything you are saying, Amal, is true. How is it going to help you if you don't translate these insights into something you want, some kind of future that you want? Because it doesn't depend only on me, I am born and I'll die, but there is a generation that is going to continue on after me. What is my responsibility to that generation? What is my responsibility to my daughter? If it was only about me—if I knew that the world began when Amal was born, the world will end when Amal dies—I would go out there and have fun and travel, and that's it! But I have a responsibility here, and I didn't come into this world for nothing.

Then when I came home, there was the trip to Germany. You called us from Neve Shalom. You were choosing people from the courses. You said, "Who wants to go? We want to do another phase with the group." I think the group was one of the strongest groups when we were together. I don't know whether you'd agree, but I thought it was a very interesting group, both on the Jewish side and the Arab side, and with Walid. So when you called about Germany and said you wanted to do more work, another phase, I thought: Why not? I'm bringing something different with me now and I want to see what I can do with it. So we went to Germany, and it was like we would be building something for me. It was unlike the Ben-Gurion University seminar, where we were the victim and all the time the Jews had to explain or apologize. Now we're in Germany, and there are three groups: the Germans, the Palestinians, and the Jews. Come let's look at all of this. It provided an opportunity to look at additional things from a different perspective. It was very meaningful for me in terms of rounding out what I had learned in Canada, and also to buttress the way I'd begun thinking there about all of this.

Then right away the second Intifada broke out. Everyone started saying, "See, coexistence has failed." I said, "Wait, is it really coexistence that has failed? Maybe it's that things are becoming visible, maybe the real picture is becoming clear and all this fogginess is disappearing, and suddenly there is a different picture, a real picture. The relations between Palestinians and Jews in Israel are in a very difficult place," I said, "and we have to think what we are going to do about that, together." At some point I organized a big demonstration in Lakiya against everything that was happening. I was in my car when a guy came on the radio from Sderot and said, "I am angry at the Bedouin, why are they burning the bank in Rahat? Why are they trashing cars? We bought them the cars, we built them the bank." Listening to that guy was the first time that I really listened and did not say, "Screw you, you're crazy! I didn't say, I'm not willing to listen to you!" I said, "Wow, this poor guy! This guy is saying things that are unreal, this guy is speaking from ignorance, from total ignorance. He thinks that if he weren't there, I'd die; he thinks that I'm only alive thanks to him; he feels important." And I thought: "This guy needs me. I have a responsibility."

TAKING RESPONSIBILITY

If I refuse to continue being a victim, and that's a decision I have made, then what is my responsibility toward the majority? Do I want to be a separatist and only deal with myself, or do I really have a responsibility toward the majority? And if I have a responsibility toward the majority, then I'm strong, and if I'm strong, then that's how I have to see myself. So I said, it can't be that I won't find partners here. It can't be that I won't find people who think just the same as I do. Surely there are other people who share the view that, because of October 2000, the need is even stronger now to learn and to act together, to learn about this conflict and not run away from it. Choosing separatism means to run away. And what is my responsibility toward Eden, my daughter, who could get to university with no preparation and meet a Jewish boy there who thinks that she is at university thanks to him. So I said to myself, that's my responsibility, and in that frame of mind, I went and founded AJEEC.

First of all, *ajeec* is an Arabic word meaning "I am coming to you." It's a community orientation because that's my approach. But the name also worked in another context because I thought: what I want is to deal with civil and political equality, I want to deal with empowerment of the Palestinian minority, and I want to deal with building partnership and creating Arab-Jewish partnership . . . and when I put all that together it came out, in English: the Arab Jewish Center for Equality, Empowerment and Cooperation: AJEEC.

Equality, empowerment, and Arab-Jewish partnership are not just a bunch of words strung together. It's about the way I look at Jewish-Arab partnership. I don't see it as optional; it's a must. If it's optional I could always say, Fine, I can live on my own, but I don't see that. I remember during the October 2000 disturbances, I was even living with a Jewish woman friend. And I asked myself, am I prepared now to give up on Jewish society, or am I prepared to give up my aunt?! Really, at that point I spent a few days with my aunt, and a few days with this Jewish woman friend, and I really love her, and I love my aunt, but suddenly my aunt became insignificant and the significant person was this friend and I said well, I won't give her up. So if I won't give that up, then evidently I don't want to throw the Jews into the sea, and if I don't want to throw the Jews into the sea, if I won't give them up, so then what kind of life do I want to live with them? I don't want the life of oppressor and oppressed, I don't want a life where someone is controlling how I live, so OK, be strong, not in the sense of dictating or not dictating, but to build some kind of life that will be right for you and also for your Jewish colleague.

NOW THEY SEE ME

So that's how AJEEC was founded. The organization is 90 percent about action in Palestinian society. You can't talk about partnership and creating partnership if the Palestinian population is not empowered. You can't talk about being empowered without seeing that translated into the language of rights and equality in the State of Israel. Thus we as an organization focus a lot on empowering the Palestinian minority. We deal a lot with the entire subject of civil equality, but we also focus a lot on Arab-Jewish partnership from the perspective of binational activism. From a place of seeing the joint space that we share, together, as Arabs and as Jews, together, and considering how we want this place to look and to be. I see this also in my daily life, and I make sure to say to Jews [who live in the same space] that I have a holiday today, for example; in the doctor's office, in the supermarket, everywhere, I have this need, I don't know if it's to educate or to affirm that I exist.

Nowadays I will suddenly catch myself going into a shop to buy milk and I'll tell the clerk, did you realize that we have a holiday today? He did not ask but I tell him anyway, and I do it in any neighborhood. Currently I am living in an area where the majority is Jewish, so I make sure to do this sort of thing all the time. Then on my holiday, people tell me "Happy Holiday," like the young guy who works at the grocery store, and I think about what it does for me when he says "Happy Holiday," what it does on the level of awareness, considering that I was once invisible. I was the Arab woman who lives in the neighborhood and I would go out to do errands and no one would see me. But now they see me, everyone in the apartment building sees me. I post things in Arabic on the bulletin board in the lobby. I do this as a way of acting out, because I'm not some transient who just sleeps there and then disappears. I have strong things to say and I'll say them, I'll put my notices in the grocery store and at the hairdresser's salon and I'll read them out loud to Eden in Arabic after I post them there. I will speak Arabic with my children in the mall without giving it a second thought, and in the park they will speak Arabic, and if some child says to them, "You're an Arab," they'll say yes without adding any sort of justification as their mother used to do back in the day, they'll just say yes and go on running around as if it's quite natural.

The other significant thing in my life currently is to establish a bilingual Arab-Jewish school in Beersheba [launched in 2009 as the Hagar Institute, by the Hagar Association, founded in 2006]. I asked myself, given that I'm living in Beersheba, do I want to send my children to a Jewish school? Absolutely not! And do I want to send my children to an Arab school? No, for two reasons: first, because the educational level in the available Arab school is very low, and secondly, because to build partnership we need to educate for it. I took the initiative and brought the idea to a group of Jews and Arabs, and we decided together to go for it. Before we approached the city, we went to Hand in Hand [the Association for Bilingual Education in Israel] to network, to learn from them, and then we brought Hand in Hand with us to the municipality. The first year we didn't have an easy time; the first year, the city did not give us a space so we rented space. We set up the kindergarten by ourselves. Now [2009] it's a flourishing school, with three grades: a kindergarten, a preschool, and a first grade class. My children are in the first group that entered. That group is in first grade now—I have twins, a son and a daughter, in the first grade class.

To recruit Jewish parents for the school, we spent some time walking around the big park in Beersheba with our children, handing out flyers and talking to people. For the Arab families, there was already a waiting list, but there were too few Jewish children enrolled. Eden and Muad, my children, were four years old at the time. Anwar and I were afraid of how people would respond; we're already adults and we've been messed up so we were afraid. We gave Eden the flyers and she ran around giving them out. At one point a woman there made an offensive gesture to her. And I thought, Oy, why have I put my daughter in this situation. This woman hurt her. But Anwar said to me, "Wait, let's see what Eden says about this." Then Eden came and told me, "Well, that lady doesn't want the flyer. I'm sure she doesn't have a child in preschool." She took the whole thing in a very healthy way, not seeing it as a negative response to her being an Arab and the flyer having Arabic writing on it. This was her response, dealing with the everyday things that happen.

Tell me more about AJEEC, about what you do there.

AJEEC, the Arab Jewish Center for Equality, Empowerment and Cooperation, is an Arab-Jewish organization for social change. As an Arab-Jewish organization, it carries the whole burden of the Arab-Jewish conflict and we have to deal with that on the level of the staff itself, which we do with what is essentially an ongoing workshop that addresses this.

We are a staff of thirty-four people; that's huge. We are Arabs and Jews who work for social change. It doesn't come easy; it's something that requires hard work with both Jews and Arabs to address their dynamic in pursuing social change. You have to talk about the best models for creating social change. And in the Arab-Jewish context, you also have to talk about the best models for Jewish-Arab partnership, so it's a compound task.

EMPOWERMENT FOR PARTNERSHIP

We work in three major areas, the first of which is economic empowerment, including promoting cooperatives as an economic model, promoting small business development, and promoting business partnerships for women, for men, everything. AJEEC today is the biggest nonprofit organization in the Negev, but it is also the second largest Arab nonprofit in Israel. So it's a really big organization, including from the standpoint of its action agenda.

The second area is about social and community empowerment. We oversee about 460 volunteers running fifty-two projects in all the Bedouin Arab villages in the Negev. We have developed models of community volunteering which have now been replicated and modified for use in Ramle, Lod, Nazareth, Sakhnin, and other places. We are the leading player in this realm. We didn't just provide a model, we also created a discourse of volunteering in Arab society. We put it on the table along with the question of civilian national service. And it definitely was not easy for us, we went through hell, but in this respect it's very important to stop saying no and start saying here is what we want as the Palestinian minority. This is valid not just regarding Jewish-Arab relations, it's also valid regarding empowerment of the Palestinian minority: What do we want for ourselves? What vision will we pursue as the Palestinian minority in Israel?

Part of this empowerment activity is our focus on early childhood development. We do a lot of work on this. We advocate for the allocation of funding for services; we lobby the various government ministries and we have been able to develop a nice model and create a precedent for the establishment of early childhood education in the unrecognized villages with subsidies from the Israeli government. This is unprecedented and thus far has not been duplicated anywhere else. You see a situation in an unrecognized village where, on the one hand, there is an outstanding demolition order because the village has no official government recognition, and on the other hand there is a big sign saying, "Under the supervision of the Ministry of Industry, Trade and Labor"—it's just incredible. This is the situation; this reflects the reality here! We created a framework that resembles day care; it's called a Mother and Child Center. It takes children aged one year to three years, and runs in the mornings from 7:30 to 12:30. We have also brought this model to Ramle-Lod, because there is a very similar population there with a reality similar to ours in the Negev.

The third major area we work on is Arab-Jewish partnership. We have a program for Arabs and Jews to give a year of their lives and volunteer. This is not just serving the Bedouin Arab population in the Negev, as a way for the Jewish side to salve its conscience. We say, for example, let Nagla from Rahat volunteer with a Jewish school, because she also has a responsibility for what goes on there; it's about Jews and Arabs together taking responsibility for the two communities and not only for one. They volunteer in pairs and spend their entire week from morning till evening in Jewish and Arab schools, in community centers for Jews and community centers for Arabs—it's really impressive. We work on a lot of women's health projects focusing on empower- ment and leadership. Recently we have gone into the schools, into the teachers' rooms; maybe it's something like what the School for Peace has done, this whole area of active citizenship, we've taken it to the teachers' lounges. How to talk about citizenship is a subject still in its infancy, but next we want to go into another eight Jewish and Arab schools in the Negev. We are a nonprofit that raises its money abroad. We rely heavily on donors and not on government funding.

You are the director of AJEEC.

I am the founder and director of the organization, but AJEEC is also a part of the Negev Institute for Strategies of Peace and Development (NISPED), of which I am a co-director, with Vivian Silver [who has since retired]. NISPED works on the international level with developing nations in the Middle East, in Palestine and Jordan, and AJEEC is actually the Israeli division.

You described earlier how you talk with your staff, in terms of their taking power—when the power is there, yet they haven't taken it. How does this training, this approach, play out? You are an Arab woman directing an organization in which a lot of Jews work, and they surely do not have an easy time accepting the authority of an Arab woman.

I don't know if they have a problem with Arab authority, but often I hear the Jewish staff talking. . . . Sometimes it's tiring to think that even if I'm just pouring out the tea, this has implications in a Jewish-Arab context, and it's about power. So I'll tell them," Yes, pay attention to this," and they'll say, "Wow. During the last war, there were rockets being fired at us here and our organization was exposed to this, on the one hand, and on the other hand we are Arabs and Jews on the staff." It was clear to me that as an Arab-Jewish organization we had to deal with this. We decided that we would address it, and we sat down and there were some very harsh things said—the most harsh statements you can imagine. This was happening within my staff, to the point that some staffers were legitimizing the war. As an organization we deal with the whole spectrum of opinion, and we dealt with this through ongoing workshops. We did not just let it go, despite how hard it was and how tiring it was to deal with this kind of thing.

I think that I am granted authority. Perhaps it's not stated outright, but probably most of the Jewish group on the staff are people who came with a prior acquaintance with me, so they knew what they were getting into. But let's take a new secretary, for instance: you can see her difficulty right away. You can almost hear her thinking, "All of a sudden you are telling me what to do, you're my boss," and you can see that the adjustment takes some time. I deal with it pleasantly; I understand it. I am aware of the dynamic and I deal with it gradually with new people, and then suddenly it becomes routine for them.

But to say that it's easy would be inaccurate. It's not easy when we are deliberating difficult issues. It's not easy when sometimes I am attempting to reflect something back through the lens of Jewish-Arab relations and then someone will say, Excuse me, but this is not the lens we need; this has to be viewed through the lens of budgets or social issues. So I say that it's really all the same lens and, incidentally, the lens of budgeting, money, power, relations between Arabs and Jews—it's nearly all the same lens.

Sometimes people don't want to look through the lens of Arab-Jewish relations and I insist; in that sense, I dictate terms. I can't look at these issues without this perspective of Jewish-Arab relations. So this perspective, which is rarely easy, nonetheless has a major presence at the organization I direct.

AFTERWORD

A Critical Analysis of the Interviews

NAVA SONNENSCHEIN

Conducting these interviews was profoundly enlightening for me. We at the School for Peace are often asked about the impact of our work and now, it seems, we have some sort of answer.

I sat down to talk with people who had participated in a School for Peace (SFP) training course sometime during the last twenty years. The common denominator was that all of them reported having been profoundly changed in meaningful ways during the course or courses in which they were participants. This impact, far from having waned in the interim, seemed if anything to have intensified with the passing years, despite the fervently conflicted reality in which we live here. This was evident in the impressive spectrum of social and political activism to which SFP course graduates committed themselves, and which they are still pursuing today, in a variety of fields.

All in all, I conducted in-depth interviews, of sixty to ninety minutes each, with twenty-seven course graduates, women and men, of whom thirteen (eleven citizens of Israel and two residents of East Jerusalem) were Palestinian Arabs. The Arab group included six men and seven women; the Israeli Jewish group, eight men and six women. All participants were given an opportunity to read their own interview transcript and all gave permission for their inclusion in this book. Two of the original twenty-seven

interviews were not published, at the request of those two participants, although all twenty-seven were addressed in this analysis of the
interviews.

The people interviewed were all graduates of one or more SFP long-term
courses of between one semester and one year in duration, offered between
1991 and 2015, at the SFP campus at Neve Shalom–Wahat al Salam or at other
academic campuses. Some participants attended courses for facilitators of
groups in conflict (120 course hours), some were students in university
courses integrating theoretical and experiential components (42 course
hours), and some were participants in training courses for social change
agents at the School for Peace over the past ten years (140 course hours).
The common denominator in all these courses was that they were of relatively long duration (as compared with, e.g., a weekend workshop or a one-
week seminar) and dealt intensively with Jewish-Palestinian dialogue using
the intergroup facilitation model and methods pioneered by the School for
Peace and described in a previous book, *Israeli and Palestinian Identities in
Dialogue* (Halabi, 2004).

As described by most of the Jewish participants and half of the Arab participants, the experience in these courses was formative and life-changing.
They said things like: "That course was transformative for me at the time, and
I think it has left its mark to this day"; and "Maybe I'll start with the bottom
line which is, without a shred of exaggeration, that the Neve Shalom course
changed my life unequivocally and is for me the point of reference in all my
development as a human being and certainly as an Israeli"; and "The course
was one of the things that changed my life, a formative experience that
changed me forever and influenced part of my identity and the agenda I take
with me everywhere." The Jewish participants called their experience in the
course a point of reference or a turning point in their lives; the Arab participants called theirs an important or significant additional layer in the fabric
of their lives. One reported outcome was that a great many of both the
Jewish and Arab participants subsequently switched careers to embrace
fields focusing on peace or on equality between Jews and Arabs. Some
became human rights lawyers. Some undertook to establish or lead nonprofit organizations focusing on relevant fields. Some turned their efforts to
peace education or related academic careers, including research dealing with
intergroup conflict.

There are a number of areas in which the Jewish and Arab participants described having undergone similar changes. The course functioned as an academy for the examination of power relations. Among the Jewish participants, both women and men, all of them said that, to this day, they continue to look at situations and analyze them in terms of power relations: "As soon as you understand power relations, your judgment is directed less toward the external [aspects of things] and more toward the internal. You can comprehend injustice and inequality." Another participant emphasized that "you begin to learn kindheartedness and concern, once you understand power relations." The participants noted that they have brought this analytical tool to bear on the analysis of other conflict situations in their personal and professional lives and in addressing conflict situations elsewhere in the world. They use it to analyze relations between genders, between religious and secular people, and between ethnic groups like Ashkenazi and Mizrahi Jews.

Eleven of the thirteen Arab graduates noted that the School for Peace taught them to look at situations from the perspective of symmetries and asymmetries of power. "Suddenly I began looking at power relations; that is the most basic thing I took away with me from Neve Shalom. Before, I looked at the occupation and at inequality and the unequal allocation of rights; I looked at those things in the [political] party [in which I was active], too, but I did not look at power relations. This may be the key point; this is evidently the change that happened to me." Graduates also said that they used what they had learned at the SFP when they began analyzing power relations in their workplace. "I started to examine the power relations on the job. Meantime, my thesis dealt with power relations between Jews and Arabs in the context of therapy. In my work as a psychotherapist, I can't look at what's happening without these lenses, neither within the therapy process itself nor in terms of the relations among the staff." The perspective of seeing things in terms of power relations also emerged in the analysis of other social situations unrelated to the Jewish-Arab context, like the relations between workers and employers. "In Tel Aviv, I was very interested in issues of socioeconomic power involving workers and employers, and all the dynamics of economic exploitation, which exist internationally and exist here, too." Several of the Arab participants noted that they had become interested in looking in this way at other conflicts and other situations of oppression around the world.

More than half the Jewish and Arab participants recounted that the course equipped them with meaningful life skills. Eight of the thirteen Arab graduates said that the course had given them a very significant set of life tools. They learned "that in every situation of conflict there is some way to proceed" and that conflict is something that can be managed. They acquired "a commitment to dialogue as a way of resolving problems." Many noted that they had learned to read group dynamics in real time, and to relate to a group as a single organism. They reported that the course taught them to read reflectively; that it helped them to learn about community resilience; that it enabled them to acquire "the ability to take a person from one place to some other place." They took these tools with them to their working environments, both on the job and as activists. Many said that it had been important to them to take ownership of this toolbox and pass it along to their children. Six of thirteen Arab participants have sent their children to bilingual schools.

About half the Jewish participants noted that they had acquired a complete set of skills in their SFP course: "I got a set of skills, like lenses, I don't know how to put it, that were the means for me to examine the behavior of all kinds of cross-sections of groups of people." These Jewish participants said they had learned "to talk with Arabs on an equal basis," to examine people's behavior, and to examine intergroup relations. They acquired "the ability to accept that there are several aspects to the same story." They learned how to see things from another's point of view; the course "offered tools for how to treat people from a culturally sensitive standpoint." They said: "The course taught me to be cautious about grandiose declarations"; the course taught "inclusiveness and more inclusiveness, a flexibility that I didn't have in me, before"; "I acquired the ability to see what isn't seen." And: "the course gave me tools for intergroup dialogue; I learned to listen and to be more attentive to people. I learned how to sit in front of a group and talk with that group."

Another area of reported change shared by both the Jewish and the Arab participants concerns the development of critical thinking. Eight of the thirteen Arab participants talked about speaking out against prevailing opinion and being people who can think critically. This was expressed in terms of a desire "not to cut corners," and to say what they think even when it isn't popular: "I have no trouble being very critical about things, for example in Arab society about things that don't seem right to me, like the oppression of women." They gave specific examples, which included going public with criticism of violent attacks when hardly anyone around them was doing so; advocating for the importance of translating for Jews on the staff, even when all the Arab facilitators think differently; or declining to appear at a conference where the prevailing attitude toward Bedouin women is Orientalist and patronizing. One man mentioned that "I could see that I can be both victim and victimizer." Others sounded a critical note in speaking about the attitude of staff members at the School for Peace: "In the facilitators group," said one Arab graduate, "there was no space to say that I'm also Israeli [as well as Palestinian]; it wasn't legitimate there, because right away they [the facilitators] would tell you that you are internalizing your oppression and it starts to choke you from the inside." These participants also talked about the personal costs of going against prevailing opinion.

All the Jewish participants said that the course gave them tools for critical thinking. "I feel that, from the moment you put these lenses on, you can't take them off again, and they're already part of your eyes, as if now this is an area I can't just decide to look at without my critical lenses. In terms of Palestinians as an occupied people, with these lenses you see the occupation everywhere." The critical thinking is further expressed in activism undertaken by the Jewish participants, who also speak out against prevailing opinion. They have paid a price for this in Israeli society, and especially in their relations with family members who are opposed to their ideas. Three Jewish participants offered criticism of the process and of the working method of the School for Peace: "A change in identity is a type of injury, because you have to decide you're cutting away something and you have to change, to graft something there instead that will fit and will 'take.' I felt alone, that I had no one to do this with. . . . Here at Neve Shalom there was no comfort, no one soothed you . . . and I expected that there would be." Another participant said: "I think that going through this process doesn't have to be at such intense levels, so hard and critical; I think there should be more tolerance for whatever place people are in, and that's also how I facilitate." Another participant: "The institution has a hard time coping with the possibility of hybrid outcomes as we expand our boundaries [in more diverse ways]."

A related area of reported change is about the participants' taking responsibility and taking action. Because the two groups come from different places with regard to the question of taking responsibility, I address this issue below along with other areas of change unique to each group.

CHANGES UNIQUE TO THE JEWISH GROUP

For both men and women in the Jewish participant group, the course was perceived as constituting "an extended process of opening our eyes to an ignorance that had been comfortable." The group began to see reality through what is happening to the Arabs. For the Jewish participants, the course developed an awareness of the unequal reality: "[There was] a process in which I was stripped of my Zionist naivety, the perspective that we are simply all human beings. [The process] raised my awareness of the significance of something being Arab or Jewish." This was a "painful process of awareness because it shattered the optimism that people originally arrive here with." The loss of that innocence was painful and sometimes experienced as actual abdominal pain. The process was about the birth of awareness; some of the participants called it a transformation or a reorientation: "I'm someone who is sitting in a different place in the world now, who acknowledges his neighbors and has compassion for them and wants to create a different reality."

Participants vividly described how painful this earthshaking process could be: A week prior to each session, said one, "that abdominal pain that the course provokes would come back: tension, pain, and guilt that was very hard for us. Plus a sense that something very, very important is happening here, if a week or two into the month we felt it coming on again" [as the next session approached]. The discovery that "I am not the most enlightened person, not the most righteous . . . creates a break, a very big question mark, and an uneasy feeling that the information we are getting [from mainstream sources on the outside] is biased." In their interviews, people gave details about this process: "I remember that feeling, repeatedly, of the penny finally dropping in terms of my awareness. For example, understanding how terrible that whole demographic concept is, that idea of [Palestinians as] a demographic threat, what that notion embodies. The dreadful fear hidden behind this idea of a threat . . . I was able to understand the fear, call it by its name, and look at it; I could be aware of that." (For more details about the pain connected with this developing awareness, see Sonnenschein & Bekerman, 2010; Sonnenschein, Bekerman, & Horenczyk, 2010.)

THE AWAKENING FROM ZIONIST NAIVETY

Another facet of the eye-opening nature of this process was "the ability to accept that there are several aspects to the same story. This is something you just don't grasp until you start to notice it. From this standpoint, one day you understand that different people can view the same reality differently, and it doesn't mean that one is wrong and one is right; they can be together in the same reality and see it differently, and what's important is that they see it differently and what's less important is to try to find what actually happened, because the fact that they see reality differently has implications for their living together." This ability is the first stage of awakening. Later on in the process there is some ambivalence between adherence to Zionist beliefs and the demand for equality.

Most of the Jewish participants described stages in an ongoing, eye-opening process of enlightenment vis-à-vis the Zionist perspective both before and after the course: "The really big change is that I arrived [at the course] very confident in my opinions, with a very positive view of myself, and left with this fracture, a big question mark, a strong sense of disruption, but with the feeling that this is right, that it's good to have this disruption of what I had before, the fake security at someone else's expense. I tried at first to bridge between the Zionist outlook and the demand for equality and wasn't able to resolve that. . . . It took me six or seven years."

The ability to talk about inner misgivings concerning Zionism in the group setting, in front of the Arab participants and also with the Jewish group by itself, is what enabled this process to occur: "I think that in the course, I found words for a lot of my feelings, and was able to explain them and also make space for the Zionist sides of me."

Another Jewish participant talked about the exclusivist basis of Zionism: "The problem is not a problem of equality or fewer resources. . . . It's a much deeper problem about how we were born, how this place was born, how it came into being as a Jewish state. I understood that there is something distorted in the foundation that was created here. I understood that the exclusivist basis of Zionism holds that this place is only ours and the memory here is only ours and the language only ours and the land only ours, so this basic orientation of Zionism is the problem. . . . I understood that we have to do as much as we can to struggle against these exclusivist components of Zionism."

This process of opening one's eyes and seeing a reality previously unseen generated new processes that functioned to reshape the identity of the Jewish participants, expanding their identity to include the other. The participants talk about an identity process during which they found themselves obliged to relinquish something before they could bring in something else. They needed to let go of the narrative within which they grew up and which they had an interest in seeing as "the right one." This is a change in identity, a change in worldview. To their preexisting identity, "another image was added, expanding our identity into something that sees in multiple ways, with other identities. . . . It's as if you are adopting something, and even if you're not aware of it, you adopt something from the person you are talking with, especially if it's done in an atmosphere that isn't about macho arguing but rather about listening. Whether you want it to happen or not, something gets into you and you change, you recalibrate. Your identity expands and turns into something that sees in multiple ways, that has other identities in it."

The intensive involvement with identities also enabled the examination of additional identities. Two Mizrahi Jewish women interviewed noted that the encounter with the Arab identity elevated their own Mizrahi identity and gave it legitimacy. "The course brought up Mizrahi identity alongside Arabness and highlighted the Arab dimension of Mizrahi identity. This raised the subject of how much I had repressed that. As an adolescent, I didn't say hello to my own grandfather on the street because he looked Arab and I was really embarrassed. . . . There, in the course, this came out for the first time, starting with my own acceptance of the Arabness in me and my willingness to admit this, which means that it's not something forbidden, it's not the evil enemy with no connection to me, it's part of who I am."

I would like to try to describe here some of the gender differences that emerged concerning the changes that the Jewish participants, men and women, reported having undergone. Most of the Jewish women and a few of the Jewish men spoke at length about their developing awareness of their own racism and of their patronizing stance—a process of humanizing the other. "The first thing you have to do is to look, and to say that they are there; that in and of itself was very difficult. It's a type of racism at your most basic, ugliest level; it's about how you apprehend the other. I told myself that everyone is equal . . . but in the encounter, everything comes out, all the stereotypes . . . the essence of who this person is who is standing in front of you, what he is experiencing, what he feels in this situation . . . the fact that maybe he doesn't need you, that you're not there in order to give him something . . . but that he has his own existence with his own separate needs." The encounter with strong Arabs brought about this higher level of awareness; one Jewish woman said: "I remember, in the course, understanding that everything about how I look at Arabs is really a product of education. I had a very condescending way of seeing them and in fact the Arabs I knew before were construction workers who worked on our house. In the course, the encounter was with Palestinian peers, an intellectual encounter on several levels with strong, smart Palestinians, and they even know more than I do, more than Jews do, about this subject, since they are living the oppression. . . . It was very powerful to talk about this and to look differently at things." All the Jewish women interviewed mentioned that the issue of racism has remained at the forefront of their attention since the SFP course, and that this is a process that they are still involved with. Another woman said, "I think that the acknowledgment of racism and coping with racism is what has preoccupied me ever since, in all kinds of ways, and that's not how it used to be." The Jewish women interviewed mentioned situations they had experienced in reality in which racist things were said about Arabs; they now took it upon themselves not to let that happen anymore. "I truly made it my job not to allow this discourse; it simply won't be on my [Facebook] wall without a response."

Another gender difference emerged concerning the attitude toward the army and toward combat service in the military. The difference arises because, in general, Israeli Jewish men must deal with this question in a more substantive way than Israeli Jewish women do. Four of the eight Jewish men interviewed refused, as a consequence of the process they went through in the SFP course and subsequently, to do reserve service in the army because of its function as an occupying force. Another of the Jewish men mentioned being supportive to his son when his son refused to serve, while three others did not mention the subject. Refusal is a difficult and lonely process, so refusers seek the company of a community. The essential thing is that this choice is a point of no return, an unequivocal and fateful decision in terms of a Zionist outlook: "Refusal enabled me to decide once and for all. . . . I understood that if I refused, it meant there was no way back. . . . It took something like six years until I decided to do it. I think the second Intifada had a lot to do with my refusal . . . it was constantly in process, one step at a time; very gradually, something was continually undermining the

Zionist perspective." There was a feeling that refusing to serve resolved one's doubts; one man explained: "I understood that this act of refusing, which seemed right to me, I understood that if I refused, then there was no going back." Another participant described a formative moment: "It's a formative moment that unquestionably emerged from the process I went through, and the main thing driving it was the course at Neve Shalom. . . . Before the course, I was a combat soldier and I was against refusal, and then I understood that, hey, the moment has come when I have to stand behind what I'm saying and stop being part of the machine. . . . The fiction of an enlightened occupation was shattered right in front of me at Neve Shalom and undoubtedly this is what led me, myself, to refuse, a long time before there was a refusal movement and a long time before the next Intifada erupted."

For the Jewish women interviewed, a parallel process was described as coping with family members on an ongoing basis and attempting to influence them, whether sons, brothers or fathers: "The whole thing about the army was very clear to me. I knew I was dealing with the issue of my son's army service as I went through the SFP course. . . . And my father, telling me about the Second Lebanon War (2006), when they asked him to come and fight and he got out of it, and when I asked him why, he said: Well, I don't know, what am I doing making war on children? This was not at all typical of my father because he's a fighter and he believes that he's acting for the good of society and for justice. I think it was my influence there."

Another way that the women dealt with this question was through volunteering with Machsom Watch, as a way of addressing the feeling of helplessness that one woman described: "What was pushing me was maybe this feeling of helplessness, that there's nothing we can do. . . . What we were able to do was still very limited, as a group of women who see, document, and publicize [what goes on at the checkpoints] in the media." While the men can refuse military service, this is a refusal of a different sort, an action that opposes what the army is doing as an occupier, a more ongoing process, not a one-time fateful decision. Another Jewish woman talked about her volunteering in Hebron with Palestinian families harmed by the occupation, and a third told about integrating a different viewpoint, a non-militaristic viewpoint, into the administration of her school. Another woman interviewed talked about her doctoral thesis in relation to this area.

These processes involving families were a bigger part of the picture in the interviews with the women. Emotional issues with their families were of great concern to these women when they were going through changes not shared by other family members. "These family conflicts are not easy; it's a difficult price to pay. My mother felt that they had taken her daughter and brainwashed her, both from a feminist standpoint and in terms of her attitude toward Arabs." Another woman reported: "I think that at this stage, people in the family had a very hard time dealing with the presence of my opinions within the family. There were heartbreaking arguments around this subject, actually to the point that there were family dinners on Friday nights that I did not want to go to." These Jewish women participants reported ongoing efforts vis-à-vis their families, sometimes successful and sometimes less so. In my judgment, the Jewish men interviewed had been through similar processes but talked about them less.

All the Jewish participants, women and men, talked about the development of a deep sense of responsibility, and the choice not to be part of the machine. "You're part of [the army and the occupation] even if you are just sitting up in a guard tower. I understood that remaining silent also means being connected" to what is going on. Many of the participants mentioned the realization that they are part of a system of occupation. One expressed the depth of this feeling of responsibility, noting that he had not changed his politics, but that "the most significant understanding that came to me in the course, more emotional than intellectual, is the understanding of my role, my partnership, as a Jew in this conflict. We Israeli Jews are totally partners in this whole project, this Zionist project. That we criticize it and act against it, this of course is very important, it's crucial, and it's great . . . but we are still a part of it. . . . We have a major task here to get rid of the colonialist component in our personality and our identity."

The Jewish men and women interviewed explained that the changes they had undergone had an impact on their activity in all areas of their life. Among the actions cited: studying Arabic; founding organizations like Zochrot; organizing the "Pilots' Letter" (September 2003) in which Israel Air Force reserve pilots declared their refusal to bomb Palestinian civilians in Gaza or anywhere else. Some of the participants changed professions; one man, for example, left a budding career in genetics to work in peace education. Some went into human rights law. Some went into advocacy for equal rights for

Arabs via nonprofit organizations such as Sikkuy; others switched their academic focus to do research in peace and conflict; still others established university courses similar to the School for Peace course they had taken as university students themselves. Some became facilitators of groups in conflict. Others, who did not go into conflict resolution as a profession or as part of their professional careers, pursued their interest in this work via political and social action, participation in demonstrations, work done in organizations like Zochrot and PsychoActive, refusal to do military service in the occupied territories, organizing alternative shared Memorial Day ceremonies, supporting Palestinian families in Hebron harmed by settler violence, volunteering with Machsom Watch or IPCRI or Hand in Hand. Many noted that they had taken on the role of bridging between worlds and responding to racist posts on social networks or in racist broadcasts. Some talked about the price they had paid for coming out publicly against prevailing opinion: Going to jail for refusal to serve in the territories, trouble finding work in their field, harsh arguments with their families, isolation and loneliness. Some talked about a process of connecting with other School for Peace graduates in search of collective support: "I call it entering a community, it's really a community that you're in touch with, even apart from facilitating at Neve Shalom; you meet them everywhere, in all kinds of places."

HOW THE ARAB PARTICIPANTS CHANGED

All the Arab participants talked about a personally and politically empowering experience. The experience was empowering in terms of being able to make their voice heard and have an influence on the Jewish participants. This differs from their daily reality as described by one of the participants: "The fear of the enemy; the fear that you can't let this fear out, that you can't make your voice heard. It eats away at you from within"; and then, in the SFP course, "the dialogue with the other side allows you to break the paralysis that has kept things inside you because of the fear. If you can sit in front of that guy and be strong and speak out about these things, it's healthy. For me as a human being it is healthier that I can speak about my pain, my fear, to the other side."

The sense of belonging and cohesion among the Arab group during the dialogue was also empowering: "I had never had this connection with an

Arab group, where we are walking along together and suddenly we're singing in Arabic on the streets of Germany. Suddenly they don't see you as a stranger; suddenly they see you as a part of us, all of us together." Coping together as a group and acting together as a group provided an empowering experience for the Arabs: "The feeling of doing things together is empowering because it's hard to deal with these things alone, and it's important that Jews also be involved with us in the political action."

Being able to speak Arabic and express oneself articulately in front of Jews and Arabs is an especially empowering experience: "The course at Neve Shalom was shocking because it was my first time in a situation where speaking Arabic was allowed. In all the other coexistence settings, it wasn't possible." The work of the School for Peace has demonstrated over decades the crucial importance of the legitimacy of speaking Arabic in these encounters, and the SFP model of working with groups in conflict accords equal status to Hebrew and Arabic in the encounter between Jews and Palestinians, because language is not just a tool for communicating in these dialogues but a central part of identity.

The dialogue allowed for touching on the most difficult points and speaking out about one's pain in a group of equals. The course provided a safe space to express anger. This was an opportunity to talk with Jews who would listen. "This was really my first chance to sit as an equal with Jews and tell them everything I had to say, without fear." This was different than the experience of their parents, who were afraid of the other side. In the course, they felt that "an Arab identity was no disgrace; the space was much more inclusive; I stopped being afraid."

For the Arab participants, the empowerment was particularly conspicuous at the level of behavior in front of the Jews: "Mainly it was about how to deal with things. That's what was empowering both individually and as a group. It was about coming to the other, or addressing the other, not from a stance of inferiority . . . asking the other to take steps toward where you are, instead of only you moving toward his side."

Two of the graduates noted that doing facilitation work themselves was empowering for them. "There was something about doing facilitation that was emotionally refreshing for me, each time, and it let me grow. And even more than that, lots of times it let me stretch my emotional boundaries." One participant from East Jerusalem spoke about how the practice of facilitation helped him to find emotional release from the occupation: "As Palestinians, we have a lot of problems among ourselves because of the occupation, and the most important thing is that you feel emotionally free, even if you are under occupation . . . because under occupation, you don't feel your own humanity very clearly. When you do facilitation work, you can really liberate people from within. I feel that if a person gets his pain out there, his fear, in front of the other side, it's healthier for him. As a facilitator, you can take a person from one place to another, and as you are doing that you are helping one or two or three people, you are building a better society with a group of people. I do feel that I am building people. It's an amazing feeling, and I love this facilitation work a lot more than I do legal work."

Eleven of the thirteen Arab graduates noted that the course shaped their political awareness. Some of the participants said that when they were at university, they did not deal with politics: "I was never into politics, or any political organization, not Fatah, not Hamas, nothing. In the course I started thinking differently. I started to see a status hierarchy. . . . My awareness about the conflict came into much clearer focus after that series of encounters." Some of them used the phrase "it opened my eyes" and said that the course had "allowed me to understand reality through a different set of spectacles," that is, through a different lens. Some of the participants had dealt with this kind of content before the course and others were dealing with it for the first time. Some noted that the course helped them to reshape their awareness by connecting the micro and the macro. Mainly, they said, it was about learning how to cope with the other side, the Jewish side. "That's what was empowering from a personal and political standpoint; everything we went through there is political education. Since leaving a small village, and having grown up in a very apolitical household, I had not had any encounters with Jews. I came from an apolitical home and turned into a political activist. There's something about the School for Peace: you learn things there and afterwards you start to act on them. After being there, I increasingly wanted to engage in activism in the field."

Another theme that emerged for ten of the thirteen Arab participants was that the SFP process helped them connect with their Palestinian national identity. If you look at identity as a developmental process in the sense of Janet Helms's developmental theory of racial and ethnic identity, then the manner in which the impact of the course would affect the developing identity of the participants would depend on their stage of identity development when they arrived at the course.

Most of the Palestinian participants reported a growing pride in belonging to their national group and more understanding of the way in which they belonged, in one case stating that the course had been "a formative experience that forced me to deal with the reality of the past. It was an experience that helped us heal the scorn we felt for our grandfathers and grandmothers." Something about the course forced the participants to address their past and that of their families as displaced families: "For the first time, I had to face it on the emotional level." All of them said that their identity was more fully formulated following the course than prior to its beginning.

About half the Arab participants mentioned feeling liberated from the internalization of oppression to varying degrees and under various circumstances. Some arrived in denial about their identity: "I didn't want the Arabness in me to be seen at all. I didn't think of myself as an Arab but as a Druze. . . . The course confronted me with the whole concept of who I am and what my identity is." This participant reported that what had made this process possible was the Arab group, the Arab facilitator, and the inclusive and supportive environment: "I must say that if the Palestinian group had not embraced me there, I think I would have got lost. . . . And the facilitation there was coming from a place that said, don't erase your identity, that's not necessary and you don't have to do it."

There were Palestinian participants who, having arrived at the course with a well-defined Palestinian national identity, nonetheless became aware that they were trying to please the Jews in various situations and learned how not to approach the other from a place of inferiority. "I don't see the Jew, as a Jew, as knowing better than I do. I see the conditions of his life, which are different, and I see his opportunities, which are different. I see this from this place that doesn't see the Jew as somehow more [than I am]."

The participants who felt inner conflicts about their identity found an opportunity in the course to make peace between the various parts of themselves. "Yes, I wanted to make peace with all the parts inside of me. By the time I began my second workshop, I was more confident of my Palestinianness and so it was harder to disparage me because I already knew who I was, so I felt more comfortable examining other parts [of myself] and saying yes, I have these parts, and then dealing with these parts, in the binational context. This is something that has to be tackled all the time." This clarification was made possible because of the way the Arab group embraced the diversity in the group as well as the way the Arab facilitator allowed for the respective developmental stages of identity formation at which the various participants found themselves.

Those whose national identity was already well established were liberated from other components like isolation and entrenchment. One participant related that he had been withdrawn, as if barricaded "in a bunker," and that the dialogue with the other liberated him to leave the bunker and opened horizons for him to act at a more inclusive level:

"The village I lived in was an Arab village. . . . I chose this for myself; I am more connected to the Arab side. I learned about Arab history, I learned about the pain and the narrative of the Arabs, I learned that if I want to live here I have to work harder and protect myself because this state, or the Jewish side, they don't want [me here] and don't think about my existence here. I grew up and lived in a situation in which the state, or the Jews, [think about] what's good for them and how to get rid of me as an Arab in this country, so I was growing up in a bunker. I never felt that I would be part of the space that exists in this country; I felt I had to take care of myself, of my nationality, of my identity, and not identify too much with the other side. That didn't interest me; what interests me is my identity, my nationality, and how to protect myself from the other side."

He went on to explain the start of his "journey" during the course: "Horizons increasingly opened up for me. I saw that it wasn't enough to think about and work on empowering your own population, the Arab population and your village, or the city where you work. You have to think more and do more at the level of what is happening in the country and what is happening on the other side, in the Jewish population as well as the Arab population. From there I began my journey about how I could contribute more on the question of conflict, mainly the Jewish-Palestinian or Jewish-Arab conflict, in all directions. I started to take more interest in what is happening on the Jewish side, what is going on with the Palestinians who live outside the boundaries of Israel and also what is happening with the Arabs inside Israel."

A CHANCE TO DEVELOP MEANINGFUL CONNECTIONS WITH JEWS AND CHANGE PRECONCEIVED IDEAS

Eight of the Arab participants noted that the course provided an opportunity to make a meaningful and ongoing connection with Jews: "If I hadn't been at Neve Shalom I don't think I would have so many connections with Jews. These are connections that endure and are important to me from a personal and political standpoint. Places like Zochrot and Neve Shalom offer a little sanity, including from the standpoint of feeling that all is not lost entirely."

Another participant said: "I felt this stigma, believing that all the Jews want to deny my rights. I started a dialogue here and I saw and felt that there is also some difficulty on the other side. It's from a different direction on the Jewish side. I and the Jews are living in one space and it's important to both of us that this space be good for both sides. So, just as I am paying a price for this conflict, the other side is also paying a price, but from a different direction. This all started to be clear to me and I began thinking about and also feeling the pain of the other side. I began feeling that the other side was starting to have a better understanding of my pain and my loss in the situation that exists here, and how together we could promote a different process that could profit both sides."

TAKING RESPONSIBILITY

All the Arab graduates talked about the role they felt called to assume following their participation in the course. "After I left here, I decided that I wanted to contribute to my people on several levels. That was one of the strongest insights I got from the course." Another said: "It's part of your dream to try to have an influence. We can't always be complaining and whining about the reality without doing anything ourselves. We have to go out and take action and try to change our reality. . . . The course was a positive experience. It lit a fire . . . it generated a lot of energy. The considerable stress from this heated encounter evidently kindled a flame and once it got going, it led to a lot of things. . . . I am a very proud person, so I am not prepared to accept the reality laid on me. I want at any price to change that reality, raising my children and passing on a legacy to them, or just by struggling against it and fighting it." The participants mentioned a moral obligation to work toward changing the reality: "I feel that I can't just let it go. Some of the commitment is a moral one, meaning, you felt solidarity with the Palestinians in the territories. This has increasingly become a part of my life, I'm concerned about it all the time, it's what I'm interested in talking about, this moral commitment to all these struggles."

As to working in this field, all of the Arab participants, both men and women, are still working in Jewish-Arab relations in various ways. Two of them are human rights lawyers. They see it as their calling. Some of the participants do group facilitation for encounters between Jews and Arabs; some have begun academic careers in the field and do research or devote their time to peace education at the college or university level; some are managers or staffers at not-for-profit associations to further equality between Jews and Arabs—such as AJEEC, Zochrot, Sadaka-Reut, Givat Haviva, the School for Peace, Hand in Hand, ACRI. Others have worked in the media and media relations. Many said that this work provides a note of sanity and helps them to avoid capitulating to despair, to keep on struggling, not to give up despite the many setbacks.

To summarize, we have seen that the SFP graduates went through profound and multilayered changes. A broader study is called for, with a greater number of participants, to examine whether this is representative of the tens of thousands of participants who have completed courses of this kind. The change that the Jewish and Arab participants underwent is in some respects very similar. For many of them, the course was a formative, even a life-changing, experience. Yet generally, the changes were more powerful and dramatic for the Jewish participants than for the Arab participants, due to the asymmetrical situation of the power relations between the two peoples. For most of the Jewish participants, this was their first significant encounter with their Arab peers whereas, for most of the Arab participants, this was one significant encounter among many that they had been through. For both groups, the course served as a mode of training in power relations and power dynamics: when the course was over, they were left with a valuable tool kit that enabled them to look at different realities and situations from a power relations standpoint. This tool kit included various skills, some similar and some quite different. Facilitation skills, the ability to read group dynamics, were cited by all the participants. But there are skills that were cited by only one national group or the other. The Palestinians talked about acquiring a commitment to dialogue as a path to resolving problems; learning to read group dynamics and to relate to a group as a single entity; to read more reflectively. They felt that the course had helped them learn about community resilience. They had acquired the ability to take someone, figuratively speaking, from one place to another. The Jews talked about acquiring the ability to talk with Arabs as equals; to examine intergroup relations; to see things from the other's point of view. They noted that the course had given them tools to relate to people in more culturally sensitive ways and to be cautious about broad general pronouncements. They had learned to contain what previously had been unsupportable, and then to contain even more. They had learned to be flexible in important new ways.

Both groups developed their critical thinking about reality. All the participants developed a sense of responsibility for changing reality although the two groups expressed their feelings about this differently, which seems unsurprising given the asymmetries of power between the two groups. The course, for Jews and Palestinians alike, kindled a burning and enduring desire to work for change, a personal sense of responsibility for changing the status quo. Both the Jews and the Arabs became, or were confirmed as, social change activists and leaders in diverse ways. Now more than ever, they see this activism as a mission and a duty.

The most conspicuous change among both the Jews and the Palestinians concerns the participants' national identity. The process they underwent allowed them to examine their identity in depth through interaction with the other. This is a dynamic developmental process encompassing multiple changes, but the changes have different orientations depending on the group. For the Arab participants, it was an empowering experience that helped them to connect with their national identity and also to accept its various parts. The change occurred along a spectrum of intensity depending on a given participant's stage of identity development at the start of the course. The Jewish participants also dealt with identity via an eye-opening process that for most of them was earthshaking and painful, involving as it did an awakening from Zionist naivety. Initially they began learning to accept that there are several facets to the same story and subsequently to understand with greater clarity the exclusivist aspects of Zionism and seek ways to narrow the gap between their political beliefs and their actions. As the Palestinian participants were experiencing empowerment in their emergence from the bunker, the Jewish participants were going through a process of expanding their identity to include the other and the reality of the other's existence.

In closing, I would like to express my thanks to all the Jewish and Palestinian graduates for agreeing to be interviewed, and for their tireless work for peace and equality.

ACKNOWLEDGMENTS

I extend my thanks to all who assisted in the birth of this book: to Deb Reich, who translated the material into English and edited it with dedication and professionalism; to Faten Abu Ghosh, for her excellent transcriptions of the audio interviews; to the American Friends of Neve Shalom–Wahat al-Salam for their generous support of the project; to all the women and men interviewed here, Palestinian and Jewish, for offering to share the story of their lives and their testimony about the process they underwent in the School for Peace courses they took and the changes they experienced; to Tamar Saguy, who kindly agreed to frame this work with a theoretical introduction; to Professor Ariella Friedman, for her comments on the draft; and to the legions of School for Peace graduates not profiled in this volume who have devoted themselves to the quest for justice and equality for Israelis, Palestinians, and others around the globe. And finally, thanks to my partner, Coby, and to our children, Nir, Ori, and Tali, for their unflagging encouragement all along the way.

BIBLIOGRAPHY

Allport, G. W. (1954). *The nature of prejudice*. Garden City, N.Y.: Doubleday.

Amir, Y. (1969). Contact hypothesis in ethnic relations. *Psychological Bulletin*, 71, 319–342.

Aronson, E., & Patnoe, S. (1997). *The jigsaw classroom*. New York: Longman.

Ayres, I. (1991). Fair driving: Gender and race discrimination in retail car negotiations. *Harvard Law Review*, 104, 817–872.

Banfield, J. C., & Dovidio, J. F. (2013). Whites' perceptions of discrimination against Blacks: The influence of common identity. *Journal of Experimental Social Psychology*, 49(5), 833–841.

Becker, J. C., Wright, S. C., Lubensky, M. E., & Zhou, S. (2013). Friend or ally: Whether cross-group contact undermines collective action depends on what advantaged group members say (or don't say). *Personality and Social Psychology Bulletin*, 39(4), 442–455.

Bertrand, M., & Mullainathan, S. (2004). Are Emily and Greg more employable than Lakisha and Jamal? *American Economic Review*, 94, 991–1013.

Bikmen, N. & Durkin, K. (2014). Equality for all? White Americans' willingness to address inequality with Asian and African Americans. *Cultural Diversity and Ethnic Minority Psychology*, 20(4), 591–600.

Bikmen, N., & Sunar, D. (2013). Difficult dialogs: Majority group members' willingness to talk about inequality with different minority groups. *International Journal of Intercultural Relations*, 37, 467–476.

Blumer, H. (1958). Race prejudice as a sense of group position. *Pacific Sociological Review*, 1, 3–7.

Bobo, L. D. (1999). Prejudice as group position: Microfoundations of a sociological approach to racism and intergroup relations. *Journal of Social Issues*, 55, 445–472.

Brewer, M., B., & Miller, N. (1984). *Groups in contact: The psychology of desegregation*. Orlando, Fla., Academic Press.

Cakal, H., Hewstone, M., Schwär, G., & Heath, A. (2011). An investigation of the social identity model of collective action and the "sedative" effect of intergroup contact among Black and White students in South Africa. *British Journal of Social Psychology*, 50(4), 606–627.

Central Bureau of Statistics (2013). Retrieved September 1, 2017, from http://www.cbs.gov.il

Crisp, R. J., & Turner, R. N. (2012). The imagined contact hypothesis. *Advances in Experimental Social Psychology*, 46, 125–182.

Demoulin, S., Leyens, J. P., & Dovidio, J. F. (Eds.). (2009). *Intergroup misunderstandings: Impact of divergent social realities*. Philadelphia, Pa.: Psychology Press.

Dixon, J., Durrheim, K., & Tredoux, C. (2005). Beyond the optimal contact strategy: a reality check for the contact hypothesis. *American Psychologist*, 60(7), 697–711.

———. (2007). Intergroup contact and attitudes toward the principle and practice of racial equality. *Psychological Science*, 18(10), 867–872.

Dixon, J., Levine, M., Reicher, S., & Durrheim, K. (2012). Beyond prejudice: Are negative evaluations the problem and is getting us to like one another more the solution? *Behavioral and Brain Sciences*, 35(6), 411–425.

Dovidio, J. F., & Gaertner, S. L. (2010). Intergroup bias. In S. T. Fiske, D. Gilbert, & G. Lindzey (Eds.), *Handbook of social psychology* (Vol. 2, 1084–1121). New York: Wiley.

Dovidio, J. F., Gaertner, S. L., & Saguy, T. (2009). Commonality and the complexity of "We": Social attitudes and social change. *Personality and Social Psychology Review*, 13, 3–20.

Dovidio, J.F., Gaertner, S., & Saguy, T. (2015). Color-blindness and commonality: Included but invisible? *American Behavioral Scientist*, 59, 1518–1538.

Emerson, R. (1962). Power-dependence relations. *American Sociological Review*, 27, 31–41.

Feagin, J. R. (2006). *Systematic racism: A theory of oppression.* New York: Routledge.

Gaertner, S. L., & Dovidio, J. F. (2012). Reducing intergroup bias: The common ingroup identity model. In P. A. M. Van Lange, A. W. Kruglanski & E. T Higgins (Eds.), *Handbook of theories of social psychology* (Vol. 2, 439–457). Thousand Oaks, Calif: SAGE Publications.

Halabi, R. (Ed.). (2004). Israeli and Palestinian identities in dialogue: The school for peace approach. New Brunswick, N.J.: Rutgers University Press.

Hayes, B. & Dowds, L. (2006). Social contact, cultural marginality, or economic self-interest? Attitudes towards immigrants in Northern Ireland. *Journal of Ethnic and Migration Studies*, 32, 455–476.

Knowles, E. D., Lowery, B. S., Chow, R. M., & Unzueta, M. M. (2014). Deny, distance, or dismantle? How White Americans manage a privileged identity. *Perspectives on Psychological Science*, 9, 594–609.

LeVine, R. A., & Campbell, D. T. (1972). *Ethnocentrism: Theories of conflict, ethnic attitudes, and group behavior.* New York: Wiley.

Maoz, I. (2000). Power relations in intergroup encounters: A case study of Jewish-Arab encounters in Israel. *International Journal of Intercultural Relations*, 24, 259–277.

———. (2011). Does contact work in protracted asymmetrical conflict? Appraising 20 years of reconciliation-aimed encounters between Israeli Jews and Palestinians. *Journal of Peace Research*, 48, 115–125.

Nadler, A., & Saguy, T. (2004). Reconciliation between nations: Overcoming emotional deterrents to ending conflicts between groups. In H. Langholtz & C. E. Stout (Eds.), *The psychology of diplomacy* (pp. 29–46). New York: Praeger.

Paluck, E. L., & Green, D. P. (2009). Prejudice reduction: What works? A review and assessment of research and practice. *Annual Review of Psychology*, 60, 339–367.

Pettigrew, T. F., & Tropp, L. R. (2006). A meta-analytic test of intergroup contact theory. *Journal of Personality and Social Psychology*, 90, 751–783.

———. (2008). How does intergroup contact reduce prejudice? Meta-analytic tests of three mediators. *European Journal of Social Psychology*, 38(6), 922–934.

Pettigrew, T. F., Wagner, U., & Christ, O. (2007). Who opposes immigration? Comparing German with North American findings. *Du Bois Review*, 4, 19–39.

Pratto, F., Sidanius, J., Stallworth, L. M., & Malle, B. F. (1994). Social dominance orientation: A personality variable predicting social and political attitudes. *Journal of Personality and Social Psychology*, 67, 741–763.

Reicher, S. (2007). Rethinking the paradigm of prejudice. *South African Journal of Psychology*, 37, 820–834.

Richeson, J. A., & Nussbaum, R. J. (2004). The impact of multiculturalism versus color-blindness on racial bias. *Journal of Experimental Social Psychology*, 40, 417–423.

Rouhana, N. N., & Korper, S. H. (1997). Power asymmetry and goals of unofficial third party intervention in protracted intergroup conflict. *Peace and Conflict: Journal of Peace Psychology*, 3, 1–17.

Ryan, C. S., Hunt, J. S., Weible, J. A., Peterson, C. R., & Casas, J. F. (2007). Multicultural and colorblind ideology, stereotypes, and ethnocentrism among Black and White Americans. *Group Processes and Intergroup Relations*, 10, 617–637.

Saguy, T., & Chernyak-Hai, L. (2012). Intergroup contact can undermine disadvantaged group members' attributions to discrimination. *Journal of Experimental Social Psychology*, 48(3), 714–720.

Saguy, T., & Dovidio, J. F. (2013). Insecure status relations shape preferences for the content of intergroup contact. *Personality and Social Psychology Bulletin*, 39, 1030–1042.

Saguy, T., Dovidio, J. F., & Pratto, F. (2008). Beyond contact: Intergroup contact in the context of power relations. *Personality and Social Psychology Bulletin*, 34, 432–445.

Saguy, T., & Kteily, N. (2014). Power, negotiations, and the anticipation of intergroup encounters. *European Review of Social Psychology*, 25(1), 107–141.

Saguy, T., Tausch, N., Dovidio, J. F., & Pratto, F. (2009). The irony of harmony: Intergroup contact can produce false expectations for equality. *Psychological Science*, 20, 114–121.

Saguy, T., Tausch, N., Dovidio, J. F., Pratto, F, & Singh, P. (2010). Tension and harmony in intergroup relations. In M. Mikulincer & P.R. Shaver (Eds.), *Human aggression and violence: Causes, manifestations, and consequences* (pp. 333–348). Washington, D.C.: American Psychological Association.

Sengupta, N. K., & Sibley, C. G. (2013). Perpetuating one's own disadvantage: Intergroup contact enables the ideological legitimation of inequality. *Personality and Social Psychology Bulletin*, 39(11), 1391–1403.

Sherif, M., Harvey, O. J., White, B. J., Hood, W., & Sherif, C. W. (1961). Intergroup conflict and cooperation: The Robbers Cave experiment (pp. 155–184). Norman, Okla.: University Book Exchange.

Sidanius, J., & Pratto, F. (1999). *Social dominance: An intergroup theory of social hierarchy and oppression*. New York: Cambridge University Press.

Simon, B., & Klandermans, B. (2001). Politicized collective identity: A social psychological analysis. *American Psychologist*, 56(4), 319–331.

Smooha, S. (2005). Index of Arab-Jewish relations in Israel 2004. Haifa, Israel: University of Haifa, Jewish-Arab Center.

Sonnenschein, N. (2008). Dialogue challenging identity: Jews constructing their identity through encounter with Palestinians (in Hebrew). Haifa, Israel: Pardes Publishing.

Sonnenschein, N., & Bekerman, Z. (2010), Who is more humane? An ethnographic account of power struggle in Jewish-Palestinian Dialogue Encounters. *Peace and Conflict Studies*, 17(2): 307–346.

Sonnenschein, N., Bekerman, Z., & Horenczyk, G. (2010). Threat and the majority identity. *Group Dynamics: Theory, Research and Practice*, 14(1): 47–65.

Tajfel, H., & Turner, J. C. (1979). An integrative theory of intergroup conflict. In W. G. Austin & S. Worchel (Eds.), *The social psychology of intergroup relations* (pp. 33–48). Monterey, Calif.: Brooks/Cole.

Tausch, N., Hewstone, M., Kenworthy, J. B., Psaltis, C., Schmid, K., Popan, J. R., Cairns, E. R., & Hughes, J. (2010). Secondary transfer effects of intergroup contact: Alternative accounts and underlying processes. *Journal of Personality and Social Psychology*, 99(2), 282–302.

Tropp, L. R., & Pettigrew, T. F. (2005). Relationships between intergroup contact and prejudice among minority and majority status groups. *Psychological Science*, 16, 951–956.

Tropp, L. R., Hawi, D., Van Laar, C., & Levin, S. (2012). Cross-ethnic friendship, perceived discrimination, and their effects on ethnic activism over time: A longitudinal investigation of three ethnic minority groups. *British Journal of Social Psychology*, 51, 257–272.

Ulmer, J., & Johnson, B. D. (2004). Sentencing in context: A multilevel analysis. *Criminology*, 42, 137–177.

van Oudenhoven, J. P., Prins, K. S., & Buunk, B. (1998). Attitudes of minority and majority members towards adaptation of immigrants. *European Journal of Social Psychology*, 28(6), 995–1013.

van Zomeren, M., Postmes, T., & Spears, R. (2008). Toward an integrative social identity model of collective action: A quantitative research synthesis of three sociopsychological perspectives. *Psychological Bulletin*, 134, 504–535.

Vezzali, L., Andrighetto, L., & Saguy, T. (2016). When intergroup contact can backfire: The content of intergroup encounters and desire for equality. Unpublished paper.

Walker, I., & Smith, H. J. (Eds.) (2002). *Relative deprivation: Specification, development, and integration*. Cambridge: Cambridge University Press.

Wolsko, C., Park, B., Judd, C. M., & Wittenbrink, B. (2000). Framing interethnic ideology: Effects of multicultural and color-blind perspectives on judgments of groups and individuals. *Journal of Personality and Social Psychology*, 78, 635–654.

Wright, S., & Lubensky, M. (2009). The struggle for social equality: Collective action vs. prejudice reduction. In S. Demoulin, J. P. Leyens, & J. F. Dovidio (Eds.), *Intergroup misunderstandings: Impact of divergent social realities* (pp. 291–310). New York: Psychology Press.

Wright, S. C., & Tropp, L. R. (2002). Collective action in response to disadvantage: Intergroup perceptions, social identification, and social change. In I. Walker, & H. Smith (Eds.), *Relative deprivation: Specification, development, and integration* (pp. 200–236). Cambridge: Cambridge University Press.

Zandberg, E. (2006). Non-cooperative housing. Retrieved March, 1, 2008, from http://www.haaretz.com.

Zúñiga, X., Nagda, B. R. A., & Sevig, T. D. (2002). Intergroup dialogues: An educational model for cultivating engagement across differences. *Equity & Excellence in Education*, 35(1), 7–17.

ABOUT THE AUTHOR

NAVA SONNENSCHEIN is the founder and director of the School for Peace (www.sfpeace.org). She has trained hundreds of Palestinian and Jewish facilitators to facilitate dialogue between groups in conflict in Israel and Palestine and between people in other areas of conflict throughout the world. She has taught the subject at the Tel Aviv University over the past twenty-six years, and in the past ten years she has developed courses specifically for Israeli and Palestinian professionals. She earned her Ph.D. from Hebrew University in 2006, with a focus on identity and conflict. In 2010 she received the "Women of Courage Certificate" from the U.S. State Department in recognition of her courage in leadership and her tireless work advocating for social change and coexistence.